PRINCIPLES OF CALIFORNIA AND FEDERAL EVIDENCE

A STUDENT'S GUIDE TO THE COURSE AND BAR

John E.B. Myers

Professor of Law
University of the Pacific
McGeorge School of Law

CONCISE HORNBOOK SERIES™

WEST
ACADEMIC
PUBLISHING

The publisher is not engaged in rendering legal or other professional advice, and this publication is not a substitute for the advice of an attorney. If you require legal or other expert advice, you should seek the services of a competent attorney or other professional.

Preface

Evidence is harder than you think! You might ask, "How hard could it be? It's just a relatively small bundle of rules." Don't be fooled by the brevity of the rules. The subject is large and complicated. In 1904, it took the great evidence scholar, John H. Wigmore, ten volumes to tell the whole story, in his classic *Evidence in Trials at Common Law*! Two of today's leading evidence scholars, Christopher B. Mueller and Laird C. Kirkpatrick, take five volumes in *Federal Evidence* (4th ed. 2013). You will not find clearer writing about the Federal Rules of Evidence than the work of Professors Mueller and Kirkpatrick. Their one volume treatise—*Evidence* (5th ed. 2012)—is superb for students and practicing attorneys alike.

The rules of evidence can be tricky. Some are simple; others give you a headache. The real challenge, however, is not the rules, but coming to grips with how the rules operate in court. Understanding the rules at work is challenging for the beginner who has not spent much, if any, time in court. It is one thing to memorize the definition of character evidence or hearsay. It is quite another to understand how the rules operate at trial.

Evidence would be challenge enough if you had one set of rules to master—you have two: The Federal Rules of Evidence (FRE) and the California Evidence Code (CEC). Although there are many similarities between the FRE and the CEC, there are important differences. The California Bar Examination, and most evidence professors, tests both sets of rules, especially the differences between the FRE and the CEC. This book describes the similarities and differences. Appendix C, at the end of the book, summarizes the major differences.

So, prepare to devote many hours to deciphering the FRE and the CEC. Study the similarities *and* the differences. As you get comfortable with the black letter rules, visualize how the rules work in court. When you have a feel for how the rules are implemented at trial, your ability to spot and analyze exam issues will be enhanced.

In court, there is a barrier—a bar—that separates the public gallery from the court itself. Only litigants, witnesses, and attorneys may pass that bar. If it is your desire to pass the bar examination so you can pass the physical bar in court, and assume the enormous responsibilities resting on the shoulders of courtroom lawyers, you will find the long hours of study worth it. Even if your only desires are to pass the evidence course and the bar exam, and you have no desire to set foot in court, you need a thorough understanding of the subject. Evidence is challenging. At the same time, evidence is interesting, and, dare I say it? Fun. The goal of this book is to help you on your journey.

John E.B. Myers

May 2017

Summary of Contents

PREFACE iii

Chapter 1. Basics of the FRE and the CEC 1
§ 1.1   The Rules of Evidence Do Not Cover All Aspects of the
        Subject 1
§ 1.2   Evidence Defined 2
§ 1.3   Rules on Substantive Evidence and Rules on Credibility
        of Witnesses... 3
§ 1.4   Rules of Evidence Apply to All Parties 3

**Chapter 2. Relevance, Unfair Prejudice, and Excluding
Evidence for Reasons of Policy** 7
§ 2.1   Basics and Rules 7
§ 2.2   Similarities and Differences Between CEC and FRE 8
§ 2.3   Direct and Circumstantial Evidence 10
§ 2.4   Questions on Relevance and Direct and Circumstantial
        Evidence 12
§ 2.5   Relevance on Exams 14
§ 2.6   Limited Admissibility 17
§ 2.7   Problem on Limited Admissibility 19
§ 2.8   Limited Admissibility on an Exam 19
§ 2.9   Rule of Completeness... 20
§ 2.10 Similarities and Differences Between CEC and FRE 21
§ 2.11 Example of the Rule of Completeness—The Rest of
        the Story 21
§ 2.12 Probative Value vs. Danger of Unfair Prejudice.............. 23
§ 2.13 Similarities and Differences Between CEC and FRE 25
§ 2.14 FRE 403 and CEC § 352 Exclude Relevant Evidence 26
§ 2.15 Party Must Object to Raise and Preserve Issue 26
§ 2.16 Meaning of Unfair Prejudice 26
§ 2.17 Factors in FRE 403 and CEC § 352 Balancing 27
§ 2.18 FRE 403 and CEC § 352 on Exams 29
§ 2.19 Additional Factors Under FRE 403 and CEC § 352 29
§ 2.20 Problems on Probative Value vs. Unfair Prejudice 30
§ 2.21 Subsequent Remedial Measures....................................... 31
§ 2.22 Settlement and Plea Negotiations 33
§ 2.23 Offer to Pay Medical Expenses 33
§ 2.24 Liability Insurance 33
§ 2.25 Answers to Chapter Problems... 34

Chapter 3. Preliminary Facts and Laying a Foundation 37
§ 3.1　　Preliminary Facts 37
§ 3.2　　Similarities and Differences Between FRE and CEC 40
§ 3.3　　Judge Decides Preliminary Facts Under FRE 104(a);
　　　　　Jury Decides Preliminary Facts Under 104(b) 40
§ 3.4　　Under the CEC, Preliminary Facts Under § 403 Are
　　　　　for the Jury. Preliminary Facts Under § 405 Are for
　　　　　the Judge 43
§ 3.5　　Problems on Preliminary Facts.. 44
§ 3.6　　Laying a Foundation: Introduction.................................. 45
§ 3.7　　Foundations Vary 45
§ 3.8　　Self-Authenticating Documents....................................... 46
§ 3.9　　Rules Regarding Authentication...................................... 46
§ 3.10　Similarities and Differences Between FRE and CEC 47
§ 3.11　Common Foundations... 47
§ 3.12　FRE 902—Self-Authentication 51
§ 3.13　Presumptive Authentication Under the CEC 53
§ 3.14　Unique Items vs. Generic Items 54
§ 3.15　Authentication of Electronic Communications 57
§ 3.16　Authentication in Practice 58
§ 3.17　Answers to Chapter Problems.. 59

Chapter 4. Objections and Offers of Proof............................. 61
§ 4.1　　Rules of Evidence 61
§ 4.2　　Objection and Motion to Strike....................................... 62
§ 4.3　　Offer of Proof.. 63
§ 4.4　　Harmless and Reversible Error 63
§ 4.5　　Plain Error 64
§ 4.6　　Constitutional Error 64
§ 4.7　　Exercise with Objections, Motions to Strike, and
　　　　　Offers of Proof 64

Chapter 5. Best and Secondary Evidence Rules;
　　　　　Judicial Notice... 75
§ 5.1　　Best Evidence Rule 75
§ 5.2　　What Is a "Writing"?... 75
§ 5.3　　What Is an "Original"?.. 76
§ 5.4　　What Is a "Duplicate?".. 76
§ 5.5　　What Is a "Copy?" 76
§ 5.6　　Four Excuses for Not Producing the Original................. 76
§ 5.7　　Summary of Voluminous Originals 77
§ 5.8　　What Is Secondary Evidence? 77
§ 5.9　　California's Secondary Evidence Rule.............................. 77
§ 5.10　BER/SER on Exams... 78
§ 5.11　Judicial Notice... 79

Chapter 6. Character Evidence 85
§ 6.1   What Is Character? 85
§ 6.2   Is Character Relevant? 86
§ 6.3   The Rule Against Character Evidence 89
§ 6.4   Exceptions to Rule Against Character Evidence 93
§ 6.5   Methods of Proving Character 94
§ 6.6   FRE 405(a)—Character Witness 94
§ 6.7   Rule 405(b)—Character "in Issue" 96
§ 6.8   CEC § 1100—Methods of Proving Character 96
§ 6.9   Defendant Offers Evidence of Good Character:
           The Mercy Rule 97
§ 6.10   Questions on Good Character Evidence 101
§ 6.11   Good Character Evidence on an Exam 102
§ 6.12   Defendant Attacks Victim's Character 103
§ 6.13   Special Rule for Homicide Cases: FRE Only 109
§ 6.14   Character Evidence to Impeach Credibility 111
§ 6.15   Selective Abolition of Rule Against Character
           Evidence 111
§ 6.16   Answers to Chapter Problems 112
§ 6.17   Answers to Questions in §§ 6.12(d) and 6.12(e) 113

Chapter 7. Habit 115
§ 7.1   Habit 115
§ 7.2   Corroboration and Eyewitness Rules 116
§ 7.3   Routine Practice of Organization 117
§ 7.4   Analysis of Questions on Habit 117

Chapter 8. Uncharged Misconduct Evidence 119
§ 8.1   Introduction and Rules 119
§ 8.2   UME Is Not Character Evidence 120
§ 8.3   UME Is Proven with Specific Instances, Not
           Character Witnesses 121
§ 8.4   Proof of UME 121
§ 8.5   Exclusion of UME for Reasons of Unfair Prejudice 121
§ 8.6   The Rubric "Uncharged Misconduct Evidence" Is
           Not Ideal 122
§ 8.7   Plan 122
§ 8.8   Motive 125
§ 8.9   Prove Intent on the Charged Occasion with Evidence
           of Intent on Uncharged Occasions 126
§ 8.10   Prove Intent by Disproving Accident 128
§ 8.11   Modus Operandi to Prove Identity 131
§ 8.12   California's Broad Approach to UME 132
§ 8.13   Third Party Culpability Evidence 134

Chapter 9. Lay and Expert Witnesses 135
§ 9.1   Competence to Testify 135

§ 9.2   Dead Man's Statute 137
§ 9.3   Personal Knowledge 138
§ 9.4   Oath or Affirmation 139
§ 9.5   Opinions from Lay Witnesses 139
§ 9.6   Exclude Witnesses While Other Witness Testify 140
§ 9.7   Refreshing Recollection 141
§ 9.8   Expert Testimony.. 142
§ 9.9   Who Qualifies as an Expert?.......................... 142
§ 9.10   Form of Expert Testimony 144
§ 9.11   Reasonable Certainty 145
§ 9.12   What Can Experts Rely on to Testify? 145
§ 9.13   Ultimate Issues 148
§ 9.14   Cross-Examination of Experts 149
§ 9.15   Impeach Expert with a Learned Treatise 149
§ 9.16   Scientific Evidence... 150

**Chapter 10. Cross-Examination, Impeachment and
    Rehabilitation of Witnesses 153**
§ 10.1   Direct, Cross, and Redirect Examination..................... 153
§ 10.2   Demeanor 154
§ 10.3   Impeachment Techniques 155
§ 10.4   Prior Inconsistent Statement........................ 156
§ 10.5   Contradiction... 160
§ 10.6   Conviction... 161
§ 10.7   Impeachment with Specific Acts.................... 168
§ 10.8   Bias, Memory, Capacity to Observe................ 170
§ 10.9   Impeach with a Character Witness 170
§ 10.10   Impeach a Character Witness......................... 171
§ 10.11   Impeach Hearsay Declarant 173
§ 10.12   Collateral Fact Rule.. 174
§ 10.13   No Impeachment for Religious Belief............ 175
§ 10.14   Rehabilitation.. 175
§ 10.15   Rape Shield Statute.. 178
§ 10.16   Analysis of Chapter Questions and Exams.................... 181

Chapter 11. Hearsay 183
§ 11.1   Hearsay Defined 183
§ 11.2   Rule Against Hearsay..................................... 184
§ 11.3   Hearsay Attack Sheet for Exams.................... 185
§ 11.4   Non-Hearsay Uses of Out-of-Court Statements 185
§ 11.5   Hearsay Exceptions 187
§ 11.6   Unavailability 187
§ 11.7   Present Sense Impressions 188
§ 11.8   Excited Utterances.. 189
§ 11.9   State of Mind Exception 190
§ 11.10   Medical Diagnosis or Treatment.................... 194

§ 11.11　Past Recorded Recollection.. 195
§ 11.12　Business Records Exception... 200
§ 11.13　If the Record Is Silent, It Didn't Happen 201
§ 11.14　Public Records... 201
§ 11.15　No Record Exists... 203
§ 11.16　Ancient Documents... 203
§ 11.17　Learned Treatises 203
§ 11.18　Former Testimony... 204
§ 11.19　Dying Declarations 209
§ 11.20　Statement Against Interest... 210
§ 11.21　Prior Inconsistent Statement... 212
§ 11.22　Prior Consistent Statement 213
§ 11.23　Out-of-Court Statement of Identification....................... 213
§ 11.24　Party Admissions 214
§ 11.25　Residual Exception 219
§ 11.26　Minor Exceptions 220
§ 11.27　Hearsay Within Hearsay—Layered Hearsay 221
§ 11.28　Impeach Hearsay Declarant 223
§ 11.29　The Confrontation Clause and Hearsay.......................... 223
§ 11.30　Bruton.. 228
§ 11.31　Forfeiture by Wrongdoing 229
§ 11.32　Analysis of Chapter Questions.. 231

Chapter 12. Privilege **237**
§ 12.1　Attorney-Client Privilege—CEC §§ 950–962 237
§ 12.2　Physician-Patient Privilege—CEC §§ 990–1007 238
§ 12.3　Psychotherapist-Client Privilege—CEC
　　　　§§ 1010–1027... 238
§ 12.4　Clergy-Penitent Privilege—CEC §§ 1030–1034.............. 239
§ 12.5　Spousal Privileges.. 239
§ 12.6　Official Information Privilege—CEC §§ 1040–1047 240
§ 12.7　Privilege Against Self-Incrimination.............................. 240

Chapter 13. Presumptions **241**
§ 13.1　Presumption and Inference Defined and Explained....... 241
§ 13.2　Burden of Producing Evidence and Burden of Proof 243
§ 13.3　Types of Presumptions 244
§ 13.4　Presumption Affecting Burden of Producing
　　　　Evidence 245
§ 13.5　Presumption Affecting Burden of Proof 247
§ 13.6　Presumptions Under the FRE.. 248

Chapter 14. Practice Exams, Answers, and Analysis **249**

APPENDIX A. FEDERAL RULES OF EVIDENCE 289

APPENDIX B. CALIFORNIA EVIDENCE CODE 323

APPENDIX C. DIFFERENCES BETWEEN FRE & CEC 393

TABLE OF CASES 403

INDEX 405

Table of Contents

PREFACE iii

Chapter 1. Basics of the FRE and the CEC 1
§ 1.1   The Rules of Evidence Do Not Cover All Aspects of the Subject 1
§ 1.2   Evidence Defined 2
§ 1.3   Rules on Substantive Evidence and Rules on Credibility of Witnesses... 3
§ 1.4   Rules of Evidence Apply to All Parties................................ 3

Chapter 2. Relevance, Unfair Prejudice, and Excluding Evidence for Reasons of Policy 7
§ 2.1   Basics and Rules... 7
§ 2.2   Similarities and Differences Between CEC and FRE 8
        § 2.2(a). Facts of Consequence 8
        § 2.2(b). Disputed Fact 9
        § 2.2(c). Witness Credibility Is Always Relevant 10
§ 2.3   Direct and Circumstantial Evidence 10
§ 2.4   Questions on Relevance and Direct and Circumstantial Evidence 12
§ 2.5   Relevance on Exams 14
§ 2.6   Limited Admissibility 17
§ 2.7   Problem on Limited Admissibility 19
§ 2.8   Limited Admissibility on an Exam 19
§ 2.9   Rule of Completeness 20
§ 2.10   Similarities and Differences Between CEC and FRE 21
§ 2.11   Example of the Rule of Completeness—The Rest of the Story 21
§ 2.12   Probative Value vs. Danger of Unfair Prejudice.............. 23
§ 2.13   Similarities and Differences Between CEC and FRE 25
§ 2.14   FRE 403 and CEC § 352 Exclude Relevant Evidence 26
§ 2.15   Party Must Object to Raise and Preserve Issue 26
§ 2.16   Meaning of Unfair Prejudice.. 26
§ 2.17   Factors in FRE 403 and CEC § 352 Balancing.................. 27
§ 2.18   FRE 403 and CEC § 352 on Exams 29
§ 2.19   Additional Factors Under FRE 403 and CEC § 352......... 29
§ 2.20   Problems on Probative Value vs. Unfair Prejudice 30
§ 2.21   Subsequent Remedial Measures.. 31
§ 2.22   Settlement and Plea Negotiations 33
§ 2.23   Offer to Pay Medical Expenses 33
§ 2.24   Liability Insurance 33
§ 2.25   Answers to Chapter Problems 34

Chapter 3. Preliminary Facts and Laying a Foundation 37

§ 3.1   Preliminary Facts 37

§ 3.2   Similarities and Differences Between FRE and CEC 40

§ 3.3   Judge Decides Preliminary Facts Under FRE 104(a);
           Jury Decides Preliminary Facts Under 104(b) 40

§ 3.4   Under the CEC, Preliminary Facts Under § 403 Are
           for the Jury. Preliminary Facts Under § 405 Are for
           the Judge 43

§ 3.5   Problems on Preliminary Facts 44

§ 3.6   Laying a Foundation: Introduction 45

§ 3.7   Foundations Vary 45

§ 3.8   Self-Authenticating Documents....................................... 46

§ 3.9   Rules Regarding Authentication 46

§ 3.10   Similarities and Differences Between FRE and CEC 47

§ 3.11   Common Foundations... 47

           § 3.11(a).   Testimony of a Witness Who Knows 47
           § 3.11(b).   Handwriting... 47
           § 3.11(c).   Reply Letter Doctrine.................................... 48
           § 3.11(d).   Information Known Only to One Person......... 48
           § 3.11(e).   Distinctive Characteristics 49
           § 3.11(f).   Voices.. 49
           § 3.11(g).   Telephone Calls 49
           § 3.11(h).   Public Records.. 50
           § 3.11(i).   Ancient Documents 50
           § 3.11(j).   Output of a Process 50
           § 3.11(k).   "I Found It on the Internet, So It Must Be
                        Reliable, Right?" 50

§ 3.12   FRE 902—Self-Authentication 51

           § 3.12(a).   Public Documents Under Seal—FRE
                        902(1)... 51
           § 3.12(b).   Public Documents Not Under Seal—
                        FRE 902(2) 51
           § 3.12(c).   Foreign Documents—FRE 902(3).................... 51
           § 3.12(d).   Certified Copies of Public Records—
                        FRE 902(4) 51
           § 3.12(e).   Government Publications—FRE 902(5).......... 52
           § 3.12(f).   Newspapers and Magazines—FRE 902(6)...... 52
           § 3.12(g).   Trade Inscriptions—FRE 902(7)..................... 52
           § 3.12(h).   Notarized Documents—FRE 902(8) 52
           § 3.12(i).   Uniform Commercial Code and Commercial
                        Paper—FRE 902(9).. 52
           § 3.12(j).   Presumptively Genuine—FRE 902(10)........... 52
           § 3.12(k).   Certified Domestic Business Record—FRE
                        902(11).. 53

§ 3.12(l). Certified Foreign Business Record—FRE 902(12) 53
§ 3.13 Presumptive Authentication Under the CEC 53
    § 3.13(a). Official Seals—CEC § 1452 53
    § 3.13(b). Signatures of Government Officials— CEC § 1453 54
    § 3.13(c). Signatures of Foreign Government Officials—CEC § 1454 54
    § 3.13(d). Official Documents and Recorded Documents—CEC §§ 1530–1532 54
    § 3.13(e). Government Publications—CEC § 644 54
    § 3.13(f). Newspaper or Magazine—CEC § 645.1 54
    § 3.13(g). Notary Public Acknowledgment—CEC § 1451 54
§ 3.14 Unique Items vs. Generic Items 54
§ 3.15 Authentication of Electronic Communications 57
§ 3.16 Authentication in Practice 58
§ 3.17 Answers to Chapter Problems 59

Chapter 4. Objections and Offers of Proof 61
§ 4.1 Rules of Evidence 61
§ 4.2 Objection and Motion to Strike 62
§ 4.3 Offer of Proof 63
§ 4.4 Harmless and Reversible Error 63
§ 4.5 Plain Error 64
§ 4.6 Constitutional Error 64
§ 4.7 Exercise with Objections, Motions to Strike, and Offers of Proof 64

Chapter 5. Best and Secondary Evidence Rules; Judicial Notice 75
§ 5.1 Best Evidence Rule 75
§ 5.2 What Is a "Writing"? 75
§ 5.3 What Is an "Original"? 76
§ 5.4 What Is a "Duplicate?" 76
§ 5.5 What Is a "Copy?" 76
§ 5.6 Four Excuses for Not Producing the Original 76
§ 5.7 Summary of Voluminous Originals 77
§ 5.8 What Is Secondary Evidence? 77
§ 5.9 California's Secondary Evidence Rule 77
§ 5.10 BER/SER on Exams 78
§ 5.11 Judicial Notice 79
    § 5.11(a). Judicial Notice Under the FRE 79
    § 5.11(b). Judicial Notice Under the CEC 82

Chapter 6. Character Evidence 85
§ 6.1 What Is Character? 85

§ 6.2   Is Character Relevant?.. 86
           § 6.2(a).   Evidence of Character Offered to Prove a
                       Person Acted in Conformity with Character:
                       Substantive Evidence.. 86
           § 6.2(b).   Character Evidence Offered to Prove Witness
                       Credibility: Not Substantive Evidence........... 87
           § 6.2(c).   Substantive Law Makes Character a Fact of
                       Consequence 87
§ 6.3   The Rule Against Character Evidence 89
           § 6.3(a).   Character Evidence on Exams......................... 91
           § 6.3(b).   Examples of Character Evidence on Exams ... 92
§ 6.4   Exceptions to Rule Against Character Evidence 93
§ 6.5   Methods of Proving Character 94
§ 6.6   FRE 405(a)—Character Witness 94
           § 6.6(a).   Reputation Character Witness 94
           § 6.6(b).   Opinion Character Witness 95
           § 6.6(c).   Character Witness May Not Describe
                       Specific Instances on Direct Examination 95
§ 6.7   Rule 405(b)—Character "in Issue"................................... 96
§ 6.8   CEC § 1100—Methods of Proving Character................... 96
§ 6.9   Defendant Offers Evidence of Good Character:
           The Mercy Rule... 97
           § 6.9(a).   FRE 404(a)(2)(A) and CEC § 1102 Apply
                       Only in Criminal Cases.................................... 97
           § 6.9(b).   Evidence of Defendant's Good Character Is
                       Provided by Character Witnesses................... 98
           § 6.9(c).   Mercy Rule 98
           § 6.9(d).   Pertinent Character Trait............................... 98
           § 6.9(e).   At What Point in a Trial Does a Defendant
                       Offer Good Character Evidence? 99
           § 6.9(f).   If a Defendant Offers Evidence of
                       Defendant's Good Character, the Prosecutor
                       Can Rebut with Evidence of Defendant's
                       Bad Character... 99
           § 6.9(g).   The Term "Character in Issue" Can Cause
                       Confusion 99
           § 6.9(h).   Can the Defendant Be His Own Good
                       Character Witness? 100
           § 6.9(i).   FRE and CEC Rules on Good Character
                       Operate Similarly.. 100
           § 6.9(j).   In California, a Defendant Charged with
                       Child Molestation May Offer Expert
                       Testimony
                       on Defendant's Character 101
§ 6.10   Questions on Good Character Evidence........................ 101

§ 6.11   Good Character Evidence on an Exam............................ 102
§ 6.12   Defendant Attacks Victim's Character........................... 103
          § 6.12(a). Similarities Between FRE 404(a)(2)(B)
                      and CEC § 1103 104
          § 6.12(b). A Discredited Theory of Proof in Sex
                      Offense Prosecutions 105
          § 6.12(c). Difference Between FRE 404(a)(2)(B) and
                      CEC § 1103.. 105
          § 6.12(d). Test Yourself with Two Multiple Choice
                      Questions About the Victim's Character 106
          § 6.12(e). A Source of Confusion Explained
                      (Hopefully) 107
§ 6.13   Special Rule for Homicide Cases: FRE Only.................. 109
§ 6.14   Character Evidence to Impeach Credibility................... 111
§ 6.15   Selective Abolition of Rule Against Character
          Evidence 111
§ 6.16   Answers to Chapter Problems 112
§ 6.17   Answers to Questions in §§ 6.12(d) and 6.12(e)............. 113

Chapter 7. Habit..**115**
§ 7.1   Habit.. 115
§ 7.2   Corroboration and Eyewitness Rules 116
§ 7.3   Routine Practice of Organization................................ 117
§ 7.4   Analysis of Questions on Habit.................................. 117

Chapter 8. Uncharged Misconduct Evidence **119**
§ 8.1   Introduction and Rules.. 119
§ 8.2   UME Is Not Character Evidence 120
§ 8.3   UME Is Proven with Specific Instances, Not
          Character Witnesses... 121
§ 8.4   Proof of UME.. 121
§ 8.5   Exclusion of UME for Reasons of Unfair Prejudice........ 121
§ 8.6   The Rubric "Uncharged Misconduct Evidence" Is
          Not Ideal.. 122
§ 8.7   Plan... 122
§ 8.8   Motive 125
§ 8.9   Prove Intent on the Charged Occasion with Evidence
          of Intent on Uncharged Occasions 126
§ 8.10   Prove Intent by Disproving Accident............................ 128
          § 8.10(a). Doctrine of Chances Proves Only Intent....... 129
          § 8.10(b). Anonymous Acts Are Admissible Under
                      the Doctrine of Chances 130
          § 8.10(c). How Many Incidents Are Needed to
                      Trigger the Doctrine of Chances? 130
          § 8.10(d). How Similar Do the Uncharged and the
                      Charged Acts Have to Be?............................. 130

§ 8.11   Modus Operandi to Prove Identity 131
§ 8.12   California's Broad Approach to UME 132
§ 8.13   Third Party Culpability Evidence 134

Chapter 9. Lay and Expert Witnesses 135
§ 9.1   Competence to Testify 135
        § 9.1(a).   Presiding Judge and Jurors Do Not
                   Testify—Impeaching a Verdict 136
        § 9.1(b).   Testimonial Competence on Exams 137
§ 9.2   Dead Man's Statute 137
§ 9.3   Personal Knowledge 138
§ 9.4   Oath or Affirmation 139
§ 9.5   Opinions from Lay Witnesses 139
§ 9.6   Exclude Witnesses While Other Witness Testify 140
§ 9.7   Refreshing Recollection 141
§ 9.8   Expert Testimony 142
§ 9.9   Who Qualifies as an Expert? 142
§ 9.10   Form of Expert Testimony 144
§ 9.11   Reasonable Certainty 145
§ 9.12   What Can Experts Rely on to Testify? 145
§ 9.13   Ultimate Issues 148
§ 9.14   Cross-Examination of Experts 149
§ 9.15   Impeach Expert with a Learned Treatise 149
§ 9.16   Scientific Evidence 150

Chapter 10. Cross-Examination, Impeachment and
       Rehabilitation of Witnesses 153
§ 10.1   Direct, Cross, and Redirect Examination 153
§ 10.2   Demeanor 154
§ 10.3   Impeachment Techniques 155
§ 10.4   Prior Inconsistent Statement 156
        § 10.4(a). Foundation 157
        § 10.4(b). Rule in the Queen's Case 157
        § 10.4(c). Extrinsic Evidence of Prior Inconsistent
                   Statement 157
        § 10.4(d). Prior Inconsistent Statement as Hearsay 158
§ 10.5   Contradiction 160
§ 10.6   Conviction 161
        § 10.6(a). Impeachment by Conviction—FRE 609 163
        § 10.6(b). Exam Questions on FRE 609 164
        § 10.6(c). How to Impeach with a Conviction 165
        § 10.6(d). Not the Gory Details 166
        § 10.6(e). The Luce Rule 166
        § 10.6(f).   Impeachment Under CEC § 788 167
§ 10.7   Impeachment with Specific Acts 168

§ 10.7(a). FRE 608(b)—Specific Instances of Untruthfulness 168

§ 10.7(b). Impeachment with Specific Instances in California 169

§ 10.8 Bias, Memory, Capacity to Observe 170

§ 10.9 Impeach with a Character Witness 170

§ 10.10 Impeach a Character Witness.. 171

§ 10.11 Impeach Hearsay Declarant 173

§ 10.12 Collateral Fact Rule.. 174

§ 10.13 No Impeachment for Religious Belief............................. 175

§ 10.14 Rehabilitation 175

§ 10.14(a). Rule Against Bolstering Prior to Impeachment.. 175

§ 10.14(b). Prior Consistent Statements....................... 176

§ 10.14(c). Not All Impeachment Triggers Rehabilitation with PCS............................. 177

§ 10.14(d). PCS Offered for Two Purposes.................... 177

§ 10.14(e). "Recently" Doesn't Mean Recently.............. 177

§ 10.14(f). The Timing Rule for PCSs........................... 178

§ 10.15 Rape Shield Statute.. 178

§ 10.16 Analysis of Chapter Questions and Exams..................... 181

Chapter 11. Hearsay 183

§ 11.1 Hearsay Defined 183

§ 11.2 Rule Against Hearsay... 184

§ 11.3 Hearsay Attack Sheet for Exams..................................... 185

§ 11.4 Non-Hearsay Uses of Out-of-Court Statements 185

§ 11.4(a). Effect on the Listener 185

§ 11.4(b). Verbal Acts, aka, Words of Independent Legal Significance 186

§ 11.4(c). Verbal Parts of an Act 186

§ 11.4(d). Effect on the Listener, Verbal Acts, and Verbal Parts of an Act Are Not Hearsay 187

§ 11.5 Hearsay Exceptions 187

§ 11.6 Unavailability 187

§ 11.7 Present Sense Impressions 188

§ 11.8 Excited Utterances 189

§ 11.9 State of Mind Exception 190

§ 11.10 Medical Diagnosis or Treatment 194

§ 11.11 Past Recorded Recollection 195

§ 11.11(a). Past Recollection Recorded on the California Bar 199

§ 11.12 Business Records Exception.. 200

§ 11.13 If the Record Is Silent, It Didn't Happen 201

§ 11.14 Public Records... 201

§ 11.14(a). End Run Around FRE 803(8)'s
             Restrictions?... 202
§ 11.14(b). Findings of Fact and Conclusions.............. 203
§ 11.15 No Record Exists.. 203
§ 11.16 Ancient Documents.. 203
§ 11.17 Learned Treatises.. 203
§ 11.18 Former Testimony.. 204
§ 11.18(a). Basic Requirements.................................... 205
§ 11.18(b). Schematic Approach to Former
             Testimony.. 206
§ 11.18(c). When the Party Against Whom Former
             Testimony Is Offered at Trial Number 2
             Was a Party to Trial Number 1.................... 206
§ 11.18(d). When the Party Against Whom Former
             Testimony Is Offered at Trial Number 2
             Was Not a Party to Trial Number 1.......... 207
§ 11.18(e). FRE 804(b)(1)'s Predecessor in Interest
             Language.. 207
§ 11.18(f). Examples of Former Testimony................. 207
§ 11.19 Dying Declarations.. 209
§ 11.20 Statement Against Interest.............................. 210
§ 11.20(a). The Williamson Issue................................ 211
§ 11.21 Prior Inconsistent Statement........................... 212
§ 11.22 Prior Consistent Statement.............................. 213
§ 11.23 Out-of-Court Statement of Identification......... 213
§ 11.24 Party Admissions... 214
§ 11.24(a). Personal Admissions.................................. 214
§ 11.24(b). Adoptive Admissions................................. 215
§ 11.24(c). Authorized Admissions.............................. 216
§ 11.24(d). Employee Admissions................................ 216
§ 11.24(e). Co-Conspirator Exception......................... 217
§ 11.25 Residual Exception.. 219
§ 11.26 Minor Exceptions.. 220
§ 11.27 Hearsay Within Hearsay—Layered Hearsay................. 221
§ 11.28 Impeach Hearsay Declarant.............................. 223
§ 11.29 The Confrontation Clause and Hearsay............ 223
§ 11.30 Bruton... 228
§ 11.31 Forfeiture by Wrongdoing................................. 229
§ 11.32 Analysis of Chapter Questions.......................... 231

Chapter 12. Privilege... 237
§ 12.1   Attorney-Client Privilege—CEC §§ 950–962................. 237
§ 12.2   Physician-Patient Privilege—CEC §§ 990–1007........... 238
§ 12.3   Psychotherapist-Client Privilege—CEC §§ 1010–
         1027.. 238
§ 12.4   Clergy-Penitent Privilege—CEC §§ 1030–1034............. 239

§ 12.5   Spousal Privileges 239
          § 12.5(a).   Spousal Testimonial Privilege 239
          § 12.5(b).   Spousal Confidential Communications
                        Privilege 240
§ 12.6   Official Information Privilege—CEC §§ 1040–1047 240
§ 12.7   Privilege Against Self-Incrimination 240

Chapter 13. Presumptions **241**
§ 13.1   Presumption and Inference Defined and Explained 241
§ 13.2   Burden of Producing Evidence and Burden of Proof 243
§ 13.3   Types of Presumptions 244
§ 13.4   Presumption Affecting Burden of Producing
          Evidence 245
§ 13.5   Presumption Affecting Burden of Proof 247
§ 13.6   Presumptions Under the FRE 248

Chapter 14. Practice Exams, Answers, and Analysis **249**
Question 1 249
Question 2 252
Question 3 257
Question 4 259
Question 5 266
California Bar Examination Questions 272
Multiple Choice Questions 274
Answers and Analysis of Multiple Choice Questions 282

APPENDIX A. FEDERAL RULES OF EVIDENCE 289

APPENDIX B. CALIFORNIA EVIDENCE CODE 323

APPENDIX C. DIFFERENCES BETWEEN FRE & CEC 393

TABLE OF CASES 403

INDEX 405

PRINCIPLES OF CALIFORNIA AND FEDERAL EVIDENCE

A STUDENT'S GUIDE TO THE COURSE AND BAR

Chapter 1

BASICS OF THE FRE AND THE CEC

The CEC went into effect in 1967; the FRE in 1975. The FRE apply in federal court. Most states have adopted the FRE, usually with few changes. California has not adopted the FRE. California has its own rules of evidence, the CEC, used in California Superior Court.

§ 1.1 The Rules of Evidence Do Not Cover All Aspects of the Subject

The FRE and the CEC do not cover every aspect of evidence law.[1] Some subjects are governed by constitutional law. For example, the Confrontation Clause of the Sixth Amendment to the U.S. Constitution limits the admissibility of hearsay in criminal cases (See § 11.29). The California Constitution was amended by the Proposition 8 initiative, the Victims' Bill of Rights. Under Prop. 8, Article I, § 29(d) of the California Constitution provides, "Relevant evidence shall not be excluded in any criminal proceeding." This aspect of Prop. 8 impacts several sections of the CEC in criminal trials (See § 10.7(b)). Prop. 8 also impacts the use of convictions to impeach witnesses in criminal cases (See § 10.6(f)). Prop. 8 does not apply in civil litigation. Prop. 8 is discussed at appropriate locations throughout the book.[2]

The FRE and CEC apply during trials of civil and criminal cases (FRE 1101(a) and (b); CEC § 300). On law school examinations and the bar, assume the rules of evidence apply. The call of the question usually tells you which set of rules to use.

Evidentiary privileges (*e.g.*, attorney-client privilege) apply in all proceedings, even when other rules of evidence do not apply (FRE 1101(c); CEC § 910). Thus, privileges apply during grand jury proceedings, although the FRE and CEC do not apply in proceedings before the grand jury (FRE 1101(d)(2); CEC § 300).

---

[1]   The CEC is much longer and more detailed than the FRE.

[2]   The late Professor Miguel Mendez was a leading expert on the CEC. According to Professor Mendez, Prop. 8 created two evidence codes, the CEC, as it is written, for civil cases, and the CEC, as it is modified by Prop. 8, for criminal cases. Miguel A. Mendez, The Victims' Bill of Rights—Thirty Years Under Proposition 8, 25 Stanford Law and Policy Review 379 (2014). I don't go so far as to say that there are two evidence codes. There is only one, the CEC. But Professor Mendez is right that Prop. 8 has a major impact on the CEC in criminal cases.

§ 1.2   Evidence Defined

The FRE does not define "evidence." The CEC does. Section 140 of the CEC defines evidence as "testimony, writings, material objects, or other things presented to the senses that are offered to prove the existence or nonexistence of a fact." Although the FRE does not define evidence, the meaning of evidence is the same under FRE and CEC. Thus, in federal and state court, evidence includes testimony from lay and expert witnesses. Evidence includes many kinds of documents, from deeds to contracts to x-rays to traffic tickets. The definition of evidence includes things, such as a gun, a knife, and a bag of narcotics.

Physical objects that played a role in the facts of the case are sometimes called real evidence. Thus, a murder weapon is real evidence. Real evidence should be contrasted with demonstrative evidence. Typically, demonstrative evidence did not play a role in the facts of the case. Demonstrative evidence consists of diagrams, charts, maps, models, photos, power point presentations, computer generated exhibits, and other items that are presented in court to help the jury understand the testimony of witnesses. Thus, a doctor might use a model of the human skeleton to explain the plaintiff's injuries. A pathologist might use a medical drawing of the human skull to help the jury understand the doctor's technical description of the brain injury that killed the victim.

With demonstrative evidence, the item typically is not formally received in evidence. The evidence consists of the witness' testimony, not the demonstrative aid. The aid is simply intended to help the jury understand the witness's testimony. The evidence is the testimony.

Sometimes, testimony, documents, and objects that are not admissible under the rules of evidence (*e.g.*, inadmissible hearsay) are nevertheless admitted by the judge because the opponent fails to object. Once admitted in evidence, such items constitute evidence. Consider, for example, the following questioning of a police officer by an attorney. The case involves a car accident:

Q: Officer, when you arrived at the accident scene, what did you do first?

A: I parked my patrol car to protect the crash scene from traffic, and I went to the cars to see if anyone was hurt.

Q: When you walked up to the first car, what did you see?

A: The driver was sitting behind the steering wheel.

Q: Did you ask the driver what happened?

A: Yes.

Q: What did the driver say?

A: She said that she had been drinking, and knew the accident was her fault.

The moment the attorney asked, "What did the driver say?", it was obvious that the question called for hearsay, and the opposing attorney should have objected if the attorney believed the hearsay inadmissible and harmful.[3] Because there was no objection, the officer answered the question, and hearsay was received. Failure to object at the proper time waived objection to the hearsay, and the hearsay constitutes evidence in the case (Chapter 4). Because the hearsay has been admitted, the jury may consider it, and this is true even if the hearsay would have been excluded upon proper objection.

§ 1.3   Rules on Substantive Evidence and Rules on Credibility of Witnesses

As you begin your journey to understanding of the FRE and the CEC, you may find it helpful to divide the rules into two categories: rules that govern admission of substantive evidence, and rules that govern the credibility of witnesses. Substantive evidence is evidence that tends to prove the facts of the case. Credibility evidence pertains to the credibility of witnesses. Dividing the rules into the two categories can help you decide which rule you are dealing with, or which rule to apply, in a particular fact situation. At appropriate locations in the book, you will be reminded of the differences between rules governing substantive evidence and rules governing credibility.

§ 1.4   Rules of Evidence Apply to All Parties

The rules of evidence apply to all parties to civil and criminal litigation. For example, the rule against hearsay applies as much to the defendant in a criminal case, as it does to the prosecution.[4] Although both sides are bound by the rules of evidence, certain rules apply to only one party. For example, in criminal cases, the defendant is permitted to offer evidence of the defendant's good

---

[3]   A trial attorney might object one question earlier, when the questioning attorney asked, "Did you ask the driver what happened?" Technically, this question calls for a "yes" or "no" answer, not the repetition of an out-of-court statement (hearsay). Yet, it is clear that the purpose of "Did you ask the driver what happened?" is to set up the next question, which does call for hearsay. Moreover, there is a high likelihood the witness will respond to, "Did you ask the driver what happened?" with hearsay rather than "yes" or "no." To forestall this possibility, object to "Did you ask . . . ."

[4]   People v. Mickel, 2 Cal. 5th 181, 385 P.3d 796, 211 Cal. Rptr. 3d 601 (2016).

character as substantive evidence of innocence (see § 6.4). The prosecutor is not permitted to be the first to offer evidence of the defendant's character. Another example is the FRE public records exception to the hearsay rule, which allows the defendant in a criminal case to offer certain documents against the prosecution, but forbids the prosecutor from doing the same (§ 11.14). The Confrontation Clause of the Sixth Amendment limits admission of "testimonial" hearsay against a defendant, but not against the prosecution (§ 11.29).

In rare circumstances, the *correct* application of a rule of evidence against a defendant in a criminal case deprives the defendant of a fair trial. When this happens—and again, it is rare—the rule of evidence must give way to the greater value of guaranteeing the accused a fair trial.[5] The most famous examples of this scenario are *Chambers v. Mississippi*, 410 U.S. 284, 93 S. Ct. 1038 (1973) and *Rock v. Arkansas*, 483 U.S. 44, 107 S. Ct. 2704 (1987). In *Rock*, defendant was charged with murder. Prior to trial, defendant underwent hypnosis. Arkansas had a rule of evidence that prohibited hypnotically refreshed testimony. The trial judge *correctly* applied the rule, and refused to allow defendant to testify on her own behalf. The U.S. Supreme Court ruled that the defendant's constitutional right to testify trumped the rule of evidence. In *Chambers*, defendant was accused of murdering a police officer. Before trial, another person signed a confession to the crime, and made inculpatory statements. At trial, the defendant called the person as a witness, but the person denied any involvement in the homicide, and repudiated the confession and the inculpatory statements. The trial judge refused to allow defense counsel to cross-examine the person because cross-examination would violate Mississippi's voucher rule. The voucher rule provided that a party calling a witness vouched for the witness's credibility, and could not impeach the witness. (FRE 607 and CEC § 785 abolish the voucher rule. See § 10.1). Although the trial judge correctly applied the voucher rule, the U.S. Supreme Court reversed the conviction because correct application of the rule deprived the defendant of the ability to offer strong exculpatory evidence. Thus, in rare circumstances, a rule of evidence must bend to allow a defendant the opportunity to testify or otherwise present a defense. The U.S. Supreme Court wrote in *Holmes v. South Carolina*, 547 U.S. 319, 325, 126 S. Ct. 1727 (2006):

---

[5]   For California cases, *see* People v. Mickel, 2 Cal. 5th 181, 385 P.3d 796, 211 Cal. Rptr. 3d 601 (2016); People v. Anderson, 207 Cal. App. 4th 1440, 144 Cal. Rptr. 3d 606 (2012).

State and federal rulemakers have broad latitude under the Constitution to establish rules excluding evidence from criminal trials. This latitude, however, has limits. Whether rooted directly in the Due Process Clause of the Fourteenth Amendment or in the Compulsory Process or Confrontation Clauses of the Sixth Amendment, the Constitution guarantees criminal defendants a meaningful opportunity to present a complete defense. This right is abridged by evidence rules that infringe upon a weighty interest of the accused and are arbitrary or disproportionate to the purposes they are designed to serve.

Chapter 2

RELEVANCE, UNFAIR PREJUDICE, AND EXCLUDING EVIDENCE FOR REASONS OF POLICY

This chapter discusses the fundamental concept of relevance. As well, the chapter describes the authority of judges to exclude relevant evidence when the probative value of the evidence is substantially outweighed by the danger the evidence will cause unfair prejudice to a party. Finally, the chapter discusses rules that exclude relevant evidence for reasons of policy.

§ 2.1 Basics and Rules

Relevant evidence is admissible unless it is excluded by law. Irrelevant evidence is not admissible. The rules defining relevance provide:

> **FRE 401. Test for Relevant Evidence**. Evidence is relevant if: (a) it has any tendency to make a fact more or less probable than it would be without the evidence; and (b) the fact is of consequence in determining the action.

> **FRE 402. General Admissibility of Relevant Evidence**. Relevant evidence is admissible unless any of the following provides otherwise: the United States Constitution; a federal statute; these rules; or other rules prescribed by the Supreme Court. Irrelevant evidence is not admissible.

> **CEC § 210. Relevant Evidence**. "Relevant evidence" means evidence, including evidence relevant to the credibility of a witness or hearsay declarant, having any tendency in reason to prove or disprove any disputed fact that is of consequence to the determination of the action.

> **CEC § 350. Only Relevant Evidence Admissible**. No evidence is admissible except relevant evidence.

> **CEC § 351. Admissibility of Relevant Evidence**. Except as otherwise provided by statute, all relevant evidence is admissible.

Although the CEC and the FRE define relevant evidence, the rules shed no light on when particular items of evidence are relevant in given cases. Relevance is evaluated case-by-case. In one case, testimony from a witness that she saw a car run a red light is relevant, whereas the same testimony in another case is irrelevant. Relevance is determined by asking whether the evidence has a tendency to prove a fact that is of consequence *in this case*. Testimony about a car running a light would likely be relevant in an auto accident case focused on the color of the light. On the other hand, if such testimony is offered in a case that has nothing to do with the color of the light, the evidence is likely irrelevant. In real trials, attorneys seldom offer evidence that has no bearing on the case, and true irrelevancy is uncommon.

§ 2.2   Similarities and Differences Between CEC and FRE

Relevance has essentially the same meaning in the CEC and the FRE, that is, does the evidence—testimony, document, thing—have "any tendency," however slight or great, to prove a fact of consequence in the action?

§ 2.2(a).   Facts of Consequence

What are the facts of consequence in a case?[1] The answer is *not* found in the FRE or the CEC. The facts of consequence are determined by the substantive law governing the case, that is, by criminal law, tort law, contract law, etc. To understand what facts are "consequential," ask yourself, what facts does the plaintiff or prosecutor have to prove to win? In criminal prosecutions, criminal law determines the elements of crimes, and, thus, the facts of consequence. For example, burglary was defined at common law as the breaking and entering of the dwelling house of another at night with the intent to commit a felony therein. In a burglary prosecution, the facts of consequence are: breaking, entry, dwelling house of another, nighttime, and intent to commit a felony. Evidence that has any tendency to prove or disprove these facts is relevant. Turning to civil litigation, in a negligence case, tort law determines the facts of consequence. In a contract case, contract law controls. In a property dispute, property law. Etc. Etc.

When a defendant in a criminal or civil case raises an affirmative defense, the elements of the defense are facts of consequence. For example, a defendant charged with murder may claim self-defense, the elements of which are: (1) the defender

---

[1]   Courts and commentators sometimes refer to facts of consequences as "material" facts.

honestly believed she was being attacked, or was about to be attacked; (2) the defender's belief in the need for self-defense was reasonable; and (3) the defender was not the first aggressor. Evidence focused on these facts is relevant.

§ 2.2(b).   Disputed Fact

CEC § 210 limits relevance to evidence that tends to prove "any disputed fact." FRE 401 and 402 do not mention "disputed facts." The different is more apparent than real. Both the CEC and the FRE refer to facts of consequence, and define this term identically. The words "material facts" are sometimes used instead of "facts of consequence," but the words have the same meaning. A material fact is a fact that matters, a fact of consequence. *Witkin's California Evidence* states, "The Evidence Code substitutes the word 'disputed' for 'material . . . .' "[2] Despite different language, the definitions of relevance in the FRE and CEC are the same: Evidence is relevant when it has any tendency to prove a fact of consequence.

There are cases where an issue that normally would be disputed is removed from the case, usually because one party admits the issue. The admission could occur in the pleadings, or at trial. In wrongful death cases, for example, defendants sometimes admit liability, and contest only damages. In such cases, the manner of death—often gruesome—may be irrelevant because it is not disputed. Under CEC § 210, the judge could rule that evidence describing the uncontested manner of death is irrelevant, because cause of death is not "disputed." Under the FRE, a judge could reach the same conclusion, either by ruling the evidence irrelevant, or by excluding the evidence under FRE 403, discussed in § 2.12.

Can a defendant in a criminal case deprive a prosecutor of the ability to offer evidence of a fact by admitting the fact, or by stating that the fact will not be disputed, or by offering to stipulate to the fact, thus rendering evidence offered to prove the fact irrelevant? If the answer is yes, the defense will occasionally have an incentive to admit, or, at a minimum, not contest, points that may cause the jury to be upset with the defendant. For example, suppose defendant is charged with murdering a baby by violently and repeatedly shaking the baby and inflicting massive bleeding inside the baby's skull. The defendant may admit that someone shook the baby to death, but claim it wasn't the defendant. Defendant argues that evidence of how the baby died is irrelevant. The only question is identity—who did it? The general rule is that pleading not guilty puts the prosecution to its burden of proof on *all* elements of the

---

[2]   5 Witkin's California Evidence § 3, p. 361 (5th ed. 2012).

crime, plus identity.[3] A defendant normally cannot dictate to a prosecutor what evidence the prosecutor will offer to prove the People's case, by expressing a willingness to stipulate to a fact the prosecutor must prove. There are times when a judge will require a prosecutor to accept an offer to stipulate to a fact. This issue is discussed in § 2.17.

§ 2.2(c).   Witness Credibility Is Always Relevant

CEC § 210 specifies that relevant evidence includes evidence relevant to the credibility of a witness or hearsay declarant. FRE 401 does not contain this language, but the result is the same. Credibility of witnesses is relevant.

§ 2.3   Direct and Circumstantial Evidence

Evidence is direct or circumstantial. To understand the difference, you need to understand inferences. CEC § 600(b) defines inference as "a deduction of fact that may logically and reasonably be drawn from another fact or group of facts found or otherwise established in the action." The FRE does not define inference, but the meaning is the same under the CEC and the FRE.

An inference is simply a thought process. A person reasons from one fact to another fact. You draw hundreds of inferences every day. For example, you are standing on a street corner, waiting to cross a busy street. Cars come to a halt, so you infer that the traffic light changed color. You don't observe the light change color. You infer the change from the behavior of the drivers. On your driveway in the morning, you find the newspaper. You infer that the delivery person for the paper tossed it on the driveway while you slept. As mentioned above, an inference is simply the process of reasoning from one fact to another. In court, jurors are instructed that they may draw reasonable inferences from the evidence.[4] Suppose, for example, that a prosecutor offers a witness who testifies that, just before the bank was robbed, she saw the defendant near the bank. The jury may infer from the testimony that the defendant was the robber because she was near the bank. In the same case, the prosecutor offers evidence that the robber wore a tan leather jacket. When police searched the defendant's

---

[3]   *See* People v. Bryant, 60 Cal. 4th 335, 407, 334 P.3d 573, 178 Cal. Rptr. 3d 185 (2014) ("Defendants pleaded not guilty, placing in issue all the elements of murder."); People v. Ranlet, 1 Cal. App. 5th 363, 204 Cal. Rptr. 3d 445 (2016).

[4]   An inference must be logical; there must be a logical connection between the evidence and the inference drawn therefrom. *See* People v. Bryant, 60 Cal. 4th 335, 405, 334 P.3d 573, 178 Cal. Rptr. 3d 185 (2014)("Inferences drawn from the evidence must be logical and reasonable, not merely speculative.").

apartment, they found a tan leather jacket. The jury may infer from these two items of evidence that the defendant was the robber.

An inference is permissive. The jury in the bank robbery case is not *required* to infer from the evidence that the defendant robbed the bank. When an inference is reasonable, the jury *may* draw the inference, but is not required to.

The defense is free to suggest competing inferences, such as, the defendant was going to the karate school next to the bank, and defendant had nothing to do with the robbery. As for the leather jacket, the defense attorney may argue the fact that the robber and the defendant own tan leather jackets has little probative value. Lots of people own such apparel. Part of your job as a trial lawyer is suggesting alternative inferences to explain away the inferences suggested by your opponent!

Evidence is circumstantial when the trier of fact must draw one or more inferences from the evidence to what the evidence is offered to prove. Thus, the fact that cars came to a halt at an intersection is circumstantial evidence that the traffic light changed color. The newspaper on your driveway is circumstantial evidence it was delivered by an employee of the paper. In the bank robbery case, testimony that the defendant was seen near the bank, and owns the same type of jacket as the robber, are circumstantial evidence that defendant is the robber. Mueller and Kirkpatrick put it this way, "Circumstantial evidence means proof that does not actually assert or describe the point or proposition to be proved, but asserts or describes something else, from which the trier of fact may either reasonably infer the truth of the proposition ... or reasonably infer an increase in the probability that a proposition that matters in the case is true . . . ."[5]

Evidence is direct when the trier of fact does not have to draw an inference from the evidence to what it is offered to prove. CEC § 410 states, " 'Direct evidence' means evidence that directly proves a fact, without an inference or presumption, and which in itself, if true, conclusively establishes that fact." The most common example of direct evidence is eyewitness testimony. If the jury believes an eyewitness, the jury need not draw any inferences from the testimony to what it is offered to prove. In the bank robbery case, eyewitness testimony from the bank teller who was robbed, identifying the defendant as the robber, is direct evidence. Regarding the traffic light, discussed above, if you testify that you were looking directly at the light and saw it change color, your

---

[5]   1 Christopher B. Mueller & Laird C. Kirkpatrick, *Federal Evidence* § 4:2, pp. 538–539 (4th ed. 2013).

testimony is direct evidence. As for the newspaper, if you were up early, and looked out your window to see the delivery person toss the paper onto your driveway, your eyewitness testimony would be direct evidence.

CEC § 411 provides that eyewitness testimony from one witness, if the witness is believed, is sufficient to prove any fact.[6] Although the FRE has no counterpart to CEC § 411, the result is the same.

A civil or criminal case can be decided on direct evidence, circumstantial evidence, or a combination of the two. Sometimes, especially on TV, you hear someone say, "You can't find me guilty. The evidence is only circumstantial." This is wrong. A criminal conviction can be based entirely on circumstantial evidence. It is true that, in criminal cases, when the prosecution's case rests entirely or primarily on circumstantial evidence, the jury must be convinced that the only reasonable conclusion to draw from the circumstantial evidence is that defendant is guilty. If two inferences can be drawn from circumstantial evidence, one inference pointing toward innocence, and the other pointing toward guilt, the jury must select the inference pointing toward innocence. This rule is tempered by the proviso that if one of the competing inferences is reasonable, while the other is unreasonable, the jury must select the reasonable inference.[7]

§ 2.4   Questions on Relevance and Direct and Circumstantial Evidence

The following questions provide an opportunity to distinguish direct from circumstantial evidence, and to determine whether evidence is relevant. Analysis of the questions may be found in § 2.25.

---

[6]   Corroboration for an eyewitness is needed to prove treason or perjury.

[7]   The Judicial Council of California publishes *California Criminal Jury Instructions: CALCRIM*. Instruction 224 provides:

Before you may rely on circumstantial evidence to conclude that a fact necessary to find the defendant guilty has been proved, you must be convinced that the People have proved each fact essential to that conclusion beyond a reasonable doubt.

Also, before you may rely on circumstantial evidence to find the defendant guilty, you must be convinced that the only reasonable conclusion supported by the circumstantial evidence is that the defendant is guilty. If you can draw two or more reasonable conclusions from the circumstantial evidence, and one of those reasonable conclusions points to innocence and another to guilt, you must accept the one that points to innocence. However, when considering circumstantial evidence, you must accept only reasonable conclusions and reject any that are unreasonable.

1.   Is Dell an Arsonist?

Dell is charged with arson, for intentionally burning a home. Dell has pleaded not guilty. Dell does not testify. At Dell's trial, Beth testifies, "I saw Dell running away from the house just as it burst into flames." Is Beth's testimony direct or circumstantial evidence of Dell running? After Beth testifies, the prosecutor argues that Dell was running away from the home because he had just set it alight, and he was making his escape. The prosecutor wants the jury to conclude that Dell was running away because he knew he was guilty. Is Dell's running direct or circumstantial evidence of his belief in his own guilt? When Dell was questioned by police a week after the home burned, he made a complete confession. Is Dell's confession direct or circumstantial evidence of guilt?

2.   International Child Abduction

The United States and nearly 100 other nations are parties to a treaty intended to deter and remedy international parental child abduction. The treaty is The Hague Convention on the Civil Aspects of International Child Abduction. Under the Convention, when a parent removes a child from the child's country of habitual residence, without the consent of the other parent, the removal is "wrongful." The left behind parent can bring an action in state or federal court, seeking an order that the child be returned to the habitual residence. The Convention also provides a return remedy when a parent wrongfully refuses to return a child to the child's habitual residence after a visit.

Mother and father divorced in California, and mother received primary custody of their son. Mother and son, who was then nine, moved to Iceland. Father lived in Sacramento. Father loved his son, but failed to pay child support, and owed mother more than $60,000 in unpaid support. At the end of a summer visit with father in Sacramento, father refused to return the child to mother in Iceland. Mother brought a case under the Hague Convention, arguing that father wrongfully refused to return the child to Iceland. The case was tried in Federal District Court in Sacramento. The only issue before the court was whether father wrongfully refused to return the child. During cross-examination of father, mother's attorney asked father if he was $60,000 in arrears on child support. Father's attorney strenuously objected that issues of child support were irrelevant to whether father's decision to keep the child was wrongful. The judge was about to sustain the objection, when mother's attorney asked the court to allow him to explain why the evidence was relevant. The attorney told the court that because father was so far behind in his child support, the state agency in charge of child support had confiscated father's passport, making it impossible for him to travel abroad, including to Iceland to visit his son. Mother's attorney argued that because father had lost his passport for failing to pay child support, father had a motive to wrongfully keep the boy with him in Sacramento, the only place father knew he could see his son. What do you think? Was the fact that father lost his passport relevant to his motive for refusing to return the child to Iceland? If the father's motive was relevant, was it proper for mother's attorney to mention that father failed to support his son to the tune of $60,000?

3.   Murder Most Foul

The murder victim was discovered tied up in her home, with her head and hands cut off. The prosecution's theory is that defendant was burglarizing victim's home when victim returned and surprised the defendant, and that defendant murdered the victim in part because he was terrified to return to prison. During the prosecution's case-in-chief, the prosecutor offers evidence that a week after the grisly murder, defendant told his girlfriend what he had done, and threatened her to keep her silent. After threatening the girlfriend, defendant purchased a pruning saw, a butcher knife, and two balls of twine. Defense counsel objects to the saw, the knife, and the twine. Is defendant's shopping spree relevant?

4.   Did Alcohol Matter?

Defendant is prosecuted for murder during the commission of unlawful sodomy. During the defense case-in-chief, defense counsel offers evidence that the victim had a blood-alcohol level of .26%. The prosecutor objects that the victim's intoxication is irrelevant to whether she consented to sodomy. The defense is not able to offer any evidence that the victim's blood-alcohol level impaired her judgment or behavior on the night she was killed. Should the judge sustain the prosecutor's relevance objection?

5.   Is the Gun Relevant?

Defendant is charged with conspiracy to distribute drugs, and with distribution. The prosecutor offers evidence that, at the time of his arrest, defendant possessed a semiautomatic handgun. Defendant is not charged with a weapons offense. Is the gun relevant?

§ 2.5   Relevance on Exams

On exams, as in real trials, the relevance of evidence is usually obvious because the evidence bears directly on the facts of the case, or the credibility of a witness. On an exam, you should be prepared to discuss relevance whenever eyewitness testimony, a document, or a thing is offered in evidence. Begin by defining relevant evidence.

Tell the examiner *why* the evidence is relevant, and do this even if relevance is obvious. For example, if the prosecutor offers an eyewitness to a crime, don't say, "Relevance is obvious." Say something like, "The testimony of the eyewitness is direct evidence of the crime itself, and therefore, if the witness is believed, the testimony has a tendency to prove the crime, which is a fact of consequence in the case."

If you are having difficulty seeing how a document or a witness's testimony has anything to do with the facts of the exam question, this may be a clue that you are faced with irrelevant evidence, or evidence the relevance of which is tricky. Think about the evidence, and see if you can connect it to the facts of consequence or to witness credibility.

When an exam question is focused on impeachment of witnesses, you will, of course, discuss whether the impeachment is proper. Do you need to mention that impeachment is relevant? You might say, credibility of witnesses is always relevant.

Exam Questions. The February, 2012, California bar had an evidence essay that focused primarily on hearsay, but the facts also afforded an opportunity to discuss relevance. Below is part of the question, reprinted with permission of the California State Bar:

> Paul sued David in federal court for damages for injuries arising from an automobile accident. At trial, in his case-in-chief, Paul testified that he was driving westbound, under the speed limit, in the right-hand lane of a highway having two westbound lanes. He further testified that his passenger, Vera, calmly told him she saw a black SUV behind them weaving recklessly through the traffic. He also stated that, about 30 seconds later, he saw David driving a black SUV, which appeared in the left lane and swerved in front of him. He testified that David's black SUV hit the front of his car, seriously injuring him and killing Vera.

For many previous bar exams, the California Bar website contains "model" answers for essays. The model answers were written by students sitting for the bar. You can access previous essays and model answers on the bar website. For the February, 2012 bar exam, both model answers begin by stating that in order to be admissible, evidence must be logically relevant. The model answers define logical relevance. They explain how weaving through traffic has a tendency to prove that David was driving negligently or recklessly, increasingly the likelihood that he caused the accident. After finishing the discussion of logical relevance, the model answers switch to discussion of what they call "legal relevance," which is the likelihood that the probative value of relevant evidence is substantially outweighed by the danger of unfair prejudice to a party. To me, it seems there is virtually no risk of *unfair* prejudice in this question. Nevertheless, experts on the California bar exam believe that you should virtually always discuss both logical and legal relevance.

Below is part of a law school evidence question:

> Ann, Beth, and Charlene devised a plan to rob a bank in Sacramento. Ann's job was to be the getaway driver in a stolen car. Beth and Charlene entered the bank and shouted, "Nobody move, this is a robbery." Ann waited outside in the getaway car. While Beth and Charlene were in the bank, police began arriving, and Ann sped off without Beth and Charlene. Ann led police on the lengthy high-speed chase. During the chase, Ann used her cell phone to call a local TV station. The TV station put Ann's call to the station on live TV. Speaking into her cell phone during the chase, Ann said, "We robbed the bank as a protest against the corrupt government. We were going to give the money to the poor, not keep it for ourselves. Beth and Charlene and I are like modern-day Robin Hoods, stealing from the rich and giving to the poor." Ann, Beth, and Charlene are charged with bank robbery, and are on trial together. None of them testify.

> Call of the question: Discuss all evidence issues raised in the following paragraphs: (1) During the prosecution's case-in-chief, the prosecutor offers a recording from the TV station of Ann's remarks during the car chase. (2) During the prosecution's case-in-chief, the prosecutor offers testimony from Bob, a teller at the bank. Bob testifies, "I was working at the bank when Beth and Charlene burst in with guns and said, 'Nobody move, this is a robbery.' Beth came to my teller window, stuck a gun next to my face and said, 'Put all the money in this bag, and no funny stuff.'"

These paragraphs are loaded with evidence issues, including the best evidence rule, authentication, hearsay, and what § 11.30 calls the *Bruton* issue, which falls under the Confrontation Clause of the Sixth Amendment to the U.S. Constitution. The evidence is quite obviously relevant, but in the part of your answer that focuses on relevance, be sure to define relevance, and analyze both probative value and the risk of unfair prejudice. For paragraph 1, you might write:

Regarding the recording of Ann's remarks, evidence must be relevant to be admissible. Under the Federal Rules of Evidence (FRE) and the California Evidence Code (CEC), only relevant evidence is admissible. Relevance is defined similarly in the FRE and the CEC, as following: Evidence having any tendency in logic to make a fact of consequence more or less likely. We can infer from the facts that Ann, Beth, and Charlene have pleaded not guilty. Whether they robbed the bank is a fact of consequence. Ann's recorded statements amount to an admission that the three robbed the bank, and Ann's statement has a tendency to prove their guilt. Thus, the recording is relevant.

The court has the discretion to exclude relevant evidence if the probative value of the evidence is substantially outweighed by the danger of unfair prejudice to the party against whom the evidence is offered. Unfair prejudice means a tendency of evidence to tempt the jury to decide the case on an improper basis such as anger or disgust directed toward a party. The fact that evidence is strong does not make it unfairly prejudicial. Ann's statement is powerful evidence of guilt. It is difficult to see any tendency in her statement to tempt the jury to decide the case on anything other than a proper evaluation of the evidence. Thus, there is no or very little danger of unfair prejudice in this evidence. Nor is there a risk that this evidence will confuse the jury or waste the court's time. An objection that the evidence is unfairly prejudicial will be overruled.

§ 2.6   Limited Admissibility

In many cases, an item of evidence that is admissible for one purpose is inadmissible for another purpose. As well, evidence that is admissible against one party may be inadmissible against another party. When these scenarios arise—and they arise frequently—the evidence is generally admissible. Upon request from an attorney, the judge instructs the jury to consider the evidence only for the purpose for which it is admissible.[8] The rules governing limited admissibility follow:

FRE 105. Limiting Evidence That Is Not Admissible Against Other Parties or for Other Purposes. If the

---

[8]   CALCRIM instruction 303 provides: "During the trial, certain evidence was admitted for a limited purpose. You may consider that evidence only for that purpose and for no other."

court admits evidence that is admissible against a party or for a purpose—but not against another party or for another purpose—the court, on timely request, must restrict the evidence to its proper scope and instruct the jury accordingly.

CEC § 355. Limited Admissibility. When evidence is admissible as to one party or for one purpose and is inadmissible as to another party or for another purpose, the court upon request shall restrict the evidence to its proper scope and instruct the jury accordingly.

Suppose Sue slips and falls on a banana peel in the produce isle of a grocery store. Twenty minutes *before* Sue slipped, a different customer, Esmerelda, told the produce manager, "Hi, there is a banana peel, on the floor in the produce isle, someone might slip on it." If Esmerelda's statement is offered to prove there really was a banana peel on the floor, the statement is hearsay (*See* § 11.1). Unless a hearsay exception applies, Esmerelda's statement is inadmissible to prove a banana peel was on the floor. However, under tort law governing slip and fall cases, the plaintiff has to prove that the defendant was on notice of the dangerous condition that caused the accident.[9] Esmerelda's statement to the produce manager, twenty minutes before the accident, provides the required notice. Offered for the limited purpose of proving notice, Esmerelda's words are not hearsay. Although Esmerelda's statement is inadmissible hearsay when it is offered to prove the truth of the matter asserted, it is admissible when it is offered to prove notice. Thus, evidence that is inadmissible for one purpose (proof the banana peel was on the floor) is admissible for another purpose (proof of notice of a dangerous condition).

Consider another example of limited admissibility. John is accused of robbing the First Bank of Redding on August 1. The prosecutor has evidence that John robbed ten other banks, but John is not charged with any those ten robberies.[10] John is on trial for only one robbery, the robbery of the First Bank of Redding on August 1. John does not deny that the First Bank of Redding was robbed. John's argument is that he didn't do it. John asserts that when the bank was robbed in Redding, he was in Paso Robles, 400 miles away. The prosecutor is not allowed to offer evidence of John's ten uncharged robberies to prove that John is the kind of guy who robs banks, and therefore John probably robbed the First Bank of

---

[9]   *See Laird v. T.W. Mather, Inc.,* 51 Cal. 2d 210, 220, 331 P.2d 617 (1958).

[10]   Why isn't John charged with all eleven robberies? There are many possible reasons. For example, some or all of the other robberies might have occurred outside the territorial jurisdiction of the trial court.

Redding. Offered for that purpose, evidence of John's ten uncharged robberies violates the rule against character evidence; the rule that evidence of a person's character or disposition is not admissible to prove that a person acted in conformity with their character or disposition on a particular occasion (FRE 404(a)(1); CEC § 1101). The rule against character evidence, and the exceptions to the rule, is discussed in Chapter 6.

Although the prosecutor can't offer John's ten uncharged robberies as character evidence, suppose *all eleven* robberies were perpetrated in a strikingly similar way. In all eleven, the robber wore a black mask like the action hero Zorro, escaped in a red Ferrari, brandished identical pearl handled pistols, and handed the bank teller a pink taffeta pillow case in which to put the money! With such a unique *modus operandi*, it appears that one and the same person robbed *all eleven* banks. You will see in § 8.11 that when uncharged and charged crimes are perpetrated with a unique *modus operandi*, the uncharged acts may be admissible to prove identity. Offered to prove identity, the evidence is *not* character evidence, and is admissible. Thus, while evidence of John's ten uncharged robberies is not admissible to prove he has a propensity to rob banks, the ten uncharged robberies are admissible to prove identity.

M.O.

Finally, suppose Raul and Claudia are on trial together for burglary. Before trial, Raul made a statement to a police officer that implicated himself and Claudia in the burglary. Suppose the statement is admissible against Raul, but not against Claudia. Under FRE 105 and CEC § 355, Raul's statement may be admitted against him, but not against Claudia, and the judge will instruct the jury not to consider the statement against Claudia. To presage an issue discussed in § 11.30, it may be that the Confrontation Clause of the Sixth Amendment prohibits the admission of Raul's statement implicating Claudia. The Confrontation Clause, and the so-called *Bruton* issue, are discussed in Chapter 11.

§ 2.7   Problem on Limited Admissibility

A small, private airplane crashed, and the pilot was badly hurt. The pilot sued the airplane manufacturer under two theories: strict product liability and negligent design. At trial, the manufacturer offers evidence of the pilot's contributory negligence. Plaintiff objects. How should the judge rule? For the answer, *see* § 2.25.

§ 2.8   Limited Admissibility on an Exam

Your professor or the bar examiners could give you an exam question that explicitly asks you to explain limited admissibility.

More likely, however, you will mention limited admissibility in conjunction with your analysis of whether evidence is admissible. For example, with John, the accused bank robber, discussed in § 2.6, you might say:

> Evidence of John's ten uncharged robberies is very likely admissible to prove his identity as the person who robbed the First Bank of Redding. As discussed earlier in my answer, the unique *modus operandi* with which John robbed the ten other banks is strikingly similar to the *modus operandi* used in the robbery of the First Bank of Redding. As well, all eleven robberies have a unique signature quality—the mark of Zorro—that points to one person—John—as the culprit in all eleven crimes. It should be added that the ten uncharged robberies would be inadmissible against John if offered as character evidence, that is, circumstantial evidence that John has a propensity to rob banks, and, therefore, robbed the First Bank of Redding. Under the principle of limited admissibility, evidence admissible for one purpose—identity—but inadmissible for another purpose—character—is admissible, unless, of course, the evidence is excluded because the danger of unfair prejudice to the defendant substantially outweighs the probative value of the evidence, or the evidence is likely to confuse the jury.

§ 2.9   Rule of Completeness

When one party offers part of a document into evidence, fairness dictates that the other party be allowed to offer other parts relating to the same subject. The so-called rule of completeness accomplishes this end. The FRE and CEC provisions follow:

> **FRE 106. Remainder of or Related Writings or Recorded Statements**. If a party introduces all or part of a writing or recorded statement, an adverse party may require the introduction, at the time, of any other part—or any other writing or recorded statement—that in fairness ought to be considered at the same time.

> **CEC § 356. Entire Act, Declaration, Conversation, or Writing May Be Brought out to Elucidate Part Offered**. Where part of an act, declaration, conversation, or writing is given in evidence by one party, the whole on the same subject may be inquired into by an adverse party; when a letter is read, the answer may be given; and when a detached act, declaration, conversation, or writing is given in evidence, another act, declaration,

conversation, or writing which is necessary to make it understood may also be given in evidence.

§ 2.10 Similarities and Differences Between CEC and FRE

The FRE rule of completeness applies only to documents. The CEC is broader, applying to documents, conversations, and acts. The California Supreme Court wrote in *People v. Arias,* 13 Cal. 4th 92, 156, 51 Cal. Rptr. 2d 770, 913 P.2d 980 (1996), "Thus, if a party's oral admissions have been introduced in evidence, he may show other portions of the same interview or conversation, even if they are self-serving, which have some bearing upon, or connection with, the admission . . . ." California courts apply the rule of completeness broadly.[11] In *People v. Harris,* 37 Cal. 4th 310, 334–335, 118 P.3d 545, 33 Cal. Rptr. 3d 509 (2005), the Supreme Court wrote, "In applying Evidence Code section 356 the courts do not draw narrow lines around the exact subject of inquiry. In the event a statement admitted in evidence constitutes part of a conversation or correspondence, the opponent is entitled to have placed in evidence all that was said or written by or to the defendant in the course of such conversation or correspondence, provided the other statements have some bearing upon, or connection with, the admission or declaration in evidence."

Despite the fact that the FRE rule of completeness is limited to writings, judges working under FRE 106 often apply the rule to oral as well as written statements.

§ 2.11 Example of the Rule of Completeness—The Rest of the Story

An auto accident between Plaintiff and Defendant happened at an intersection regulated by a traffic light. Plaintiff sues Defendant for negligently causing the accident by running a red light. At trial, plaintiff offers testimony from a police officer who spoke with Defendant after the accident. In response to questions from Plaintiff's attorney, the officer testifies, "Defendant told me that he was going about 30 miles an hour when he entered the intersection against a red light." On cross-examination of the officer by Defendant's attorney, the following occurs:

Cross-Examination by Defense Counsel: Officer, during your direct testimony, in response to questions by Plaintiff's attorney, you described a conversation you had with my client, the Defendant, correct?

---

[11]   People v. Clark, 63 Cal. 4th 522, 372 P.3d 811, 203 Cal. Rptr. 3d 407 (2016).

A: Correct.

Q: During your direct testimony, you did not describe the entire conversation you had with my client, did you?

A: No. Your client had other things to say about the accident.

Q: What else did my client say about the accident?

Plaintiff's Counsel: Your honor, I object to this question. It calls for hearsay that is not within any exception to the hearsay rule.

Defense Counsel: Your honor, the objection should be overruled. During direct examination, Plaintiff's attorney elicited part of the conversation between the officer and my client, but more was said between them about how the accident happened. Under the rule of completeness, I am entitled to offer the rest of the conversation, and plaintiff's counsel can't raise a hearsay exception.

Court: Counsel approach the bench.

[Whereupon the following bench conference was held, outside the hearing the jury.]

Court: Asking the officer to repeat what your client told the officer would be hearsay, and there is no hearsay exception for it, is there?

Defense Counsel: Your honor, normally the hearsay objection would be well taken, but in this case, the rule of completeness trumps the hearsay objection. Plaintiff's counsel elicited from the officer part, and only part, of what my client told the officer. Fairness dictates that I be allowed to bring out the rest of what my client told the officer. What my client said on the same subject, the accident, tells the rest of the story.

Court: What did your client tell the officer?

Defense Counsel: My client told the officer that as he approached the intersection, he knew the light was red for him, so he stepped on the brakes to stop, but the brakes didn't work. My client told the officer that he pumped the brake pedal, but nothing happened. He told the officer he had recently had the brakes repaired, and they were working fine just before the accident.

Court: Well, that does seem to be the whole story, doesn't it counsel?

Plaintiff's Counsel: Your honor, the problem is, defense counsel is offering inadmissible hearsay. If defense counsel wants his client to give his version of what happened, the proper way to proceed is for defendant to testify and tell his story, not to violate the hearsay rule.

How should the judge rule on the objection? The judge should overrule the objection under the CEC and the FRE. Although the

FRE rule of completeness applies only to documents, and the conversation between the officer and defendant was oral, as mentioned above, judges applying the FRE often apply the completeness doctrine to oral as well as written statements.

As for the hearsay objection, a party's self-serving statement, offered for the truth of the matter asserted (here that the brakes didn't work), is hearsay, and, unless a hearsay exception applies, the statement is inadmissible. However, when the rule of completeness applies, the hearsay objection is not well taken, and the rest of the conversation is admissible. Fairness dictates this result.

The judge called the lawyers to the bench for a bench conference. Some bench conferences are recorded, others are not. The bench conference is a common practice, especially in jury trials, when the judge wants to discuss matters with counsel that the jury should not hear. The lawyers gather close to the bench and everyone speaks in hushed tones so the jury cannot overhear. Most of the time, it is more convenient, and quicker, to call the attorneys to the bench, rather than to have the jury leave the room. If you become a trial lawyer, you will often participate in bench conferences.

In the new courthouse for Yolo County, the judge can push a button on the bench, and white noise fills the courtroom to prevent anyone from hearing what transpires at the bench. In neighboring Colusa County, the historic courthouse opened for business during the first year of the Civil War, 1861, when Abe Lincoln was President. It will probably not surprise you to learn that in the historic Colusa courtroom, there is no button for white noise. Depending on where you practice, you make take an interest in courthouses. California has quite a few interesting old courthouses.

§ 2.12 Probative Value vs. Danger of Unfair Prejudice

Occasionally, a judge excludes relevant evidence because the probative value of the evidence is substantially outweighed by the danger the evidence will tempt the jury to decide the case on an improper basis, usually an emotional one. Imagine you are sitting on a criminal jury. The prosecution alleges that the defendant killed his elderly grandmother in her kitchen by shooting her in the head. The defendant admits he shot his grandmother, but defendant claims he acted in self-defense when the elderly lady attacked him with a knife. At trial, the prosecutor offers 20 photographs of the victim. Five photos show the victim alive and smiling, surrounded by her children, grandchildren, and great-grandchildren. Eight photos show various angles of the deceased victim on the floor of her kitchen, lying in a large pool of blood. Two pictures show the kitchen wall, spattered with blood and pieces of the victim's brain and skull stuck to the wall. Five of the photos are of the autopsy. One of the autopsy photos shows the victim's head, with the top of the skull blown off. One autopsy photo shows the victim's skull after the pathologist has removed the remaining portion of the top of the skull to expose what is left of the brain. One photo shows the remnants of the victim's brain, in a bowl. Two autopsy photos are of the victim's naked body lying on the metal autopsy table. As a juror, unless you work in the medical field, are a paramedic or a police officer, such photos must be deeply troubling. Indeed, even if you have seen severe trauma, the emotional impact of such photos is significant.

The photos are relevant because they show that, at one time, the victim was alive, and murder is the killing of a *living* human being. As well, the photos show where and how death occurred. The defense attorney will argue that some or all of the photos should be excluded from evidence despite their relevance. The defense will argue that the photos are so horrible, so gruesome, that the jury will be carried away with emotion, and will convict the defendant even if he acted in self-defense. According to the defense, the emotional impact of the photos will make it too difficult for the jury to calmly and methodically consider all the evidence, and to reach a just verdict. The prosecutor will respond that murder is not pretty. Although the photos are gruesome, the jury needs to see the photos to fully understand what happened. The photos undercut the defendant's argument that he killed in self-defense. Finally, some of the photos are needed to help the jury understand the testimony of the pathologist who performed the autopsy. The photos will help the jury understand the doctor's technical medical testimony about the nature of the wound and the cause of death. What should the judge do? Admit all the photos? Exclude them all? Admit some and exclude others?

The FRE and the CEC contain a rule that allows judges to balance the probative value of relevant evidence against the danger the evidence will unfairly prejudice a party, and to exclude the evidence if the probative value is substantially outweighed by the danger of unfair prejudice. The rules follow:

FRE Rule 403. Excluding Relevant Evidence for Prejudice, Confusion, Waste of Time, or Other Reasons. The court may exclude relevant evidence if its probative value is substantially outweighed by a danger of one or more of the following: unfair prejudice, confusing the issues, misleading the jury, undue delay, wasting time, or needlessly presenting cumulative evidence.

CEC § 352. Discretion of Court to Exclude Evidence. The court in its discretion may exclude evidence if its probative value is substantially outweighed by the probability that its admission will (a) necessitate undue consumption of time or (b) create substantial danger of undue prejudice, of confusing the issues, or of misleading the jury.

§ 2.13 Similarities and Differences Between CEC and FRE

Although the language of FRE 403 and CEC § 352 differ, the rules work identically in practice: The judge admits relevant evidence unless the probative value of the evidence is substantially outweighed by the danger of unfair prejudice.

With most types of evidence, the balancing of probative value against the danger of unfair prejudice under CEC § 352 and FRE 403 is identical. The FRE has 2 situations where the balancing is different.

First, FRE 609(a)(1)(B) deals with impeaching the defendant in a criminal case with the defendant's prior felony conviction. On objection to the impeachment, the judge balances the probative value of the conviction for purposes of impeachment against the danger of unfair prejudice to the defendant. The conviction is only admissible to impeach the defendant if the probative value of the conviction for purposes of impeachment outweighs the prejudicial effect on the defendant. Do you see the difference between regular 403 balancing, and balancing under FRE 609(a)(1)(B)? In both situations, the judge balances the probative value of evidence against the danger of unfair prejudice. With regular balancing, evidence is admissible unless the probative value is substantially outweighed by the danger of unfair prejudice. With balancing under FRE 609(a)(1)(B), the probative of the conviction must outweigh the prejudicial effect to the defendant. The factors that are balanced are the same. It is the balancing test that differs.

Second, FRE 703 deals with expert testimony. Rule 703 provides that when an expert's opinion is based on inadmissible information, the expert may only disclose the inadmissible information in court if the probative value of the information in helping the jury evaluate the expert's opinion substantially outweighs the prejudice to the opposing party. Again, the factors to be balanced are the same. Only the balancing test differs.

The CEC has no counterpart to the altered balancing tests of FRE 609(a)(1)(B) and FRE 703. In these situations, California judges employ regular Section 352 balancing. In most cases, however, a California Superior Court judge is likely to reach the same result as her counterpart in the Federal District Court.

§ 2.14   FRE 403 and CEC § 352 Exclude *Relevant* Evidence

FRE 403 and CEC § 352 exclude *relevant* evidence. If the evidence is not relevant, then 403 and 352 do not come into play. On an examination, the best approach is usually to analyze relevance first. If you conclude the evidence is not relevant, then it is excluded by FRE 402 and CEC § 350, not by FRE 403 and CEC § 352. If the evidence is relevant—if it has some probative value on a fact of consequence—then it is time to balance the probative value against the dangers catalogued in FRE 403 and CEC § 352.

§ 2.15   Party Must Object to Raise and Preserve Issue

The party seeking to exclude relevant evidence under FRE 403 or CEC § 352 must object: "Your honor, the defense objects on the basis of FRE 403 to the photographs offered by the prosecution. The probative value of the photographs is substantially outweighed by the danger of unfair prejudice to the defendant." Failure to object waives any claim of unfair prejudice.[12] Once a party objects, the judge balances the probative value of the evidence against the danger of unfair prejudice.

§ 2.16   Meaning of Unfair Prejudice

FRE 403 and CEC § 352 exclude evidence that is unfairly prejudicial to a party. Evidence that is powerful is not, for that reason, unfairly prejudicial. By unfair prejudice, the rules mean evidence that is likely to distract the jury from its duty to impartially and dispassionately evaluate the evidence. Evidence that may tempt jurors to decide the case based on strong emotion rather than the facts, is prejudicial. When evidence may incline the jury to dislike the party against whom evidence is offered, and to decide against the person whether or not that is the correct result, the evidence is unfairly prejudicial.

---

[12]   *See* People v. Landry, 2 Cal. 5th 52, 86, 385 P.3d 327, 211 Cal. Rptr. 3d 160 (2016)("As a general rule, the failure to object to errors committed at trial relieves the reviewing court of the obligation to consider those errors on appeal. This rule applies equally to any claim on appeal that the evidence was erroneously admitted, other than the stated rule for the objection at trial.").

§ 2.17　Factors in FRE 403 and CEC § 352 Balancing

When an attorney makes a FRE 403 or CEC § 352 objection, the judge balances the probative value of the evidence against the danger of unfair prejudice to the objecting party. The stronger the probative value of the evidence, the less likely any risk of unfair prejudice will substantially outweigh the probative value. Thus, it is not uncommon for evidence that carries a significant risk of unfair prejudice to be admissible because the probative value of the evidence is strong, and the risk of unfair prejudice simply cannot substantially outweigh the probative value. Even when the danger of unfair prejudice is greater than probative value, the evidence is admissible. Only when the danger of unfair prejudice *substantially* outweighs the probative value does the judge sustain a FRE 403/CEC § 352 objection.

Factors influencing the degree of prejudice include the remoteness of the evidence. Old evidence may have little probative value today, yet may carry significant risk of prejudice.

In criminal cases, the more similar proffered evidence is to the charged crime, the greater the risk of unfair prejudice to the defendant because the jury may misuse the evidence as proof defendant is guilty because "he's the kind of guy who would do such a thing."[13]

Defense counsel nearly always objects to evidence that is shocking or gruesome, such as autopsy and crime scene photographs in murder cases. Courts are clear, however, that gruesome photos are admissible if they help the jury understand what happened, or if they assist a medical expert to explain injuries and cause of death. With gruesome photos, it is not uncommon for the prosecution to offer more photos than necessary. When the defense makes a 403/352 objection, the judge goes through the photos, and admits some and excludes others.

When the party offering evidence has great need for particular evidence, the judge is not likely to exclude it, even though the evidence carries the risk of unfair prejudice. If the party's need for "dangerous" evidence is low because the party has other, equally probative evidence, the judge may exclude the "dangerous" evidence, especially if the other evidence has little or no risk of unfair prejudice.

---

[13] The risk is that the jury will use the proffered evidence as proof that the defendant has a propensity for certain types of conduct, and acted in conformity with that propensity to commit the charged crime. Such reasoning violates the rule against character evidence, FRE 404(a)(1) and CEC § 1101(a).

A factor in 403/352 balancing is whether the issue on which evidence is offered is disputed. When an issue is hotly disputed, the need for evidence is great, even if the evidence might unfairly prejudice. On the other hand, when there is no dispute, the need for evidence on the non-disputed point is low. A party seeking to avoid admission of prejudicial evidence sometimes offers to stipulate to the issue on which the prejudicial evidence is offered. The leading case is *Old Chief v. United States*, 519 U.S. 172, 117 S. Ct. 644 (1997). Mr. Old Chief was charged with assault with a dangerous weapon and possession of a firearm by a person with a prior felony conviction. The prosecutor had to prove the prior conviction, which was for assault causing serious injury. Defense counsel informed the judge that Old Chief was willing to stipulate that he had a prior felony conviction. The defense asked the judge to order the prosecutor not to mention the fact that the earlier crime, like the crime in the present trial, was assault. Defense counsel argued that because it was willing to admit the prior conviction, the issue was not disputed. It would unfairly prejudice Old Chief for the prosecutor to mention the name of the prior crime because the jury might use the earlier assault for the impermissible purpose of proving Old Chief's character. The prosecutor refused to agree to the stipulation, and informed the judge the prosecution intended to mention to the jury that the earlier crime was assault. The trial judge ruled in favor of the prosecution.

The issue before the U.S. Supreme Court was whether the trial court erred when it ruled the prosecution did not have to accept the defense offer to stipulate. The Court stated that in most cases, lawyers are free to prove their case with whatever admissible evidence they think best. Normally, one side cannot force the other side to stipulate to a fact, thus removing the need for evidence on that fact. In rare cases, however, when a fact is not essential to a party's ability tell a coherent and convincing story, the judge may order one side to accept the other side's offer to stipulate. The fact of a prior conviction is such a situation. Requiring the prosecution to stipulate to Old Chief's earlier conviction did nothing to weaken the government's evidence. Mentioning the name of the earlier conviction carried a risk of unfair prejudice, strengthening the argument in favor of the stipulation.

In California, Prop. 8 provides that when a prior felony conviction "is an element of any felony offense, it shall be proven to the trier of fact in open court."[14] When a defendant is charged with a felony, and an element of the crime is being an ex-felon in possession of a firearm, the defendant cannot prevent the

---

[14]   Cal. Const. Art. I, § 28(f)(4).

prosecutor from proving the earlier conviction. However, the nature of the prior conviction is inadmissible if the defendant offers to stipulate to the conviction.[15]

§ 2.18   FRE 403 and CEC § 352 on Exams

On exams, professors take different approaches to how much they want students to emphasize 403/352. For example, should you mention 403/352 with every item of evidence on an exam, even if a particular item carries no potential for unfair prejudice? This is a good question for your prof. Issues of unfair prejudice are most likely to arise with uncharged misconduct evidence (Chapter 8), impeachment by conviction (§ 10.6), and gruesome photographs (§ 2.12). If an item of evidence seems to you to have the potential for unfair prejudice, discuss 403/352, engage in the balancing that the trial court would do, and put your conclusion in your answer.

On the bar exam, the bar examiners like it when candidates discuss logical relevance first (FRE 401–402; CEC §§ 210, 350–351), followed by discussion of 403/352. Some bar prep courses teach students to use this approach. Some prep courses describe relevance as "logical relevance," and 403/352 as "legal relevance." Some professors use this terminology, others don't. Some professors refer to 403/352 as "pragmatic relevancy." Again, ask your prof.

§ 2.19   Additional Factors Under FRE 403 and CEC § 352

Most 403/352 issues concern claims of unfair prejudice. In addition to prejudice, the rules allow judges to exclude relevant evidence that would confuse or mislead the jury, waste time, cause unnecessary delay, or result in needless presentation of cumulative evidence. Obviously, in many cases there is overlap between unfair prejudice, misleading the jury, and confusion of the issues. Little separates delay from time wasting.

The Court of Appeal's decision in *Thompson v. Los Angeles*, 142 Cal. App. 4th, 47 Cal. Rptr. 3d 702 (2006) is instructive. Thompson tried unsuccessfully to steal two cars. Sheriff's deputies spotted Thompson, who ran and hid under a car. Deputies searching for Thompson announced by loud speaker that a police dog would be used. The dog located Thompson in his hiding place. A deputy ordered Thompson to come out with his hands in the open. As Thompson started to comply, the dog bit him on the leg. Thompson started hitting the dog, and, in the end, Thompson had bites on his leg, hand, and butt. Thompson sued the deputies and the county for

---

[15]   People v. Valentine, 42 Cal. 3d 170, 720 P.2d 913, 228 Cal. Rptr. 25 (1986).

excessive force in the use of the dog. At the civil trial, Thompson's attorney sought to introduce a report of bites inflicted by a *different* police dog. The trial judge excluded the report under CEC § 352 because the evidence was likely to confuse the jury. The Court of Appeal affirmed. Any small probative value was outweighed by the possibility of jury confusion.

§ 2.20   Problems on Probative Value vs. Unfair Prejudice

1.   Torture Murder

Dell is charged with torture murder, which requires the prosecutor to prove that Dell intended to inflict cruel or extreme pain and suffering. Dell had a history of inflicting domestic violence on the victim. In a public parking lot, Dell beat and kicked the victim. Dell retrieved a can of gas from his car, poured the gas on the victim, and set her on fire. The victim suffer massive burns that took her life. At trial, the prosecutor offers expert testimony describing the burns suffered by the victim, photographs of the burns, and a tape recording of the victim's screams while in the ambulance. Defense counsel objects on the basis of CEC § 352 because the evidence is extremely gruesome. How should the judge rule?

2.   Are the Videos Too Much?

After a night of heavy drinking with friends, Dell was driving the friends to a restaurant when he lost control of the speeding car and crashed. One of the friends was killed. Dell is charged with murder under a theory requiring proof that he was aware of the high degree of risk involved in drunk driving, but drove anyway. California decisions state that in order to prove the defendant's awareness, the prosecutor may offer evidence that the defendant had prior DUI convictions. Dell had such convictions. In conjunction with his earlier DUI convictions, Dell watched two videos on the dangers and consequences of drunk driving. The videos contained gruesome footage of fatal car crashes. As well, the videos contained tearful testimonials from surviving family members of victims of drunk driving. At Dell's murder trial, the prosecutor offers the two videos as evidence of Dell's awareness of the risks of drunk driving. Defense counsel objects on the basis of CEC § 352. The defense argues that the graphic accident footage, and the sad comments by surviving relatives, will tempt the jury to convict Dell whether or not he is guilty. Defense counsel cites *People v. Doolin*, 45 Cal. 4th 390, 439, 198 P.3d 11, 87 Cal. Rptr. 3d 209 (2009), where the Supreme Court wrote, "Evidence should be excluded as unduly prejudicial when it is of such nature as to inflame the emotions of the jury, motivating them to use the information, not to logically evaluate the point upon which it is relevant, but to reward or punish one side because of the jurors' emotional reaction. In such a circumstance, the evidence is unduly prejudicial because of the substantial likelihood the jury will use it for an illegitimate purpose." Assume that the prosecutor is allowed to establish defendant's awareness of the risks of drunk driving with his earlier convictions. Should the judge exclude the highly emotional videos as overkill? See § 2.25 for answers.

§ 2.21   Subsequent Remedial Measures

In the FRE, rules 407 to 411 exclude relevant evidence for reasons of policy. The CEC has counterparts for these rules.

FRE 407 and CEC § 1151 exclude evidence of subsequent remedial measures. The rules provide:

> **FRE 407. Subsequent Remedial Measures**. When measures are taken that would have made an earlier injury or harm less likely to occur, evidence of the subsequent measures is not admissible to prove: negligence; culpable conduct; a defect in a product or its design; or a need for a warning or instruction. But the court may admit this evidence for another purpose, such as impeachment or—if disputed—proving ownership, control, or the feasibility of precautionary measures.

> **CEC § 1151. Subsequent Remedial Conduct**. When, after the occurrence of an event, remedial or precautionary measures are taken, which, if taken previously, would have tended to make the event less likely to occur, evidence of such subsequent measures is inadmissible to prove negligence or culpable conduct in connection with the event.

FRE 407 and CEC § 1151 are similar. The rules are designed to encourage people to take steps to increase safety after an accident, without worrying that remedial measures will be used as evidence of fault. Consider the follow exam question:

> Travis is an excellent skier. Travis decided to go skiing at a ski resort near Lake Tahoe, California. Travis took the ski lift to the top of the mountain, and decided to ski down the most difficult ski run. A sign at the entrance to the ski run said, "Difficult run. Recommended for experienced skiers only." Half way down the run, Travis hit a tree and was seriously injured. Travis is suing the ski resort based on the theory that the resort was negligent in

allowing people to use the ski run on which Travis was injured. The ski resort denies any negligence. **Call of the question:** Apply the Federal Rules of Evidence (FRE) and the California Evidence Code (CEC). However, you should only mention the CEC if there is a difference between the FRE and the CEC on a particular issue. Assume all proper objections and offers of proof are made. Discuss all evidence issues in the numbered paragraphs. Paragraphs are not weighted equally for grading.

* * *

2.   Travis's lawyer offers the testimony of Thor Billings, who states: "After this accident, the ski resort replaced the sign at the top of the run. The new sign states: 'EXTREMELY DANGEROUS RUN, WITH EXPOSED TREES AND ROCKS; ENTER AT YOUR OWN RISK.'"

This is an example of a subsequent remedial measure that is barred by FRE 407 and CEC § 1151. Travis is suing based on negligence. The new sign was placed *after* Travis's accident. The sign is a remedial measure that may have made the accident less likely to occur. Evidence of the new sign might be relevant to prove negligence, but the sign is not admissible for that purpose.

The facts do not indicate that the ski resort is arguing that it was not feasible to take precautionary measures. If the ski resort took the position that there was nothing it could have done to make the ski run safer, the evidence of the sign would be admissible.

There is no issue of ownership or control of the ski run. Thus, the new sign is not admissible to prove ownership or control. Nor do the facts indicate the new sign would be relevant for purposes of impeachment.

FRE 407 and CEC § 1151 bar evidence of remedial measures taken subsequent to an accident. Remedial measures that were taken *before* an accident happened are not barred by the rules, so long as they are relevant.

FRE 407 and CEC § 1151 bar evidence of remedial measures taken by the defendant. If a third party, not connected to the defendant, made subsequent remedial measures, and the measures are relevant, the measures are not barred by the rules.

FRE 407 bars subsequent remedial measures in negligence and strict product liability cases. CEC § 1151 bars subsequent remedial measures in negligence cases, but not in strict product liability cases.

§ 2.22   Settlement and Plea Negotiations

Most civil litigation settles. The rules of evidence encourage settlement by providing that statements made during efforts to settle disputed claims are inadmissible if the case goes to trial (FRE 408, CEC § 1152).

Most criminal cases are resolved through plea negotiations. To encourage candid discussions during plea bargaining, FRE 410 and CEC § 1153 limit admission of statements made during such negotiations.

§ 2.23   Offer to Pay Medical Expenses

To encourage acts of beneficence, FRE 409 provides that an offer to pay medical expenses resulting from an injury cannot be used as evidence that the offeror felt responsible for the injury. The CEC counterpart is Section 1160. Section 1160 is broader than FRE 409. The CEC provision excludes from evidence statements or benevolent gestures expressing sympathy for a person involved in an accident.

Sometimes, an offer to pay medical expenses, or some other gesture of sympathy, is accompanied by an admission of fault. For example, after Dell ran over Vic with Dell's car, Dell visited Vic in the hospital, and said, "Vic. I feel terrible about your injuries. May I offer to pay your medical expenses? I wasn't watching the road when I hit you. It was my fault. I apologize." CEC § 1160(a) provides that the section does not apply to statements of fault. Under the FRE, a judge might admit the part of the statement that admits fault, and exclude the part that offers to pay medical expenses.

§ 2.24   Liability Insurance

The fact that a person had or lacked insurance to pay for injuries is probably irrelevant to whether the person was at fault. Assuming, arguendo, that insurance has some probative value regarding negligence, FRE 411 and CEC § 1155 exclude evidence that a person was or was not insured to prove negligence or other wrongdoing.

Occasionally, evidence of insurance is relevant to prove something other than fault. For example, a vehicle is involved in an accident, and the injured party sues Dell, claiming Dell owns the vehicle. Dell denies ownership. Through discovery, the injured party learns that Dell's insurance policy covers the vehicle. Evidence of insurance would be admissible at trial to prove ownership.

§ 2.25   Answers to Chapter Problems

1.   Is Dell an Arsonist? (§ 2.4)

Beth's testimony is direct evidence, as is Dell's confession. From Beth's eyewitness testimony, it is reasonable to infer that Dell was fleeing to escape capture. Evidence of flight is often admitted as circumstantial evidence of consciousness of guilt. From consciousness of guilt, it is reasonable to infer actual guilt.

2.   International Child Abduction (§ 2.4)

I was mother's attorney. I thought the loss of father's passport, and the reason for the loss, were relevant because the loss of his ability to travel meant that if mother refused to send the child to Sacramento, father would have no way to spend time with his son. At first, the child support evidence seemed entirely irrelevant, and the judge nearly sustained the objection. Luckily, the judge let me explain, and he was persuaded. The evidence was admitted. Mother won, and her son was returned to her care.[16]

3.   Murder Most Foul (§ 2.4)

Problem 3 is based on *People v. Hamilton,* 41 Cal. 3d 408, 710 P.2d 981, 221 Cal. Rptr. 902 (1985), *vacated,* 478 U.S. 1017 (1986). The California Supreme Court ruled the prosecution's evidence was relevant to show defendant's consciousness of guilt and his identity as the killer. The fact that defendant went shopping for tools that would allow him to do to the girl friend what had been done to the murder victim had a tendency to prove that defendant was the killer.

4.   Did Alcohol Matter? (§ 2.4)

Problem 4 is based on *People v. Stitely,* 35 Cal. 4th 514, 108 P.3d 182, 26 Cal. Rptr. 3d 1 (2005). The trial judge excluded the evidence of the victim's intoxication, and the Supreme Court approved. Absent some evidence that the victim's intoxication was relevant to her giving or withholding consent, the evidence was irrelevant.

5.   Is the Gun Relevant? (§ 2.4)

Courts generally hold that guns are "tools of the trade" of drug dealers, and are relevant.

---

[16]   Interestingly, after a few years, the parents agreed to resume summer visits in Sacramento, and all went well.

Problem on Limited Admissibility (§ 2.7)

The problem is based on *McGee v. Cessna Aircraft Co.*, 139 Cal. App. 3d 179, 188 Cal. Rptr. 542 (1983). The Court of Appeal ruled that contributory negligence was irrelevant on the issue of strict product liability, but relevant to plaintiff's negligence claim.

Problems on Probative Value vs. Unfair Prejudice (§ 2.20)

1.   Torture Murder

In *People v. Streeter*, 54 Cal. 4th 205, 236, 278 P.3d 754, 142 Cal. Rptr. 3d 481 (2012), the Supreme Court ruled that the evidence was admissible to prove defendant's intent to torture the victim. The evidence accurately illustrated the horrible nature of defendant's crime.

2.   Are the Videos Too Much?

The Court of Appeal in *People v. Diaz,* 227 Cal. App. 4th 362, 173 Cal. Rptr. 3d 594 (2014), ruled it was reversible error to admit the videos. The Court of Appeal considered quite a few factors that are not repeated in the problem, including the fact that the prosecution's case for murder was not strong. The Court placed particular emphasis on the emotional content of the videos to support the court's decision that the videos unfairly prejudiced defendant.

Chapter 3

PRELIMINARY FACTS AND LAYING A FOUNDATION

This chapter discusses issues that arise *before* evidence is admitted. The chapter begins with discussion of preliminary facts, that is, facts that must be decided in order to determine whether evidence is admissible. That done, the chapter discusses ways to prove preliminary facts, typically called laying a foundation.

§ 3.1   Preliminary Facts

Before proffered evidence is admissible, certain facts must be established.[1] For example, before evidence is admitted, a decision must be made whether the evidence is relevant. Before a person may testify as an expert witness, a decision must be made whether the person is an expert. Before a lay witness may testify, a decision must be made whether the person is competent to testify. Before an out-of-court statement is admitted, someone needs to decide whether the statement is hearsay, and, if it is, whether it meets the requirements of a hearsay exception. Before a bag of narcotics is admissible against a defendant, a decision must be made whether the drugs belong to the defendant. If the drugs are not the defendant's, the drugs are not relevant. Before a letter bearing a signature is admissible against the alleged author, someone must decide whether the person actually wrote the letter. And so it goes with virtually all evidence. Before evidence is admissible, someone must decide certain facts, called preliminary facts, that is, preliminary to admissibility.

You are familiar with the division of labor between judge and jury. The jury decides the facts. The judge determines the law, and instructs the jury on the law it is to apply to the facts. But what about preliminary facts? Are preliminary facts decided by the jury? Or does the judge decide preliminary facts? The answer is, it depends on what kind of preliminary fact you have in mind. Some preliminary facts are decided by the judge, with no input from the jury. Other preliminary facts are decided by the jury, after the judge makes a screening decision that there is enough evidence of

---

[1]   CEC § 401 defines "proffered evidence" as evidence, the admissibility or inadmissibility of which, is dependent upon the existence or nonexistence of a preliminary fact. The FRE has no definition of proffered evidence, but the meaning is the same under the FRE.

the preliminary fact to justify giving the issue to the jury. The rules on preliminary facts follow:

FRE 104. Preliminary Questions. (a) In General. The court must decide any preliminary question about whether a witness is qualified, a privilege exists, or evidence is admissible. In so deciding, the court is not bound by evidence rules, except those on privilege. **(b) Relevance That Depends on a Fact**. When the relevance of evidence depends on whether a fact exists, proof must be introduced sufficient to support a finding that the fact does exist. The court may admit the proposed evidence on the condition that the proof be introduced later. **(c) Conducting a Hearing So That the Jury Cannot Hear It**. The court must conduct any hearing on a preliminary question so that the jury cannot hear it if: (1) the hearing involves the admissibility of a confession; (2) a defendant in a criminal case is a witness and so requests; or (3) justice so requires. **(d) Cross-Examining a Defendant in a Criminal Case**. By testifying on a preliminary question, a defendant in a criminal case does not become subject to cross-examination on other issues in the case. **(e) Evidence Relevant to Weight and Credibility**. This rule does not limit a party's right to introduce before the jury evidence that is relevant to the weight or credibility of other evidence.

CEC § 312. Jury as Trier of Fact. Except as otherwise provided by law, where the trial is by jury: (a) All questions of fact are to be decided by the jury. (b) Subject to the control of the court, the jury is to determine the effect and value of the evidence addressed to it, including the credibility of witnesses and hearsay declarants.

CEC § 400. Preliminary Fact. As used in [§§ 400–406], "preliminary fact" means a fact upon the existence or nonexistence of which depends the admissibility or inadmissibility of evidence. The phrase "the admissibility or inadmissibility of evidence" includes the qualification or disqualification of a person to be a witness and the existence or nonexistence of a privilege.

CEC § 401. Proffered Evidence. As used in [§§ 400–406], "proffered evidence" means evidence, the admissibility or inadmissibility of which is dependent upon the existence or nonexistence of a preliminary fact.

CEC § 402. Procedure for Determining Foundational and Other Preliminary Facts. (a) When the existence of a preliminary fact is disputed, its existence or nonexistence shall be determined as provided in [§§ 400–406]. (b) The court may hear and determine the question of the admissibility of evidence out of the presence or hearing of the jury; but in a criminal action, the court shall hear and determine the question of the admissibility of a confession or admission of the defendant out of the presence and hearing of the jury if any party so requests. (c) A ruling on the admissibility of evidence implies whatever finding of fact is prerequisite thereto; a separate or formal finding is unnecessary unless required by statute.

CEC § 403. Determination of Foundation and Other Preliminary Facts Where Relevancy, Personal Knowledge, or Authenticity Is Disputed. (a) The proponent of the proffered evidence has the burden of producing evidence as to the existence of the preliminary fact, and the proffered evidence is inadmissible unless the court finds that there is evidence sufficient to sustain a finding of the existence of the preliminary fact, when: (1) The relevance of the proffered evidence depends on the existence of the preliminary fact; (2) The preliminary fact is the personal knowledge of a witness concerning the subject matter of his testimony; (3) The preliminary fact is the authenticity of a writing; or (4) The proffered evidence is of a statement or other conduct of a particular person and the preliminary fact is whether that person made the statement or so conducted himself. (b) Subject to Section 702 [the requirement that a witness have personal knowledge], the court may admit conditionally the proffered evidence under this section, subject to evidence of the preliminary fact being supplied later in the course of the trial. (c) If the court admits the proffered evidence under this section, the court: (1) May, and on request shall, instruct the jury to determine whether the preliminary fact exists and to disregard the proffered evidence unless the jury finds that the preliminary fact does exist. (2) Shall instruct the jury to disregard the proffered evidence if the court subsequently determines that a jury could not reasonably find that the preliminary fact exists.

CEC § 404. Determination of Whether Proffered Evidence Is Incriminatory. Whenever the proffered evidence is claimed to be privileged under Section 940 [the privilege against self-incrimination], the person claiming the privilege has the burden of showing that the proffered evidence might tend to incriminate him; and the proffered evidence is inadmissible unless it clearly appears to the court that the proffered evidence cannot possibly have a tendency to incriminate the person claiming the privilege.

CEC § 405. Determination of Foundational and Other Preliminary Facts in Other Cases. With respect to preliminary fact determination not governed by Section 403 or 404: (a) When the existence of a preliminary fact is disputed, the court shall indicate which party has the burden of producing evidence and the burden of proof on the issue as implied by the rule of law under which the question arises. The court shall determine the existence or nonexistence of the preliminary fact and shall admit or exclude the proffered evidence as required by the rule of law under which the question arises. (b) If a preliminary fact is also a fact in issue in the action: (1) The jury shall not be informed of the court's determination as to the existence or nonexistence of the preliminary fact. (2) If the proffered evidence is admitted, the jury shall not be instructed to disregard the evidence if its determination of the fact differs from the court's determination of the preliminary fact.

CEC § 406. Evidence Affecting Weight or Credibility. This article [§§ 400–406] does not limit the right of a party to introduce before the trier of fact evidence relevant to weight or credibility.

§ 3.2   Similarities and Differences Between FRE and CEC

The language of the rules is different. In practice, however, the FRE and the CEC rules on preliminary facts operate similarly. One difference is that under the FRE, the judge who is deciding a preliminary fact is not bound by the rules of evidence, except rules of privilege (FRE 104(a)), whereas a California judge applying the CEC to preliminary facts is bound by the rules of evidence.

§ 3.3   Judge Decides Preliminary Facts Under FRE 104(a); Jury Decides Preliminary Facts Under 104(b)

FRE 104(a) states that the "the court decides" certain preliminary facts. The words "the court decides" means the judge *alone* decides preliminary facts that fall within Rule 104(a). The standard of proof for 104(a) preliminary questions is a preponderance of the evidence. The jury plays no role in determining 104(a) preliminary facts. The jury decides how much, if any weight, to give the evidence *after* it is admitted, but the jury plays no role in deciding the facts that determine admissibility. For example, when a party offers expert testimony, the preliminary fact is whether the witness is qualified to testify as an expert. Qualification to provide expert testimony is a Rule 104(a) question for the judge. The jury plays no role in deciding whether a person qualifies to testify as an expert. The jury decides whether to believe the expert, but not whether the person qualifies to testify as an expert.

Preliminary facts that fall within FRE 104(b) are decided by the jury, *after* the judge makes an initial screening decision that there is enough evidence of the preliminary facts that a reasonable jury could find the preliminary facts true. If the judge concludes that no reasonable juror could find the preliminary facts true, the judge excludes the evidence. Assuming the judge admits the evidence, the jury decides the existence of the preliminary facts by a preponderance of the evidence. For example, if the plaintiff offers a document allegedly signed by the defendant, the preliminary fact is whether the defendant signed the document. This is a Rule 104(b) question. The judge listens to evidence about the signature, and decides whether a reasonable juror could determine from the evidence that the signature is genuine. If so, then the document may be admitted.[2] The jury will be instructed that if it finds the signature genuine, it may give the document whatever weight it deserves, but if the signature is not genuine, the document should be ignored.

Under the FRE, it is important to determine whether the existence of a preliminary fact is a 104(a) question for the judge to decide, or a 104(b) question for the jury to decide. Rule 104(b) draws the distinction with words that are not a model of clarity. Rule 104(b) states that when the relevance of proffered evidence depends on whether a preliminary fact exists, the preliminary fact is for the jury to decide under 104(b). In other words, if the preliminary fact exists, *then* the proffered evidence is relevant, as relevance is defined in FRE 401—the proffered evidence has a tendency to prove a fact of consequence. However, if the preliminary fact does not exist, then the proffered evidence is irrelevant, in the FRE 401

---

[2]   Other evidence issues will need to be determined too, including the best evidence rule and hearsay. Each of those issues comes with its own questions of preliminary fact, decided under 104(a) or 104(b).

sense. To return to the document in the previous paragraph, the preliminary question is whether the defendant signed the document. If defendant signed it, then the document is relevant. If defendant did not sign it, the document is irrelevant. The preliminary fact of whether defendant signed the document is for the jury to decide under Rule 104(b).[3]

The following preliminary facts fall within 104(a): Whether evidence is relevant; whether a privilege applies; whether a witness is competent; whether a person qualifies as an expert witness; most hearsay issues; whether a hearsay declarant is unavailable; and most issues under the best evidence rule.

Suppose you encounter an item of evidence. You know that preliminary facts must be established before the evidence is admissible, and you determine what the preliminary facts are. However, you don't know whether the preliminary facts are for the judge to decide under Rule 104(a), or for the jury to decide under Rule 104(b). How do you figure out whether to apply 104(a) or 104(b)? Rule 104 does not answer the question for all types of preliminary facts. You could do research in cases or treatises. But you can figure it out on your own. Here's how. First, if the evidence is *relevant,* in the Rule 401 sense, only if the preliminary facts are true, then the preliminary facts are for the jury under Rule 104(b). Second, if the evidence would be relevant *whether or not* the preliminary facts are true, the preliminary facts are probably for the judge to decide under Rule 104(a).

Consider an example involving a claim of privilege—the psychotherapist-client privilege (See § 12.3). Assume there was a confidential communication between a psychotherapist and the therapist's client. Assume that what was said is highly relevant. In court, the communication may be privileged. If the privilege applies, the jury will not hear the communication. If the privilege does not apply, the jury will hear the communication. In either case, the communication is relevant. Who decides the preliminary facts that determine whether the communication is privileged, judge or jury? The answer is, the judge alone decides questions of privilege. Rule 104(a) so provides, and you can see why. The reason has nothing to do with whether the evidence is relevant. It has to do with whether it is reasonable to expect a jury to be able to listen to the evidence of the preliminary facts, including the communication, and to

---

[3]   Some courts refer to 104(b) questions as matters of conditional relevancy, that is, the relevance of evidence is conditioned upon the truth of some preliminary fact. Don't confuse conditional relevance, FRE 104(b), with relevance, defined in FRE 401. Rule 401 tells you what evidence is relevant. Rule 104(b) tells you what preliminary facts are decided by the jury. They are related, but separate concepts.

rationally decide whether the preliminary facts are established. If the jury decides the preliminary facts are not established, the jury will conclude no privilege applies, and will consider the communication. If the jury decides the preliminary facts are established, the jury will have to conclude the privilege applies, and pretend it never heard the communication. But is that realistic? Is it realistic to ask lay jurors to listen to evidence, and then, if the evidence is inadmissible, pretend they never heard it? It is asking a lot. It is asking too much. The better approach is for the judge to rule on privilege issues. That way, if a privilege applies, the jury never hears the communication. Thus, you can see why preliminary facts related to privileges fall under Rule 104(a).

Consider another example, this time involving whether a confession was voluntary. If the confession was voluntary, the jury will hear it. If the confession was involuntary, the jury won't hear it. The preliminary fact is whether or not the confession was voluntary. Who decides voluntariness, judge or jury? Answer, the judge. To decide whether a confession was voluntary, it is typically necessary to listen to the confession itself. Is it realistic to expect a jury to listen to the defendant confessing the very crime on trial, to conclude that it was involuntary, and then to completely erase the confession from their minds? No. So, the judge decides whether the confession was voluntary. The FRE and CEC feel so strongly about confessions that the rules require the judge to make sure the jury does not inadvertently hear any preliminary evidence on the matter (FRE 104(c)(1); CEC § 402(b)).

If you encounter preliminary facts, and you don't know whether to apply Rule 104(a) or Rule 104(b), ask yourself: Is it realistic to ask jurors to evaluate the preliminary facts, and, as is often the case, the evidence itself, and to disregard the evidence if it inadmissible? If your answer is no, it is not realistic, then the preliminary facts should be decided by the judge under Rule 104(a).

§ 3.4   Under the CEC, Preliminary Facts Under § 403 Are for the Jury. Preliminary Facts Under § 405 Are for the Judge

CEC § 403 provides that when the relevance of evidence depends on the existence of a preliminary fact, the jury decides the preliminary fact (CEC § 403(a)(1)).[4] This is the same as FRE 104(b).

CEC § 403(a) allocates to the jury preliminary facts related to whether a witness has personal knowledge, whether a writing is

---

[4]   CEC § 403(c) describes the instruction the judge gives the jury regarding preliminary facts. A similar instruction would be given under the FRE.

authentic, and whether a person is properly identified. The FRE treats these the same, under Rule 104(b).

Under the CEC, when a preliminary fact does not fall under CEC § 403, then it falls under § 405, and is decided by the judge. The following preliminary facts are for the judge under § 405: whether a witness is competent, whether a person qualifies to testify as an expert, privileges, and whether an out-of-court statement is hearsay.[5] The same is true under the FRE; these are FRE 104(a) preliminary facts for the judge.

§ 3.5   Problems on Preliminary Facts

Try your hand with a few problems on preliminary facts. Are the preliminary facts for the judge or for the jury? You will find analysis in § 3.17.

1.   Did Wendy See It?

An auto accident occurred at a city intersection. Plaintiff is suing Defendant, claiming that Defendant ran a red light and caused the accident. Plaintiff offers testimony from Wendy, who will testify that she saw the accident. Defendant has information that, at the time of the accident, Wendy was out of town, and could not have witnessed what happened. What preliminary fact has to be decided before Wendy testifies? Is the preliminary fact for the judge under Rule 104(a) or the jury under Rule 104(b)? What about in California? Section 403, or Section 405?

2.   Who Penned the Missive?

In a personal injury suit arising out of a car accident, defendant offers testimony from Plaintiff's treating doctor. The doctor testifies that Plaintiff was not seriously injured in the accident. To impeach the doctor, Plaintiff's attorney offers in evidence a copy of a letter allegedly written by the doctor, in which, whoever wrote the letter, wrote that Plaintiff's injuries were serious. What preliminary facts must be decided? Are the preliminary facts for the judge or the jury under the FRE and the CEC?

3.   This Pizza Is Cold!

In yet another car accident, Plaintiff sues the Defendant Pizza Company, claiming that Plaintiff, was struck by Joe—Starving Student—Johnson, who was delivering pizzas for Pizza Company, and that Joe caused the accident. What preliminary facts must be decided? Who decides them?

---

[5]   The judge decides whether a statement is hearsay (§ 405), but the jury decides whether a person made a statement (§ 403).

§ 3.6   Laying a Foundation: Introduction

"Objection, lack of foundation." This objection is heard every day in courtrooms across America. Before a judge admits evidence, the proponent must lay the necessary foundation. Failure to lay a foundation results in exclusion of the evidence, unless the opponent fails to object.

It is important to understand that preliminary facts (FRE 104/CEC §§ 403–405) and foundation (FRE 901/CEC § 1400) are not separate issues. They are different aspects of the same issue, namely: The what, the who, and the how of admissibility. First, *what* preliminary facts must be established before evidence is admissible? Second, *who* decides the preliminary facts, judge or jury? Third, *how* are the preliminary facts established: What foundation must be laid?

Authentication and identification are types of foundations. You lay the foundation for a document by authenticating the document. You lay the foundation for a bag of cocaine by identifying the cocaine as the cocaine seized from the defendant. At trial, an attorney hoping to exclude a document might say, "Objection, failure to authenticate" or "Objection, failure to lay the necessary foundation." The words differ, but the complaint is the same. The attorney is arguing that the proponent has not taken the steps necessary to justify receipt of the evidence by establishing the necessary preliminary facts.

In practice, the word "authenticate" typically refers to documents, and "identify" refers to things and voices. Thus, you authenticate documents and identify things and voices.

§ 3.7   Foundations Vary

Every kind of evidence has a foundation. For example, to admit a document, three foundations are typically required: (1) authentication, (2) best evidence,[6] and (3) hearsay. The foundation for lay witness testimony is proof of personal knowledge. To admit an audio recording of a voice, three foundations may be needed: (1) identification of the voice, (2) proof that the recording is accurate, and (3) hearsay. The foundation for a character witness is proof that the witness knows the person they are testifying about well enough to have an opinion, or knows the person's reputation well enough to relate the reputation to the jury.

---

[6]   California has the secondary evidence rule rather than the best evidence rule.

Laying a foundation is not rocket science. Once you understand the necessity of a foundation, you will get it right. As a neophyte lawyer, you will write out the necessary questions for each foundation. As you gain experience, laying a foundation becomes second nature, and you won't need a script. There are books that tell you exactly how to lay the foundation for just about every kind of evidence you can imagine. Two excellent resources are *California Evidentiary Foundations* by professors Edward J. Imwinkelried and Thomas J. Leach, and *Evidentiary Foundations* by Edward J. Imwinkelried.

§ 3.8   Self-Authenticating Documents

The law does not assume a document is genuine. The proponent must establish genuineness, that is, authenticate the document. Certain documents, however, are so likely to be genuine that they are self-authenticating—they authenticate themselves. FRE 902 specifies twelve types of self-authenticating documents. FRE 902 is discussed in § 3.12.

The CEC does not speak of self-authentication. The California approach to documents that are likely to be genuine is to presume the genuineness of such documents (CEC §§ 644–645.1; 1451–1454; 1530–1532). The CEC approach is discussed in § 3.13.

When a document is not self-authenticating under the FRE, or presumed genuine under the CEC, genuineness is established with evidence in addition to the document—called extrinsic evidence. The extrinsic evidence is often a witness, who testifies that the document is genuine.

§ 3.9   Rules Regarding Authentication

The FRE rule requiring authentication states:

FRE 901(a). Authenticating or Identifying Evidence.
(a) In General. To satisfy the requirement of authenticating or identifying an item of evidence, the proponent must produce evidence sufficient to support a finding that the item is what the proponent claims it is.

After you read Rule 901(a), return to § 3.1, and reread Rule 104(b). Do you see the similar wording? This is deliberate. In the FRE, 104(b) questions of preliminary fact are decided by the jury. Rule 901(a) uses very similar language to make clear that authentication is a preliminary fact for the jury.

The CEC rules on authentication follow:

CEC § 1400. Authentication Defined. Authentication of a writing means (a) the introduction of evidence sufficient to sustain a finding that it is the writing that the proponent of the evidence claims it is or (b) the establishment of such facts by any other means provided by law.

CEC § 1401. Authentication Required. (a) Authentication of a writing is required before it may be received in evidence. (b) Authentication of a writing is required before secondary evidence of its content may be received in evidence.

Read Section 1400 in conjunction with Section 403(a). As with the FRE, the parallel language is deliberate. Authentication is a preliminary fact for the jury to decide.

§ 3.10 Similarities and Differences Between FRE and CEC

FRE 901 refers to authenticating documents and identifying things. CEC §§ 1400 and 1401 refer only to documents. This is a distinction without a difference, however. To be relevant under the CEC, all evidence—documents, things, voices, etc.—must be authenticated or identified.

§ 3.11 Common Foundations

It would take hundreds of pages to fully explore foundations. Our mission is less lofty. The goal is to help you understand the basics so you are ready for exams. This section discusses some of the most common foundations. When the occasion arises in other chapters, other foundations are discussed.

§ 3.11(a). Testimony of a Witness Who Knows

If you need to authenticate a document or identify a thing, the easiest way to do it is with a witness who knows. FRE 901(b)(1) authorizes authentication and identification with "testimony that an item is what it is claimed to be." CEC § 1413 provides, "A writing may be authenticated by anyone who saw the writing made or executed, including a subscribing witness."

§ 3.11(b). Handwriting

FRE 901(b)(2) provides a simple way to authenticate handwriting; use "a nonexpert's opinion that handwriting is genuine, based on familiarity with it that was not acquired for the current litigation." CEC § 1416 is similar.

A more complicated way to authenticate handwriting is provided by FRE 901(b)(3): "A comparison with an authenticated specimen by an expert witness or the trier of fact." CEC §§ 1417–1418 are similar. A handwriting expert may compare the disputed handwriting with exemplars of handwriting that have been authenticated. In a wire fraud case, for example, the defendant did not admit that his signature appeared on a document that was vital to the prosecution's case. The government found defendant's signature on a Department of Motor Vehicles (DMV) document and on a return receipt for registered mail. After the DMV and postal service documents were authenticated, a handwriting expert compared the exemplars to the disputed signature, and concluded one and the same person signed all three documents.

FRE 901(b)(3) and CEC § 1417 allow the comparison to be made by an expert or by the jury. As a trial attorney, I would never trust a jury to do the comparison. I can't control what a jury decides. I can control what my expert says. If my expert tells me in advance of trial that the signature is not genuine, I won't offer the expert's testimony. Is that ethical? Yes. So as long as I don't suppress evidence or mislead the court.

§ 3.11(c).   Reply Letter Doctrine

A letter, email, text message, or similar two-way communication can be authenticated with evidence that the document is a response to a known document. This is called the reply letter doctrine, and it is authorized by CEC § 1420, which provides, "A writing may be authenticated by evidence that the writing was received in response to a communication sent to the person who is claimed by the proponent of the evidence to be the author of the writing." The FRE does not expressly authorize the reply letter doctrine, but the doctrine is well accepted in federal court.

§ 3.11(d).   Information Known Only to One Person

A document can be authenticated with evidence that the document contains information known only to one person. This method is sanctioned CEC § 1421, which states, "A writing may be authenticated by evidence that the writing refers to or states matters that are unlikely to be known to anyone other than the person who is claimed by the proponent of the evidence to be the author of the writing."

§ 3.11(e).   Distinctive Characteristics

FRE 901(b)(4) allows authentication based on "the appearance, contents, substance, internal patterns, or other distinctive characteristics of the item, taken together with all the circumstances." Authorship is sometimes established under 901(b)(4) with evidence that a communication contains misspellings, phrases, or words that only one person employs.

FRE 901(b)(4) is also used to authenticate things. For example, it may be critical to prove that the bullet retrieved from the victim's body was fired from the defendant's gun. An expert can test-fire bullets from defendant's gun, and compare the unique markings on the test bullets with markings on the fatal bullet.

§ 3.11(f).   Voices

When it is necessary identify a voice, someone familiar with the speaker can do so (FRE 901(b)(5)).

§ 3.11(g).   Telephone Calls

When it comes to phone calls, different rules apply to identify the caller and the callee. Regarding the caller, courts agree that self-identification is not sufficient, by itself, to identify the caller. Thus, if you pick up the phone, and the voice on the other end says, "Hello, this is Susan," this self-identification is not sufficient to identify Susan as the caller. There must be additional evidence. If you are able to identify Susan's voice from experience, that will suffice (FRE 901(b)(1)). If the caller said, "Hello, this is Susan. I'm responding the voicemail message you left me earlier tonight about the party," the reply letter doctrine can be enlisted. If your phone is equipped with caller ID, and the number that shows up can be traced to Susan, her voice can be authenticated. Thus, self-identification, in conjunction with other evidence, authenticates the caller.

To identify the callee, simply offer testimony from someone familiar with the callee's voice. Alternatively, FRE 901(b)(6) allows identification of a callee with evidence that a call was made to the phone number assigned to the callee, and the person answering the phone self-identified as the callee. If the call was to a business, identification of the business is accomplished with evidence the phone number was assigned to the business, and the substance of the call related to business reasonably transacted over the phone.

§ 3.11(h).   Public Records

The law authorizes certain documents to be filed in government offices. Consider deeds to land, recorded in the office of the county recorder of deeds. Such a document can be authenticated with testimony that the document was recorded or filed in the appropriate public office (FRE 901(b)(7)(A); CEC § 1600).

Documents prepared by government workers can be authenticated with testimony that the record is from the office where such records are kept (FRE 901(b)(7)(B)).

§ 3.11(i).   Ancient Documents

The CEC and FRE have rules to authenticate so-called ancient documents. Under the FRE, a document must be at least 20 years old. In California, 30 years is required. California's ancient document rule is narrower than the FRE rule. The CEC rule applies only to deeds, wills, and other documents affecting an interest in real or personal property, whereas the FRE rule applies to all documents. Under the CEC and the FRE, the document must be in a condition that raises no concerns about its authenticity, and must be found in a place where such a document would likely be kept. What is such a place? Examples include a safe deposit box, and a dusty old box in the attic.

When an ancient document is offered for the truth, it is hearsay. The FRE and the CEC contain a hearsay exception for ancient documents (FRE 803(16); CEC § 1331). *See* § 11.16.

§ 3.11(j).   Output of a Process

Computers, laboratory devices, certain machines, and various processes and systems generate results. The results can be authenticated with evidence that the computer, device, machine, process, or system produces accurate results (FRE 901(b)(9)).

§ 3.11(k).   "I Found It on the Internet, So It Must Be Reliable, Right?"

You grew up with the internet, and you know that just because it's on the internet doesn't mean it's true. Many judges grew up before the internet, (amazing but true), yet those old timers in black robes share your lack of confidence in the accuracy of internet material. The Court of Appeal, in *People v. Stamps*, 3 Cal. App. 5th 988, 996, 207 Cal. Rptr. 3d 828 (2016), wrote, "The cases reflect a common judicial skepticism of evidence found on the internet: While some look to the Internet as an innovative vehicle for communication, the courts continue to view it warily and wearily as a catalyst for rumor, innuendo, and misinformation."

So, to authenticate material from the internet, you need to do more than say, "I found it on the internet" or "I Googled it."

§ 3.12 FRE 902—Self-Authentication

Section 3.8 mentions that some documents are so likely to be genuine that the law dispenses with the requirement of witnesses to authenticate—the document authenticates itself. FRE 902 describes a variety of self-authenticating documents. The CEC uses a different vehicle to arrive at the same destination. The CEC approach is discussed in Section 3.13.

§ 3.12(a).   Public Documents Under Seal—FRE 902(1)

Many agencies of government in the United States have an official seal. Under FRE 902(1), a document of an agency of federal, state, or local government, in the U.S., is self-authenticating when it bears such a seal, accompanied by an official signature.

§ 3.12(b).   Public Documents Not Under Seal—FRE 902(2)

A government document without a seal is self-authenticating when it bears the signature of an employee of the agency, plus the signature of another government employee, who has a seal or its equivalent, attesting that the document is genuine.

§ 3.12(c).   Foreign Documents—FRE 902(3)

A document of a foreign government is self-authenticating when it is signed by a person authorized by foreign law to sign, and the document is accompanied by a certification that the signature on the document is genuine. FRE 902(3) is a little more complex than just described, but the details would put you to sleep, so I'll spare you.

§ 3.12(d).   Certified Copies of Public Records—FRE 902(4)

A copy of a government document, or a private document filed in a public office (think deeds filed with the county recorder of deeds), certified as correct by a person authorized to make the certification, is self-authenticating.

§ 3.12(e).   Government Publications—FRE 902(5)

Agencies of federal, state, and local governments issue all kinds of publications, pamphlets, and books. Many documents issued by the federal government bear the words U.S. Government Printing Office. Such words are enough to self-authenticate the publication. The same is true for documents published by the California Office of State Publishing.

§ 3.12(f).   Newspapers and Magazines—FRE 902(6)

To authenticate a copy of the *New York Times* or the *Los Angeles Times*, just hand a copy to the judge. The document speaks for itself.

§ 3.12(g).   Trade Inscriptions—FRE 902(7)

After class, you purchase a can of your favorite energy or soft drink. You open the can and take a big gulp. As you raise the can a second time, a mouse tail slides out! The rest of the mouse is still in the can!! What do you do? Sue the producer of the drink, of course. With the millions you recover, you can leave law school and retire to a tropical island. Before your retire to paradise, however, you'd better win your lawsuit. You have to prove that the can with the mouse was produced by the defendant. In other words, you have to authenticate the can. FRE 902(7) provides your answer. The rule states that trade inscriptions—Coke, Pepsi, Red Bull, Monster Energy—are self-authenticating. So, all you have to do is cite Rule 902(7) and offer the can. Viola! (I don't know how you authenticate the mouse).

§ 3.12(h).   Notarized Documents—FRE 902(8)

A document accompanied by a certificate from a notary public is self-authenticating.

§ 3.12(i).   Uniform Commercial Code and Commercial Paper—FRE 902(9)

"Commercial paper" is a term that applies to several types of documents. The UCC recognizes four kinds of commercial paper: promissory notes, drafts, checks, and certificates of deposit. FRE 902(9) makes commercial paper, and the signatures on it, self-authenticating.

§ 3.12(j).   Presumptively Genuine—FRE 902(10)

Scattered through the United States Code are statutes declaring certain signatures and documents presumptively genuine.

FRE 902(10) provides that when such a statute applies, the signature or document is self-authenticating.

§ 3.12(k).   Certified Domestic Business Record— FRE 902(11)

The business records exception to the hearsay rule is found in FRE 803(6). (*See* § 11.12). One way to authenticate a business record is to call the custodian of records as a witness, and have the custodian lay the foundation for the exception. FRE 902(11) eliminates the need for live testimony from the custodian of records. Under Rule 902(11), the custodian executes a certification that the document is a business record. The document is then self-authenticating as a business record.

Like the FRE, the CEC has a mechanism to eliminate the need for live foundation testimony from the custodian of records. (*See* § 11.12). In California, the business records exception is found in CEC § 1270. Sections 1560 to 1567, set forth procedures for the authentication, production, and copying of business records. *See* California Judicial Council form SUBP–002.

§ 3.12(*l*).   Certified Foreign Business Record— FRE 902(12)

Rule 902(12) allows a foreign business record to be certified in a manner similar to a domestic business record, covered by Rule 902(11).

§ 3.13   Presumptive Authentication Under the CEC

Unlike the FRE, the CEC does not deem certain documents self-authenticating. Instead, California uses presumptions to support authentication of selected documents. The subject of presumptions is covered in Chapter 13. For present purposes, it is enough to say that when certain facts are proven, California law presumes the existence of another fact, the presumed fact. When it comes to documents, if certain facts are proven, there is a rebuttable presumption that the document is genuine.

§ 3.13(a).   Official Seals—CEC § 1452

CEC § 1452 presumes the validity of official seals of the United States and its agencies, as well as official seals of selected foreign governments. Section 1452 also presumes the validity of the seal of a notary public from any U.S. state. The FRE counterpart is Rule 902(1).

§ 3.13(b).   Signatures of Government Officials— CEC § 1453

Section 1453 creates a presumption of validity for official signatures of employees of federal, state, and local governments. Section 1453 extends the presumption of validity to the signature of a notary public. The FRE counterpart is Rule 902(2).

§ 3.13(c).   Signatures of Foreign Government Officials—CEC § 1454

Section 1454 presumes the validity of properly certified signatures of officials of foreign governments. The FRE counterpart if Rule 902(3).

§ 3.13(d).   Official Documents and Recorded Documents—CEC §§ 1530–1532

Section 1530 establishes a presumption of validity for copies of domestic and foreign government documents, stored with a government agency, and certified as correct by a public employee with proper authority. The FRE counterpart if Rule 902(4).

§ 3.13(e).   Government Publications—CEC § 644

A book purportedly printed or published by a public authority is presumed to have been printed by the government. The FRE counterpart if Rule 902(5).

§ 3.13(f).   Newspaper or Magazine—CEC § 645.1

Newspapers and periodicals issued at least every three months are presumed to be genuine. The FRE counterpart if Rule 902(6).

§ 3.13(g).   Notary Public Acknowledgment—CEC § 1451

A notary public's certificate of acknowledgement of a writing (other than a will) is prima facie evidence of the facts in the certificate and the genuineness of the signature of the persons signing before the notary public.

§ 3.14   Unique Items vs. Generic Items

Some things are unique; one of a kind. The foundation to identify a unique item has the following elements: (1) The witness observed the item at an earlier time, (2) The item is unique, (3) The item offered in evidence is the same item that was observed at the earlier time, and (4) The item has not changed, or, if it has changed, the witness explains the changes.

Many items are not unique. For example, drugs seized from a defendant cannot typically be distinguished from other similar drugs. Yet, at trial, the prosecutor must prove that the drugs offered in evidence are the very drugs seized from the defendant. If the drugs offered are not the defendant's drugs, they are irrelevant. An attorney identifies non-unique items with a chain of custody. Each link in the chain is the person or place where the item was located, from the relevant time to the time the evidence is offered in court. A simple example will be useful. Defendant is on trial for possession of 20 ounces of methamphetamine. Police seized 20 ounces of powder from defendant at the time of his arrest. The police crime lab tested the power and confirmed that it is meth. To lay the foundation to offer the powder into evidence, the following exchange occurs between the prosecutor and the police officer who seized the powder from the defendant:

Prosecutor: What did you seize from the defendant after he was arrested?

A: I seized from his person a quantity of white power, found in a clear plastic bag.

Q: What did you do with the powder while at the scene?

A: Following the protocol of the police department, I placed the plastic bag containing the powder inside what we call an evidence bag, which is a plastic bag with the word Evidence stamped on it. I sealed the evidence bag, and wrote on the evidence bag what the bag contained, as well as the time, date, and place where I placed the items in the evidence bag.

Q: What did you do next?

A: I placed the evidence bag in the locked trunk of my police car. I had the only key to the trunk. I then completed my work at the scene.

Q: What did you do next?

A: I drove in my police car to police headquarters. I opened the trunk and removed the evidence bag, which was exactly where I placed in when I put it in the trunk. The seal on the evidence bag was intact.

Q: Then what did you do?

A: I weighed the evidence bag and its contents. Before weighing it, I checked the scale to make sure it was correctly calibrated.

Q: What did it weigh?

A: Subtracting the weight of the empty evidence bag, the contents of the bag was exactly 20 ounces.

Q: What did you do next?

A: I logged the evidence bag into the evidence room at the police department. I followed all the steps required by the department's evidence logging protocol. I personally placed the bag in the evidence room, and locked the door behind me.

Q: Did you bring anything with you to court today?

A: Yes. This morning, on the way to court, I went to the locked evidence room at the police department, and I retrieved the evidence bag for this case. The bag remained with me until I handed it to you just before court started this morning.

Q: Before you left the evidence room, did you open the evidence bag to check the contents.

A: Yes. The contents were undisturbed from the time I first sealed the bag.

Q: Did you weigh the contents of the bag today?

A: Yes, after checking the scale for accuracy, and subtracting the weight of the evidence bag, the contents of the bag weighed just under 20 ounces. This was slightly less than it weighed the first time I weighed it. The difference can be accounted for by the tiny amount of powder the crime lab used to test the substance.

Q: Did you check the log book to see if anyone else had logged out the evidence?

A: Yes, technician Rene Renoldo, from the crime lab, checked out the bag on September 1 of this year, and checked it back in the next day, September 2.

Q: Did the log book indicate that anyone else had removed the bag?

A: The log book stated that no one else had removed the evidence bag from the evidence room.

Q: I hand you now what has been marked People's Exhibit 5 for identification, and ask if you can identify it.

A: Yes, this is the evidence bag I retrieved from the evidence room this morning.

Q: How are you sure?

A: I see my handwriting on the bag. Looking inside the bag, I see the same contents I have seen before. Nothing has changed.

Q: Your honor, the People now offer People's Exhibit 5 for identification into evidence as People's 5.

Defense counsel: No objection.

Court: It is admitted.

The lab tech, Rene Renoldo, is another link in the chain of custody and it may be necessary to offer testimony from Renoldo, if the defense insists on it. To prove that the bag contains meth, the prosecutor will call the appropriate expert.

§ 3.15   Authentication of Electronic Communications

The CEC went into force in 1967; the FRE in 1975. At that time, no one imagined cell phones, tablets, the internet, Facebook, text messages, etc. etc. The rules on authentication were created for a different time, a time when people wrote letters to each other, and made phone calls on rotary phones connected by landlines. Times have changed. Late in the twentieth century, some experts argued that new rules should be drafted for the authentication of digital communications. For the most part, courts rejected the call for new rules, and adapted existing rules to electronic communications. This section briefly summarizes the law on authentication of electronic communications.

Email. An email typically begins with "From" and "To." Because it is possible to fake emails, the fact that an email states that it is From "John Brown" is *not* sufficient, by itself, to authenticate John as the author.[7] The "From" portion of the email is admissible for authentication, but it must be fortified with other evidence. The reply letter doctrine, in conjunction with the "From" line, is often sufficient.[8] In many cases, the evidence necessary to authenticate is gleaned from the contents of the email—for example, "I dropped the kids off at soccer practice. Sally still has a band aid on her arm, but I put antibiotic on it, and it is better." In *State v. Manuel*, 357 S.W.3d 66, 75 (Tex. Ct. App. 2011), the Texas Court of Appeals explained: "Characteristics to consider in determining whether e-mail evidence has been properly authenticated include (1) consistency with the e-mail address in another e-mail sent by the alleged author; (2) the author's awareness, shown through the e-mail, of the details of the alleged

---

[7]   *See State v. Eleck*, 130 Conn. App. 632, 23 A.3d 818, 822 (2011); *Sublet v. State*, 442 Md. 632, 113 A.3d 695, 711 (2015); *Tienda v. State*, 358 S.W.3d 633, 641–642 (Tex. Ct. App. 2012).

[8]   *See People v. Downin*, 357 Ill. App. 3d 193, 828 N.E.2d 341, 293 Ill. Dec. 371 (2005).

author's conduct; (3) the e-mail's inclusion of similar requests that the alleged author had made by phone during the time period; and (4) the e-mail's reference to the author by the alleged author's nickname." A witness could describe a history of email communications to and from a particular email address. A party's admission that he sent an email will suffice.[9] In most cases, authentication is achieved without resort to expert testimony tracing the electronic communication to a particular device.

Text Messages. Text messages typically contain the name of the sender, and, often, a phone number or a photo. Like emails, texts can be faked, and judges want evidence in addition to a screen shot or photo of the text.[10] In many cases, the necessary evidence is found in a string of back and forth text messages. Often, a text makes no sense unless it is from a particular person.[11] The authentication factors that work for emails, work for texts.[12]

Facebook. Authorship of a message posted to Facebook can be authenticated with circumstantial evidence similar to that employed for emails and texts.[13] In *United States v. Barnes*, 803 F.3d 209 (5th Cir. 2015), the prosecution offered enough evidence to authenticate defendant as the author of Facebook posts. A witness testified she had observed defendant using Facebook, she recognized his Facebook account, and the Facebook messages matched the defendant's manner of communicating.

§ 3.16 Authentication in Practice

In civil litigation, documents are often authenticated before trial. Attorneys agree in advance that various documents are authentic, removing the need for formal, time consuming authentication at trial. Many judges expect attorneys to work cooperatively this way. California law requires attorneys to meet and confer in an effort to resolve matters such as authentication. At a trial readiness conference, the judge may ask the attorneys about progress on authenticating documents, and you don't want to upset your judge before trial with excuses about why you have not made progress.

---

[9]   *Kearley v. State*, 843 So. 2d 66 (Miss. Ct. App. 2002).

[10]   *See State v. Eleck*, 130 Conn. App. 632, 23 A.3d 818, 822 (2011).

[11]   *See People v. Green*, 107 A.D.3d 915, 967 N.Y.S.2d 753 (2013).

[12]   *See State v. Koch*, 334 P.3d 280 (Idaho 2014); *State v. Davis*, 61 N.E.3d 650 (Ohio Ct. App. 2016).

[13]   *See United States v. Hassan*, 742 F.3d 104 (4th Cir. 2014); *State v. Palermo*, 168 N.H. 387, 129 A.3d 1020 (2015); *State v. Ford*, 782 S.E.2d 98 (N.C. Ct. App. 2016); *Manuel v. State*, 357 S.W.3d 66 (Tex. Ct. App. 2011).

Discovery tools are used to discover *and* authenticate documents. Thus, depositions, requests for production of documents, requests for admission, and interrogatories play roles in authentication before trial. Documents that are produced in response to discovery requests are generally considered authenticated.

You are most likely to encounter formal authentication issues in criminal trials, where pretrial discovery is limited. Even in criminal cases, however, attorneys often agree upon the admissibility of documents and things.

§ 3.17 Answers to Chapter Problems

This section contains analysis of questions in Chapter 3.

Problems on Preliminary Facts: § 3.5

1. Did Wendy See It?

The preliminary question is whether Wendy has personal knowledge of the accident. Lay witnesses must have personal knowledge to testify (FRE 602; CEC § 702. See § 9.3). If the opponent objects that Wendy lacks personal knowledge, the preliminary fact is decided under FRE 104(b) or CEC § 403(a)(2). The judge listens to the evidence pro and con on personal knowledge. If there is enough evidence of personal knowledge that a reasonable juror could find personal knowledge, the judge admits Wendy's testimony, and instructs the jury, at the end of the case, that it is for the jury to decide whether Wendy had personal knowledge. If so, the jury may give Wendy's testimony whatever weight the jury thinks proper. If the jury concludes that Wendy lacked personal knowledge, the jury disregards her testimony.

2. Who Penned the Missive?

This question has several preliminary facts. First, is the letter relevant? This is for the judge under FRE 104(a) or CEC § 405. Second, Plaintiff is seeking to prove the contents of a document, therefore, the best evidence rule (FRE 1002) or the secondary evidence rule applies (CEC § 1521). Third, the letter must be authenticated. Authentication is a FRE 104(b)–CEC § 403 issue for the jury. Fourth, Plaintiff is seeking to impeach the doctor with a prior inconsistent statement. The judge decides whether the earlier statement is indeed inconsistent. Fifth, if, in addition to impeachment, the Plaintiff offers the doctor's letter to prove that Plaintiff was in fact seriously injured, the letter is hearsay. Preliminary questions under the hearsay rule and its exceptions are for the court.

3.   This Pizza Is Cold!

You know from torts that the preliminary facts are: (1) was Joe College employed by Pizza Company, and was he within the scope of his employment when the accident happened? These issues are for the jury under FRE 104(b) or CEC § 403.

Chapter 4

OBJECTIONS AND OFFERS
OF PROOF

In trials, both sides offer evidence. If your opponent offers evidence that you believe is inadmissible, you object. Failure to object waives any argument that the judge was wrong to admit the evidence.[1] If you are the one offering evidence, and your opponent objects, the judge rules on the objection. If the judge overrules the objection, your evidence is admitted. However, if the judge sustains the objection, your evidence is excluded. When a judge sustains an objection to your evidence, and you believe the judge is wrong, you make an offer of proof. Failure to make an offer of proof waives any argument that the judge erred in excluding your evidence.

§ 4.1   Rules of Evidence

The rules governing objections and offers of proof provide:

FRE 103. Rulings on Evidence (a) Preserving a Claim of Error. A party may claim error in a ruling to admit or exclude evidence only if the error affects a substantial right of the party and: (1) if the ruling admits evidence, a party, on the record; (A) timely objects or moves to strike; and (B) states the specific ground, unless it was apparent from the context; or (2) if the ruling excludes evidence, a party informs the court of its substance by an offer of proof, unless the substance was apparent from the context. . . .[2] **(e) Taking Notice of Plain Error**. A court may take notice of a plain error affecting a substantial right, even if the claim of error was not properly preserved.

CEC § 353. Erroneous Admission of Evidence; Effect. A verdict or finding shall not be set aside, nor shall the

---

[1]   *See* People v. Landry, 2 Cal. 5th 52, 86, 385 P.3d 327, 211 Cal. Rptr. 3d 160 (2016) ("As a general rule, the failure to object to errors committed at trial relieves the reviewing court of the obligation to consider those errors on appeal. This rule applies equally to any claim on appeal that the evidence was erroneously admitted, other than the stated rule for the objection at trial.").

[2]   Subparts (b), (c), and (d) are omitted. Subpart (b) provides that an attorney doesn't have to renew an objection if the judge has made a definitive ruling on the matter. Subpart (c) addresses the judge's authority to discuss evidence and to direct how offers of proof are made. Subpart (d) directs the court to make sure that the jury does not overhear inadmissible evidence. For example, the judge might exclude the jury during an offer of proof.

judgment or decision based thereon be reversed, by reason of the erroneous admission of evidence unless: (a) There appears of record an objection to or a motion to exclude or to strike the evidence that was timely made and so stated as to make clear the specific ground of the objection or motion; and (b) The court which passes upon the effect of the error or errors [the appellate court] is of the opinion that the admitted evidence should have been excluded on the ground stated and that the error or errors complained of resulted in a miscarriage of justice.

CEC § 354. Erroneous Exclusion of Evidence; Effect. A verdict or finding shall not be set aside, nor shall the judgment or decision based thereon be reversed, by reason of the erroneous exclusion of evidence unless the court which passes upon the effect of the error or errors is of the opinion that the error or errors complained of resulted in a miscarriage of justice and it appears of record that: (a) the substance, purpose, and relevance of the excluded evidence was made known to the [trial] court by the questions asked, an offer of proof, or by any other means; (b) the rulings of the court made compliance with subdivision (a) futile; or (c) The evidence was sought by questions asked during cross-examination or recross-examination.

§ 4.2   Objection and Motion to Strike

The FRE and CEC are very similar regarding objections to the opponent's evidence. Failure to make a timely and specific objection waives any error by the judge in admitting evidence. To be timely, an objection must be made as soon as the ground for objection is apparent. An objection is specific if it states a rule or a law that justifies the objection: "Objection, the question calls for hearsay." "Objection, irrelevant." "Objection under Rule 403; the probative value of the evidence is substantially outweighed by the danger of unfair prejudice to my client." "Objection, leading on direct." Etc. Etc. Simply stating, "Objection," will not suffice: It is not specific.

If improper evidence is admitted before there is an opportunity to object, the procedure is to object and move to strike the objectionable evidence. For example, if the opponent's question called for hearsay, and the witness answered before it was possible to object, the attorney could say, "Your honor, the answer was hearsay. I object, move to strike the answer, and request the court to instruct the jury to disregard it."

§ 4.3   Offer of Proof

When an attorney offers evidence, and the opposing attorney objects, the judge either sustains or overrules the objection. If the judge sustains the objection, the proponent must make an offer of proof in order to preserve any error for appeal. Failure to make an offer of proof waives error in admitting the evidence.

An offer of proof consists of the substance and relevance of the excluded evidence. (*See* CEC § 354(a)). The most frequent way to make an offer of proof is for the attorney offering the evidence to describe the excluded evidence. For example, the attorney might say, "Your honor, may I make an offer of proof?" The judge will oblige. The attorney says, "Your honor, if the witness were permitted to answer the question, the witness would testify that she overheard the victim say that the victim had just been shot by the defendant. Her statement would be hearsay, as counsel suggests, however, the statement is an excited utterance, and is admissible. I can lay the necessary foundation."

There are two reasons for an offer of proof. First, when a trial judge hears an offer of proof, the judge may change her mind and admit the evidence. Second, if the trial judge does not change her mind, the offer of proof creates a record for appellate judges to read.

§ 4.4   Harmless and Reversible Error

The fact that an attorney makes a proper objection, motion to strike, or offer of proof—thus preserving for appeal the claim that the trial court erred—does not mean the attorney wins the appeal. This is true even if the attorney is right! Even if the trial judge erred in admitting or excluding evidence, and the attorney did everything necessary to preserve the error for review, not all errors warrant reversal of the trial court decision. Some errors are harmless, which is another way of saying that the outcome would probably have been the same without the error. If error is harmless, the lower court decision is affirmed. Errors that require reversal, and a new trial, are reversible errors.

The FRE states that an error is reversible when the error affects a "substantial right" of the party. The CEC uses the words "miscarriage of justice." The terms "substantial right" and "miscarriage of justice" have the same meaning. When an appellate court determines that an error occurred in the trial court, and the error was preserved for review, the appellate court decides whether the error likely influenced the outcome of the trial. The appellate court examines the entire record of the trial, and considers the seriousness of the error or errors, and the probable impact the error had on the outcome. If the outcome probably would have been the same despite the error, the appellate court labels the error harmless. On the other hand, if the error likely influenced the verdict, then the error is reversible.

§ 4.5   Plain Error

Plain error is error that was *not* preserved for appeal by proper objection or offer of proof. Nevertheless, the error is so serious, so prejudicial, that the appellate court considers it despite the fact that it was not preserved (FRE 103(d)). Plain error requires reversal of the lower court decision. The CEC does not contain a provision on plain error.

§ 4.6   Constitutional Error

A trial court error that violates a criminal defendant's constitutional rights often requires reversal of a conviction. However, not all constitutional error is reversible error. If the properly admitted evidence of guilt is strong, a constitutional error may be harmless. With constitutional error, however, the prosecutor must prove the error was harmless beyond a reasonable doubt. (Chapman v. California, 386 U.S. 18, 87 S. Ct. 824 (1967)).

§ 4.7   Exercise with Objections, Motions to Strike, and Offers of Proof

A good way to get comfortable with objections, motions to strike, and offers of proof is to study a transcript of testimony. The following transcript is from a bank robbery trial. The witness is the first police officer to arrive at the bank, just after the robbers fled. The officer is testifying for the prosecution. The three accused robbers are on trial together. None of them testify. As you read the transcript, note objections, motions to strike, and offers of proof. With each one, did the attorney act properly? Just as important, look for places where an attorney could have taken action, but didn't. What are the consequences of silence when action is required?

Questioning by Prosecutor: Please state your full name, and where you work.

A: Able Amir. I am a police officer with the City Police Department.

Q: Were you working on August 1st of this year?

A: Yes.

Q: Did you respond to a bank robbery in progress call on that day?

A: Yes. The call came over the radio at 1:30 p.m., and I immediately drove to the bank, arriving two minutes after the robbers fled.

Q: What did you do when you first arrived?

A: I informed dispatch that I had arrived. I was the first officer to arrive, so I didn't know if the robbery was over. I entered the bank with my service weapon drawn to see if the robbery was still in progress. It was apparent that the robbery was over.

Q: Who did you first speak to inside the bank?

A: The manager came running up to me and said, "There were three of them. All young white men, in their twenties. They have guns."

Defense counsel: Objection, your honor. Move to strike.

Prosecutor: Your honor, this was an excited utterance.

Court: Overruled.

Prosecutor: What happened next?

A: By this time, there were ten or more officers at the bank. I wanted to get a better description of the robbers, so I took the manager to her office and we sat down. I gave her a cup of water. I asked her to describe what the robbers looked like.

Q: What did the manager tell you?

A: She described the three robbers in detail. She said each was carrying a handgun. She described one as about five feet ten inches tall, with brown hair and a brown beard. He was wearing Levis and white t-shirt. He was white, but tan, from being in the sun. Maybe a construction worker, given how tan his skin was. This robber was the only one to speak. He said, "Nobody move, and nobody gets hurt. This is a robbery. Get all the money out of the cash drawers and put it in these bags. He spoke in an accent. He sounded Russian."

Q: Did you write a report of the robbery?

A: Yes.

Q: Do you have the report with you?

A: Yes. I have my report here with me.

Prosecutor: Your honor, at this time, the People offer People's Exhibit Number 1, the police officer's report, into evidence as People's Number 1.

Q: Now officer, I want to ask you some questions about your report. On page 1, you indicate that the getaway car was a 2006

Honda Civic, green in color, with California license number VCU 345, is that correct?

A: That's right.

Q: On page two of your report . . .

Defense counsel, interrupting: Your honor, I'm sorry to interrupt, but I object to the police report. No foundation has been laid for this report. It is hearsay, and it is not admissible.

Court: Well, counsel, your objection comes too late. Overruled. The report is admitted as People's number 1.

Prosecutor: Did you have an opportunity to question defendant Jones, in this case?

A: Yes, I arrested Mr. Jones. I read him his Miranda rights, and he said he would talk to me.

Q: Where and when did this questioning occur?

A: Two weeks after the robbery. I arrested Mr. Jones at his home, and I interviewed him at the police station an hour later, in an interview room.

Q: What did he tell you?

A: He admitted he robbed the bank, along with the two other defendants. He said they had spent three months planning the robbery, and that all had agreed on how it should go down.

Q: Was this interview recorded?

A: Yes. I video recorded the entire interview.

Q: Did you bring the video recorded interview to court today?

A: Yes.

Q: Is the video recording of the interview the video recording that is marked as People's exhibit number 2, for identification?

A: Yes.

Q: How do you know the video is the right one?

A: I looked at and listened to the entire video recording today. It is correct. The video recorder was working properly. The video recording has not been altered in any way. Nor has it been edited.

Prosecutor: Your honor, at this time, the People offer People's number 2, for identification, into evidence as People's number 2.

Defense counsel: Objection, your honor, this is hearsay. The foundation is inadequate. The probative value of the video is substantially outweighed by the danger of unfair prejudice. Finally, the officer failed to properly inform my client of his right to remain silent, and the video violates my client's constitutional rights.

Court: Objection sustained.

Prosecutor: Now officer, did you have occasion to speak to anyone other than the bank manager, about the robbery?

A: I spoke with Anne Taylor, one of the tellers during the robbery. She corroborated the description of the Mr. Jones as one of the robbers.

Defense counsel: Objection, hearsay. Move to strike.

Court: Sustained. Ladies and gentlemen of the jury, I instruct you to disregard the officer's last answer.

Prosecutor: Did the teller write down a description of the three robbers?

A: Yes she did.

Q: I hand you what has been marked as People's Exhibit number 3, for identification, and ask if you can identify it?

A: Yes, this is the handwritten note written by the bank teller describing the robbers.

Q: Will you please read aloud that the note says.

A: Sure, it says, "Three young white males entered the bank with guns. One of them did all the talking. He was about 5 feet ten inches tall, and quite tan."

Prosecutor: Thank you. No further questions.

Hopefully, you worked through the transcript on your own. That's the best way to learn. To check your work, the transcript is repeated below, with analysis **bold and underlined.**

Questioning by Prosecutor: Please state your full name, and where you work.

No problem with this question.

A: Able Amir. I am a police officer with the City Police Department.

Q: Were you working on August 1st of this year?

Not objectionable.

A: Yes.

Q: Did you respond to a bank robbery in progress call on that day?

Not objectionable. Is it leading? Maybe a little, but this type of question is used all the time to introduce a subject, without objection.

A: Yes. The call came over the radio at 1:30 p.m., and I immediately drove to the bank, arriving two minutes after the robbers fled.

Q: What did you do when you first arrived?

This is a proper question.

A: I informed dispatch that I had arrived. I was the first officer to arrive, so I didn't know if the robbery was over. I entered the bank with my service weapon drawn to see if the robbery was still in progress. It was apparent that the robbery was over.

Q: Who did you first speak to inside the bank?

If I was defense counsel, I would object to this question, "Objection, calls for inadmissible hearsay." Technically, the question does not ask the officer to repeat what anyone said, but it is clear that the prosecutor is about to elicit hearsay; just look at the witness's answer!

A: The manager came running up to me and said, "There were three of them. All young white men, in their twenties. They have guns."

Defense counsel: Objection, your honor. Move to strike.

The objection is timely, but it is not specific. Simply saying, "I object" is not sufficient—it does not specify the ground for the objection. Sometimes the judge says, "On what basis?" Other times, the judge overrules the objection for failing to specify the basis for the objection. In this case, the objection is timely because the attorney objected as soon as the officer repeated hearsay. The argument that the objection is timely is strengthened because the question that elicited the hearsay did not, technically speaking, ask for hearsay. Defense counsel should not be penalized for not objecting at the time the question was asked.

Prosecutor: Your honor, this was an excited utterance.

When an attorney objects, it is common for the judge to allow the attorneys to argue both sides of the objection, before the judge rules on the objection. If I was the defense attorney, I would add that the prosecutor failed to lay any foundation for the exited utterance exception. If an attorney fails to object on the basis of lack of foundation, any error is waived.

Court: Overruled.

Prosecutor: What happened next?

This is a proper question.

A: By this time, there were ten or more officers at the bank. I wanted to get a better description of the robbers, so I took the manager to her office and we sat down. I gave her a cup of water. I asked her to describe what the robbers looked like.

Q: What did the manager tell you?

Aaggghhh! Where is defense counsel's objection? This question obviously calls for hearsay, and the attorney must object before the witness answers.

A: She described the three robbers in detail. She said each was carrying a handgun. She described one as about five feet ten inches tall, with brown hair and a brown beard. He was wearing Levis and white t-shirt. He was white, but tan, from being in the sun. Maybe a construction worker, given how tan his skin was. This robber was the only one to speak. He said, "Nobody move, and nobody gets hurt. This is a robbery. Get all the money out of the cash drawers and put it in these bags. He spoke in an accent. He sounded Russian."

Because defense counsel failed to object, all this hearsay is admitted as evidence. The jury may consider it, and this is true even if some or all of the hearsay would have been excluded on proper objection! If the defendant is convicted and appeals, the appellate court will not consider the hearsay issue because there was no objection. Defendant's only hope on appeal under the FRE is to argue that admitting the hearsay was plain error. To be plain error, the error must be egregious. I doubt very much that admitting this hearsay would amount to plain error. The CEC does not have the plain error rule.

Q: Did you write a report of the robbery?

The question is ok, but an experienced attorney knows hearsay is about to be offered, and might object at this stage.

A: Yes.

Q: Do you have the report with you?

A: Yes. I have my report here with me.

Prosecutor: Your honor, at this time, the People offer People's Exhibit Number 1, the police officer's report, into evidence as People's Number 1.

Unless defense counsel *wants* the police report admitted in evidence, the attorney should object. First, the prosecutor has failed to authenticate the report. Second, because the prosecutor is seeking to prove the contents of a document, the best evidence rule or the secondary evidence rule needs to be satisfied. Third, the police report is hearsay, and no foundation has been laid to offer the report under the business records exception or the public records exception. Failure to object waives any error in admitting the report.

Q: Now officer, I want to ask you some questions about your report. On page 1, you indicate that the getaway car was a 2006 Honda Civic, green in color, with California license number VCU 345, is that correct?

A: That's right.

Q: On page two of your report . . .

Defense counsel, interrupting: Your honor, I'm sorry to interrupt, but I object to the police report. No foundation has been laid for this report. It is hearsay, and it is not admissible.

This objection should have come before the officer started talking about the contents of the report.

Court: Well, counsel, your objection comes too late. Overruled. The report is admitted as People's number 1.

The judge is right, the objection is not timely.

Prosecutor: Did you have an opportunity to question defendant Jones, in this case?

A: Yes, I arrested Mr. Jones. I read him his Miranda rights, and he said he would talk to me.

Q: Where and when did this questioning occur?

A: Two weeks after the robbery. I arrested Mr. Jones at his home, and I interviewed him at the police station an hour later, in an interview room.

Q: What did he tell you?

At this point, or earlier, defense counsel should object if there is a valid basis to object. Anything the defendant told the officer would be admissible as a party admission, but are there *Miranda* issues? Fourth or Fifth Amendment issues?

A: He admitted he robbed the bank along with the two other defendants. He said they had spent three months planning the robbery, and that all had agreed on how it should go down.

Defendant's statement that he robbed the bank is admissible against the defendant as a party admission, assuming there are no impediments to admission. (*See* § 11.24(a)). However, defendant stated that he robbed the bank "with the two other defendants." This part of defendant's statement may violate the Confrontation Clause of the Sixth Amendment. Specifically, this testimony raises the so-called *Bruton* issue (§ 11.30).

Q: Was this interview recorded?

A: Yes. I video recorded the entire interview.

Q: Did you bring the video recorded interview to court to day?

A: Yes.

Q: Is the video recording of the interview the video recording that is marked as People's exhibit number 2, for identification?

A: Yes.

Q: How do you know the video is the right one?

A: I looked at and listened to the entire video recording today. It is correct. The video recorder was working properly. The video recording has not been altered in any way. Nor has it been edited.

These are typical questions to authenticate a recording.

Prosecutor: Your honor, at this time, the People offer People's number 2, for identification, into evidence as People's number 2.

Defense counsel: Objection, your honor, this is hearsay. The foundation is inadequate. The probative value of the video is substantially outweighed by the danger of unfair prejudice. Finally, the officer failed to properly inform my client of his right to remain silent, and the video violated my client's constitutional rights.

Court: Objection sustained.

The judge sustained the defense objection to the recording. If the prosecutor believes the judge erred in sustaining the objection, the prosecutor needed to make an offer of proof. The prosecutor failed to make an offer of proof, and any error in excluding the evidence is waived.

Prosecutor: Now officer, did you have occasion to speak to anyone other than the bank manager, about the robbery?

Again, although this question technically asks for a "yes" or "no" answer, a trial lawyer would object on the basis of hearsay before the witness answers.

A: I spoke with Anne Taylor, one of the tellers during the robbery. She corroborated the description of the Mr. Jones as one of the robbers.

Defense counsel: Objection, hearsay. Move to strike.

I suppose, for the reason outlined above, that this objection is timely. I would have objected earlier.

Court: Sustained. Ladies and gentlemen of the jury, I instruct you to disregard the officer's last answer.

Prosecutor: Did the teller write down a description of the three robbers?

A: Yes she did.

Q: I hand you what has been marked as People's Exhibit number 3, for identification, and ask if you can identify it?

A: Yes, this is the handwritten note written by the bank teller describing the robbers.

Defense counsel might want to object that the answer is not responsive. The question called for a "yes" or "no" answer, but the officer provided additional information. Of course, there was no objection. If the answer was improper, any error in allowing it was waived.

Q: Will you please read aloud that the note says.

Object! Object! Object! Hearsay! Hearsay! Hearsay! Since there was no objection, any error in admitting the note is waived.

A: Sure, it says, "Three young white males entered the bank with guns. One of them did all the talking. He was about 5 feet ten inches tall, and quite tan."

Prosecutor: Thank you. No further questions.

You can see from this short exercise, that a trial lawyer has to pay strict attention to opposing counsel's questions, and witness answers. You snooze, you lose, or, more aptly, you snooze, your client loses.

Here is a bit of advice. Some lawyers wait to ask an improper question until they observe that the opposing attorney is not paying attention. This happened to me. My expert was on the stand. The cross-examiner was asking questions. However, the cross-examiner was not looking at the expert. The cross-examiner was watching me! When I started looking through some papers, the cross-examiner realized I was not paying attention, and he took the

opportunity to ask a highly improper question. Because I was not paying attention, I didn't hear the question, and I failed to object. What result? Any objection was waived, and I felt like an idiot (which I was).

Chapter 5

BEST AND SECONDARY EVIDENCE RULES; JUDICIAL NOTICE

This chapter discusses the best evidence rule of the FRE, and the secondary evidence rule of the CEC. The best evidence rule (BER) and the secondary evidence rule (SER) apply when a party seeks to prove the contents of a writing. The chapter also addresses judicial notice.

§ 5.1   Best Evidence Rule

Under the FRE, when a party seeks to prove the contents of a writing, the party must offer the original writing. This is the BER. (FRE 1002). California replaced the BER with the secondary evidence rule (SER). Most of the time, the results are the same under the BER and the SER.

§ 5.2   What Is a "Writing"?

Under the BER and the SER, the word "writing" is defined broadly. FRE 1001(a) defines a writing as "letters, words, numbers, or their equivalent set down in any form." The term includes recordings of words and numbers, as well as photographs. The CEC is the same (CEC § 250).

Suppose an object has writing on it, and a party wants to prove what is written. Can an object be a writing? Yes. Thus, if a party wants to prove what is written on a California Highway Patrol officer's badge, the badge is a writing. The BER rules requires the badge itself to be brought into court. Suppose a party wants to prove the Vehicle Identification Number (VIN) of a McLaren P1 sports car. The VIN is attached to the car. Should the car be considered a writing and driven into court? Of course not. In this case, a photo of the VIN plate will suffice. What if a party wants to prove what is carved into a gravestone at a cemetery. Is the gravestone a writing? Should we dig it up and haul it to court? When an object has writing on it, the judge has discretion to require the production of the original, if that is convenient, or to allow other evidence of the contents of the original.

§ 5.3   What Is an "Original"?

The "original" is a term of art in the BER/SER (FRE 1001(d); CEC § 255). The original is the document that played a role in a litigated event. For example, Ned types a document on his computer, and prints it out. Fran takes a piece of paper and prepares a handwritten version of Ned's typed document. Fran then uses the handwritten version to perpetrate a fraud of Vic. What is the original? Fran's hand written version is the original because it is the document that played a role in the litigated facts. In this case, the typed document might be an original too. Thus, in some cases, there is more than one original.

§ 5.4   What Is a "Duplicate?"

A duplicate is an exact reproduction of an original (FRE 1001(e); CEC § 260). A photocopy is a duplicate. A handwritten version of an original cannot be a duplicate. Just to make your life interesting, if the original is hand written, a photocopy of the original is a duplicate. A duplicate is admissible to the same extent as an original, unless there is reason to suspect the duplicate (FRE 1003).

§ 5.5   What Is a "Copy?"

A copy is a version of a writing that does not qualify as a duplicate. Thus, a handwritten version of an original can't qualify as a duplicate, so it is a copy. You should know that the word "copy" is used elsewhere in the FRE, and has a different meaning outside the confines of the BER. (*See, e.g.,* FRE 902(11); 902(12)).

§ 5.6   Four Excuses for Not Producing the Original

FRE 1004 sets out four excuses for the nonproduction of the original. First, the original is lost or destroyed in the ordinary course of business. To claim loss, the proponent must convince the judge that a search was conducted for the original. The more important the document, the more diligent the search. Second, the original can't be obtained by subpoena or other process. Third, the other party has the original and won't produce it despite request. Fourth, the original isn't important.[1]

---

[1]   I tell my students never to rely on the fourth excuse. You might think a document is unimportant, but that doesn't mean the judge will agree with you. If you are going to prove the contents of a writing, offer the original.

§ 5.7   Summary of Voluminous Originals

Imagine a case where there are thousands of originals. Must the proponent bring in boxes of originals to prove what's in them? It makes more sense to summarize the documents, and offer the summary in evidence. FRE 1006 allows this procedure, so long as the opponent has access to the originals. (*See* CEC § 1523(d)).

§ 5.8   What Is Secondary Evidence?

The best evidence rule requires the original. Evidence of the content of a writing that is *not* the original, and not a duplicate, is secondary evidence. Consider the tombstone mentioned above. The original is the tombstone itself. Testimony from a witness who read the words on the tombstone, and who repeats the words from memory, is secondary evidence. A photograph of the tombstone is secondary evidence. A rubbing on paper of the tombstone is secondary evidence (or is it a duplicate? Hmm. I don't know). Consider another example, an x-ray of a patient's arm. An x-ray is a writing. If a party wants to prove the contents of an x-ray, the original x-ray must be produced. Testimony from the radiologist who "read" the x-ray, and who describes it from memory, is secondary evidence. The radiologist's written report about the x-ray is secondary evidence.

§ 5.9   California's Secondary Evidence Rule

California's SER states, "The content of a writing may be proved by otherwise admissible secondary evidence" (CEC § 1521(a)). Although the SER allows secondary evidence, a judge will exclude secondary evidence, and require the original, if there is a dispute about important terms of a writing, or if it would be unfair to admit secondary evidence (CEC § 1521(a)(1), (2)). Oral testimony is not admissible to prove the content of a writing unless the original is lost or destroyed, the original cannot be obtained by subpoena or other process, or the writing is not very important (CEC § 1523). In criminal cases, secondary evidence is inadmissible if the original is in the proponent's possession or control, and the proponent has not made the original available for inspection (CEC § 1522(a)). In practice in California, if you have the original, offer it. On exams, the result is usually the same under the FRE and the CEC. In particular, a witness's memory about what a writing says is viewed with skepticism, and is not admissible unless the original is lost or destroyed.

§ 5.10 BER/SER on Exams

Professors often raise the BER by having a witness testify to what is in a document. Here are examples from real exams:

> Fawn is on trial for robbing a jewelry store. Fawn offers an alibi. During the prosecution's case-in-chief, the prosecutor offer testimony from the detective who investigated the robbery. The detective testifies, "The jewelry store has surveillance cameras. I downloaded the content of the recordings at the time of the robbery onto my computer. The recordings show the actual robbery as it happened. It is clear from the recording that the defendant, Fawn, was the robber."

Your answer should mention[2] (1) relevance of the evidence, (2) authentication of the recording, and (3) the BER and the SER. The original is the recording. The detective's testimony is secondary evidence, and none of the FRE's four excuses for the production of the original apply. Whenever you see a witness describing what is in a document, think BER! Here is another example:

> Andy and Dell are charged with robbing a Wells Fargo bank in San Diego. During the prosecution's case-in-chief, the prosecutor offers testimony from Captain Smith of the San Diego Police Department. Captain Smith was in charge of investigating the robbery. Smith testifies, "The day after the robbery, I recovered a 2006 white Chevrolet minivan that matched the description of the van used by the robbers. Official police department records indicate that two weeks prior to the robbery, Andy stole a white Chevrolet minivan."

Issues to discuss include the recovery of the white minivan. Smith testifies that she recovered the van, so she apparently has personal knowledge of the van. But is the van relevant? It is relevant if the rest of Smith's testimony is admissible, but there are problems with Smith's testimony. How does Smith know the recovered van matches the description of the van used by the robbers? Smith must have spoken with someone who knows that, or read about it. In either case, Smith's statement is hearsay, sometimes called "masked" hearsay. If Smith read it, then you have a BER issue. Where is the original from which Smith read? Smith's testimony about what she read is secondary evidence. I suppose you could argue that where she read it is not very important, that is,

---

[2] Your answer would not discuss hearsay because the video recording is not hearsay. Machines, including surveillance cameras, do not make hearsay statements. Only people make hearsay statements; not machines.

"not closely related to a controlling issue," (FRE 1004(d)), thus excusing the production of the original, but I'm not sanguine that the judge will agree. You definitely have a BER issue when Smith testifies, "Official police department records indicate that two weeks prior to the robbery, Andy stole a white Chevrolet minivan." Your answer might say, "The prosecutor is seeking to prove, by Smith's testimony, the contents of police department records. The BER applies in this situation. The original is the records themselves. Smith's testimony is secondary evidence of the contents of the records. None of the excuses for the production of the original applies. Smith's testimony about the contents of the records is inadmissible because it violates the BER. If the prosecutor produces the original police department records, then the records will have to be authenticated and satisfy an exception to the hearsay rule (the public records exception (§ 11.14) or the business records exception (§ 11.12)). Under California's SER, oral testimony is not admissible to prove the contents of a material document. Thus, the answer is the same under the BER and the SER: Smith's testimony about the contents of the police department records violates both sets of rules."

§ 5.11   Judicial Notice

When a court takes judicial notice of a fact, there is no need for evidence of the fact. As Christopher Mueller and Laird Kirkpatrick put it, "[J]udicial notice is a substitute for evidence."[3] Courts do not take judicial notice of disputed facts. In *Barreiro v. State Bar,* 2 Cal. 3d 912, 1000, 471 P.2d 992, 88 Cal. Rptr. 192 (1970), the Supreme Court wrote, "If there is any doubt whatever as to the fact itself or as to its being a matter of common knowledge, evidence should be required." An attorney who wants a judge to take judicial notice of a fact, requests the court to do so.

§ 5.11(a).   Judicial Notice Under the FRE

FRE 201 provides:

> **Rule 201. Judicial Notice of Adjudicative Facts. (a) Scope**. This rule governs judicial notice of an adjudicative fact only, not a legislative fact.[4] **(b) Kinds of Facts That May Be Judicially Noticed**. The court may judicially notice a fact that is not subject to reasonable dispute because it: (1) is generally known within the trial court's

---

[3]   1 Christopher B. Mueller & Laird C. Kirkpatrick, *Federal Evidence* § 2:2, p. 319–320 (4th ed. 2013).

[4]   Legislative facts are facts outside the court record that a court—often an appellate court—considers as background supporting the court's decision.

territorial jurisdiction;[5] or (2) can be accurately and readily determined from sources whose accuracy cannot reasonably be questioned.[6] **(c) Taking Notice**. The court: (1) may take judicial notice on its own;[7] or (2) must take judicial notice if a party requests it and the court is supplied with the necessary information. **(d) Timing**. The court may take judicial notice at any stage of the proceeding.[8] **(e) Opportunity to Be Heard**. On timely request, a party is entitled to be heard on the propriety of taking judicial notice and the nature of the fact to be noticed. If the court takes judicial notice before notifying a party, the party, on request, is still entitled to be heard. **(f) Instructing the Jury**. In a civil case, the court must instruct the jury to accept the noticed fact as conclusive. In a criminal case, the court must instruct the jury that it may or may not accept the noticed fact as conclusive.

Rule 201 regulates judicial notice of adjudicative facts, which are the who, what, where, and when of a case. Mueller and Kirkpatrick write, "[A]djudicative facts include everything that parties must prove in order to prevail because they amount to elements in claims, charges, or defenses."[9]

Courts take judicial notice of the court's own records. Thus, a court would take judicial notice of a judgment from the same court, entered by the same or a different judge, involving the same parties.[10] Also, a court generally will take judicial notice of court orders and judgments pertaining to the same parties from other courts.[11]

---

[5]   It does not matter whether the judge herself knows the fact. Nor is it necessary that everybody within the court's jurisdiction know the fact. What is required is that most people living in the area know the fact. Thus, a judge would take judicial notice that the Golden Gate Bridge connects San Francisco to Marin County.

[6]   A judge will take judicial notice of the exact time the sun set in San Diego on January 3, 2018, if the judge is presented with a reliable almanac or document showing sunset times. Could you Google the time and give the judge a printout from your computer? I don't know. I do know that judges are suspicious of information from the internet. I would make sure that the internet page appears to be an official government site.

[7]   Judges sometimes take notice of a fact *sua sponte*. More often, however, an attorney asks a judge to take judicial notice of a fact.

[8]   An appellate court may take judicial notice.

[9]   1 Christopher B. Mueller & Laird C. Kirkpatrick, *Federal Evidence* § 2:2, p. 321 (4th ed. 2013).

[10]   Sullivan v. Doe, 100 A.3d 171 (Me. 2014) (court took judicial notice of pending criminal charges).

[11]   Lockley v. Law Office of Cantrell, Green, Pekich, Cruz & McCort, 91 Cal. App. 4th 875, 882, 110 Cal. Rptr. 2d 877, 882 (2001) ("The court may in its discretion take judicial notice of any court record in the United States.").

Judges are cautious about taking judicial notice of court documents involving different parties. Suppose, for example, that Juan and Maria divorce in 2017, and the family court judge enters a judgment of divorce. In 2018, Juan declares bankruptcy, and receives a discharge from the federal bankruptcy court. In 2019, Maria takes Juan back to family court to increase child support, and Juan asks the family court to take judicial notice of the document evidencing discharge in bankruptcy. The family court judge should oblige, despite the fact that Maria was not a party to the bankruptcy. Mueller and Kirkpatrick write, "Rule 201(b)(2) does not limit judicial notice of court proceedings [to cases involving the same parties], and there is no reason in policy or doctrine to impose such a limit. Records of any court can properly be noticed . . . ."[12]

Note that, in addition to judicial notice, Juan must authenticate the bankruptcy document. He also has to satisfy the best evidence rule or the secondary evidence rule. Finally, the document is hearsay, although it should satisfy the public records exception to the hearsay rule. (See § 11.14).

A court that takes judicial notice of a court document may accept as true statements of fact contained in the document, when those facts are not subject to dispute.[13] Thus, a court taking judicial notice of a divorce decree will take notice that the divorce was final on the date specified in the decree. A court will not, however, take judicial notice of facts that are subject to dispute.[14] *Marriage of Carter-Scanlon*[15] illustrates the point. Joe and Lona divorced. They had two kids. The divorce court ordered Joe to pay monthly child support. Later, Joe had a child with Joann. Joann opened a child

---

[12]　1 Christopher B. Mueller & Laird C. Kirkpatrick, *Federal Evidence* § 2:5, p. 345 (4th ed. 2013). *See also,* Kowalski v. Gagne, 914 F.2d 229, 305 (1st Cir. 1990).

[13]　*See* Hennessy v. Penril Datacomm Networks, 69 F.3d 1344, 1354 (7th Cir. 1995) ("In order for a fact to be judicially noticed, indisputability is a prerequisite."); *In re* Vicks, 56 Cal. 4th 274, 314, 295 P.3d 863, 892, 153 Cal. Rptr. 3d 471, 506–507 (2013); Hawkins v. Suntrust Bank, 246 Cal. App. 4th 1387, 206 Cal. Rptr. 3d 681, 685 (2016).

[14]　Guarantee Forklift, Inc. v. Capacity of Texas, Inc., 2017 WL 2267270 (Cal. Ct. App. 2017) ("we generally do not take judicial notice of the truth of the matter asserted in such documents, and many decline to take judicial notice of matters not relevant to dispositive issue on appeal."); Licudine v. Cedars-Siani Medical Center, 3 Cal. App. 5th 881, 901, 208 Cal. Rptr. 3d 170 (2016); Lockley v. Law Office of Cantrell, Green, Pekich, Cruz & McCort, 91 Cal. App. 4th 875, 882, 110 Cal. Rptr. 2d 877, 882 (2001) ("The court may in its discretion take judicial notice of any court record in the United States. . . . However, while courts are free to take judicial notice of the *existence* of each document in a court file, including the truth of results reached, they may not take judicial notice of the truth of hearsay statements in decisions and court files. Courts may not take judicial notice of allegations in affidavits, declarations and probation reports in court records because such matters are reasonably subject to dispute and therefore require formal proof.")

[15]　322 P.3d 1033 (Mont. 2014).

support case, and pegged Joe's yearly income at $74,000. Joe disputed the amount, and an administrative law judge (ALJ) lowered Joe's annual income to $25,000. Joe then returned to family court, and asked the court to lower the child support owed to Lona each month. Joe asked the family court to take judicial notice of the ALJ's finding that his income was $25,000. Lona objected to judicial notice because she received no notice of the proceedings before the ALJ, and had no opportunity to participate. Moreover, Lona argued that Joe was deliberately underemployed. The family court ruled that it was not bound by the ALJ's decision.

On appeal, Joe argued the family court was required to take judicial notice of the ALJ's income determination. The Montana Supreme Court rejected Joe's contention. The Supreme Court noted that "Joe has presented no evidence that Lona knew about, or participated in" the ALJ proceedings.[16] More to the point, "[A] court may not take judicial notice of a fact from a prior proceeding when the fact is reasonably disputed . . . . [T]he matter to be judicially noticed here, that of Joe's yearly income, was subject to reasonable, and vigorous, dispute by the parties."[17]

When an attorney asks a judge to take judicial notice, failure by the opponent to object, waives objection.[18] *Marriage of Harpenau,*[19] dealt with child support. The children's father asked the judge to take judicial notice of an unsigned and unverified child support worksheet attached to the divorce decree. The judge obliged. The mother's failure to object to judicial notice of the worksheet waived the right to raise the issue on appeal.[20]

§ 5.11(b).   Judicial Notice Under the CEC

The CEC contains detailed provisions on judicial notice. Section 451 *requires* judges to take judicial notice of constitutional, statutory, and case law from California and the federal government. Judicial notice is also required of "Facts and propositions of generalized knowledge that are so universally known that they cannot reasonably be the subject of dispute" (CEC § 451(f)).

Section 452 *allows* judges to take judicial notice of the law of other states, and "facts and propositions that are not reasonably subject to dispute and are capable of immediate and accurate determination by resort to sources of reasonably indisputable accuracy" (CEC § 452(h)). In *In re Cook,* 7 Cal. App. 5th 393, 212

---

[16]   322 P.3d at 1037.

[17]   *Id.* at 1038.

[18]   *See* Marriage of Harpenau, 17 N.E.3d 342 (Ind. Ct. App. 2014).

[19]   *Id.*

[20]   *Id.* at 349.

Cal. Rptr. 3d 646 (2017), the Court of Appeal took judicial notice of
the online Court of Appeal docket. In *Gould v. Maryland Sound
Industries, Inc.,* 31 Cal. App. 4th 1137, 1145, 37 Cal. App. 2d 719
(1995), the Court wrote that judges take judicial notice of "facts
which are widely accepted as established by experts and specialists
in the natural, physical, and social sciences which can be verified by
reference to treatises, encyclopedias, almanacs and the like or by
persons learned in the subject matter." The *Gould* court ruled that
it would be improper to take judicial notice of the existence of a
contract between two parties. In *Licudine v. Cedars-Sinai Medical
Center,* 3 Cal. App. 5th 881, 208 Cal. Rptr. 3d 170 (2016), the court
refused to take judicial notice of average salaries for attorneys.
Attorney income is not a fact that is "capable of immediate and
accurate determination by resort to sources of reasonably
indisputable accuracy."

Chapter 6

CHARACTER EVIDENCE

The two most difficult areas of evidence are character and hearsay, and, of the two, character is the greater challenge. The rules on character are complex, and are easily confused with rules that do not concern character. To add to the complexity, there are important similarities and differences between the Federal Rules of Evidence (FRE) and the California Evidence Code (CEC). This chapter is not a cake walk, but once you figure character evidence out, you are on your way toward understanding evidence.

§ 6.1   What Is Character?

In daily life, it is common to judge others: "That guy is generous to a fault." "She's a liar; I wouldn't believe a word she says." "You can trust him. His word is his bond." "Be careful around her, she has a short temper, so don't make her mad." "He's a thief. He'd steal your last dime." "She is always careful behind the wheel." In 1972, Rock singer and composer, Carly Simon, released a famous song, "You're So Vain," in which she describes a guy who is so vain he "probably thinks this song is about [him]."

It seems to be part of human nature to draw conclusions about other people's character. But what is character? What do we mean when we say a person has a particular character? People are complicated. Is anyone all bad or all good; always honest or always a liar; invariably violent or invariably peaceful? Of course not. The worst villain isn't villainous 24/7/365. And yet, it does seems that people—at least most people—have an approach to life, a style of living, a way about them, that allows us to say, "She's *that* kind of person."

Consider two famous figures from the last century: Mother Teresa and Al Capone. Mother Teresa, now Saint Teresa of Calcutta, was the Catholic nun who devoted her life to helping the poor. Al Capone was the American gangster famous for ruthless violence to prop up his criminal empire. Your reaction to these individuals is different. At a basic level, one is very very good; the other very very bad. Mother Teresa's character is one of generosity and benevolence. Al Capone's character is that of a criminal, and a violent criminal, at that. Thus, when we say that a person has a particular character, we mean a person's disposition to think and act in a certain way. A violent person is inclined to violence. A liar is disposed to lie. A careless person is likely to act carelessly. And so on.

§ 6.2   Is Character Relevant?

You recall from Chapter 2 that evidence is relevant if it has *any* tendency to make a fact of consequence more or less likely. Evidence of a person's character can be relevant three ways: (1) to prove a person acted in conformity with her character on a particular occasion, (2) to shed light on a witness's credibility, and (3) as proof of character when a trait of character is *itself* a fact of consequence.

§ 6.2(a).   Evidence of Character Offered to Prove a Person Acted in Conformity with Character: Substantive Evidence

People tend to act in accordance with their character. Thus, a violent person is prone to act violently, while a peaceful person is not. An untruthful person is more apt to lie than a truth teller. Do people always act in conformity with their character? Of course not. I assume there were days when Mother Teresa was grumpy, and acted accordingly (although I wouldn't bet on it). As well, Al Capone loved his son, Albert, and treated him with affection. The point is not that people *always* act in conformity with their character, but that character predisposes people to act in particular ways.

In court, proof of a person's character could be offered as circumstantial evidence that the person acted in conformity with their character on a particular occasion. The reasoning is simple. First, evidence of a person's character is admitted. Second, from the evidence, we infer that the person has a particular character. Third, because the person has a particular character, we infer that the person probably acted in conformity with character on a particular occasion. Why? Because people often act in conformity with character.[1]

Suppose you are on jury duty in a civil case. Your task is to determine whether the defendant drove negligently on December 1, causing an accident. The plaintiff offers evidence that on five separate occasions before December 1, the defendant drove negligently. Are the five episodes of negligent driving relevant? Sure. You can infer from the five episodes that defendant is a terrible driver. From this, you can further infer that on December 1,

---

[1]   Evidence of character is relevant to prove a person acted in conformity with the person's character. People v. Jackson, 1 Cal. 5th 269, 376 P.3d 528, 205 Cal. Rptr. 3d 386 (2016).

defendant probably acted in conformity with his character and drove negligently, causing the accident.

Switch trials, and imagine you are a juror in the trial of John, who is charged with robbing the First Bank of Redding on August 1. You met John in § 2.6. Recall that the prosecutor has evidence that John robbed ten other banks, but John is *not* currently charged with any those ten robberies. John is charged only with robbing the First Bank of Redding on August 1. Is evidence of John's ten uncharged bank robberies relevant? Sure! The fact that John robbed ten other banks makes it more likely he robbed the First Bank of Redding. Why? Because he's a bank robber!

Thus, evidence of character can be relevant as substantive evidence in civil and criminal litigation, to prove that a person acted in conformity with character. Whether such character evidence is admissible is another story, but relevance is clear.

§ 6.2(b).   Character Evidence Offered to Prove Witness Credibility: *Not* Substantive Evidence

Evidence pertaining to the credibility of witnesses is relevant, and a character for truthfulness or its opposite has much to say. A liar is more likely to lie on the witness stand than a truthful person. Who would you believe, Mother Teresa or Al Capone? Thus, evidence of a witness's character for truthfulness or lying is relevant to credibility.

Note that the use of character evidence to attack or support witness credibility is really just an application of character evidence offered to prove that a person acted in conformity with character on a particular occasion. In this case, the occasion is testifying in court.

Recall from Chapter 1, that you are urged to categorize rules of evidence into rules related to substantive evidence and rules related to witness credibility. Character evidence fits both categories. Sometimes, character evidence is relevant as substantive evidence of facts of consequence. In other cases, character evidence is relevant to witness credibility. Separate rules govern each use of character.

§ 6.2(c).   Substantive Law Makes Character a Fact of Consequence

In a small number of civil cases, substantive law makes a person's character a fact of consequence. As FRE 405(b) puts it, substantive law makes a person's character "an essential element of a charge, claim or defense ...." When this is so, evidence of character is *not* offered to prove that a person acted in conformity with the person's character on a particular occasion. That is, character evidence is not offered as circumstantial evidence of conduct. Rather, the governing substantive law (*e.g.*, tort law) provides that in order to win the case, a party must prove some aspect of a person's character. In such cases, courts and commentators often say "character is in issue."

The best way to understand this use of character "in issue" is through examples. First, consider the tort of negligent entrustment. Joe asks Fran to borrow Fran's car. Fran knows Joe is a bad driver, who often drives drunk. Nevertheless, Fran tosses the keys to Joe and says, "Have fun." Joe drunkenly crashes into Plaintiff's car. Plaintiff sues *Fran* for negligent entrustment. In negligent entrustment cases, tort law states that the plaintiff must prove that the defendant (Fran) was aware that the driver (Joe) was a danger behind the wheel. The substantive law makes Joe's character as a bad driver a fact of consequence. Joe's character is "in issue." In the negligent entrustment case, evidence of Joe's character as a bad driver is *not* offered to prove that Joe acted in conformity with his character and caused the accident. Rather, the evidence is offered to prove that Joe was a menace on the roadway. Other evidence is offered to prove that Fran *knew* this, and negligently entrusted her car to Joe.

Another example of character in issue is child custody litigation. When parents battle over custody, the judge uses the "best interests of the child" standard to decide custody. Parental fitness is key, and evidence of parental character—parental strengths and weaknesses—is relevant. Parental character is "in issue."

Character is often in issue in defamation cases. Suppose Dell goes on TV and says of Paul, "Paul is a good for nothing lazy bum, who would just as soon steal from an old lady as look at her." Paul sues Dell for defamation. Dell's defense is, "Everything I said is true." When the defense is truth, the plaintiff's character is "in issue" for the character traits mentioned by the defendant.

When character is "in issue," remember three things. First, when character is in issue, evidence of character is *not* offered to prove that a person acted in conformity with their character. Rather, the substantive law makes an aspect of character a fact of consequence. Second, character is only in issue in a few types of civil cases. In most civil cases, character is *not* in issue. Thus, character is not in issue in the typical negligence case. Character is not in issue in contract, property, or business litigation. The best way to spot "character in issue" on exams is to know the types of cases where this use of character is allowed. Third, with one exception, character is not in issue in criminal cases. The exception is the entrapment defense. There are two approaches to entrapment, the subjective approach and the objective approach. The subjective approach is employed in federal court and most states. California and a few other states adhere to the objective approach. With the subjective approach to entrapment, the defendant's predisposition (*i.e.*, character) to engage in the charged crime is relevant. To that extent, in subjective entrapment jurisdictions, character is in issue. Apart from the subjective approach to entrapment, character is not in issue in criminal cases. Thus, character is not in issue in cases of murder, rape, robbery, burglary, assault, arson, etc. Turning to defenses, character is not in issue when a defendant claims self-defense, necessity, duress, or insanity.

§ 6.3   The Rule Against Character Evidence

Section 6.2(a) makes clear that evidence of a person's character can be relevant to prove that the person acted in conformity with their character on a particular occasion. However, a cardinal principle of evidence law holds that proof of a person's character generally is not admissible to establish that the person acted in conformity with the person's character on a particular occasion. In other words, although character evidence is relevant to prove conduct, it is not admissible to prove conduct. This is the rule against character evidence. The rule is found in FRE 404(a)(1) and CEC § 1101(a):

> **Rule 404(a)(1). Prohibited Uses**. Evidence of a person's character or character trait is not admissible to prove that on a particular occasion the person acted in accordance with the character trait.

> **CEC § 1101(a)**. Except as provided [by other rules], evidence of a person's character or a trait of his or her character (whether in the form of opinion, evidence of reputation, or evidence of specific instances of his or her conduct) is inadmissible when offered to prove his or her conduct on a specified occasion.

The rule against character evidence forbids circumstantial use of character to prove that a person acted in a certain way. In other words, the rule forbids the inferential reasoning that makes character evidence relevant. That reasoning is, first, evidence is offered to establish character. Second, from evidence of character, you infer that a person possesses a particular character. Third, because people often act in accordance with character, you infer that the person acted in conformity with the person's character on a particular occasion. It is this inferential reasoning that is barred by FRE 404(a)(1) and CEC § 1101(a). Because the rule against character evidence forbids such inferential reasoning, this book sometimes refers to the reasoning as the forbidden chain of inferences.

With the forbidden chain of inferences in mind, recall the prosecution of John for robbing the First Bank of Redding on August 1. (§ 2.6). The prosecutor has evidence that John robbed ten other banks. Under the rule against character evidence, the prosecutor cannot offer the ten other robberies to prove that John is a thief and, because he is a thief, he probably robbed the First Bank of Redding. The result is the same under the FRE and the CEC.

But why? Evidence of John's ten other bank robberies tends to prove that John is a thief, and his character as a thief makes it more likely that he robbed the First Bank of Redding. The evidence is relevant. Why do the rules make evidence of John's ten other robberies inadmissible to prove his character, and, from his character, his guilt? The answer is not that the evidence lacks relevance. The answer lies in the fact that if the jury hears about the ten other robberies, they might convict John *whether or not* he is guilty of robbing the First Bank of Redding. Even if the evidence of John's guilt falls short of proof beyond a reasonable doubt, the jury may engage in the following erroneous reasoning: "He got away with those other robberies. Maybe he didn't rob the bank in Redding, but this guy is a menace to society, and needs to be locked up. Guilty!" Or, the jury might think, "He must be guilty. He's a bank robber!" Of course, the judge could instruct the jury not to engage in such reasoning, but the worry is that the jury can't or won't obey the instruction. Thus, the law makes the value judgment that character evidence, although relevant, should not be admissible to prove that a person acted in conformity with the person's character on a particular occasion. The evidence is not excluded because it is irrelevant, but because the jury may misuse the evidence.

Consider the rule against character evidence in the context of a civil suit alleging negligence. In a car accident case, plaintiff sues defendant, claiming that defendant negligently caused the accident. Through discovery, plaintiff learns that during the past five years, defendant negligently caused five other traffic accidents. At trial, plaintiff's attorney offers evidence of the five other accidents to prove that defendant is a negligent driver, and, because he is a negligent driver, he acted in conformity with his negligent character and caused the accident. Defendant objects on the basis of the rule against character evidence. Should the judge sustain the objection? Yes. The rule against character evidence applies in civil cases as well as in criminal cases.

The CEC contains a section specifically addressed to negligence cases. CEC § 1104 provides: "[E]vidence of a trait of a person's character with respect to care or skill is inadmissible to prove the quality of his conduct on a specific occasion." Technically, Section 1104 is unnecessary because the same result would be reached under the general rule against character evidence contained in Section 1101(a). Under the CEC and the FRE, in negligence cases, evidence of a person's prior negligence is not admissible to prove that the person acted negligently on the occasion that is the subject of the law suit.

§ 6.3(a).   Character Evidence on Exams

You might think it is easy to spot character evidence on a test, and apply the rule against it. Don't get your hopes up. The issue is complicated by the fact that there are exceptions to the rule against character evidence. That is, there are times when it is proper to offer character evidence to prove that a person acted in conformity with the person's character. And that's not all, in many cases, evidence that is inadmissible, if it is offered to prove character, is admissible if it is offered for another, non-character purpose. This other, non-character purpose is typically governed by FRE 404(b)(2) and CEC § 1101(b), and involves proof of intent, identity, and *actus reus*. (See Chapter 8). The issue is further complicated by the fact that some of the rules on character evidence apply to character evidence offered as substantive evidence, while other rules on character evidence apply to character evidence that is offered to impeach witnesses. On an exam, you have to know *all* of these principles so well that you can look at a set of facts and see which of the various principles apply. The rule against character evidence applies to keep evidence out *only* when there is no permissible purpose for the evidence. Thus, you have to determine whether an exception to the rule against character evidence applies, and check that off. Then you have to see whether a non-character use of the evidence applies, and check that off. Only when you conclude that the *only* logical relevance of the evidence is the chain of inferences that is forbidden by the rule against character evidence do you apply the rule and conclude that the evidence is barred by the rule against character evidence. Fun stuff, huh?

§ 6.3(b).   Examples of Character Evidence on Exams

It may be useful to look at two exam questions where you would probably conclude that the rule against character evidence prohibits evidence offered by a prosecutor:

> Juan is on trial for assault on a police officer. According to the prosecution, Juan struck the officer with a stick as the officer was attempting to arrest Juan. During the prosecution's case-in-chief, the prosecutor offers testimony from Juan's neighbor, Sylvia. Sylvia testifies, "A year ago, Juan was upset with something my little boy did. Juan came onto my property and hit me in the face with his fist."

Your answer might look like this:

> Defense counsel should object because Sylvia's testimony violates the rule against character evidence. Although evidence of the assault on Sylvia may have some tendency to prove that Juan is violent, and therefore more likely than a non-violent person to commit assault, that theory of relevance of exactly what the rule against character evidence forbids. The rule excludes evidence of character that is offered to prove that a person acted in conformity with the person's character on a particular occasion. There are exceptions to the rule against character evidence; however, none of those exceptions apply here. As well, there is no non-character use of the evidence. The assault on Sylvia does not prove plan, intent, or any other permissible use of uncharged misconduct evidence. Even if it could be argued that the assault on Sylvia has some small probative value to prove intent, the probative value of the evidence for that purpose would be substantially outweighed by the danger of unfair prejudice to the defendant. Uncharged misconduct evidence offered against a defendant in a criminal trial is often highly prejudicial. In the final analysis, the only logical relevance of the assault on Sylvia is the very theory of relevance prohibited by the rule against character evidence. The judge should sustain the defense objection to the evidence.

Consider the following, taken from an actual exam:

> Fawn is prosecuted for robbing a jewelry store on June 1. Fawn has pleaded not guilty. Fawn does not deny

that someone robbed the jewelry store. Fawn's defense is that she was out of town when the store was robbed. During the prosecution's case-in-chief, the prosecutor offers the testimony of Abigail who testifies: "Once two years ago, I was with Fawn when she committed burglary. And again, three years ago, I was with her when she committed burglary."

Abigail's testimony should be rejected because it is evidence of Fawn's character, offered to prove that Fawn is a bad person, and, because she is a bad person, she probably acted in conformity with her bad character and robbed the jewelry store. In Chapter 8, you study uncharged misconduct evidence. Fawn's previous crimes do not fit any theory of uncharged misconduct evidence. The only logical relevance of Fawn's burglaries is precisely the theory of relevance that is prohibited by the rule against character evidence.

§ 6.4   Exceptions to Rule Against Character Evidence

The FRE provides four exceptions to the rule against character evidence. First, the defendant in a criminal case can offer evidence of defendant's good character as substantive evidence of innocence (FRE 404(a)(2)(A)). Second, the defendant in a criminal case, who claims self-defense, can offer evidence of the victim's violent character as substantive evidence that the victim was the first aggressor (FRE 404(a)(2)(B)). Third, in a homicide prosecution, the prosecutor can offer evidence of the victim's peacefulness, after the defendant offers evidence that the victim was the first aggressor (FRE 404(a)(2)(C)). Fourth, witnesses in criminal *and* civil trials can be impeached with evidence of character for untruthfulness (FRE 404(a)(3)).

The CEC has three of the four exceptions found in the FRE. First, CEC § 1102 provides that in a criminal case, the defendant can offer evidence of the defendant's good character as substantive evidence of innocence. Second, CEC § 1103 allows a criminal defendant who claims self-defense to offer evidence of the victim's violent character as substantive evidence that the victim was the first aggressor. Third, CEC § 1101(c) provides that witnesses in civil *and* criminal trials can be impeached with character evidence of untruthfulness. California does not have a counterpart to FRE 404(a)(2)(C), the rule that allows a prosecutor in a homicide case to offer evidence that the victim was a peaceful person, after the defendant offers evidence that the victim was the first aggressor. The exceptions are explained in following sections.

§ 6.5 Methods of Proving Character

There are three ways to prove a person's character. First, offer evidence of specific instances of the person's conduct that shed light on the person's character. For example, to prove that a person is violent, offer witnesses to describe fights the person started over the years. Second, offer testimony from a witness who knows the person well, and who has an opinion about the person's character. For example, offer testimony from the person's long-time friend, that the person is honest. Third, offer testimony from a witness who knows the person's reputation in the community for a character trait. The witness need not know the person. What is important is that the witness knows the person's reputation. For example, a witness who has lived for years in the same community could testify that the person has a bad reputation for honesty.

§ 6.6 FRE 405(a)—Character Witness

The three methods of proving character—specific instances, opinion, and reputation—are addressed in FRE 405. FRE 405(a) is discussed in this section. FRE 405(b) is discussed in § 6.7.

> **Rule 405. Methods of Proving Character. (a) By Reputation or Opinion**. When evidence of a person's character or character trait is admissible, it may be proved by testimony about the person's reputation or by testimony in the form of an opinion. . . .

When Rule 405(a) speaks of "Reputation or Opinion," the Rule refers to a character witness. A character witness is a lay witness, not an expert witness.[2] A properly qualified character witness may testify about a person's reputation for a particular character trait. Alternatively, a properly qualified character witness may offer the character witness's own opinion about a person's character. Whether a character witness testifies in the form of reputation or opinion, the purpose is the same, prove a person's character.

§ 6.6(a).   Reputation Character Witness

A person qualifies to testify as a reputation character witness when the witness is sufficiently familiar with a person's reputation in a geographic (e.g., neighborhood) or social (e.g., workplace) community. As mentioned above, a reputation character witness does not need to know the person personally. The important thing is that the character witness knows of the person's reputation in the community. There is no hard-and-fast rule on how long it takes to

---

[2]   In California, a defendant charged with child molestation may be allowed to offer expert testimony about his character. *See* § 6.9(j).

gain a reputation, or on how familiar the witness must be with the reputation. The longer the time, and the more familiar, the better.

The proponent of a reputation character witness must satisfy the judge that the witness qualifies to testify. The proponent asks questions to demonstrate that the witness knows the person's reputation. This is laying the foundation for a character witness.

§ 6.6(b).   Opinion Character Witness

A person qualifies to testify as an opinion character witness if the witness knows the person sufficiently well to have an opinion on the person's character. How long is long enough? No rule exists. Is three months long enough? Probably not. Three years? Likely.

The proponent of an opinion character witness must lay a foundation. The proponent asks questions to satisfy the judge that the witness has a solid basis for the opinion.

§ 6.6(c).   Character Witness May Not Describe Specific Instances on Direct Examination

The direct examination of a character witness is very short. It begins with the foundation questions. That done, the witness states the person's reputation or offers an opinion. For example, direct examination of an opinion character witness might go as follows:

Q: Do you have an opinion on Mr. Jones' character for violence or peacefulness?

A: Yes.

Q: What is your opinion?

A: In my opinion, Mr. Jones is a violent man.

That's it! No more. On direct examination, a character witness cannot say *why* he has this opinion. The character witness cannot describe the specific things the witness observed that led to the opinion. All the character witness can say is, "In my opinion, Mr. Jones is a violent man."

Testimony from a reputation character witness is similarly short. For example:

Q: Are you familiar with Mr. Jones' reputation in the community for truth?

A: Yes.

Q: What is that reputation?

A: Bad.[3]

A reputation character witness cannot describe the things the person did to earn the reputation.

§ 6.7   Rule 405(b)—Character "in Issue"

Rule 405(b) allows character to be proven with a character witness *or* with specific instances of a person's conduct. When proof is by specific instances, testimony is provided by witnesses who observed the conduct, or with documents.

Rule 405(b) applies *only* when character is "in issue," as discussed in § 6.2(c). Rule 405(b) makes this clear when the rule states that specific instances are allowed "[w]hen a person's character or character trait is an essential element of a charge, claim, or defense . . . ."

Recall from § 6.2(c) that character is not in issue in criminal cases, with the exception of the subjective approach to entrapment. Because character is not in issue in criminal cases, FRE 405(b) does not apply in criminal cases.[4] The result under the FRE is that when character evidence is admissible in a criminal case, specific instances of conduct are *not* allowed to prove character because Rule 405(b), the rule allowing specific instances, does not apply. The party seeking to prove character under the FRE is limited to character witnesses who testify in the form of reputation or opinion, and who may *not,* on direct examination, describe specific instances of the person's conduct.

Character is not "in issue" in most civil litigation. For example, character is not in issue in garden variety negligence cases. Character *is* "in issue" in negligent entrustment cases, child custody litigation, certain defamation cases, and in a few other scenarios. When character is "in issue," FRE 405(b) allows proof of character with specific instances of conduct or with a character witness.

§ 6.8   CEC § 1100—Methods of Proving Character

Like the FRE, the CEC specifies three ways to prove character: specific instances, reputation, and opinion. CEC section 1100 provides:

> **§ 1100. Manner of Proof of Character**. Except as otherwise provide by statute, any otherwise admissible evidence (including evidence in the form of an opinion,

---

[3]   The character might say more than "Bad." She might say, "Mr. Jones' reputation for truth is bad," or similar words.

[4]   Again, the entrapment defense is the exception to the rule that FRE 405(b) does not apply in criminal cases.

evidence of reputation, and evidence of specific instances of such person's conduct) is admissible to prove a person's character or a trait of his character.

Regarding character witnesses, the CEC and the FRE are similar, allowing testimony in the form of reputation or opinion. As for specific instances of conduct to prove character, there are similarities and differences between the CEC and the FRE. When character is "in issue," the CEC and FRE are the same: character may be established in any of the three ways. When character is *not* "in issue," there are similarities and differences, described below.

§ 6.9   Defendant Offers Evidence of Good Character: The Mercy Rule

The most frequently deployed exception to the rule against character evidence allows the defendant in a criminal case to offer evidence of defendant's good character as substantive evidence of innocence. The idea is simple: The defendant is a good person. Good people don't commit crimes. Therefore, defendant probably acted in conformity with his good character and didn't commit the crime. The FRE and CEC rules follow:

> **FRE 404(a)(2)(A). Exceptions for a Defendant** . . . .
> The following exceptions [to the rule against character evidence] apply in criminal cases: (A) a defendant may offer evidence of the defendant's pertinent trait [of character], and if the evidence is admitted, the prosecutor may offer [character] evidence to rebut it.

> **CEC § 1102. Opinion and Reputation Evidence of Character of Criminal Defendant to Prove Conduct**. In a criminal action, evidence of the defendant's character or a trait of his character in the form of an opinion or evidence of his reputation is not made inadmissible by Section 1101 [the rule against character evidence] if such evidence is: (a) Offered by the defendant to prove his conduct in conformity with such character or trait of character. (b) Offered by the prosecution to rebut evidence adduced by the defendant under subdivision (a).

§ 6.9(a).   FRE 404(a)(2)(A) and CEC § 1102 Apply Only in Criminal Cases

The rule allowing a defendant to offer evidence of good character applies only in criminal cases. Thus, the defendant in civil litigation cannot offer such evidence.

§ 6.9(b). Evidence of Defendant's Good Character Is Provided by Character Witnesses

As discussed earlier, there are three ways to prove character: specific instances of conduct, reputation, and opinion. The latter two are provided by character witnesses. When a defendant in a criminal case uses FRE 404(a)(2)(A) or CEC § 1102 to offer evidence of good character, the defendant is limited to a character witness who testifies in the form of reputation or opinion.[5] The defendant may not prove good character with specific instances of defendant's good conduct. (FRE 405(a); CEC § 1102).

§ 6.9(c). Mercy Rule

Note that the defendant in a criminal case is *allowed* to do precisely what the prosecutor is *forbidden* to do. The rule against character evidence prohibits the prosecutor from offering evidence of the defendant's bad character to prove guilt. Yet, FRE 404(a)(2)(A) and CEC § 1102 allow the defendant to offer evidence of the defendant's good character to prove innocence. This is sometimes called the Mercy Rule. Why the unequal treatment, favoring defendants? Because the defendant has so much at stake in a criminal trial that the law takes mercy on the defendant and affords him the option of offering evidence of good character; an option foreclosed to the prosecution.

§ 6.9(d). Pertinent Character Trait

When a defendant offers evidence of good character, the character evidence must be relevant to the crime charged. Thus, if defendant is charged with a violent crime, the relevant character trait is non-violence. If the crime involves deceit or lying, the relevant character trait is truthfulness or honesty. FRE 404(a)(2)(A) uses the word "pertinent" to express this requirement. The CEC is to the same effect.

---

[5]　　FRE 405(a) specifies that when a defendant offers evidence of good character as substantive evidence of innocence, defendant is limited to character witnesses, and cannot offer specific instances of defendant's good conduct. CEC § 1102 specifies that defendant is limited to character witnesses. The Law Revision Comments on Section 1102 provide: "Section 1102 codifies the general rule under existing law which precludes evidence of specific acts of the defendant to prove character as circumstantial evidence of his innocence or of his disposition to commit the crimes with which he is charged."

§ 6.9(e). At What Point in a Trial Does a Defendant Offer Good Character Evidence?

If a defendant decides to offer evidence of her good character, the defendant's character witnesses testify during the defense case-in-chief. A defendant may offer evidence of good character whether or not the defendant testifies.

§ 6.9(f). If a Defendant Offers Evidence of Defendant's Good Character, the Prosecutor Can Rebut with Evidence of Defendant's Bad Character

When a defendant offers evidence of good character to prove innocence, the prosecutor may rebut with evidence that defendant has a bad character. The FRE language authorizing the prosecutor's rebuttal is, "[T]he prosecutor may offer evidence to rebut it." The CEC language is, "Offered by the prosecution to rebut evidence adduced by the defendant." The prosecutor's rebuttal character witnesses testify during the prosecution's case-in-rebuttal.[6]

The defense attorney's decision to offer good character evidence often turns on what the prosecutor can throw at the defendant in rebuttal. If the defendant is a good person, with no or few skeletons in the closet, then it may be safe to offer evidence of good character because the prosecutor won't have ammunition for rebuttal. On the other hand, if the defendant is a scoundrel, then it isn't a good idea to offer evidence of good character because the prosecutor will fire back with *bad* character witnesses. But that's not all. When a defendant offers evidence of good character, the prosecutor is allowed to cross-examine the defendant's character witnesses. Such cross-examination can be disastrous for the defense because the prosecutor is allowed to ask the character witness about specific instances of the *defendant's conduct!* Cross-examination of character witnesses is discussed in § 10.10.

§ 6.9(g). The Term "Character in Issue" Can Cause Confusion

The rules on character evidence are confusing enough, but when the same term—"character in issue"—is used to describe two different things, the potential for confusion expands. Often, when a

---

[6]   When a defendant offers evidence of defendant's good character to prove innocence, the evidence is substantive evidence. When a prosecutor offers rebuttal character evidence of defendant's bad character, the rebuttal evidence is substantive evidence of guilt.

defendant in a criminal case offers evidence of the defendant's good character as substantive evidence of innocence (FRE 404(a)(2)(A); CEC § 1102), the court says defendant has placed his character in issue. Fair enough. It is true that the defendant introduced his character into the case, and, in that sense, character is "in issue." This meaning of character in issue should not be confused with civil cases where an aspect of a person's character is a fact of consequence (FRE 405(b)). In the latter situation too, courts say that character is in issue.[7]

§ 6.9(h).   Can the Defendant Be His Own Good Character Witness?

A defendant in a criminal case has a constitutional right to testify in his own behalf. When a defendant testifies, and tells his version of events, he is not acting as a character witness. Sometimes, however, a defendant strays beyond the facts, and crosses the blurry line that separates factual testimony from character testimony.[8] For example, if a defendant testifies, "I would never do that kind of thing," or "I'm not that kind of person," or "I am an honest, upstanding member of my community," then the defendant becomes his own good character witness. When this happens, the prosecutor is allowed to rebut the defendant with character witnesses who testify that defendant's character is bad.

§ 6.9(i).   FRE and CEC Rules on Good Character Operate Similarly

When it comes to a defendant in a criminal case offering evidence of the defendant's good character as substantive evidence of innocence, the FRE and the CEC are virtually identical. The defendant can offer evidence of a pertinent trait of defendant's good character. It is up to the defendant to decide whether to open the door to character. The prosecutor can't be the first to introduce evidence of defendant's character as substantive evidence.[9] That

---

[7]   I encourage students to avoid using "character in issue" to describe the situation where the defendant uses the Mercy Rule to offer evidence of his good character. I tell students it will avoid confusion if they limit the phrase "character in issue" to those civil cases where the substantive law makes an aspect of a person's character a fact of consequence (*e.g.*, negligent entrustment case). Your professor may have a different approach.

[8]   *See* People v. Wagner, 13 Cal. 3d 612, 618, 532 P.2d 105, 119 Cal. Rptr. 457 (1975), in which defendant was charged with selling an illegal drug. In his testimony denying guilt, defendant became his own good character witness when he described his civic activities in his community, his family background, and like matters of good conduct.

[9]   Things can get tricky. Suppose defendant does not offer evidence of his good character. That keeps the door shut to his character, and the prosecutor can't offer evidence of defendant's bad character as *substantive evidence*. However, suppose the defendant testifies and denies guilt. When the defendant testifies, and gives his

would violate the cardinal principle that the prosecutor can't prove the defendant is guilty with character evidence. When the defendant offers evidence of good character—Mercy Rule (FRE 404(a)(2)(A); CEC § 1102)—the evidence comes through a character witness. The character witness can testify to defendant's reputation in the community, or to the character witness's opinion of the defendant's character. On direct examination, a character witness may not mention specific instances of defendant's conduct.

§ 6.9(j).   In California, a Defendant Charged with Child Molestation May Offer Expert Testimony on Defendant's Character

In *People v. Stoll*, 49 Cal. 3d 1136, 783 P.2d 698, 265 Cal. Rptr. 111 (1989), the defendant was charged with child molestation. The Supreme Court ruled that defendants in such cases can offer expert testimony that the defendant is not psychologically disposed to commit the charged sex offense. The evidence is admissible under CEC § 1102. *Stoll* represents the minority approach. In *State v. Hughes*, 841 So. 2d 718, 721 (La. 2003), the Louisiana Supreme Court wrote, "The overwhelming weight of recent authority in other state jurisdictions considering the question of whether the accused may present expert testimony that he is psychologically unlikely to commit the charged offense has been to exclude expert evidence offered by the defendant .... California stands as a notable exception to the overwhelming majority rule on this point . . . ."

§ 6.10 Questions on Good Character Evidence

Try your hand at a couple of questions. You will find answers in § 6.16.

1.   Is This a Smart Move on John's Part?

Recall John, who stands accused of robbing the First Bank of Redding on August 1. (§ 2.6). John robbed ten other banks. At trial, would it be a good strategy for John to offer character witnesses to testify to John's good character?

---

version of the facts, he is NOT offering evidence of good character. However, he is a witness, and like all witnesses, he can be impeached. One way to impeach a witness—including the defendant, if he testifies—is with a character witness who testifies that the defendant has a bad reputation for honesty, or that, in the character witness's opinion, the defendant is a liar. This character evidence is NOT offered as substantive evidence. It is offered on the issue credibility. *See* FRE 608(a); CEC § 786. This use of character witnesses to attack credibility does not violate the rule that a prosecutor cannot use character evidence as substantive evidence of the defendant's conduct in conformity with defendant's character. Why not? Because character evidence to impeach credibility is not offered as substantive evidence.

2.   Are Specific Instances Allowed?

June is charged with assault with a deadly weapon on Hanna. June denies that she attacked Hanna. During the defense case-in-chief, June offers testimony from Juanita, who has been friends with June for many years. On direct examination, Juanita states, "June is a peaceful, non-violent person. I have often been with her at social gatherings and not once has she ever been aggressive with anyone else. Once, at a party, some gang banger got in her face, and tried to pick a fight, but June just walked away." Is Juanita's testimony admissible?

§ 6.11 Good Character Evidence on an Exam

Consider the following portion of an exam question:

Nancy was charged with murder, and has pleaded not guilty. The victim was shot and killed. During the defense case-in-chief, the defense offers the testimony of Ursula, who testifies, "I have known Nancy all her life. We grew up together. Nancy is not a violent person. She would not deliberately hurt someone."

It is easy to see that the facts call for analysis of character evidence. Your answer might say:

The defendant in a criminal case may offer evidence of defendant's good character as substantive evidence of innocence. This is the so-called "Mercy Rule." The rule exists under the FRE and the CEC. Under both sets of rules, the defendant must use a character witness who testifies in the form of reputation or opinion. The character witness describes a trait of defendant's character that is pertinent to the crime charged. On direct examination, a good character witness offered by a defendant may not describe specific instances of the defendant's conduct.[10] A foundation must be laid for a person to qualify as a character witness. In this case, Ursula testifies as an opinion witness, so it is necessary to establish, by way of foundation, that Ursula knows Nancy well enough to have an opinion of her character. Ursula has known Nancy all her life, so this is adequate for the foundation. With the foundation laid, Ursula offers her opinion of Nancy's character. The testimony appears proper, although one could argue that the words, "She

---

[10]   Check with your professor on this point. Some professors may be of the opinion that under the CEC, Proposition 8 would allow a character witness to describe specific instances on direct exam, despite the fact that CEC § 1102 limits evidence to a character witness who testifies in the form of reputation or opinion.

would not deliberately hurt someone" might stray over the line into specific instances. The judge will probably allow Ursula's testimony.

§ 6.12 Defendant Attacks Victim's Character

The FRE and CEC allow the defendant in a criminal case to attack the victim's character. At first glance, this seems like open season on victims, but first glances are often wrong, and so it is here. It turns out that the only time a defendant can attack a victim's character is when the defendant claims self-defense, and the defendant asserts that the victim was the first aggressor.[11] The rules provide:

> **FRE 404(a)(2)(B). Exceptions for a Defendant in a Criminal Case.** The following exceptions [to the rule against character evidence] apply in a criminal case: (B) subject to the limitations of Rule 412 [the rape shield statute], a defendant may offer evidence of an alleged victim's pertinent trait [of character], and if the evidence is admitted, the prosecutor may (i) offer evidence to rebut it [about the victim]; and (ii) offer evidence of the defendant's same trait . . . ."

> **CEC § 1103. Character of Crime Victim to Prove Conduct; Evidence of Defendant's Character or Trait for Violence; Evidence of Manner of Dress of Victim; Evidence of Complaining Witness' Sexual Conduct.** (a) In a criminal action, evidence of the character or a trait of character (in the form of an opinion, evidence of reputation, or evidence of specific instances of conduct) of the victim of the crime for which the defendant is being prosecuted is not made inadmissible by section 1101 [the rule against character evidence] if the evidence is: (1) Offered by the defendant to prove conduct of the victim in conformity with the character or trait of character. (2) Offered by the prosecution to rebut evidence adduced by the defendant under paragraph (1).

> (b) In a criminal action, evidence of the defendant's character for violence or trait of character for violence (in the form of an opinion, evidence of reputation, or evidence of specific instances of conduct) is not made inadmissible by Section 1101 if the evidence is offered by the

---

[11] The affirmative defense of self-defense has the following elements: (1) Defendant believed that she was under attack or that an attack was imminent, (2) Defendant's belief in the need for self-defense was reasonable, and (3) Defendant was not the first aggressor, that it, defendant didn't start the fight.

prosecution to prove conduct of the defendant in conformity with the character or trait of character and is offered after evidence that the victim had a character for violence or a trait of character tending to show violence has been adduced by the defendant under paragraph (1) of subdivision (a).

(c)(1) Notwithstanding any other provision of this code to the contrary, and except as provided in this subdivision, in any prosecution under [Penal Code sections defining rape, child molestation, and other sex offense], opinion evidence, reputation evidence, and evidence of specific instances of the complaining witness' sexual conduct, or any of that evidence, is not admissible by the defendant in order to prove consent by the complaining witness.[12]

§ 6.12(a).   Similarities Between FRE 404(a)(2)(B) and CEC § 1103

The FRE and CEC allow the defendant in a criminal case who claims self-defense to offer evidence of the victim's violent character to prove that the victim was the first aggressor. The only character trait that is pertinent is violence or its opposite, peacefulness. Evidence of the victim's violent character is offered as substance evidence that because the victim is violent, the victim acted in conformity with his violent character, and was the first aggressor. The prosecutor cannot initiate evidence of the victim's character. The defendant decides whether to make an issue of the victim's character. If the defendant attacks the victim with character evidence that the victim is violent, the prosecutor may respond with character evidence the victim is peaceful.

FRE 405(a) and CEC 1103(a) allow a defendant to use character witnesses to attack the victim's character. A character witness testifies in the form of reputation or opinion. In response, the prosecutor may offer rebuttal character witnesses who testify that the victim was a peaceful person. The rebuttal character witnesses also testifies in the form of reputation or opinion.

When the defendant attacks the *victim's* character as a violent person, the prosecutor may respond with character evidence not only about the victim, but also about the *defendant*. By attacking the victim, the defendant opens the door to evidence of defendant's character for violence.

---

[12]   CEC § 1103(c)(2) limits admissibility of evidence of the way a sex offense victim was dressed at the time of the offense.

When a defendant attacks a victim's character, the prosecutor may respond about the victim's peacefulness *and* the defendant's violence! A defendant with a history of violence needs to think carefully before attacking the victim's character.

§ 6.12(b).   A Discredited Theory of Proof in Sex Offense Prosecutions

In the past, defendants charged with rape often attacked the victim's character for chastity, or, rather, unchastity. The theory was that an unchaste woman is more likely to consent to sex than a chaste woman. If such evidence were admissible today, it would fall under FRE 404(a)(2)(B) and CEC § 1103. However, because the theory of relevance underlying such an attack has been discredited, the rules do not allow the attack. The FRE and CEC contain rape shield laws that bar most evidence that a victim consented to sex with persons other than the defendant. The FRE rape shield statute is Rule 412, and FRE 404(a)(2)(B) specifically mentions Rule 412 to ensure that defendants charged with rape cannot use Rule 404(a)(2)(B) to offer evidence of the victim's unchastity. CEC § 1103(c)(1) achieves the same result. The rape shield statute is discussed in § 10.15.

§ 6.12(c).   Difference Between FRE 404(a)(2)(B) and CEC § 1103

The FRE and the CEC are the same insofar as they allow criminal defendants claiming self-defense to offer character evidence about the victim's violent character, in an effort to prove the victim was the first aggressor. The FRE and CEC differ not in theory, but in execution. Under the FRE, the defendant is limited to character witnesses who testify in the form of reputation or opinion. The CEC allows character witnesses. However, in addition to character witnesses, the CEC allows a defendant to offer evidence of specific instances of the victim's conduct to prove the victim's character for violence (CEC § 1103(a)). Thus, under the CEC, to prove that a victim was a violent person, the defendant may offer lay witnesses to describe the victim's prior acts of violence. The FRE is limited to character witnesses, and does not allow evidence of specific instances to prove the victim's violent character.

Under the FRE, when a defendant attacks a victim's character, the prosecutor may respond about the victim *and* the defendant. The same is true under the CEC. The difference lies again in execution, specifically, in the use of specific instances. The FRE forbids specific instances, while the CEC permits specific instances. Thus, under the CEC, when a defendant attacks a victim's character, the prosecutor can fire back with specific instances of the victim's peacefulness *and* specific instances of the defendant's violence.

§ 6.12(d).   Test Yourself with Two Multiple Choice Questions About the Victim's Character

To lock down your understanding of character evidence to attack a victim's character, try your hand at the following multiple choice questions. See the answers in § 6.17.

1.   Brenda is charged in California Superior Court with assault with a deadly weapon during a fight with Claudia. Brenda admits she hit Claudia with a stick, but Brenda asserts she acted in self-defense after Claudia attacked her. During the defense case-in-chief, Brenda offers testimony from Bill, that Bill witnessed Claudia start fights on three occasions. The prosecutor objects to Bill's testimony. How should the judge rule?

A.   Sustain the objection because evidence of a person's character is not admissible to prove that the person acted in conformity with their character on a specific occasion.

B.   Overrule the objection because character is in issue when the defendant claims self-defense.

C.   Sustain the objection because the probative value of the specific instances is substantially outweighed by the danger of unfair prejudice.

D.   Overrule the objection because the evidence is admissible.

2.   Dell is on trial in Federal District Court, charged with murder. Dell admits he shot and killed Vic, but Dell claims he acted in self-defense. Dell had never met Vic prior to their fatal encounter, and Dell knew nothing about Vic. During Dell's case-in-chief, Dell offers testimony from Zeek, who will testify that he knew Dell since they were kids. Over the years, Zeek watched Dell attack many people for no reason. The Assistant United States Attorney objects to Zeek's testimony. How should the judge rule?

A.   Overrule the objection and admit Zeek's testimony because Dell is claiming self-defense, and has opened the door to evidence of the victim's character.

B.   Sustain the objection and prohibit Zeek from testifying because the rules of evidence do not permit attacks on the victim's character unless the prosecutor first introduces evidence that the victim is a peaceful person.

C.   Sustain the objection and prohibit Zeek from testifying because Zeek is not qualified to testify to the victim's character.

D.   Sustain the objection and prohibit Zeek from testifying because Zeek is describing specific instances of Dell's conduct.

§ 6.12(e).   A Source of Confusion Explained (Hopefully)

Law professors and bar examiners love to torture students with the following scenario: Dell is charged with murder. Dell admits he shot Vic, but Dell claims self-defense. Defense counsel offers a witness, Thelma, to testify as follows, "I knew Vic since high school. In high school, Vic started fights with other kids." The question for you is, is Thelma's testimony admissible? The answer depends on two things. First, what is Thelma's testimony offered to prove? Second, did Dell know of Vic's violence before the fatal encounter between Vic and Dell?

Put on your character evidence hat. You know that under the FRE and CEC, Dell can attack Vic's character for violence. Under FRE 404(a)(2)(B), Thelma's testimony is objectionable because she mentions specific instances of Vic's conduct. Under CEC § 1103(a), Thelma's testimony is ok because Section 1103(a) allows specific instances. So far so good.

Now, take off your character evidence hat, and put on your relevance hat (FRE 401 & 402; CEC §§ 210 & 350). Don't think about character. Just think about when evidence is relevant. According to Thelma, Vic picked fights with kids at school. Suppose Dell was also a student at the school, and witnessed Vic picking the fights described by Thelma. Is Dell's knowledge of Vic's earlier violence relevant to the claim of self-defense? Yes. Dell's knowledge sheds light on whether Dell honestly and reasonably believed he needed to defend himself from Vic. The honesty and reasonableness of a defendant's belief in the need for self-defense are elements of the defense. If Dell's trial occurs under the FRE, Thelma's testimony is admissible because it is relevant to Dell's knowledge, and his knowledge is relevant to self-defense. Offered to prove Dell's knowledge, Thelma's testimony has nothing to do with Vic's character—it is not character evidence. Because Thelma's testimony is not character evidence, her testimony is not governed by Rule 405 because Rule 405 applies only to character evidence. Since Thelma's testimony is not character evidence governed by Rule 405(a), that rule's prohibition on evidence of specific instances doesn't apply to Thelma's testimony. Because Rule 405(a) does not apply, Thelma can describe specific instances of Vic' violence that are relevant to Dell's claim of self-defense. The result is the same under the CEC.

Change the facts. On the night of the fatal encounter between Dell and Vic, the two were complete strangers. They had never met, and Dell knew nothing about Vic or his violence. In this scenario, Thelma's testimony describing Vic's high school fights sheds no light on Dell's knowledge, since he had no knowledge of Vic. Thelma's testimony is *irrelevant* regarding Dell's knowledge, and irrelevant evidence is not admissible.

Now, put your character evidence hat back on. You know that a defendant in a criminal case who claims self-defense can attack the victim's character. Because the evidence is character evidence, Rule 405(a) applies,[13] and limits the evidence to character witnesses who testify in the form of reputation or opinion. On direct examination, a character witness may not describe specific instances of the victim's conduct. Offered to prove Vic's character, Thelma's testimony describing specific instances of Vic's violence is inadmissible under the FRE. Things are different under the CEC because Section 1103(a) allows specific instances.

Whew, that's confusing! No wonder professors torture students with this scenario. Try your hand at the following question:

GUNFIGHT AT THE OK CORRAL

Dell is charged with the murder of Vic. Dell admits he shot Vic, but Dell claims he acted in self-defense. Dell drove to a convenience store called the OK Corral, and parked in front of the store. Vic and his friend, Elenore, were standing in the parking lot. Dell had never met Vic, and knew nothing about him. Dell went into the store, made his purchases, and was walking back to his car. Elenore testifies for the prosecution, as follows, "As Dell approached his car, Dell looked at Vic and said, 'Where are you from?' which gang members sometimes say to people they suspect might be a member of a rival gang. Vic replied, 'I don't bang.' Dell then drew a pistol from his waistband and fired twice at Vic, killing him. Vic had no weapon." In the defense case-in-chief, Dell testifies in his own behalf, as follows, "I was walking back to my car, minding my own business, when Vic said to me, 'Hey man, you Surenos?' I ignored him. I was getting into my car when I looked at Vic, and he was pulling a gun on me, so I pulled my gun and shot him before he could shoot me." After Dell's testimony, Dell's attorney offers testimony from Rafa, who will testify that he had been friends with

---

[13]   Character is not in issue when a defendant claims self-defense, so Rule 405(b) does not apply.

Vic for five years, and that Vic often started fights, including gun fights, with other people. The prosecutor objects to Rafa's testimony. How should the judge rule under the FRE and under the CEC?

See the analysis in § 6.17.

§ 6.13 Special Rule for Homicide Cases: FRE Only

Normally, the prosecutor cannot be the first to offer character evidence as substantive evidence. If the defendant offers evidence of defendant's good character, the prosecutor can offer rebuttal character evidence about the defendant's bad character (FRE 404(a)(2)(A), CEC § 1102), but the prosecutor can't *start* the character evidence ball rolling. Similarly, if the defendant offers character evidence of the victim's violence, the prosecutor can rebut about the victim *and* the defendant (FRE 404(a)(2)(B); CEC § 1103(a) and (b)), but the prosecutor can only do so in response to the defendant's decision to attack the victim's character.

Under the FRE, there is one scenario in which a prosecutor is allowed to be the first to offer character evidence as substantive evidence. In homicide prosecutions, the FRE allows a prosecutor to offer character witnesses to testify that the victim was a peaceful person *after* the defendant offers evidence—but not character evidence—that the victim was the first aggressor (FRE 404(a)(2)(C)). The CEC does not have a counterpart to FRE 404(a)(2)(C).

FRE 404(a)(2)(C) provides:

> The following exceptions [to the rule against character evidence] apply in a criminal case: (C) in a homicide case, the prosecutor may offer evidence of the alleged victim's trait of peacefulness to rebut evidence that the victim was the first aggressor.

FRE 404(a)(2)(C) is narrow. Rule 404(a)(2)(C) applies only in homicide cases. If the defendant attacks the victim's character with character witnesses, as the defendant can do under Rule 404(a)(2)(B), then the prosecutor doesn't need Rule 404(a)(2)(C), because Rule 404(a)(2)(B) allows the prosecutor to offer rebuttal character witnesses about the victim's peacefulness.

Rule 404(a)(2)(C) applies only when a defendant offers evidence—*but not character evidence*—that the victim was the first aggressor. When the defendant does so, the prosecutor can be the first to offer a character witness. The character witness testifies that the victim was a peaceful person.

Here are facts that trigger Rule 404(a)(2)(C): Defendant is on trial for murder. Defendant claims self-defense. During the prosecution's case-in-chief, the prosecutor offers the following testimony from Nan Hui: "I was sitting in the bar when the fight started. I heard yelling behind me, and turned around to see what was going down. I could see the defendant and the victim tussling with each other. The defendant pulled a knife and stabbed the victim." On cross-examination of Nan Hui by defense counsel, the following occurs:

Q: When you saw the fight, you were sitting about 25 feet away, right?

A: Correct.

Q: The lights in the bar were low, weren't they?

A: The lights were low, but I could see ok.

Q: You testified you saw defendant pull a knife, right?

A: Right.

Q: Given the distance and the low lighting, isn't it possible that the victim might have had something in his hand too?

A: As best as I can recall, you are right. The victim did have something in his hand. I think it was a glass.

Q: From that distance, it would have been hard to tell what the victim had in his hand, wouldn't it?

A: Yes.

Q: From that distance, the thing you saw in the victim's hand could have been a knife, couldn't it?

A: It could have been a knife, I guess.

Q: So, just to be clear, the victim may have been holding a knife in his hand, right?

A: Yes. It could have been a knife.

Q: And it is possible, too, that the victim was the first one to draw a weapon.

A: Well, I didn't see who drew first, but it is possible the victim was first with a weapon.

Answers to questions on cross-examination constitute "evidence." In this case, the prosecutor might argue that defense counsel's questions elicited evidence that the victim was the first aggressor. If the judge agrees, then the prosecutor might elect to use Rule 404(a)(2)(C) to offer a character witness to testify that the victim was a peaceful person.

Another scenario that triggers Rule 404(a)(2)(C) occurs when a defendant charged with homicide testifies, and describes how the victim attacked the defendant with deadly force. The defendant's testimony is evidence the victim was the first aggressor, and the prosecutor may utilize Rule 404(a)(2)(C) to offer evidence of the victim's peaceful disposition. The prosecutor's Rule 404(a)(2)(C) character evidence would be offered during the prosecutor's case-in-rebuttal.

In both of the forgoing scenarios, the prosecutor was the first to offer a character witness. In both scenarios, the defendant offered evidence—but not character evidence—that the victim was the first aggressor.

California does not have a counterpart to FRE 404(a)(2)(C). What would a California prosecutor do in the two scenarios? There are many avenues open to the prosecutor, but not the one made available by FRE 404(a)(2)(C).

§ 6.14   Character Evidence to Impeach Credibility

Impeachment is discussed in Chapter 10. Suffice it to say, here, that several theories of impeachment utilize character evidence. FRE 404(a)(3) and CEC § 1101(c) authorize evidence of untruthful character to impeach witness credibility.

§ 6.15   Selective Abolition of Rule Against Character Evidence

FRE 413, 414, and 415 abolish the rule against character evidence in sex offense cases. Thus, in a child molest trial, the prosecutor could offer evidence that the defendant molested other children to prove that defendant is a child molester, and, because he is a child molester, he probably molested the child in this case. This is evidence of defendant's character offered as substantive evidence that defendant acted in conformity with his character on a particular occasion, but it is allowed by FRE 413–415.

The CEC abolished the rule against character evidence in sex offense cases (CEC § 1108), and in domestic violence (CEC § 1107) and elder and child abuse cases (CEC § 1109).

When character evidence is offered against a defendant under these rules, defense counsel often objects that the evidence is unfairly prejudicial to the defendant (FRE 403; CEC § 352). Upon objection, the trial court balances the probative value of the character evidence against the danger of unfair prejudice to the defendant. Of course, the defendant can't argue that the jury will misuse the evidence as proof that the defendant has a character flaw because that is precisely what the rules permit!

§ 6.16 Answers to Chapter Problems

1. Is This a Smart Move on John's Part?

John is accused of robbing the First Bank of Redding on August 1. John has the right to offer evidence of his good character as substantive evidence of innocence (FRE 404(a)(2)(A); CEC § 1102). John could offer character witnesses to testify in the form of opinion or reputation about John's character as a nonviolent, honest man. But should John offer such evidence? I'd say no. If John offers character witnesses, the prosecutor will be able to rebut with character witnesses who testify that John's character for these traits is bad. More importantly, if John offers good character witnesses, his witnesses can be impeached. If John offers a reputation witness, the prosecutor can ask the witness, "Have you heard that John robbed ten other banks?" Yikes! What will members of the jury think when they hear that? If John offers an opinion character witness, the prosecutor will ask, "Did you know that John robbed ten other banks?" Ouch! By offering evidence of his good character, John invited the prosecutor to ask these damaging questions. So, should John offer evidence of his good character? NO!

2. Are Specific Instances Allowed?

June is charged with a violent offense, and she can offer evidence of good character—non-violence—as substantive evidence of innocence (FRE 404(a)(2)(A); CEC § 1102). What form must the evidence take? Under the FRE, the answer is clear. Rule 405(a) provides that evidence of June's character must come from a character witness who testifies in the form of reputation or opinion. On direct examination, June's character witness may not describe specific instances of June's peaceful, non-violent conduct. June's character witness started off ok by stating that, in the character witness's opinion, June is a peaceful, non-violent person. However, the character witness ran afoul of Rule 405(a) when the character witness described specific instances of June's conduct.

Section 1102 of the CEC specifies that a good character witness must testify in the form of opinion or reputation, not specific instances. However, Proposition 8 states that all relevant evidence is admissible. Specific instances of good character can be relevant. Does Prop. 8 overrule Section 1102's exclusion of specific instances to prove defendant's good character? Can June's character witness describe specific instances of June's non-violent conduct on direct examination? The answer is unclear. There does not appear to be a California case on point. The best advice on an exam is to apply Section 1102 as it is written, and to mention that Prop. 8 may influence the outcome.

§ 6.17   Answers to Questions in §§ 6.12(d) and 6.12(e)

Test yourself with two multiple choice questions—§ 6.12(d)

1.   The fact that the trial is in California Superior Court means you use the CEC. The correct answer is D.; overrule the objection because the question is proper. CEC § 1103(a) allows a criminal defendant who claims self-defense to offer specific instances of the victim's violence to prove the victim is violent and was the first aggressor. It is character evidence, but it is permitted.

A.   Is wrong. Answer A states the general rule against character evidence, but the question invokes an exception to the general rule. B. is wrong because character is not in issue when a defendant claims self-defense. C. is wrong. There is nothing unfairly prejudicial about the evidence.

2.   Trial is in U.S. District Court, which means the FRE govern. Rule 404(a)(2)(B) allows a defendant claiming self-defense to attack the victim's character with character witnesses who testify to victim's reputation for violence, or who offer an opinion on the victim's violence.

A.   Is wrong because Dell can't use specific instances of Vic's violence. B. is wrong because the rules of evidence do allow the defendant to attack the victim's character. The prosecutor cannot be the first to offer evidence of the victim's character. It must be the defendant that starts the character evidence ball rolling. C. is wrong because Zeek has known Vic long enough to qualify as a character witness. D. is correct because Zeek is testifying to specific instances, and that is not allowed under the FRE.

If this trial occurred in California Superior Court, the defendant could offer specific instances of the victim's character for violence.

Gunfight at the OK Corral—§ 6.12(e)

Under the FRE, Rafa's testimony is not admissible because it is specific instances of violence to attack the victim's character, and Rule 405(a) states that only reputation or opinion may be used to prove the victim was the first aggressor. Under the CEC, by contrast, Rafa's testimony is admissible because Section 1103(a) allows the attack on the victim's character to be by reputation, opinion, or specific instances of the victim's character.

Chapter 7

HABIT

Evidence of character is *inadmissible* to prove a person's conduct in conformity with the person's character. By contrast, evidence of a person's habit is *admissible* to prove conduct in conformity with the person's habit. What this means, of course, is that you have to be able to distinguish habit from character. Sometimes it's easy, sometimes it isn't. The rules state:

> **Rule 406. Habit; Routine Practice**. Evidence of a person's habit or an organization's routine practice may be admitted to prove that on a particular occasion the person or organization acted in accordance with the habit or routine practice. The court may admit this evidence regardless of whether it is corroborated or whether there was an eyewitness.

> **CEC § 1105. Habit or Custom to Prove Specific Behavior**. Any otherwise admissible evidence of habit or custom is admissible to prove conduct on a specified occasion in conformity with the habit or custom.

§ 7.1 Habit

Character is a broad description of a person's approach to life. Thus, a person has a character as honest or deceitful, peaceful or violent. Habit is much more specific. Thus, a person has a habit of always (or nearly always) stopping at the same Starbucks on the way to work, running up the stairs two steps at a time, leaving the car keys in the bowl next to door, always turning on an electric fan to fall asleep. What are your habits? Constantly studying evidence, right?

Are the following scenarios evidence of habit or character? See the analysis in § 7.4.

1.   Dell is charged with rape and murder of Vic. Vic's body was found naked. The prosecutor seeks to prove that Dell forced Vic to remove her pajamas. Thus, the prosecutor needs to prove Vic was wearing pajamas. Vic's father testifies that he stayed with Vic for six months during the winter, and observed Vic wearing flannel PJs on a regular basis. Is the father's testimony admissible? Does Vic's wearing of PJs speak to habit or character?

2.   Dell is charged with driving under the influence of alcohol, having been convicted of DUI in the past. The prosecutor needs to prove Dell's previous DUI. Unfortunately, Dell's previous DUI occurred more than ten years ago, and court records that are more than ten years old are routinely destroyed. Dell admits he plead guilty to DUI eleven years ago, but Dell argues he was not informed by the judge that he had a right to counsel, thus the old conviction is unconstitutional. To prove that Dell *was* informed of the right to counsel, the prosecutor offers testimony from the retired judge who took Dell's plea. The judge can't remember Dell or Dell's case, but the judge testifies that before taking pleas, he always informed defendants of their right to counsel. Is the judge's testimony admissible to prove that Dell was informed?

3.   Pauline was killed when her car was broadsided by a train at a rural grade crossing. There are no warning lights or barricades at the remote crossing. Pauline's survivors sue the railroad on the theory that the engineer failed to sound the horn as the train approached the crossing. The railroad asserts that the horn was sounded, and that Pauline was negligent for entering the grade when she did. The survivors' attorney offers testimony from Pauline's adult daughter that the daughter rode in the car with Pauline hundreds of times at that crossing, and Pauline always slowed down and looked both ways before crossing the tracks. The survivors' attorney offers the testimony as evidence of habit. The railroad's attorney objects that the testimony amounts to inadmissible character evidence. Who is right?

The engineer of the train can't remember whether she blew the train whistle at the grade crossing where the accident happened. Should the engineer be permitted to testify that she always sounds the whistle as the train approaches crossings?

§ 7.2   Corroboration and Eyewitness Rules

Rule 406 provides that habit is admissible "regardless of whether it is corroborated or whether there was an eyewitness." In the past, some courts were suspicious of habit evidence, and admitted such evidence only if it was corroborated by other, non-habit, evidence. As well, some courts held that if there was an eyewitness to an event, as well as habit evidence to prove the event, the eyewitness had to testify. The FRE abolish both "rules." Habit need not be corroborated, and habit evidence is admissible whether or not an eyewitness testifies. California law is the same.

§ 7.3   Routine Practice of Organization

People have habits, organizations (businesses, agencies) have routine practices. The routine practice of an organization is admissible to prove the organization followed the practice on a particular occasion.

§ 7.4   Analysis of Questions on Habit

1.   Is wearing PJs a habit? In *People v. Tully*, 54 Cal. 4th 952, 1017, 282 P.3d 173, 145 Cal. Rptr. 3d 146 (2012), the Supreme Court ruled the testimony of Vic's father was admissible to prove Vic's habit of wearing PJs, which made it more likely she was wearing PJs when defendant attacked her.

2.   The judge's testimony should be admissible to prove the judge had a habit of advising defendants. The judge's habit is admissible to prove that the court advised Dell.

3.   Was Pauline's behavior of slowing and looking both ways evidence of habit or character? This is a tough one. On one hand, the testimony portrays Pauline as a careful person, and that's character evidence. CEC § 1104 specifies that "evidence of a trait of a person's character with respect to care or skill is inadmissible to prove the quality of his conduct on a specified occasion." On the other hand, Pauline's repetitive conduct is very specific and regular. It looks like a habit. The judge has discretion, but may put this one in the habit category. The train engineer's habit of blowing the whistle should be admitted.

Chapter 8

UNCHARGED MISCONDUCT EVIDENCE

This chapter discusses theories of proof that fall under the rubric "uncharged misconduct evidence," or UME. The subject is large and complex. The FRE and the CEC rules on UME are essentially identical.

§ 8.1   Introduction and Rules

In criminal trials, the prosecutor must prove *actus reus, mens rea*, and identity. The defendant has the burden of going forward with evidence of affirmative defenses, and, depending on the defense, has the burden of proving the defense. In civil litigation, the plaintiff has the burden of proof on the elements of a cause of action. The defendant typically has the burden of proof on defenses.[1] The UME theories discussed in this chapter are used in criminal and civil litigation to prove the elements of crimes, causes of action, identity, and defenses.

The FRE and CEC rules on UME follow:

FRE 404(b). Crimes, Wrongs, or Other Acts. (1) Prohibited Uses. Evidence of a crime, wrong, or other act is not admissible to prove a person's character in order to show that on a particular occasion the person acted in accordance with the character.[2] **(2) Permitted Uses**. This evidence [*i.e.*, evidence of crimes, wrongs, or other acts] may be admissible for another purpose [*i.e.*, other than character evidence], such as proving motive, opportunity, intent, preparation, plan, knowledge, identity, absence of mistake, or lack of accident.[3]

---

[1]   In some civil litigation, the party with the burden of proof on an issue may be able to shift the burden of proof to the opposing party via a presumption. See Chapter 13, on presumptions.

[2]   FRE 404(b)(1) does not deal with UME. Rather, 404(b)(1) restates the rule against character evidence contained in FRE 404(a)(1). It is FRE 404(b)(2) that addresses UME.

[3]   FRE 404(b)(2) provides: "On request by a defendant in a criminal case, the prosecutor must: (A) provide reasonable notice of the general nature of any such evidence that the prosecutor intends to offer at trial; and (B) do so before trial—or during trial if the court, for good cause, excuses lack of pretrial notice." The CEC rule on uncharged misconduct evidence (CEC § 1101(b)) does not contain a similar notice requirement.

CEC § 1101(b). [Uncharged Misconduct Evidence].
Nothing in [the rule against character evidence] prohibits the admission of evidence that a person committed a crime, civil wrong, or other act when relevant to prove some fact (such as motive, opportunity, intent, preparation, plan, knowledge, identity, absence of mistake or accident . . .).

§ 8.2   UME Is *Not* Character Evidence

Before you dive into the deep end of UME, it is important to understand that UME is *not* character evidence. UME is *not* offered to prove that a person has a character trait, and acted in conformity with that trait of character. It can be difficult to distinguish UME from character evidence because, in many cases, the very evidence that is offered as UME could also be offered to prove character. The evidence will be admissible as UME, but inadmissible if offered to prove character.[4]

The best way to understand the difference between admissible UME and inadmissible character evidence is with an example. You remember John, who is accused of robbing the First Bank of Redding on August 1. (§ 2.6). John does not deny the bank was robbed. John says, "I didn't rob it. You charged the wrong guy." Thus, the issue is identity. Recall that the prosecutor has evidence John robbed ten other banks. John is not charged with those robberies. He is charged only with robbing the First Bank of Redding. The prosecutor may not offer evidence of John's ten uncharged bank robberies to prove that John has a character trait for robbery, and, therefore, probably robbed the First Bank of Redding. Such use of the uncharged robberies violates the rule against character evidence (FRE 404(a)(1); CEC § 1101(a)). Suppose, however, that in his ten uncharged robberies, John employed a unique *modus operandi*. John wore a black mask like the action hero Zorro, escaped in a red Ferrari, brandished identical pearl handled pistols, and handed the bank teller a pink taffeta pillow case in which to put the money. Lo and behold, whoever robbed the First Bank of Redding wore a black mask like the action hero Zorro, escaped in a red Ferrari, brandished identical pearl handled pistols, and handed the bank teller a pink taffeta pillow case in which to put the money! Is this just a coincidence? Could be, but not likely. The odds are tremendous that one and the same person robbed *all eleven* banks, namely, John. When evidence of John's ten uncharged robberies is offered to prove identity, it is not

---

4   FRE 105 takes care of admissibility issues by providing that evidence that is admissible for one purpose (UME), but inadmissible for another purpose (character), is admissible. CEC § 355 is to the same effect.

offered to prove John's character, and is admissible UME. John's case is one of the thousands in which a person's conduct is admissible when offered as UME, but would be inadmissible if offered to prove character.

§ 8.3   UME Is Proven with Specific Instances, Not Character Witnesses

When character evidence is admissible under the FRE, the proponent must use character witnesses who testify in the form of opinion or reputation. The character witness cannot mention specific instances of conduct of the person they are describing (FRE 405(a)). The same is true in California, except when the defendant attacks the victim's character in a self-defense scenario (CEC §§ 1102 & 1103. *See* § 6.12). *UME is not character evidence.* Therefore, the testimonial restrictions on character witnesses have no application to UME. UME is proven with relevant, admissible evidence, including eyewitness testimony of specific instances of conduct.[5]

§ 8.4   Proof of UME

Before UME is admitted, the offering party, usually a prosecutor, must establish that the uncharged act occurred. Additionally, under most theories of UME, the prosecutor must establish that the defendant committed the uncharged act. Courts vary regarding the degree of proof imposed on the prosecutor. A few courts insist on clear and convincing evidence. A rare decision appears to require proof beyond a reasonable doubt. Most courts require the uncharged acts to be established by a preponderance of the evidence. In *Huddleston v. United States*, 485 U.S. 681, 108 S. Ct. 1496 (1988), the U.S. Supreme Court opted for a standard less demanding than a preponderance. In federal court, admissibility of uncharged misconduct is governed by Rule 104(b), which merely requires the judge to determine that a reasonable juror could find the uncharged act occurred. In California Superior Court, UME must be established by a preponderance of the evidence.

§ 8.5   Exclusion of UME for Reasons of Unfair Prejudice

UME may be excluded if its probative value is substantially outweighed by the danger of unfair prejudice (FRE 403; CEC § 352). There is no doubt that UME can prejudice criminal defendants. The California Supreme Court observed in *People v. Smallwood*, 42 Cal.

---

[5]   UME must be proven with admissible evidence. For example, you cannot prove UME with inadmissible hearsay.

3d 415, 429, 722 P.2d 197, 228 Cal. Rptr. 913 (1986) that uncharged misconduct is "the most prejudicial evidence imaginable against an accused."

The stronger the probative value of UME, the greater the likelihood the probative value is not substantially outweighed by unfair prejudice. When UME is offered on an important issue, the proponent's need for the evidence is often high. When an issue is hotly contested, the need for evidence is greater than when an issue is nominally disputed or conceded. When an issue is not disputed, courts sometimes exclude UME directed to the issue.

When evaluating the potential for unfair prejudice, judges are particularly sensitive to how similar the UME is to the charged crime. If the UME and the charged offense are identical, there is a high probability the jury will have difficulty confining its consideration of the UME to permissible purposes. Jurors may be unable to resist the temptation to use the UME for the improper purpose of proving character. On request, jurors are instructed to limit use of UME to permissible purposes, but obeying the instruction can be difficult, especially when the UME and the charged offense are identical.

§ 8.6   The Rubric "Uncharged Misconduct Evidence" Is Not Ideal

The methods of proof that fall under the rubric UME go by other names: "prior bad acts evidence" and "extrinsic acts evidence." None of the rubrics is very good. UME is imperfect because conduct that qualifies as UME does not have to be misconduct. The conduct can be entirely legal. For example, one UME theory is plan. Purchasing an airline ticket may be part of a criminal plan, but booking a ticket is hardly misconduct. As well, uncharged misconduct does not have to be uncharged. The word "uncharged" means uncharged in *this* case. To go back to John, the accused bank robber, if John had been charged in a different proceeding with all or any of the ten other robberies, they would nevertheless be uncharged in the case involving the First Bank of Redding. If you can think of a better rubric to describe UME, let me know, and we will name it in your honor.

§ 8.7   Plan

If someone has a plan to do something, the plan increases the odds the person followed the plan. We don't always follow our plans, but the existence of a plan is relevant evidence of conduct. UME establishing plan is admissible to prove identity, *mens rea*, and *actus reus*. When identity is disputed, the fact that defendant had a plan to commit the crime increases the odds defendant was the culprit. As for *mens rea*, a plan to commit a crime is powerful evidence of intent. Finally, evidence of plan is admissible to establish the criminal act. Anonymous acts are not admissible to prove plan. The plan must be tied to the planner.

There are two theories of plan evidence: one narrow, the other broad. Most states, including California, adhere to both theories of plan.

Under the narrow theory of plan, a plan exists only when a person's plan incorporates the uncharged acts *and* the charged act into one continuous undertaking. The uncharged acts and the charged crime are stages of a single plan. Under the narrow theory of plan, the uncharged acts and the charged crime do not have to be similar. For example, the charged offense might be robbing a jewelry store. The uncharged acts that make up the plan might include stealing a getaway car, making a reservation at a hotel near the jewelry store, watching the store from across the street to determine when the store is crowded, and stealing guns.

When the uncharged acts and the charged crime *are* similar, it is important to remember that the narrow theory of plan does not apply unless the uncharged and charged acts are part of a single, unified plan. The narrow theory does not apply to a series of similar but unrelated acts. Moreover, the fact that unrelated acts were carefully planned does not invoke the plan theory. The narrow theory of plan applies *only* when the uncharged acts and the charged crime are stages of the same plan.[6]

Under the broad theory of plan, the uncharged acts and the charged crime do not have to be connected, that is, they do not have to be part of a single plan. The broad theory applies to a series of unrelated, similar acts. In *People v. Ewoldt*, 7 Cal. 4th 380, 402, 867 P.2d 757, 27 Cal. Rptr. 2d 646 (1994), the Supreme Court explained, "In establishing a common design or plan, evidence of uncharged misconduct must demonstrate not merely a similarity in the results, but such a concurrence of common features that the various acts are naturally to be explained as caused by a general plan of which they are the individual manifestations."

Do You See a Plan? Dell was employed as a psychotherapist at a hospital. Dell is charged with having sexual relations with a fifteen-year-old minor he was seeing in counseling. Dell denies

---

[6]   At one time, the California Supreme Court adhered to the narrow approach to plan. *See* People v. Tassell, 36 Cal. 3d 77, 679 P.2d 1, 201 Cal. Rptr. 567 (1984). The Supreme Court overruled *Tassell* in People v. Ewoldt, 7 Cal. 4th 380, 867 P.2d 757, 27 Cal. Rptr. 2d 646 (1994), and adopted, or, as the Court put it, re-adopted the broad theory of plan.

anything inappropriate happened. The prosecutor's evidence shows that almost from the outset of counseling, Dell focused sessions on sexual matters. During sessions, Dell massaged the minor and gave her marijuana, ostensibly to help her relax. Dell sought to develop a trusting and uninhibited relationship with the minor. Finally, Dell convinced the minor to have sex with Dell in his office. Dell urged the minor not to tell anyone because, in his words, revelation would destroy their relationship. Following the initial molestation, intercourse occurred at other counseling sessions. Later, Dell took the minor on a weekend trip to another state, where frequent acts of intercourse occurred. Dell is charged only with acts of intercourse occurring at his office. The prosecution offers to prove Dell's massages, the marijuana, the out-of-town trip, and the constant talk of sex during sessions, to prove that Dell had a plan to gain the minor's confidence so he could molest her. But that's not all. Prior to counseling the minor, Dell counseled the minor's mother, and used similar tactics to have sex with her. Should the uncharged misconduct be admitted? Did Dell have a plan? Do these facts meet the requirements of the narrow and the broad theories of plan? If Dell's attorney objects that the probative value of the evidence is substantially outweighed by the danger of unfair prejudice to Dell, how should the judge rule on the objection?

The judge should overrule the objection. The uncharged misconduct evidence is admissible under the narrow and the broad theories of plan. Under the narrow theory, the evidence establishes that Dell formulated a step-by-step scheme to seduce the teenager, just as he had seduced her mother. The massages and the marijuana were steps in the plan. Each step was intended to weaken the minor's resistance so Dell could reach his goal of sexual intercourse. The uncharged intercourse occurring in another state further evidences Dell's plan of molestation. The fact that the out-of-state intercourse occurred after the charged offense does not undermine its relevance. Under the broad theory of plan, the uncharged acts are part of an overall scheme.

It should be remembered that in sex offense cases, the rule against character evidence has been abolished (FRE 413–415; CEC § 1108). All of Dell's uncharged misconduct would be admissible to prove he is a child molester, and, because he is a child molester, he probably molested the child in this case. The prosecutor would not need the plan theory of UME.

Plan on an Exam. The following is part of an exam question:

Ann, Beth, and Charlene devised a scheme to rob a bank. Ann's job was to be the getaway driver. Beth and Charlene entered the bank with guns and announced,

"This is a robbery." Ann, Beth, and Charlene were caught, and are on trial, charged with bank robbery. **Call of the Question**: Discuss the evidence issues in the following facts: During the prosecution's case-in-chief, the prosecutor offers testimony from Slim, who owns a used car lot. Slim testifies that a month before the bank robbery, he was working late at his used car lot, when he saw Ann steal a car from the lot and drive off.

Your answer should discuss the uncharged misconduct theory of plan. Stealing a car is often part of a plan to commit a robbery. This would satisfy the narrow theory of plan. Stealing the car is a link in the chain of events that led to the robbery. Your answer should explain why the car theft is relevant. It is relevant because it is part of the plan, and the plan tends to prove identity. You could also discuss the danger of unfair prejudice, but that danger seems pretty low, and the probative value of the theft, as evidence of plan, seems pretty high.

§ 8.8   Motive

A motive is a reason to do something. You have a motive to read this book to increase your understanding of evidence, to do well on the final exam, to pass the bar, and to become a famous trial lawyer, right? Motive is not an element of most crimes. Nevertheless, evidence of motive is relevant and admissible.[7] When identity is disputed, existence of a motive increases the likelihood defendant is the culprit. Likewise, when the occurrence of the act is disputed, the fact that defendant was motivated to commit the act increases the probability the act occurred. Finally, evidence of motive is admissible to prove defendant's intent. In a murder prosecution, for example, earlier episodes of intimate partner violence by the defendant against the murder victim may shed light on defendant's motive to kill the victim.

Two UME theories prove motive. Most courts, including California courts, approve both theories. First, an uncharged act may give rise to the motive for the charged act. Murder, for example, is sometimes committed to silence someone who "knows too much." In a homicide case, the prosecutor may establish motive to kill with evidence that the defendant knew the murder victim had witnessed the defendant commit uncharged crimes, and that the victim was about to inform police. The defendant's knowledge of what the victim knew, supplied a motive to kill.

---

[7]   *See* People v. Thompson, 1 Cal. 5th 1043, 384 P.3d 693, 210 Cal. Rptr. 3d 693 (2016).

The second UME theory to establish motive applies when the uncharged and charged acts are products of the same underlying motive. That is, a single motive produces the uncharged and the charged acts. To establish motive for the charged act, the prosecutor offers evidence of uncharged acts. Suppose, for example, that Dell is charged with burglary. The state has evidence that Dell committed five other burglaries. The prior burglaries are offered to prove that Dell had a motive to commit the charged burglary.

Which Theory of Motive? Which theory of motive applies to the following facts? Defendant is charged with incest. The victim is defendant's fifteen-year-old daughter. Defendant denies the abuse. The prosecutor offers testimony from the victim's adult sister that when the sister was a minor, defendant had sexual intercourse with her. The uncharged abuse of the sister took place years before the charged offense. The prosecutor argues that the prior abuse is evidence of defendant's motive to commit incest.

These facts fit the second theory of motive. The earlier offense was a product of defendant's motive to commit incest. Proof of motive on the prior occasion increases the likelihood that defendant was similarly motivated to commit the charged offense.

The second theory of motive looks a lot like character evidence, doesn't it? The prior incest proves little more than a propensity for deviant sexual conduct. Despite arguments that the second theory of motive is just bad character evidence, courts generally approve the theory.

If this case is tried in California, or under the FRE, it is unnecessary to go through the mental gymnastics of fitting the uncharged misconduct into a UME theory because, in sex offense cases, the rule against character evidence has been abolished. Offer the uncharged acts as character evidence. What should you do on an exam if you encounter a set of facts involving sexual assault and UME? This is a good question for your professor. I tell my students to apply the UME theories first, and then, state that the evidence rules have abolished the rule against character evidence in sex offense cases.

§ 8.9   Prove Intent on the Charged Occasion with Evidence of Intent on Uncharged Occasions

Several UME theories prove intent. Thus, a plan is evidence of intent, as is a motive. This section describes an additional use of UME to prove intent. The theory is pretty simple: To prove defendant's intent on the charged occasion, evidence is offered that defendant committed similar acts in the past. From evidence of those acts, the jury draws an inference of defendant's intent on the uncharged occasions. Finally, the jury concludes that because the uncharged and the charges acts are similar, the defendant probably entertained the same intent on the uncharged and the charged occasions. A shorthand for theory is: Intent on the uncharged occasion is offered to prove intent on the charged occasion.

This UME theory proves only intent, not *actus reus* or identity. Anonymous acts are not admissible.

Examples illustrate this method of proving intent. Dell is charged burglarizing a home at the end of Main Street. Dell was arrested in the home. At common law, burglary was the breaking and entering of the dwelling house of another at night, with the intent to commit a felony therein. Dell admits he broke into the house, but Dell claims he lacked the specific intent to commit a felony inside. Dell claims he broke in because the night was cold, he was far from home, and he had to get out of the cold or freeze to death. Thus, Dell claims he lacked the *mens reas* for the crime— intent to commit a felony therein. The prosecutor wants to introduce evidence that there are ten other homes on Main Street, and that, on the night in question, Dell broke into each of those homes to steal, before he entered the home he is charged with burglarizing.[8] Defense counsel makes a three part objection. First, evidence of Dell's burglaries of the other ten houses is irrelevant. Second, the evidence of the other burglaries is character evidence that violates the rule against character evidence. Third, even if the evidence is relevant for a reason other than character, the probative value is substantially outweighed by the danger of unfair prejudice to the defendant.

The court will probably overrule the objections. First, evidence of the ten uncharged burglaries on Main Street has a tendency to prove that Dell intended to commit a felony in the home where he was caught. From each of the uncharged acts, we infer criminal intent. It is reasonable to conclude Dell had the same intent in the final home. Evidence of the uncharged acts undermines Dell's claim that he broke in just to get out of the cold. Second, the theory of UME discussed in this section does come perilously close to character evidence. Yet, there is a difference. With character, you reason from conduct to character to conduct in conformity with character. With this UME theory, you reason from conduct to *intent*, to conduct in conformity with intent. This is a distinction with a difference. Third, we have the FRE 403/CEC § 352 argument. It is true that a jury might misuse evidence of the ten uncharged

---

8   This example finds its inspiration in State v. Lapage, 57 N.H. 245 (1876).

burglaries for the impermissible purpose of character evidence. On the other hand, Dell has squarely placed his intent in issue by claiming innocent intent. The prosecutor needs the evidence, and the evidence is highly probative to intent. Very likely, the judge will rule that the probative value of the UME is not substantially outweighed by the danger of unfair prejudice to the defendant.

One more example. Denise is a letter carrier for the postal service. The postal service suspects Denise is stealing from the mail while she is on her route. To catch Denise, the postal service plants a letter in the mail containing a silver dollar. A postal service investigator conducts surveillance of Denise delivering mail. At one point, Denise leaves her route and goes into a store, where she spends an hour. At the end of the day, the investigator approaches Denise as she is walking to her car. The investigator informs Denise that she is suspected of stealing a silver dollar from a letter. The investigator asks Denise to empty her pockets. When Denise turns out her back pocket, the silver dollar falls to the ground. Denise tells the investigator the silver dollar fell out of the letter while she was delivering the mail, and that she (Denise) was trying to find her supervisor to tell the supervisor what happened, and to give the supervisor the silver dollar. At Denise's trial for theft of the silver dollar, the prosecutor offers evidence that after Denise was arrested, a search of her purse disclosed two stolen credit cards. The cards had been sent months earlier to people on Denise's delivery route. Defense counsel objects to the two credit cards. How should the judge rule?[9]

The judge will overrule the objection. The UME is possession of the two credit cards. It is reasonable to infer that Denise stole the credit cards. Her intent to steal the credit cards increases the likelihood that she had the intent to steal the silver dollar. Her intent to steal on the uncharged occasion tends to prove her intent to steal on the charged occasion.

§ 8.10   Prove Intent by Disproving Accident

In some cases, the defense argues that injury or death was accidental. When accident is the defense, the prosecutor must prove intent. Sometimes, the doctrine of chances or probabilities helps disprove accident. The idea is that uncommon events occur by accident, but when similar uncommon events happen again and again, in short succession, the odds of accident decline, and the odds of intentional conduct increase. John Wigmore gave the following example: Abe and Ben are hunting. Ben's shotgun fires, narrowly

---

[9]   This example is based on United States v. Beechum, 582 F.2d 898 (5th Cir. 1978).

missing Abe. Ben says, "I'm so sorry, it went off accidently. I'll be more careful." Abe accepts Ben's explanation because, as Abe says, "Accidents happen." Ten minutes later, Ben's gun again fires in Abe's direction, and again Ben says, "Oh geeez, how did that happen? I'm so sorry." At this point, Abe is suspicious, but he accepts Ben's excuse with, "Good grief dude. Be more careful." Ten more minutes pass, and yet again, Ben's gun fires. This time, Abe is hit. If Ben is charged with attempted murder, and claims the gun went off accidently, the prosecutor will offer the two uncharged blasts to undercut the accident defense. It is possible to explain away one shooting as accidental, maybe even two, but three?[10]

Consider the Following: Two years ago, Denise was living in Arizona, where she gave birth to an apparently healthy baby, who died in its crib at one month of age. No one suspected child abuse, no autopsy was performed, and the death certificate read Sudden Infant Death Syndrome (SIDS). Denise moved to Los Angeles, where she gave birth to an apparently healthy baby, who died in its crib within a month. Again, the death was attributed to SIDS. A detective became suspicious and checked into Denise's background. The detective learned of the death in Arizona. Before living in Arizona, Denise lived in Utah, where she gave birth to a child who died mysteriously at one month of age. Prior to that, Denise lived in Idaho, where she gave birth to her first child. That baby died in its crib at one month of age. Denise is charged with murdering the child born in Los Angeles. Denise claims the baby died of natural causes. The prosecutor offers evidence of the three other deaths. Denise's attorney objects that the other deaths are irrelevant, and that evidence of the other deaths would unfairly prejudice Denise in the eyes of jurors. Should the judge admit the evidence? Yes. No one knows what causes SIDS, and there may a genetic component which increases the risk of SIDS in some families. But is it likely that four children in the same family will die of SIDS?[11]

§ 8.10(a).   Doctrine of Chances Proves Only Intent

The doctrine of chances helps disprove accident, thereby proving intent. You should only mention the doctrine of chances when accident is a viable defense. Thus, if the defendant is charged with bank robbery, don't mention the doctrine. People don't rob banks by accident. Similarly, if the defendant arms herself with a

---

[10]   2 John H. Wigmore, *Evidence at Trials in Common Law* § 302, p. 241 (Chadbourn rev. ed. 1979).

[11]   *See* the notorious case of United States v. Woods, 484 F.2d 127 (4th Cir. 1973). Beginning in 1945, Mrs. Woods had access to nine children who suffered episodes of cyanosis. Seven of the children died.

fully automatic machine gun and shoots up a shopping mall, don't discuss the doctrine of chances. This crime is no accident.

§ 8.10(b).   Anonymous Acts Are Admissible Under the Doctrine of Chances

The doctrine of chances does not require proof that the defendant committed the uncharged or the charged acts. Under the doctrine, the identity of the person who committed the uncharged and charged acts is immaterial. Thus, anonymous acts are admissible to prove that a charged act was deliberate. The force of the doctrine of chances lies in its ability to prove that the charged act was deliberately caused by *someone*. The doctrine of chances sheds no light on the identity of the perpetrator. Other evidence must be adduced to tie the defendant to the crime.

Although anonymous acts are admissible under the doctrine of chances, before anonymous acts are received, the prosecutor must establish a connection between the defendant and the victim. For example, suppose defendant is charged with murdering a child. The defense argues the child suffered accidental head injury. The prosecutor cannot disprove accident with evidence that during the past year, five other children in the city suffered head injuries. The other injuries have no connection to defendant. However, if the prosecutor establishes that the other victims were all the defendant's children, or were all under the defendant's care, the evidence becomes highly probative of intent. Probative force exists even though the prosecutor cannot prove that the defendant inflicted the other injuries.

The doctrine of chances is the one UME theory under which the prosecutor does not have to prove that the defendant committed the uncharged acts. With the other theories—motive, plan, *modus operandi*, etc.—anonymous acts are *not* admissible.

§ 8.10(c).   How Many Incidents Are Needed to Trigger the Doctrine of Chances?

How often must an unusual event occur to trigger the doctrine of chances? There is no hard-and-fast rule. Sometimes, one prior incident is enough. Other times, several incidents are needed.

§ 8.10(d).   How Similar Do the Uncharged and the Charged Acts Have to Be?

Here too, there is no hard-and-fast rule. Similarity is required, of course, because it is the repetition of similar unusual events that gives the doctrine power. Although similarity is required, the acts do not have to be identical.

§ 8.11 *Modus Operandi* to Prove Identity

When identity is disputed, the prosecution may offer evidence of uncharged acts that are strikingly similar to the charged offense. The fact that the same *modus operandi* was used in the uncharged and the charged crimes permits an inference that the same person committed them all.

Evidence of *modus operandi* to prove identity requires a very high degree of similarity between the charged and uncharged acts. There must be a shared unique methodology. Courts use a variety of terms, including distinguishing, handiwork, idiosyncratic, signature quality, unique, and mark of Zorro. The similarity required for *modus operandi* is greater than the similarity required under the doctrine of chances or the broad theory of plan.

Does the *modus operandi* theory apply to the following facts?

The victim in the charged offense is a thirteen-year-old girl who was awakened at 2:30 a.m., when the light came on in her bedroom. A man was standing in the doorway. The man motioned with his hand for the victim to come to him. He held a baseball bat. As the victim walked toward him, the man grabbed the victim's pajamas and asked her whether any men were in the house. The victim said no. The man then ordered the victim to kiss him, which she did. The man grabbed the victim by the hair, dragged her to her bed, and anally raped her. Following the assault, the man fled. At trial, the defendant, Dell, offers an alibi. The prosecutor proposes to call two witnesses. Witness A is a thirteen-year-old girl who will testify that 10 days after the charged offense, Dell entered her bedroom at about 9:30 p.m. Dell grabbed her by the hair after she did not respond to his command to come to him. When A screamed, her mother came into the room. Dell asked the mother whether any men were in the house. The mother said there were, and Dell fled. Witness B is a nine-year-old girl who will testify that 10 days before the charged offense, during the early morning hours, Dell entered her bedroom, picked her up, and took her to a field across the street from the house. Dell removed her nightgown and began fondling her genitals. When the victim saw her mother arrive home, Dell allowed the girl to put her nightgown back on, and walked her part way back to her house. Dell fled into the night. All three assaults occurred within a four-block radius. Dell lives in the same area. Do the uncharged crimes point to Dell as the perpetrator of the charged rape?

The testimony of victim B should probably be excluded because the uncharged acts and the charged act are not sufficiently similar and unique to trigger the *modus operandi* theory. It is true that there are similarities between the assault on B and the charged assault: both victims were minors, the uncharged assault occurred near the time of the charged offense, both acts occurred in the same neighborhood, both assaults occurred at night, the perpetrator entered a bedroom on each occasion, and each case involved a sex offense. However, there are dissimilarities. No weapon was involved in the assault on B, the sexual acts were different, defendant took B outside, and defendant did not ask whether any men were in the house. Furthermore, the *modus operandi* of the two offenses is not distinguishing or unique. Nothing about these crimes ties them together as the work of one person. Rather, they are the work of ordinary, if somewhat daring, criminals.

The testimony of victim A presents a closer case. Note the similarities between the uncharged and the charged acts: both victims were minors, the crimes occurred within days of one another, each occurred at night and in the same neighborhood, the assailant entered a bedroom in both cases, the man ordered each victim to come to him, he grabbed each victim, and, in each case, he asked whether any men were in the house. But note the dissimilarities: no weapon was involved in the offense against A, and no sexual assault occurred.

The shared elements of the assault on A and the charged offense come closer to the similarity required by the *modus operandi* theory. Yet, the extent of similarity arguably falls short of the mark. What is more, there is little that is unique about these crimes. The combination of weak similarity and lack of uniqueness undercuts the argument for admission under the *modus operandi* theory. You are free to disagree.

§ 8.12   California's Broad Approach to UME

California courts are broadly receptive of UME. As mentioned in Section 8.7, California approves the broad theory of plan, also called "design" or "common scheme." Plan may be proven with evidence that the defendant performed uncharged acts that are similar to the charged offense.

In the leading case of *People v. Ewoldt,* 7 Cal. 4th 380, 403–403, 867 P.2d 757, 27 Cal. Rptr. 2d 646 (1984), the Supreme Court discussed the degrees of similarity required to prove intent, plan, and *modus operandi*:

> The least degree of similarity (between the uncharged act and the charged offense) is required in order to prove intent. . . . In order to be admissible to prove intent, the uncharged misconduct must be sufficiently similar to support the inference that the defendant probably harbored the same intent in each instance.[12]

> A greater degree of similarity is required in order to prove the existence of a common design or plan. . . . In establishing a common design or plan, evidence of uncharged misconduct must demonstrate not merely a similarity in the results, but such a concurrence of common features that the various acts are naturally to be explained as caused by a general plan of which they are the individual manifestations. . . .

> To establish the existence of a common design or plan, the common features must indicate the existence of a plan rather than a series of similar spontaneous acts, but the plan thus revealed need not be distinctive or unusual. For example, evidence that a search of the residence of a person suspected of rape produced a written plan to invite the victim to his residence and, once alone, to force her to engage in sexual intercourse would be highly relevant even if the plan lacked originality.[13] In the same manner, evidence that the defendant has committed uncharged criminal acts that are similar to the charged offense may be relevant if these acts demonstrate circumstantially that the defendant committed the charged offense pursuant to the same design or plan he or she used in committing the uncharged acts. . . .[14]

> The greatest degree of similarity is required for evidence of uncharged misconduct to be relevant to prove identity. For identity to be established, the uncharged misconduct and the charged offense must share common features that are sufficiently distinctive so as to support

---

[12]   The Court is talking about the UME theory of intent discussed in § 8.9.

[13]   The note found in the apartment is evidence of a "true" plan to commit the charged offense—the narrow theory of plan.

[14]   Evidence that the defendant committed uncharged similar offenses is the broad theory of plan, which California courts accept, but which some (including, for what it's worth, your author) believe is really just bad character evidence. Critics of the broad theory call the broad theory a specious plan, that is, no plan at all; just bad character evidence dressed up to look like UME.

the inference that the same person committed both acts. The pattern and characteristics of the crimes must be so unusual and distinctive as to be like a signature.

§ 8.13 Third Party Culpability Evidence

Most of the time, UME is offered by prosecutors against defendants. Occasionally, the defendant offers UME to prove someone else committed the crime. This use of UME is called third party culpability evidence. The theories are the same, *e.g.,* plan, *modus operandi*, etc. In *People v. Hall*, 41 Cal. 3d 826, 718 P.2d 99, 226 Cal. Rptr. 112 (1986), the Supreme Court discussed the requirements for third party culpability evidence:

> To be admissible, the third-party evidence need not show substantial proof of a probability that the third person committed the act; it need only be capable of raising a reasonable doubt of defendant's guilt. At the same time, we do not require that any evidence, however remote, must be admitted to show a third party's possible culpability. Evidence of mere motive or opportunity to commit the crime in another person, without more, will not suffice to raise a reasonable doubt about a defendant's guilt: there must be direct or circumstantial evidence linking the third person to the actual perpetration of the crime.

Chapter 9

LAY AND EXPERT WITNESSES

This chapter describes rules governing lay and expert witnesses. In most respects, the Federal Rules of Evidence (FRE) and the California Evidence Code (CEC) are similar regarding witnesses.

§ 9.1   Competence to Testify

The rules of evidence provide that nearly everyone is competent to testify. The elements of testimonial competence are: (1) Capacity to communicate so the jury can understand; (2) Sufficient memory capacity to remember events;[1] (3) Understanding of the difference between truth and falsehood; and (4) Appreciation of the duty to tell the truth in court.

With adults, questions about testimonial competence do not arise unless there are signs the adult is out of touch with reality, or incapable of understanding what's happening. Issues of testimonial competence usually arise with children. Thousands of cases, supported by psychological research, confirm that children as young as four can be competent witnesses. When a child's testimony is offered, the opposing attorney may ask the judge to question the youngster to determine whether the child understands the difference between truth and lies, and the duty to tell the truth.[2] When children are questioned properly, they demonstrate the necessary understanding. Testifying is no fun for kids, but with emotional support and preparation, most child witnesses testify capably, and do not experience long-lasting trauma from testifying.

The rules governing witness competency provide:

FRE 601. Competency to Testify in General. Every person is competent to be a witness unless these rules provide otherwise.[3]

---

[1]   What is required is general memory capacity, not memory for the events the witness will testify about.

[2]   Although the rules of evidence state that "every person" is competent, judges question children when legitimate questions are raised about a child's ability to testify.

[3]   FRE 601 also provides: "But in a civil case, state law governs the witness's competency regarding a claim or defense for which state law supplies the rule of decision." This aspect of Rule 601 deals with diversity jurisdiction in federal court. In diversity cases where state law governs, federal district court judges apply state law regarding witness competence.

CEC § 700. General Rule as to Competency. Except as otherwise provided by statute, every person, irrespective of age, is qualified to be a witness and no person is disqualified to testify to any matter.

CEC § 701. Disqualification of Witnesses. (a) A person is disqualified to be a witness if he or she is: (1) Incapable of expressing himself or herself concerning the matter so as to be understood, either directly or through interpretation by one who can understand him; or (2) Incapable of understanding the duty of a witness to tell the truth.

In practice, there is no difference between the FRE and CEC rules on testimonial competence.

§ 9.1(a).   Presiding Judge and Jurors Do Not Testify—Impeaching a Verdict

Clearly, the judge presiding over a trial should not also be a witness. FRE 605 provides that the judge may not testify. CEC § 703 allows the judge to testify if no party objects, but it is difficult to imagine a California Superior Court judge testifying in a trial over which the judge presides.

When it comes to jurors, FRE 606(a) provides that a juror may not testify as a witness before the other jurors at trial. CEC § 704 is worded differently, but the result is generally the same.

After a jury returns a verdict, information may come to light that jurors acted improperly, or that outside influences were brought to bear on jurors. FRE 606(b)(1) provides: "During an inquiry into the validity of a verdict or indictment, a juror may not testify about any statement made or incident that occurred during the jury's deliberations; the effect of anything on that juror's or another juror's vote; or any juror's mental processes concerning the verdict or indictment. The court may not receive a jurors' affidavit or evidence of a juror's statement on these matters." This is often called the rule against impeaching the verdict—the no-impeachment rule.

CEC § 1150(a) provides: "Upon an inquiry as to the validity of a verdict, any otherwise admissible evidence may be received as to statements made, or conduct, conditions, or events occurring, either within or without the jury room, of such a character as is likely to have influenced the verdict improperly. No evidence is admissible to show the effect of such statement, conduct, condition, or event upon a juror either in influencing him to assent or dissent from the verdict or concerning the mental processes by which it was determined."

Under CEC § 1150(a), a California juror could testify to events occurring in the jury room. Not so under FRE 606(B)(1), which prohibits juror testimony describing incidents occurring during deliberations.

FRE 606(b)(2) carves out exceptions to the no-impeachment rule. Rule 606(b)(2) allows a juror to "testify about whether extraneous prejudicial information was improperly brought to the jury's attention; an outside influence was improperly brought to bear on any juror; or a mistake was made in entering the verdict on the verdict form." In *Pena-Rodriguez v. Colorado*, 137 S.Ct. 855 (2017), the Supreme Court carved out a constitutional exception to the rule against impeaching a verdict, for cases in which there is evidence that a juror "relied on racial stereotypes or animus to convict a criminal defendant." The Court held that "the Sixth Amendment requires that the no-impeachment rule give way in order to permit the trial court to consider the evidence of the juror's [racially motivated] statement and any resulting denial of the jury trial guarantee."

§ 9.1(b).   Testimonial Competence on Exams

When should you discuss testimonial competence on exams? This is a fair question for your professor. I tell my students, "With adult witnesses, there is no need to write about competence unless there are facts suggesting the person is not competent. With child witnesses, write about competence, and set forth the elements of competence."

When the witness is an adult, and there appear to be no issues related to competence, some students write, "All witnesses must be competent, must have personal knowledge, and must take an oath of affirmation. I assume all three of these are satisfied with Mr. X."

§ 9.2   Dead Man's Statute

Many states, but not California, have a law called a dead man's statute. The idea is pretty simple. Two people enter into a binding oral contract. Before performance of the contract is complete, one of them dies. The survivor sues to enforce the contract, but the relatives of the deceased party dispute the existence or terms of the contract. At trial, the deceased—for obvious reasons—cannot tell her side of the story. To make things equal, a dead man's statute prevents the survivor from testifying about the contract.

Neither the FRE nor the CEC contain a dead man's statute. In California, the surviving party to an oral contract can testify. In the effort to achieve fairness, CEC § 1261 creates a hearsay exception for statements by the deceased.

§ 9.3   Personal Knowledge

Lay witnesses must have personal knowledge. The witness must use one or more of the five senses—usually sight or hearing—to gain a sensory impression of events. The rules provide:

> **FRE 602. Need for Personal Knowledge.** A witness may testify to a matter only if evidence is introduced sufficient to support a finding that the witness has personal knowledge of the matter. Evidence to prove personal knowledge may consist of the witness's own testimony. This rule does not apply to a witness's expert testimony under Rule 703. [Many experts have personal knowledge, but with some expert testimony, personal knowledge is not required.[4]]

> **CEC § 702. Personal Knowledge of Witness.** (a) Subject to Section 801 [governing expert witnesses, who don't always need personal knowledge], the testimony of a witness concerning a particular matter is inadmissible unless he has personal knowledge of the matter. Against the objection of a party, such personal knowledge must be shown before the witness may testify concerning the matter. (b) A witness's personal knowledge of a matter may be shown by any otherwise admissible evidence, including his own testimony.

Regarding personal knowledge, there is no real difference between the FRE and CEC. The normal trial practice is to call the witness to the stand, administer the oath, and begin questioning. The witness's personal knowledge is usually evident from their testimony. In the rare case where personal knowledge is an issue, the problem usually arises well into the witness's testimony, when it becomes apparent that the witness lacks the necessary knowledge.[5] At that point, an attorney may say, "Your honor, it has

---

[4]   For example, a doctor testifying as an expert may have personal knowledge of the patient because the doctor examined and treated the patient. Another doctor could offer expert testimony even though the doctor had no personal knowledge of patient, if the doctor reviewed the patient's medical record.

[5]   How does it become apparent that a witness lacks personal knowledge? Here's an example: Mary, the witness, gets on the stand and describes the accident in detail. From her testimony, it appears that Mary witnessed the accident. However, half an hour into Mary's testimony, she says something that reveals that she did not witness the accident. Mary has simply repeated what her roommate told her about

become clear that the witness lacks personal knowledge. I object to the witness's testimony, due to lack of personal knowledge, and move to strike the testimony." If an attorney thinks a witness who is about to testify lacks personal knowledge, the attorney may ask the judge to require opposing counsel to establish personal knowledge before the witness testifies. CEC § 702(a) specifically mentions such a procedure. FRE 602 contains no such procedure, but a judge using the FRE has the same authority.

§ 9.4　　Oath or Affirmation

Witnesses take an oath or affirm to testify truthfully. The FRE and CEC are the same. The rules provide:

> **FRE 603. Oath or Affirmation to Testify Truthfully**. Before testifying, a witness must give an oath or affirmation to testify truthfully. It must be in a form designed to impress that duty on the witness's conscience.

> **CEC § 710. Oath Required**. Every witness before testifying shall take an oath or make an affirmation or declaration in the form provided by law, except that a child under the age of 10 or a dependent person with a substantial cognitive impairment, in the court's discretion, may be required to promise to tell the truth.

§ 9.5　　Opinions from Lay Witnesses

Lay witnesses describe *facts*. For example, "The car went through the red light." "He picked up the gun and fired." "The bank robber wore a mask of President Trump." In addition to factual testimony, lay witnesses testify in the form of *opinion*, so long as the opinion will help the jury, and the opinion is rationally based on the witness's perception. The rules on lay opinion follow:

> **FRE 701. Opinion Testimony by Lay Witnesses**. If a witness is not testifying as an expert, testimony in the form of an opinion is limited to one that is: (a) rationally based on the witness's perception; (b) helpful to clearly understanding the witness's testimony or to determining a fact in issue; and (c) not based on scientific, technical, or other specialized knowledge within the scope of Rule 702. [Rule 702 deals with expert testimony. Subjection (c) simply means that lay witnesses don't offer expert testimony.]

---

the accident. That is the point at which the opposing lawyer objects that Mary lacks personal knowledge. This scenario is rare because attorneys seldom offer testimony from witnesses who lack personal knowledge.

CEC § 800. Lay Witnesses; Opinion Testimony. If a witness is not testifying as an expert his testimony in the form of an opinion is limited to such an opinion as is permitted by law, including but not limited to an opinion that is: (a) Rationally based on the perception of the witness; and (b) Helpful to a clear understanding of his testimony.

FRE 701 and CEC § 800 are the same. Under the rules, lay witnesses can opine on a broad range of issues, including: speed, color, distance, shape, texture, and smell. Lay witnesses may testify that someone appeared sober or drunk, happy or sad, angry or sanguine, even crazy.[6] May a lay witness opine on what someone else was thinking or feeling?[7] In *People v. DeHoyos*, 57 Cal. 4th 79, 131, 303 P.3d 1, 158 Cal. Rptr. 3d 797 (2013), the Supreme Court wrote, "A lay witness generally may not give an opinion about another person's state of mind, but may testify about objective behavior and describe behavior as being consistent with a state of mind."

§ 9.6   Exclude Witnesses While Other Witness Testify

If witnesses sit in court and observe other witnesses testify, a witness with an incentive to do so could shape testimony to conform or contrast with other witnesses. To avoid this, the rules of evidence permit a party to ask the judge to exclude witnesses from the courtroom while they are not testifying. The rules state:

FRE 615. Excluding Witnesses. At a party's request, the court must order witnesses excluded so that they cannot hear other witnesses' testimony. Or the court may do so on its own. But this rule does not authorize excluding: (a) a party who is a natural person; (b) an officer or employee of a party that is not a natural person, after being designated as the party's representative by its attorney; (c) a person whose presence a party shows to be essential to presenting the party's claim or defense; or (d) a person authorized by statute to be present.

---

[6]   *See* CEC § 870, which provides: "A witness may state his opinion as to the sanity of a person when: (a) The witness is an intimate acquaintance of the person whose sanity is in question; (b) The witness was a subscribing witness to a writing, the validity of which is in dispute, signed by the person whose sanity is in question and the opinion relates to the sanity of such person at the time the writing was signed or; (c) The witness is qualified under Section 800 or 801 to testify [as an expert witness] in the form of an opinion."

[7]   *See* People v. Seumanu, 61 Cal. 4th 1293, 355 P.3d 384, 192 Cal. Rptr. 3d 195 (2015).

CEC § 777. Exclusion of Witnesses. (a) Subject to subdivisions (b) and (c), the court may exclude from the courtroom any witness not at the time under examination so that such witness cannot hear the testimony of other witnesses. (b) A party to the action cannot be excluded under this section. (c) If a person other than a natural person is a party to the action, an officer or employee designated by its attorney is entitled to be present.

The FRE and CEC provisions on witness exclusion operate the same in practice.

§ 9.7   Refreshing Recollection

Do witnesses forget? Of course they do. No matter how well witnesses are prepared, the natural weaknesses of memory, coupled with the stress of testifying, lead occasionally to memory lapse. When this happens on direct examination, the attorney may ask the judge's permission to ask some leading questions to jog the witness's memory.[8] Another way to refresh memory is to show the witness a document to trigger recollection. When a document is used for the limited purpose of refreshing recollection, the document is not admitted into evidence. The document is not evidence; it is a mere memory stimulant. Because the document is not evidence, it is not hearsay, it does not have to be authenticated, and the best evidence rule does not apply. After the witness examines the memory stimulating document, the attorney asks, "Does the document refresh your recollection?" If the answer is "Yes," many attorneys take the document from the witness so there is no question that the witness is testifying from memory, instead of reading what is on the page. The rules on refreshing recollection follow:

FRE 612. Writing Used to Refresh a Witness's Memory. **(a) Scope**. This rule gives an adverse party certain options when a witness uses a writing to refresh memory: (1) while testifying; or (2) before testifying, if the court decides that justice requires the party to have those options. **(b) Adverse Party's Options; Deleting Unrelated Matter**. Unless 18 U.S.C. § 3500 provides otherwise in a criminal case,[9] an adverse party is entitled to have the writing produced at the hearing, to inspect it, to cross-examine the witness about it, and to introduce in

---

[8]   "Your honor, it appears the witness is having difficulty remembering. May I attempt to refresh the witness's memory with a few suggestive questions?"

[9]   18 U.S.C. § 3500 limits the production in criminal cases of documents prepared by government witnesses until the witness has testified.

evidence any portion that relates to the witness's testimony. If the producing party claims that the writing includes unrelated matter, the court must examine the writing in camera, delete any unrelated portions, and order that the rest be delivered to the adverse party. Any portion deleted over objection must be preserved for the record. **(c) Failure to Produce or Deliver the Writing**. If a writing is not produced or is not delivered as ordered, the court may issue any appropriate order. But if the proponent does not comply in a criminal case, the court must strike the witness's testimony or—if justice so requires—declare a mistrial.

CEC § 771. Production of Writing Used to Refresh Memory. (a) Subject to subdivision (c), if a witness, either while testifying or prior thereto, uses a writing to refresh his memory with respect to any matter about which he testifies, such writing must be produced at the hearing at the request of an adverse party and, unless the writing is so produced, the testimony of the witness concerning such matter shall be stricken. (b) If the writing is produced at the hearing, the adverse party may, if he chooses, inspect the writing, cross-examine the witness concerning it, and introduce in evidence such portion of it as may be pertinent to the testimony of the witness. (c) Production of the writing is excused, and the testimony of the witness shall not be stricken, if the writing: (1) Is not in the possession or control of the witness or the party who produced his testimony concerning the matter; and (2) Was not reasonably procurable by such party through the use of the court's process or other available means.

The FRE and the CEC rules on refreshing recollection operate similarly.

§ 9.8   Expert Testimony

Expert and scientific evidence is a vast, complex, and ever-changing subject. It may surprise you to learn that the rules on expert testimony are short and simple. The FRE and the CEC rules on experts are similar. The few differences are explained below.

§ 9.9   Who Qualifies as an Expert?

Expert testimony is admissible when the trier of fact—judge or jury—needs help to decide some technical, scientific, or clinical issue. The issue does not have to be completely beyond the ken of the jury. In many cases, the jury already knows something about the subject, and the expert adds depth to the jury's knowledge. An expert is someone whose training, experience, or education equips the expert to help the jury. The rules provide:

FRE 702. Testimony by Expert Witnesses. A witness who is qualified as an expert by knowledge, skill, experience, training, or education may testify in the form of an opinion or otherwise if: (a) the expert's scientific, technical, or other specialized knowledge will help the trier of fact to understand the evidence or to determine a fact in issue; (b) the testimony is based on sufficient facts or data; (c) the testimony is the product of reliable principles and methods; and (d) the expert has reliably applied the principles and methods to the facts of the case.

CEC § 720. Qualifications as an Expert Witness. (a) A person is qualified to testify as an expert if he has special knowledge, skill, experience, training, or education sufficient to qualify him as an expert on the subject to which his testimony relates. Against the objection of a party, such special knowledge, skill, experience, training, or education must be shown before the witness may testify as an expert. (b) A witness' special knowledge, skill, experience, training, or education may be shown by any otherwise admissible evidence, including his own testimony.

CEC § 801. Expert Witnesses; Opinion Testimony. If a witness is testifying as an expert, his testimony in the form of an opinion is limited to such an opinion as is: (a) Related to a subject that is sufficiently beyond common experience that the opinion of an expert would assist the trier of fact; and (b) Based on matter (including his special knowledge, skill, experience, training, and education) perceived by or personally known to the witness or made known to him at or before the hearing, whether or not admissible, that is of a type that reasonably may be relied upon by an expert in forming an opinion upon the subject to which his testimony relates, unless an expert is precluded by law from using such matter as a basis for his opinion.

The judge decides whether a person qualifies to testify as an expert (FRE 104(a); CEC § 405). Sometimes, parties stipulate that a person is an expert.[10] Absent agreement, the usual practice is for

---

[10]   Sometimes the attorney opposing a proposed expert would prefer that the jury not hear about the witness's impressive credentials. In an effort to eliminate qualification questions that highlight credentials, the attorney offers to stipulate

the proposed expert to take the witness stand, be sworn, and answer questions from the lawyer who offers the expert. The lawyer asks about the person's qualifications. The questioning takes place in front of the jury. Opposing counsel has a right to challenge the witness's qualifications to testify, a process called *voir dire*. If the person is clearly qualified, *voir dire* is typically waived.

§ 9.10   Form of Expert Testimony

The most common form of expert testimony is an opinion. For example, the pathologist who performed an autopsy might testify, "In my opinion, the victim died of blunt force trauma to the head."

Less often than an opinion, an expert gives the jury background information on a technical, scientific, or clinical issue so the jury can better understand the other evidence in the case. An example of background information comes from child sexual abuse prosecutions. The defense attorney sometimes tries to undermine the child's credibility by emphasizing that the child delayed reporting the alleged abuse, and was inconsistent in descriptions of the abuse. This is legitimate impeachment. However, when the defense adopts this approach, judges allow the prosecutor to offer expert testimony that many children who have been sexually abused delay reporting and are inconsistent.[11] The expert does not offer an opinion about whether the child was abused. Indeed, the expert need never have met the child. The expert's description of how sexually abused children disclose simply gives the jury background information that helps the jury evaluate the child's credibility, after the defense has attacked the child's credibility.

In some cases, an expert answers a hypothetical question posed by the attorney who offers the expert's testimony. The attorney asks a lengthy question about a hypothetical set of facts. The hypothetical facts must be supported by evidence admitted in the case. Thus, the facts in the hypothetical question mirror the facts established by the evidence. At the end of the hypothetical question, the attorney asks, "Based on these hypothetical facts, do you have an opinion about _____?" In California today, hypothetical questions are regularly used with police officers who are experts on gangs. The prosecutor describes a hypothetical crime, and asks for

---

that the person qualifies as an expert. Generally, judges do not require the proponent of an expert to accept such an offer to stipulate.

[11]   With this kind of expert testimony, the expert may describe the Child Sexual Abuse Accommodation Syndrome. The Syndrome describes the disclosure process in children, and testimony on the syndrome is well accepted in California to help jurors evaluate children's credibility. The syndrome does not prove sexual abuse. Rather, it helps the jury understand why it is difficult for some victims to disclose.

the expert's opinion on whether the crime was gang related, or committed for the benefit of a gang.

It is not required that the attorney offering expert testimony elicit the expert's opinion with a hypothetical question. In most cases, the attorney simply asks the expert her opinion. Indeed, in trials today, you are more likely to encounter hypothetical questions on cross-examination than direct examination of experts. The cross-examiner might ask the following hypothetical, "Doctor, if the following facts are true, would your opinion change?"

§ 9.11   Reasonable Certainty

When an expert offers an opinion, it is common for the attorney to elicit the opinion with the following question: "Do you have an opinion, based on a reasonable degree of certainty, whether _____." The so-called reasonable certainty standard is not mandated by the rules of evidence, yet, it is common. Given the ubiquity of the reasonable certainty standard, you'd think, surely, there must be a clear definition of reasonable certainty. Nope. The term has no clear meaning. It is clear that experts may not speculate or guess. It is equally clear that experts don't have to be 100% certain they are right. Reasonable certainty lies somewhere between guesswork and certainty, closer to the latter.[12]

§ 9.12   What Can Experts Rely on to Testify?

To formulate testimony, the law allows experts to rely on the kinds of information experts utilize in their day-to-day professional work. For example, physicians rely on x-rays, laboratory reports, physical examination, patient history, consultation with other doctors, and research in the medical literature. Automotive engineers rely on examination of car parts, manuals, engineering principles, designs, and relevant research. The fact that some of the information relied on by an expert might not be admissible in

---

[12]   The concept of reasonable certainty should not be confused with the burden of proof. The burden of proof is the level of certainty by which a jury must be persuaded by the evidence that is presented by the party with the burden of proof. Three burdens of proof are used: (a) Beyond a reasonable doubt; (b) Preponderance of the evidence; and (c) Clear and convincing evidence. The certainty needed for expert testimony does *not* vary with the type of litigation. Experts do not have to be more certain in criminal cases, where the burden of proof is highest, than in civil cases. Regardless of the type of litigation—criminal or civil—experts should ensure the correctness of opinions. Occasionally, attorneys ask experts whether they are certain of their opinion beyond a reasonable doubt or by a preponderance of the evidence. An accurate response to such a question is, "Counsel, when I reach an opinion, I do not employ the legal concept of burden of proof. Burdens of proof are legal constructs, and are not used in my profession of psychology. Instead, I use clinical and scientific principles to reach my opinion. In reaching my opinion, I took all the steps I could to ensure that my opinion is correct. I am reasonably certain of my opinion, and, by reasonably certain, I mean I am confident my opinion is correct."

evidence (*e.g.*, hearsay) does not make the expert's reliance unreasonable, or the expert's opinion inadmissible. The rules provide:

FRE 703. Bases of an Expert's Opinion Testimony. An expert may base an opinion on facts or data in the case that the expert has been made aware of or personally observed. If experts in the particular field would reasonably rely on those kinds of facts or data in forming an opinion on the subject, they need not be admissible for the opinion to be admitted. But if the facts or data would otherwise be inadmissible, the proponent of the opinion may disclose them to the jury only if their probative value in helping the jury evaluate the opinion substantially outweighs their prejudicial effect.

FRE 705. Disclosing the Facts or Data Underlying an Expert's Opinion. Unless the court orders otherwise, an expert may state an opinion—and give the reasons for it—without first testifying to the underlying facts or data. But the expert may be required to disclose those facts or data on cross-examination.

CEC § 801. Expert Witnesses; Opinion Testimony. If a witness is testifying as an expert, his testimony in the form of an opinion is limited to such an opinion as is: (a) Related to a subject that is sufficiently beyond common experience that the opinion of an expert would assist the trier of fact; and (b) Based on matter (including his special knowledge, skill, experience, training, and education) perceived by or personally known to the witness or made known to him at or before the hearing, whether or not admissible, that is of a type that reasonably may be relied upon by an expert in forming an opinion upon the subject to which his testimony relates, unless an expert is precluded by law from using such matter as a basis for his opinion.

CEC § 803. Opinion Based on Improper Matter. The court may, and upon objection shall, exclude testimony in the form of an opinion that is based in whole or in significant part on matter that is not a proper basis for such an opinion. In such case, the witness may, if there remains a proper basis for his opinion, then state his opinion after excluding from consideration the matter determined to be improper.

Under the FRE, an expert's opinion may be based on inadmissible evidence, including inadmissible hearsay. However, Rule 703 provides, "But if the facts or data would otherwise be inadmissible, the proponent of the opinion may disclose them to the jury only if their probative value in helping the jury evaluate the opinion substantially outweighs their prejudicial effect." If an attorney objects to an expert disclosing inadmissible evidence that supports the expert's opinion, the judge balances the utility of the inadmissible evidence to assist the jury in reaching a proper understanding of the expert's testimony, against the possibility that the jury will place too much emphasis on the inadmissible evidence. Depending on how the judge views this balance, the judge may prohibit the expert from disclosing some or all of the inadmissible evidence that supports the expert's testimony. The expert testimony is still admissible; only the inadmissible evidence that supports the testimony is kept from the jury.

When an expert relied on inadmissible hearsay to formulate the expert's opinion, and the judge rules the expert may mention the hearsay in court, the opposing attorney can ask the judge to instruct the jury not to consider the out-of-court statements for the truth. The judge instructs the jury that it may consider the statements only insofar as the statements help the jury understand and value the expert's testimony.

When it comes to expert reliance on hearsay, and an expert disclosing hearsay to the jury, California does not have the balancing approach set forth in FRE 703. A California attorney could ask a Superior Court judge to perform a similar balancing by making a Section 352 objection, and asking the judge to balance the probative value of the hearsay as support for the expert's opinion against the danger the jury will use the inadmissible hearsay for the truth, and consider the hearsay against the defendant.

In *People v. Sanchez*, 63 Cal. 4th 665, 676, 374 P.3d 320, 204 Cal. Rptr. 3d 102 (2016), the Supreme Court drew a distinction between (1) expert testimony describing general background information that is based on hearsay, and (2) case-specific facts based on hearsay. Case-specific facts are "those relating to the particular events and participants alleged to have been involved in the case being tried." No problem arises when an expert describes general background information. However, case-specific facts that are hearsay are only admissible if they meet the requirements of a hearsay exception. In criminal cases, if hearsay statements are testimonial (*See* § 11.29), they are inadmissible.

§ 9.13 Ultimate Issues

In every case, there are ultimate facts and ultimate legal issues. The ultimate facts are the facts that one side must prove to win. Lay and expert witnesses may testify to ultimate facts. Suppose, for example, that Sue broke into a house in order to steal. Sue is charged with burglary, which was defined at common law as the breaking and entering of the dwelling house of another at night with the intent to commit a felony therein. The ultimate facts are: (1) breaking, (2) entering, (3) the dwelling house, (4) of another, (5) at night, (6) with the intent to commit a felony inside the dwelling.

In a rape prosecution, the crime is defined as sexual intercourse accomplished by force and against the will of the victim. Penetration is an element of the crime, and is an ultimate fact.

In the burglary case, lay witnesses could testify to the ultimate facts required for conviction. In the rape case, the victim, the defendant, and/or an expert witness could testify regarding penetration.

The ultimate legal issue in the burglary and rape cases is whether the defendant is guilty or innocent. Witnesses may testify to ultimate facts, but *not* ultimate legal issues such as guilt or innocence. Thus, an expert should not venture an opinion on whether the defendant in a criminal case is guilty or innocent. Nor should an expert express an opinion on *who* committed a crime. Guilt, innocence, and identity are for the jury to decide, not experts. The rules on ultimate issue testimony provide:

> **Rule 704. Opinion on an Ultimate Issue. (a) In General—Not Automatically Objectionable**. An opinion is not objectionable just because it embraces an ultimate issue. **(b) Exception**. In a criminal case, an expert witness must not state an opinion about whether the defendant did or did not have a mental state or condition that constitutes an element of the crime charged or of a defense. Those matters are for the trier of fact alone.

> **CEC § 805. Opinion on Ultimate Issue**. Testimony in the form of an opinion that is otherwise admissible is not objectionable because it embraces the ultimate issue to be decided by the trier of fact.

FRE 704(b) is intended to prohibit expert testimony by mental health professionals that a defendant had the *mens rea* required for the charged crime. Thus, first degree murder is the willful, deliberate, and premeditated killing of a human being. A psychiatrist or psychologist should not say that, due to mental illness, the defendant did not premeditate, deliberate, or pull the trigger with the intent to kill. The ultimate issues of premeditation, deliberation, and intent to kill are for the jury to decide. What the expert can do is describe the defendant's mental illness, its impact on defendant's thinking (*e.g.*, delusions, hallucinations) and defendant's ability to control her/his behavior. Rule 704(b) applies to the insanity defense, which is defined in many states as a mental disease or defect that deprives a person of capacity to understand the nature and quality of the act, or to understand that the act is wrong. Under FRE 704(b), the expert should not phrase an expert opinion in the legal language of the defense. Rather, the expert should take a verbal step away from the precise language of the insanity defense, and confine testimony to the defendant's mental illness and its impact on the defendant's cognitive functioning.

§ 9.14   Cross-Examination of Experts

Expert witnesses are subject to cross-examination. CEC § 721(a) provides that "a witness testifying as an expert may be cross-examined to the same extent as any other witness and, in addition, may be fully cross-examined as to (1) his or her qualifications, (2) the subject to which his or her expert testimony relates, and (3) the matter upon which his or her opinion is based and the reasons for his or her opinion." A cross-examiner has broad latitude to question opposing experts.

§ 9.15   Impeach Expert with a Learned Treatise

One method to impeach an expert is with statements in professional books, journal articles, or publications that are inconsistent with, or that undermine, the expert's opinion. This technique is called impeachment with a learned treatise. If the expert relied on or considered a learned treatise in forming the expert's opinion, the cross-examiner may ask about the treatise.[13] If the expert did not rely on or consider the learned treatise, questioning is proper if the treatise is established as reliable.

---

[13]   *See* CEC § 721(b), Law Revision Commission Comments: "If an expert witness has relied on a particular publication in forming his opinion, it is necessary to permit cross-examination in regard to that publication in order to show whether the expert correctly read, interpreted, and applied the portions he relied on. Similarly, it is important to permit an expert witness to be cross-examined concerning those publications referred to or considered by him even though not specifically relied on by him in forming his opinion. An expert's reasons for not relying on particular publication that were referred to or considered by him while forming his opinion may reveal important information bearing upon the credibility of his testimony."

In California, CEC § 721(b) governs impeachment with learned treatises, and provides:

CEC § 721(b). [Cross-Examination of Expert with a Learned Treatise]. If a witness testifying as an expert testifies in the form of an opinion, he or she may not be cross-examined in regard to the content or tenor of any scientific, technical, or professional text, treatise, journal, or similar publication unless any of the following occurs: (1) The witness referred to, considered, or relied upon such publication in arriving at or forming his or her opinion. (2) The publication has been admitted in evidence. (3) The publication has been established as a reliable authority by the testimony or admission of the witness or by other expert testimony or by judicial notice. If admitted, relevant portions of the publication may be read into evidence but may not be received as exhibits.

Section 721(b) allows impeachment with a learned treatise, but the contents of the treatise are not admissible under Section 721(b) for the truth of the matter asserted. When the contents of a learned treatise are offered for the truth of what is written, the treatise is hearsay. The FRE and the CEC contain a hearsay exception for learned treatises, discussed in § 11.17). The FRE hearsay exception for learned treatises is broad. The California exception is quite limited.

What qualifies as a learned treatise? Certainly, well accepted medical texts, such as *Gray's Anatomy* qualify, as do articles from peer reviewed scientific journals. But what about material found on the internet? In *Kace v. Liang*, 36 N.E.3d 1215 (Mass. 2015), the Massachusetts Supreme Judicial Court ruled that materials downloaded from the web sites of the Mayo Clinic and John's Hopkins Medical Center do not qualify as learned treatises.

§ 9.16 Scientific Evidence

Some scientific principles and devices are well established, and have a track record of reliability.[14] DNA evidence, for example, has been thoroughly vetted by the scientific community. The electrocardiograph is generally accepted in medicine as a reliable method to assess heart activity. Occasionally, expert testimony comes along that is based on principles of unknown reliability. In some cases, novel scientific evidence is nothing more than "junk

---

[14]   Scientists distinguish validity from reliability. Courts generally use the word "reliable" for both.

science" that should not find its way to the jury. Judges have screening tools to keep unreliable expert testimony out of court.

The first screening tool appeared long ago in *Frye v. United States,* 293 F. 1013 (D.C. Cir. 1923). The court ruled that novel scientific evidence is not admissible until the underlying principle is generally accepted as reliable in the scientific community. *Frye* is called the general acceptance test. An attorney opposing expert testimony objects that the testimony is based on novel scientific principles, and the attorney requests a *Frye* hearing. If the judge grants the hearing, the sole issue at the hearing is whether the principle has achieved general acceptance. If the answer is no, expert testimony based on the principle is excluded. If the answer is yes, the testimony is admissible.

California is a *Frye* state. In California, the test is often called *Kelly* or *Kelly/Frye,* from *People v. Kelly,* 17 Cal. 3d 24, 549 P.2d 1240, 130 Cal. Rptr. 144 (1976). In California, *Kelly/Frye* applies to expert evidence that is based on a new scientific technique.[15] The proponent must persuade the judge that the technique is (1) Generally accepted as reliable by the scientific community, (2) The witness is qualified to discuss the technique, and (3) The person who used the technique did so properly.

In California, *Kelly/Frye* applies only to expert testimony based on new scientific techniques, particularly machines and procedures that analyze physical data. California courts have applied *Kelly/Frye* a horizontal gaze nystagmus test for intoxication, the polygraph, "truth serum," voiceprint analysis, and bite mark evidence. A California judge is likely to apply *Kelly/Frye* when a new technique, procedure, or device has features that can blindside, mislead, or over impress a jury.

It is not always easy to tell when a court will apply *Kelly/Frye.* For example, judges refused to apply the test to expert testimony on blood spatter evidence,[16] and to testimony describing why it is possible to tell on which side of a cell phone tower a particular phone was located at a particular time.[17]

Kelly/Frye applies to novel techniques, machines, and procedures. *Kelly/Frye* does not apply to expert opinion. The reason is that jurors may be overawed by a scientific machine that purports to provide definitive answers to complex questions. Jurors

---

[15]   *See* People v. Jackson, 1 Cal. 5th 269, 376 P.3d 528, 205 Cal. Rptr. 3d 386 (2016).

[16]   People v. Clark, 5 Cal. 4th 950, 857 P.2d 1099, 22 Cal. Rptr. 2d 689 (1993).

[17]   People v. Garlinger, 247 Cal. App. 4th 1185, 203 Cal. Rptr. 3d 171 (2016).

are not likely to be swept away by an expert's opinion, especially when the expert is effectively cross-examined.

In *Daubert v. Merrell Dow Pharmaceuticals, Inc.*, 509 U.S. 579, 113 S. Ct. 2786 (1993), the U.S. Supreme Court replaced *Frye* for the federal courts with a more liberal test for novel scientific evidence.[18] Under *Daubert,* the judge considers all evidence shedding light on reliability, not just general acceptance. Thus, the judge considers whether the technique has been subjected to testing by the scientific method, whether there are standards governing use of the technique, whether the technique has a known error rate, and whether the technique has been described in peer reviewed literature. In addition, the judge determines whether the technique has reached the level of general acceptance (*Frye*). Under *Daubert*, the judge is the gatekeeper of all scientific evidence. When objection is made that particular evidence may be unreliable, the judge may conduct a *Daubert* hearing, which is similar to a *Frye* hearing.

---

[18]   *Frye* is a conservative test because it excludes scientific evidence until the evidence reaches the level of general acceptance. *Daubert* is more liberal because scientific evidence that does not pass muster under *Frye* may be admissible under *Daubert*. For example, a scientific principle or device that has not quite achieved general acceptance is inadmissible under *Frye*, but might be sufficiently reliable for *Daubert*.

Chapter 10

CROSS-EXAMINATION, IMPEACHMENT AND REHABILITATION OF WITNESSES

When you watch trials on TV, much of the drama is on cross-examination. In real courtrooms, there are fewer theatrics, but the importance of cross-examination cannot be denied. This chapter introduces you to the rules governing cross-examination and impeachment of witnesses.

§ 10.1   Direct, Cross, and Redirect Examination

Testimony begins with direct examination by the party offering the witness's testimony. During direct examination, the attorney is not supposed to use leading questions, except for questions on preliminary matters like the witness's name, address, occupation, etc. The substance of a witness's testimony comes in response to non-leading questions. The rules on leading questions follow:

> **FRE 611(c). Leading Questions**. Leading questions should not be used on direct examination except as necessary to develop the witness's testimony.

> **CEC § 764. Leading Question**. A "leading question" is a question that suggests to the witness the answer that the examining party desires.

> **CEC § 767. Leading Questions**. (a) Except under special circumstances where the interests of justice otherwise require: (1) A leading question may not be asked of a witness on direct or redirect examination.

Direct examination is followed by cross-examination, during which the attorney may ask leading questions. FRE 611(c) and CEC § 767(a)(2) provide that leading questions are allowed on cross-examination.

Cross-examination is followed by re-direct examination. During re-direct, the witness can explain issues brought up by the cross-examiner. Re-direct can be described with three words: Repair the damage.[1]

Not all cross-examination involves an effort to undermine a witness. In what may be called "positive" cross-examination, a cross-examiner seeks, in a cooperative way, to clarify issues discussed on direct exam. The positive cross-examiner endeavors, in a non-confrontational manner, to bring out facts that favor the attorney's client.

When a cross-examiner believes it is necessary to undermine a witness's credibility, the process is called impeachment. The rules provide:

> **FRE 607. Who May Impeach a Witness**. Any party, including the party that called the witness, may attack the witness's credibility.

> **CEC § 785. Parties May Attack or Support Credibility**. The credibility of a witness may be attacked or supported by any party, including the party calling him.

Cross-examination is the linchpin of impeachment. The right of cross-examination is guaranteed by the FRE and CEC. In addition, in criminal cases, the defendant's right to cross-examine prosecution witnesses is protected by the Confrontation Clause of the Sixth Amendment.[2] This is not to say that a defendant's right to cross-examine is limitless. The trial judge has authority to curtail cross-examination that is unnecessarily embarrassing, harassing, wasteful of the court's time, or tangential to the issues (FRE 611(a); CEC § 765).[3]

§ 10.2 Demeanor

A witness' demeanor while testifying is an intangible that can be difficult to put into words, but there is no denying its importance. Jurors study witnesses to determine whether to believe them. The FRE do not contain a rule on demeanor evidence. CEC § 780(a) provides, "The court or jury may consider in determining the credibility of a witness . . . his demeanor while testifying and the

---

[1]   CEC § 772(a) provides, "The examination of a witness shall proceed in the following phases: direct examination, cross-examination, redirect examination, recross-examination, and continuing thereafter by redirect and recross-examination."

[2]   In civil litigation, the Due Process Clause of the Fourteenth Amendment protects the right to cross-examination. The due process right to cross-examine is not as strong as the Confrontation Clause guarantee.

[3]   *See* People v. Sanchez, 63 Cal. 4th 411, 450–451, 375 P.3d 812, 204 Cal. Rptr. 3d 682 (2016)("The trial court retains wide latitude to restrict repetitive, prejudicial, confusing, or marginally relevant cross-examination.").

manner in which he testifies." Regarding demeanor evidence, there is no difference between trials under the FRE and the CEC.

§ 10.3   Impeachment Techniques

Eight impeachment techniques are addressed in this chapter: (1) Prior inconsistent statements; (2) Contradiction; (3) Conviction; (4) A character witness to impeach; (5) Specific instances of untruthfulness; (6) Bias; (7) Defects in capacity or opportunity to observe; and (8) Impeachment *of* a character witness.

With each impeachment technique, you should be prepared on an exam to explain: (1) How the technique affects credibility—the theory of impeachment; (2) The mechanics of the technique; and (3) Whether extrinsic evidence can be admitted if the witness denies the impeachment.

The word extrinsic means "coming or operating from outside." Extrinsic evidence is evidence *other than* words spoken by a witness on the witness stand. Typically, extrinsic evidence is another witness or a document. Consider an example: Abe testifies that the traffic light was red. The cross-examiner asks, "Abe, not long after the accident, when you were discussing the accident with your friend Samantha, at Samantha's house, you said, 'The light was green,' didn't you?" This is impeachment with a prior inconsistent statement. If Abe admits the statement to Samantha, impeachment is complete. However, what if Abe says, "That's not true. I never said any such thing." Abe denies the impeaching statement. The question then becomes, may the cross-examiner offer testimony from Samantha—extrinsic evidence—that Abe made the statement to her? Another example: Juan testifies for the plaintiff in a civil case. The cross-examiner asks, "Juan, isn't it a fact that the plaintiff is your employer?" The cross-examiner is seeking to establish bias. If Juan says, "Yes, that's true," impeachment is complete. If Juan denies the plaintiff is his employer, will the cross-examiner be allowed to offer extrinsic evidence of the employment relationship? Each impeachment technique has its own rules regarding the admissibility of extrinsic evidence when a witness denies an impeaching fact.

When a party—including the defendant in a criminal case—testifies, the party is a witness, and is subject to impeachment.[4]

---

[4]   *See* People v. Wagner, 13 Cal. 3d 612, 618, 532 P.2d 105, 119 Cal. Rptr. 457 (1975) ("When a defendant testifies in his own behalf, his character *as a witness* may be impeached in the same manner as any other witness.").

§ 10.4   Prior Inconsistent Statement

A witness may be impeached with an out-of-court statement that is inconsistent with the witness's testimony at trial. The theory is simple: The witness is inconsistent, making it difficult to believe anything the witness says. The rules provide:

> **FRE 607. Who May Impeach a Witness**. Any party, including the party that called the witness, may attack the witness's credibility.

> **FRE 613. Witness's Prior Statement. (a) Showing or Disclosing the Statement During Examination**. When examining a witness about the witness's prior statement, the party need not show it or disclose its contents to the witness. But the party must, on request, show it or disclose its contents to an adverse party's attorney. **(b) Extrinsic Evidence of a Prior Inconsistent Statement**. Extrinsic evidence of a witness's prior inconsistent statement is admissible only if the witness is given an opportunity to explain or deny the statement and an adverse party is given an opportunity to examine the witness about it, or if justice so requires. This subdivision (b) does not apply to an opposing party's statement under Rule 801(d)(2). [Rule 801(d)(2) defines party admissions].

> **FRE 801(d)(1)(A). Statements That Are Not Hearsay**. A statement that meets the following conditions is not hearsay: (1) The declarant testifies and is subject to cross-examination about a prior statement, and the statement: (A) is inconsistent with the declarant's testimony and was given under penalty of perjury at a trial, hearing, or other proceeding or in a deposition.

> **CEC § 769. Inconsistent Statement or Conduct**. In examining a witness concerning a statement or other conduct by him that is inconsistent with any part of his testimony at the hearing, it is not necessary to disclose to him any information concerning the statement or other conduct.

> **CEC § 770. Evidence of Inconsistent Statement of Witness**. Unless the interests of justice otherwise require, extrinsic evidence of a statement made by a witness that is inconsistent with any part of his testimony at the hearing shall be excluded unless: (a) The witness was so examined while testifying as to give him an opportunity to explain or

to deny the statement; or (b) The witness has not been excused from giving further testimony in the action.

CEC § 780(h). Testimony; Proof of Truthfulness; Considerations. Except as otherwise provided by statute, the court or jury may consider in determining the credibility of a witness any matter that has any tendency in reason to prove or disprove the truthfulness of his testimony at the hearing, including but not limited to any of the following: (h) A statement made by him that is inconsistent with any part of his testimony at the hearing.

CEC § 1235. Inconsistent Statements. Evidence of a statement made by a witness is not made inadmissible by the hearsay rule if the statement is inconsistent with his testimony at the hearing and is offered in compliance with section 770.

§ 10.4(a).   Foundation

By long tradition, before a witness can be impeached with a prior inconsistent statement, the impeaching attorney asks four foundation questions: (1) When was the prior statement made? (2) Who was present? (3) Where was the statement made? and (4) What was the subject matter of the statement? The FRE and CEC do not require the traditional foundation, but many attorneys and judges adhere to it.

§ 10.4(b).   Rule in the Queen's Case

If a prior inconsistent statement was in writing, the practice before enactment of the FRE and the CEC required the cross-examiner to hand the document to the witness, and give the witness an opportunity to read the document, *before* asking the witness about the inconsistency. This requirement was called the rule in the Queen's Case, or the rule in Queen Caroline's case. The FRE and CEC abolish this requirement. FRE 613(a) states, "When examining a witness about the witness's prior statement, the party need not show it or disclose its contents to the witness." CEC § 769 is to the same effect.

§ 10.4(c).   Extrinsic Evidence of Prior Inconsistent Statement

When a witness is asked about a prior inconsistent statement, the witness admits or denies the statement. If she admits it, impeachment is complete, and the cross-examiner moves onto to something else. If the witness denies the prior statement, the cross-examiner can accept the denial or offer extrinsic evidence to prove the inconsistent statement. The extrinsic evidence could be a document containing the inconsistent statement, or testimony from a witness who heard the inconsistent statement. If the prior inconsistent statement is in writing, the judge generally allows the cross-examiner to confront the witness with the statement and, if the statement is admissible, to admit the statement during the cross-examination.[5] If the extrinsic evidence is another witness, the cross-examiner typically is not allowed to interrupt the opponent's case to offer the witness. Rather, the cross-examiner waits until it is her turn to offer witnesses, and offers the extrinsic evidence witness at that time.

When the extrinsic impeachment evidence is a witness, an issue of trial management arises. It takes time to offer testimony from witnesses. Is it worth taking valuable trial time to listen to a witness whose only purpose is impeachment? This question raises the so-called collateral fact rule, discussed in Section 10.12.

FRE 613(b) and CEC § 770 require that a witness have an opportunity to respond to extrinsic evidence of a prior inconsistent statement. The response can occur while the witness is still on the witness stand, or the witness can be recalled for further testimony.[6]

§ 10.4(d).   Prior Inconsistent Statement as Hearsay

A prior inconsistent statement may be offered for two purposes: first, to impeach and, second, to prove the truth of the prior statement. When a prior inconsistent statement is offered for both purposes, the statement is hearsay. Hearsay is an out of court statement—in this case, a prior inconsistent statement—offered to prove the truth of the matter asserted. Hearsay is inadmissible unless it meets the requirements of an exception to the rule against hearsay.

---

[5]   At trial, the parties generally introduce evidence during their case-in-chief, rather than during the opponent's case-in-chief. When impeaching with a document, the judge may allow the cross-examiner to offer the document into evidence during the cross-examination. This approach is logical, saves time, and avoids confusion.

[6]   When a witness finishes testifying, it is customary for the judge to ask counsel whether the witness is excused from further testimony, or whether the witness may be recalled for further testimony. If the witness is excused from further testimony, the judge would have to give permission for the witness to be recalled. If a witness has been excused, it is generally improper, at that stage, to offer the witness's prior inconsistent statement. CEC § 770(b) specifically refers to this situation when the rule states, "The witness has not been excused from giving further testimony in the action." The result is the same under the FRE. In both sets of rules, the judge has discretion. The judge might say, "You should have offered the prior inconsistent statement before I excused the witness. Your effort comes too late." If the witness's testimony is particularly important, the judge may order the party wishing to impeach to issue a fresh subpoena for the witness.

If the prior inconsistent statement does not meet the requirements of an exception to the hearsay rule, the statement is not admissible to prove the truth of the statement, but the statement *is* admissible for the limited purpose of impeaching the witness with the inconsistency.

The CEC has a hearsay exception for all prior inconsistent statements, CEC § 1235. Thus, in California, prior inconsistent statements are admissible to impeach *and* for the truth of the matter asserted.

The FRE is more complicated. Under the FRE, you can always use a prior inconsistent statement for the limited purpose of impeachment. However, only some prior inconsistent statements are admissible to impeach *and* to prove the truth of the matter asserted. FRE 801(d)(1)(A) provides that a prior inconsistent statement is admissible for the truth of the matter asserted only if the statement "was given under penalty of perjury at a trial, hearing, or other proceeding or in a deposition."

Consider the example which appeared in § 10.3: Abe testifies that a traffic light was red. The cross-examiner asks, "Abe, not long after the accident, when you were discussing the accident with your friend Samantha, at Samantha's house, you said, 'The light was green,' didn't you?"[7] Under the CEC and the FRE, Abe's prior inconsistent statement is admissible to impeach Abe. In California, Abe's out-of-court statement is also admissible to prove the color of the light, pursuant to Section 1235. If the trial occurred in federal court, Abe's statement would be admissible to impeach, but not for the truth of the matter asserted because the statement was not under oath, subject to the penalty of perjury.

Another example: Dell is charged with armed robbery. The robber drove a brown Toyota Prius. At Dell's preliminary hearing, Dell's cousin, Mary, testified for the prosecution as follows: "On the day of the robbery, I loaned my brown Toyota Prius to Dell for the day." At trial, Mary is called as a witness by the prosecution. The prosecutor asks, "On the day of the robbery, what did you do with your car?" Mary answers, "My car was in the garage all day that day." The prosecutor asks the judge for permission to ask leading questions of Mary.[8] The judge gives permission, and the prosecutor asks, "At the preliminary hearing, you testified that on the day of

---

[7] Note that these questions satisfy the foundation to impeach with a prior inconsistent statement.

[8] This is direct examination, and normally, leading is not allowed on direct exam. However, it appears that Mary is not cooperating with the prosecutor. When this happens, it is common for an attorney to ask the judge's permission to lead on direct because the witness is hostile.

the robbery, you loaned your brown Toyota Prius to Dell, didn't you?" This question is proper to impeach Mary with her prior inconsistent statement. Is Mary's prior statement admissible for the truth of the matter asserted? In California, the answer is yes, under Section 1235. Under the FRE, the answer is yes, under Rule 801(d)(1)(A), because Mary's prior statement was under oath at the preliminary hearing.

Change the facts. Mary's earlier statement was not at a court hearing. Rather Mary was talking to her friend when Mary said, "On the day of the robbery, I loaned my brown Toyota Prius to Dell for the day." May the prosecutor impeach Mary with her out-of-court statement? Yes. May the prosecutor also offer the out-of-court statement to prove that Dell had the Prius that day, that is, for the truth of the matter asserted? Yes, under CEC, Section 1235. No, under FRE 801(d)(1)(A), because Mary's statement to her friend was not under oath, subject to perjury.

The difference between the CEC and the FRE regarding admissibility of prior inconsistent statements for the truth of the matter asserted is tested by evidence professors. Be on the lookout for it.

§ 10.5 Contradiction

With contradiction, the cross-examiner tries to get the witness to change some aspect of her testimony. If the witness contradicts herself, the contradiction raises questions about the witness's testimony. The FRE does not have a specific rule on contradiction. The technique is authorized by Rule 607, which provides, "Any party, including the party that called the witness, may attack the witness's credibility." The CEC does have a rule, Section 780(i), which allows impeachment by proof of "the existence or nonexistence of any fact testified to by him."

Suppose Sue testifies the light was red. The cross-examiner asks, "Isn't it possible the light was yellow, rather than red?" If Sue agrees, then Sue contradicts herself. If Sue sticks to her story, and answers, "No, the light was red," then the effort to contradict fails, and the question becomes, will the cross-examiner be allowed to offer extrinsic evidence to prove that the light was yellow? See § 10.12 for the answer.

It is easy to confuse impeachment by prior inconsistent statement with impeachment by contradiction. To keep them separate, remember that impeachment with a prior inconsistent statement *requires a prior statement*. With contradiction, no prior statement is involved. Which type of impeachment is involved in the following example? Rachel testifies as an alibi witness for Randy, who is accused of robbing a bank, "I was with Randy at the museum of modern art at the time the bank was robbed." On cross-examination, the prosecutor asks, "Rachel, isn't it true that on the day after the bank robbery, you told your aunt, 'Yesterday, I went by myself to the museum of modern art.'?" Contradiction or prior inconsistent statement? Change the cross-examination to the following, "Rachel, isn't it a fact that on the day of the robbery, you went to the museum all by yourself?" Contradiction or prior inconsistent statement?

Practice Exam: Which Is Which? With the difference in mind between prior inconsistent statements and contradiction, consider the following exam question:

> Ann, Beth, and Charlene devised a plan to rob a bank. Ann's job was to be the getaway driver. Beth and Charlene entered the bank with guns and announced, "This is a robbery." Ann, Beth, and Charlene were caught and are on trial together, charged with bank robbery. **Call of the Question**: Discuss the evidence issues in the following paragraphs: (1) During the prosecution's case-in-chief, the prosecutor offers testimony from Bob, a teller at the bank. Bob testifies, "I was working at the bank when Beth and Charlene burst in with guns and said, 'This is a robbery.' Beth came to my teller window, stuck a gun in my face, and said, 'Put all the money in this bag, and no funny stuff.' " (2) On cross-examination of Bob, defense counsel asks, "Not long after the robbery, didn't you tell a police officer that you could not remember which robber came to your teller window?" (3) On further cross-examination of Bob, defense counsel asks, "Isn't it possible that the robber who came to your window was not Beth, but was someone who looked like Beth?"

> You might want to outline an answer under the FRE and the CEC.

§ 10.6   Conviction

Would you believe a liar? Someone with a penchant for lying is more likely to lie on the witness stand than a person who seldom strays from the truth. The FRE and the CEC allow evidence that a witness has a character for untruthfulness. Three impeachment techniques are employed to prove this character flaw: (1) Impeachment by conviction, (2) Impeachment with specific instances of the witness's untruthfulness, and (3) A character witness who testifies that the witness is untruthful. Each technique is based on the same theory: An untruthful person is likely to act in conformity with their character as a liar, and lie on the witness stand. Impeachment by conviction is addressed in this section. Impeachment with specific instances of untruthfulness in discussed in § 10.7. Impeachment with a character witness is analyzed in § 10.9. The rules governing impeachment by conviction follow:

Rule 609. Impeachment by Evidence of a Criminal Conviction. (a) In General. The following rules apply to attacking a witness's character for truthfulness by evidence of a criminal conviction: (1) for a crime that, in the convicting jurisdiction, was punishable by death or by imprisonment for more than one year, the evidence: (A) must be admitted, subject to Rule 403, in a civil case or in a criminal case in which the witness is not a defendant; and (B) must be admitted in a criminal case in which the witness is a defendant, if the probative value of the evidence outweighs its prejudicial effect to that defendant; and (2) for any crime regardless of the punishment, the evidence must be admitted if the court can reasonably determine that establishing the elements of the crime requires proving—or the witness's admitting—a dishonest act or false statement.[9]

CEC § 788. Conviction of a Witness for a Crime. For the purpose of attacking the credibility of a witness, it may be shown by the examination of the witness or by the record of the judgment that he has been convicted of a felony . . . .

---

[9]   FRE 609(b) states that convictions more than ten years old are not admissible because the issue is the witness's credibility *today,* and a conviction more than a decade old is generally not relevant to credibility *now.* The rule allows the proponent of the old conviction to attempt to persuade the judge that the conviction is still relevant to impeach. The CEC has no counterpart to the FRE's ten year rule, although a California judge could well reach the same conclusion using Section 352, by concluding that any probative value of the old conviction is substantially outweighed by the danger of unfair prejudice, especially if the witness being impeached is the defendant.

FRE 609(c) provides that a conviction is not admissible to impeach if "the conviction has been the subject of a pardon, annulment, certificate of rehabilitation, or other equivalent procedure based on a finding that the person has been rehabilitated . . ., or a finding has been made that the person was innocent."

CEC § 788(a) through (d) contain similar limits on use of convictions. The limits in Section 788 apply only in civil cases due to Prop. 8, which provides that any felony conviction can be used to impeach. The limits in Section 788 are good law in civil cases because Prop. 8 has no application in civil litigation.

FRE 609(d) places limits of use to impeach of juvenile court adjudications of delinquency.

FRE 609(e) provides that a conviction can be used to impeach while the conviction is on appeal.

Prop. 8. Cal. Const. Art. I, § 28(f)(4). Any prior felony conviction of any person in any criminal proceeding, whether adult or juvenile, shall subsequently be used without limitation for purposes of impeachment or enhancement of sentence in any criminal proceeding. . . .

The theory of impeachment by conviction is the same under the CEC and the FRE: Liars lie. However, there are important differences between the FRE and the CEC.

§ 10.6(a).   Impeachment by Conviction—FRE 609

Rule 609(a)(2) allows impeachment with conviction of so-called *crimen falsi* crimes, that is, crimes that involve false statement, deceit, or lying. Examples of *crimen falsi* crimes include perjury, fraud, embezzlement, and false pretenses. A Rule 609(a)(2) conviction is admissible whether the crime was a felony or a misdemeanor.[10] As well, when a conviction falls within 609(a)(2), the conviction is admissible without balancing the probative value of the conviction against the danger of unfair prejudice.[11]

If a conviction does not satisfy 609(a)(2) because the crime was not *crimen falsi*, then attention shifts to 609(a)(1). Rule 609(a)(1) deals with felonies.[12] A misdemeanor conviction is not admissible under 609(a)(1). When a felony conviction falls within 609(a)(1), it is necessary to balance to the probative value of the conviction for purposes of impeachment against the danger of unfair prejudice.

If the witness being impeached is *not* the defendant in a criminal case, then a "regular" Rule 403 balancing is performed (FRE 609(a)(1)(A)). The conviction is admissible to impeach unless the probative value of the conviction to impeach is substantially outweighed by the danger of unfair prejudice to a party, usually the defendant. The Rule does not concern itself with prejudice to the witness. The Rule is concerned with prejudice to a party.

If the witness being impeached under 609(a)(1) is the defendant in a criminal case, the judge balances the probative value of the conviction to impeach against the danger of unfair prejudice to the defendant. However, when the witness to be impeached is the defendant, the court does *not* do "regular" Rule 403 balancing (Rule 609(a)(1)(B)). When the witness is the defendant, Rule 609(a)(1) is structured to protect the defendant from impeachment with

---

[10]   The language "for any crime regardless of punishment" signifies that felonies and misdemeanors are admissible under FRE 609(a)(2).

[11]   The ten years is too long provision of Rule 609(b) applies to convictions admissible under 609(a)(2).

[12]   The words "punishable by death or by imprisonment for more than one year" signify that 609(a)(1) applies only felonies.

convictions that are only marginally valuable to impeach. A conviction that would survive 403 balancing with a witness other than the defendant often fails to survive the protective balancing afforded defendants who testify.

§ 10.6(b).   Exam Questions on FRE 609

When you see impeachment by conviction on an exam, it is a good idea to with begin your analysis with 609(a)(2). If the crime is *crimen falsi*, it is automatically admissible to impeach, and no 403-type balancing occurs. This is true even when the witness is the defendant. To repeat, if the witness—including a defendant who testifies—was convicted of a 609(a)(2), *crimen falsi* crime, do not balance the probative value of the conviction against the danger of unfair prejudice. Such balancing occurs under FRE 609(a)(1), *not* FRE 609(a)(2).

Suppose you don't know whether a crime is *crimen falsi*? The professor may have deliberately picked a crime that was not discussed in class. The professor is looking for something like, "I do not know whether this crime is *crimen falsi*. A crime is *crimen falsi* when it involves lying, deceit, or untruthful statement. It is unclear whether the crime here is *crimen falsi*. If the court concludes the crime is *crimen falsi*, then the conviction is automatically admissible to impeach, and the probative value of the conviction is not balanced against the danger of unfair prejudice. On the other hand, if the judge concludes that the crime is not *crimen falsi*, then it must be a felony, and the judge balances the probative value of the conviction for purposes of impeachment against the danger of unfair prejudice." Professors generally want you to do the balancing, and reach a conclusion about whether or not the conviction can be used to impeach.

A common trap on exams consists of facts that tempt you to analyze Rule 609 when it doesn't apply. Here is how I set the trap for my students: Early in the exam question, the facts state that the defendant does not testify. Later, the exam states, "The prosecutor offers a three-year-old conviction of the defendant for perjury." Students who fall into the trap think, "Ah ha, Myers is testing on impeachment by conviction. This is a *crimen falsi* offense. I'll tell him about Rule 609. I got this!" No you don't. Only witnesses can be impeached, and the facts told you that the defendant did not testify, thus the defendant was not a witness. Any discussion of Rule 609 is wrong!

One more thing to watch for on exams. When a crime is not *crimen falsi*, it is necessary to balance the probative value of the conviction against the danger of unfair prejudice. It is common for students to misunderstand the nature of the probative value of convictions for purposes of impeachment. Consider this example: Dell is charged with murder. Dell testifies and offers an alibi. The prosecutor wishes to impeach Dell with a prior conviction for murder. Murder is not *crimen falsi*. Thus, the probative value of the conviction for purposes of impeachment must be balanced against the danger of unfair prejudice. Does the earlier conviction have high or low probative value? Answer: low, very low. Remember, the theory of impeachment by conviction is that a conviction tells us something about a person's truthfulness. Murder has to do with violence, not truthfulness. Crimes of violence typically have low probative value for purposes of impeachment. The mistake students make is thinking that the greater the similarity between the conviction and the current crime, the higher the probative value of the conviction. Under this mistaken reasoning, a conviction for murder has high probative value because the defendant is charged with murder. In fact, the similarity of the conviction and the charged crime has no bearing on the probative value of the conviction to impeach. What *is* important is the relation of the conviction to truthfulness; not the similarity of the conviction to the charged crime. In Dell's case, the murder conviction says little about Dell's truthfulness, but it speaks volumes about Dell's character for violence. There is a high probability that if the judge admits the murder conviction to impeach Dell, the jury will misuse the conviction as *substantive evidence* of Dell's guilt because he is a violent man. Such use violates the rule against character evidence (FRE 404(a)(1); CEC § 1101(a)). So, here is the take away message: When the conviction is similar to the charged crime, do not assume high probative value of the conviction to impeach. Assume instead a high degree of prejudice. The prejudice is the likelihood the jury will use the earlier crime as evidence the defendant is a bad person, and, because he is bad, he committed the charged offense.

§ 10.6(c).   How to Impeach with a Conviction

The rules governing impeachment by conviction are complex. Actual impeachment is simple. Just ask the witness, "Sir, is it not a fact that two years ago, in this county, you were convicted of fraud?" That's it! If the witness admits it, move on. But what if the witness denies the conviction? When you know in advance that you are probably going to impeach a witness with a conviction, get a certified copy of the judgment of conviction. Have the certified copy ready in case the witness denies the conviction. After the denial, hand a copy of the conviction to opposing counsel. Then ask the judge's permission to approach the witness. By the way, you *always* ask the judge's permission to approach a witness, even your

witness. While we are on the subject, don't cross the well of the
court—the area that separates counsel table from the bench—
without asking permission.[13] Hand the certified copy of the
judgment of conviction to the witness and ask the witness to read it.
Then say, "Have you had all the time you need to read the
document? I ask you again, sir, is it not a fact that two years ago, in
this county, you were convicted of fraud." When the witness knows
you have him over a barrel, he may admit it. If the witness persists
in denial, have the conviction marked as an exhibit, and offer it into
evidence as proof of the conviction.[14] The conviction is extrinsic
evidence, but extrinsic evidence of conviction is admissible when a
witness denies the conviction. If opposing counsel objects based on
authentication, best evidence rule, and hearsay, you need to be
ready. The fact that the judgement is certified will make it self-
authenticating (FRE 902). The best evidence rule is satisfied
because the judgment is a duplicate (FRE 1003). The judgment is
hearsay, but there is a hearsay exception specifically for judgments
(FRE 803(22)).

§ 10.6(d).   Not the Gory Details

When impeaching with a conviction, it is proper for the cross-
examiner to ask the name of the crime, the date and place of
conviction, and the punishment. The cross-examiner may not go
into the factual details of the underlying crime. This is true under
the FRE and the CEC.

§ 10.6(e).   The *Luce* Rule

As defense counsel prepares for a criminal trial, a vital
consideration is whether the defendant will testify. If the defendant
has prior convictions, defense counsel typically files a motion before
trial—an *in limine* motion—asking the trial judge to rule that if the
defendant testifies, the prosecution may not impeach with the
defendant's convictions. If the judge grants the motion, it is safer for
the defendant to testify. If the judge denies the motion, and rules
that the prosecutor may use some or all of defendant's convictions,
the defendant may decide against testifying. If a defendant who
does not testify is convicted, the defendant would like to complain
on appeal that the trial judge erred in ruling that the prosecutor
could use the convictions. In *Luce v. United States*, 469 U.S. 38, 105
S. Ct. 460 (1984), the Supreme Court ruled "that to raise and
preserve for review [on appeal] the claim of improper impeachment

---

[13]   Of course, if you have permission to approach a witness, then you also have
permission to cross the well.

[14]   This is one of the times when it is proper to offer evidence during your
opponent's case.

with a prior conviction, a defendant must testify." Failure to testify waives any argument that the trial judge erred. California follows the *Luce* rule.[15]

§ 10.6(f).   Impeachment Under CEC § 788

CEC § 788 seems simple; a witness can be impeached by asking if the witness has been convicted of a felony. But that's where simplicity ends. Over the years, California courts interpreted Section 788 to exclude more and more felonies from the list of felonies that could be used to impeach. Eventually, only *crimen falsi* felonies were allowed. Prosecutors did not like the judicial narrowing of Section 788, and, in 1982, prosecutors succeeded in winning voter approval for Prop. 8, the relevant part of which reads, "Any prior felony conviction of any person in any criminal proceeding, whether adult or juvenile, shall subsequently be used without limitation for purposes of impeachment . . . in any criminal proceeding." Well, that seems clear, doesn't it? "Any" felony means any felony, right? Not so fast. In *People v. Castro*, 38 Cal. 3d 301, 696 P.2d 111, 211 Cal. Rptr. 719 (1985), the Supreme Court ruled that despite the clear language of Prop. 8, trial judges can balance the probative value of any felony conviction against the danger of unfair prejudice, and disallow impeachment when probative value is substantially outweighed by the risk of unfair prejudice (CEC § 352).[16] *Castro* also held that due process limits felonies that can be used to impeach to felonies that are *crimen falsi* or that involve moral turpitude. Moral turpitude is readiness to do evil.[17] The Supreme Court ruled that distribution of heroin can be used to impeach. Although drug dealing is not *crimen falsi,* drug dealing involves moral turpitude. On the other hand, possession of drugs for personal use involves neither *crimen falsi* nor moral turpitude, and cannot be used to impeach.

The CEC does not allow impeachment with a misdemeanor. However, another part of Prop. 8 provides that all relevant evidence is admissible. As a result, in criminal cases, while the misdemeanor conviction itself remains inadmissible hearsay,[18] the underlying

---

[15] People v. Collins, 42 Cal. 3d 378, 722 P.2d 173, 228 Cal. Rptr. 899 (1986); People v. Sanghera, 6 Cal. App. 5th 365, 211 Cal. Rptr. 3d 382 (2016).

[16] When conducting Section 352 balancing, the judge considers the degree to which the crime is related to honesty, how old the conviction is—the older it is, the less it tells us about the witness's credibility today—and, when the witness is the defendant, the similarity of the prior crime to the crime now on trial.

[17] People v. Aguilar, 245 Cal. App. 4th 1010, 200 Cal. Rptr. 3d 202, 208 (2016). To determine whether a crime involves moral turpitude, the judge does not consider the facts of the case. The judge determines whether the elements of the conviction necessarily involve moral turpitude.

[18] People v. Wheeler, 4 Cal. 4th 284, 288, 841 P.2d 938, 14 Cal. Rptr. 2d 418 (1992).

criminal conduct can be used to impeach, provided the conduct involves *crimen falsi* conduct or moral turpitude. In *People v. Wheeler*, 4 Cal. 4th 284, 296–297, 841 P.2d 938, 14 Cal. Rptr. 2d 418 (1992), the Supreme Court noted, "In general, a misdemeanor—or any other conduct not amounting to a felony—is a less forceful indicator of immoral character or dishonesty than is a felony. Moreover, impeachment evidence other than felony convictions entails problems of proof, unfair surprise, and moral turpitude evaluation which felony convictions do not present. Hence, courts may and should consider with particular care whether the admission of such evidence might involve undue time, confusion, or prejudice which outweighs its probative value."

Do the following offenses involve moral turpitude? Disturbing the peace? No. Prostitution? Yes. Burglary? Yes. Theft? Yes. Carrying a concealed firearm in a vehicle? Yes.

You can impeach with a conviction, but not an arrest. In *People v. Medina*, 11 Cal. 4th 694, 769, 906 P.2d 2, 47 Cal. Rptr. 2d 165 (1995), the Supreme Court wrote, "[M]ere arrests are usually inadmissible, whether as proof of guilt or impeachment."

§ 10.7 Impeachment with Specific Acts

Under the FRE, a witness can be impeached by asking the witness about specific instances of the witness's conduct. Because the rules on this technique differ in the FRE and the CEC, it is useful to discuss the rules in separate sections.

§ 10.7(a).   FRE 608(b)—Specific Instances of Untruthfulness

Under FRE 608(b), a witness can be impeached by asking the witness about specific instances of the witness's untruthful conduct. The theory is the same as the theory of impeachment by conviction. A liar is likely to lie on the witness stand. Thus, impeachment under FRE 608(b) *is* character evidence, but it is allowed by FRE 404(a)(3). An example of FRE 608(b) impeachment is, "Mr. Witness, is it not a fact that two months ago, you lied on an employment application?" If the witness admits the lie, impeachment is complete. If the witness denies it, STOP! The cross-examiner cannot offer extrinsic evidence to prove the witness lied on the application. The cross-examiner must "take the witness's answer," even if the denial is itself a lie! Rule 608(b) states:

FRE 608(b). Specific Instances of Conduct. Except for a criminal conviction under Rule 609, extrinsic evidence is not admissible[19] to prove specific instances of a witness's conduct in order to attack or support[20] the witness's character for truthfulness. But the court may, on cross-examination, allow them to be inquired into if they are probative of the character for truthfulness or untruthfulness of: (1) the witness . . . .

§ 10.7(b).   Impeachment with Specific Instances in California

Federal courts and most states have the FRE, including Rule 608(b), which allows impeachment with specific instances of a witness's untruthfulness. California is among the minority of states that do not permit this impeachment technique. CEC § 787 provides that "evidence of specific instances of his conduct relevant only as tending to prove a trait of his character is inadmissible to attack or support the credibility of a witness."

In California civil litigation, it is not permissible to impeach a witness by asking about specific instances of the witness's conduct, including untruthful acts, to prove a character flaw regarding truthfulness. It is permissible, however, to ask about specific instances for other purposes. Thus, to prove bias, a witness may be asked, "Isn't it true that you started living with the plaintiff two weeks ago?" A witness may be asked about a specific prior inconsistent statement. The limitation imposed by Section 787 applies to impeachment *of character*.

Prop. 8 supersedes Section 787 in criminal cases.[21] Thus, in criminal cases, it is proper to impeach a witness by asking the witness about specific instances of the witness's untruthfulness. That's not all. The cross-examiner may ask not only about lying, but also about specific instances of conduct that involve moral turpitude.[22] The judge can balance the probative value of the

---

[19]   When you use Rule 609 to impeach by conviction, if the witness denies the conviction, you *can* use extrinsic evidence in the form of a copy of the judgment of conviction. By contrast, when you use Rule 608(b) to impeach, by asking about a specific instance of the witness's untruthfulness, if the witness denies the specific instance, you *cannot* use extrinsic evidence to prove the specific instance. You must accept the witness's denial of the specific instance, even if the denial it itself a lie!

[20]   After a witness's truthfulness has been attacked, the witness can be rehabilitated. *See* § 10.14.

[21]   Prop. 8 provides, in part, that all relevant evidence is admissible, and this type of impeachment is relevant. In People v. Wheeler, 4 Cal. 4th 284, 291, 841 P.2d 938, 14 Cal. Rptr. 2d 418 (1992), the Supreme Court wrote, "We and the Court of Appeal have consistently held that in criminal proceedings, section 28(d) [Prop. 8] supersedes all California restrictions except those preserved or permitted by the express words of section 28(d) itself."

[22]   People v. Wheeler, 4 Cal. 4th 284, 295, 841 P.2d 938, 14 Cal. Rptr. 2d 418 (1992)("Misconduct involving moral turpitude may suggest a willingness to lie.").

impeachment against the danger of unfair prejudice to a party (CEC § 352).

What if a cross-examiner in a California criminal trial asks a witness about a specific instance of misconduct, but the witness denies it. Under FRE 608(b), the cross-examiner must take the witness's answer, and may not offer extrinsic evidence of the misconduct. Under the CEC, however, because of Prop. 8, it appears that the cross-examiner does not have to take the witness's answer, but may offer extrinsic evidence, subject to the judge's authority to exclude the evidence under Section 352.[23]

§ 10.8   Bias, Memory, Capacity to Observe

A cross-examiner can inquire about possible bias (FRE 607; CEC § 780(f), (j)). A common example occurs in criminal cases, where multiple people commit a crime, and one of them testifies for the prosecution in exchange for lenience. Defense counsel asks, "Isn't it true that the prosecution dismissed the charges against you in exchange for your testimony?" If a witness denies bias, the cross-examiner may offer extrinsic evidence to prove the bias, subject to the court's discretion to exclude the extrinsic proof under FRE 403/CEC § 352.

A witness's memory can be challenged, as can the witness's opportunity to observe what occurred. Thus, a cross-examiner could ask, "Isn't it true that it was a dark and stormy night?" "There are no streetlights at that intersection, are there?" "There was no moon, was there?" "You were more than 200 yards from the intersection, isn't that right?"

§ 10.9   Impeach with a Character Witness

There is an impeachment tool that is not very powerful, and that you probably won't use in practice, but that is available, so you need to understand it. You can impeach a witness with another witness—a character witness. The character witness testifies that the first witness—the witness to be impeached—is a liar. FRE 608(a) provides: "A witness's credibility may be attacked . . . by testimony about the witness's reputation for having a character for . . . untruthfulness, or by testimony in the form of an opinion about that character."

The proponent of the FRE 608(a) character witness begins by laying the necessary foundation. The character witness either knows the reputation of the witness to be impeached for lying, or

---

[23]   *See* Miguel A. Mendez, The Victims' Bill of Rights—Thirty Years Under Proposition 8, 25 Stanford Law and Policy Review 379, 393 (2014).

the character witness has an opinion about the untruthfulness of the witness to be impeached. Having qualified to testify as a character witness, the testimony of a reputation character witness looks like this:

Q: What is the witness's reputation in the community for truthfulness?

A: It is bad. [or] The witness has a reputation as a liar.

If the character witness testifies in the form of opinion, the testimony goes:

Q: Do you have an opinion about the witness's truthfulness?

A: Yes.

Q: What is your opinion?

A: In my opinion, the witness is a liar. [Or] In my opinion, the witness is not a truthful person.

Hardly dynamite, right? Remember, this is a character witness. A reputation character witness can't describe *why* the witness being impeached has a reputation as a liar. Nor can an opinion character witness disclose the basis for the opinion. Just, "He's a liar." That's all folks.

This mode of impeachment can be used in California.

§ 10.10 Impeach a Character Witness

Character witnesses testify about a criminal defendant's good character—The Mercy Rule. (§ 6.9). Character witnesses testify about a victim's violence when a criminal defendant claims self-defense (§ 6.12). Finally, character witnesses testify to impeach a witness's credibility. (§ 10.9).

A character witness can be impeached like any other witness.[24] In addition, there is an impeachment technique that applies only to character witnesses.[25] In order to determine whether a character witness really knows the person the character witness testified about, the cross-examiner asks the character witness about specific instances of the conduct of the person the character witness testified about. You remember John, who is accused of robbing the First Bank of Redding on August 1 (*See* § 2.6). The prosecutor has evidence that John robbed ten other banks, but John is not charged

---

[24] Thus, you could impeach a character witness with the character witness's own conviction, with the character witness's prior inconsistent statement, with the character witness's bias, etc.

[25] The leading case is *Michelson v. United States*, 335 U.S. 469, 69 S. Ct. 213 (1948).

with those robberies. John (unwisely) offers a character witness to testify to John's character as a non-violent, law abiding person (FRE 404(a)(2)(A); CEC § 1102). On cross-examination of John's character witness, the prosecutor asks, "Mr. character witness, did you know that John robbed ten other banks?" This question is permitted by FRE 405(a), which states, "On cross-examination of the character witness, the court may allow an inquiry into relevant specific instances of the person's conduct." The CEC does not contain language that is equivalent to FRE 405(a), but this type of impeachment is allowed in California.[26]

What is the purpose of the prosecutor's question? The purpose is to test whether the character witness really knows John's character. The purpose is *not* to besmirch John's character.[27] The judge will instruct the jury that the question is not offered to prove that John actually robbed other banks. The question is asked only to test the character witness's knowledge of John. Yet, imagine the jury's reaction when they hear the question! "Ten other bank robberies!! Are you kidding me? John *must* be guilty of robbing the First Bank of Redding *because he's a bank robber!*" Such reasoning violates the rule against character evidence, of course, and is not allowed. The judge will instruct the jury not to consider the question as evidence of John's character or conduct, but will the instruction be effective? Could any instruction unring the bell? The jury has heard of the ten uncharged robberies. You might say, defense counsel should invoke FRE 403 or CEC § 352, and ask the judge to rule the prosecutor can't ask the question because there is too great a chance the jury will use the question as evidence of John's bad character. The judge is unlikely to oblige. After all, it was John who decided to offer evidence of his good character. If John didn't want his character witness to be impeached, John should not have offered the character witness. John invited the question.

When impeaching a character witness in this manner, the form of the question depends on the type of character witness. If the character witness offers an opinion, the proper cross-question is

---

[26]   *See* People v. Wagner, 13 Cal. 3d 612, 532 P.2d 105, 119 Cal. Rptr. 457 (1975); People v. Tuggles, 178 Cal. App. 4th 1106, 100 Cal. Rptr. 3d 820 (2009).

[27]   By the way, the prosecutor does not care how the character witness answers. This is a win-win-win for the prosecutor. If the character witness says, "No, I didn't know about any other robberies," then the jury will conclude the character witness is not well informed about John's character. If the character witness says, "Yes, I know John robbed ten other banks, but I still think he is a non-violent, law abiding person," the jury will discount the character witness's opinion because the character witness has, to say the least, an odd understanding of non-violence and obedience to law. Regardless of the character witness's answer, the jury heard about the other robberies, and the prosecutor doesn't mind that!

"Did you know?" If the character witness describes a person's reputation, the proper cross-question is "Have you heard?"

§ 10.11   Impeach Hearsay Declarant

A hearsay declarant who does not testify at trial cannot be cross-examined. Yet, when the declarant's hearsay is admitted, the absent declarant is very much a "witness." The rules of evidence allow the opponent to impeach a hearsay declarant's credibility. The rules state:

> **Rule 806. Attacking and Supporting the Declarant's Credibility**. When a hearsay statement—or a statement [by a party's agent, employee, or co-conspirator]—has been admitted in evidence, the declarant's credibility may be attacked, and then supported, by any evidence that would be admissible for those purposes if the declarant had testified as a witness. The court may admit evidence of the declarant's inconsistent statement or conduct, regardless of when it occurred or whether the declarant had an opportunity to explain or deny it. If the party against whom the statement is admitted calls the declarant as a witness, the party may examine the declarant on the statement as if on cross-examination.

> **CEC § 1202. Credibility of Hearsay Declarant**. Evidence of a statement or other conduct by a declarant that is inconsistent with a statement by such declarant received in evidence as hearsay evidence is not inadmissible for the purpose of attacking the credibility of the declarant though he is not given and has not had an opportunity to explain or deny such inconsistent statement or other conduct. Any other evidence offered to attack or support the credibility of the declarant is admissible if it would have been admissible had the declarant been a witness at the hearing. For the purposes of this section, the deponent of a deposition taken in the action in which it is offered shall be deemed to be a hearsay declarant.[28]

---

[28]   The Law Revision Commission Comments to Section 1202 state in part: "Section 1235 provides that evidence of inconsistent statements made by a trial witness may be admitted to prove the truth of the matter stated. No similar exception to the hearsay rule is applicable to a hearsay declarant's inconsistent statements that are admitted under Section 1202. Hence, the hearsay rule prohibits any such statement from being used to prove the truth of the matter stated." Such statements are admissible to impeach, but not for the truth.

§ 10.12   Collateral Fact Rule

Throughout this chapter, the text specifies when extrinsic evidence is admissible to impeach. When a witness is impeached under FRE 608(b), with a specific instance of the witness's untruthfulness, and the witness denies the specific instance, the cross-examiner is bound by the witness's answer.[29] Extrinsic evidence of the specific instance is not admissible.[30] When a witness is impeached by conviction, and the witness denies the conviction, extrinsic evidence in the form of the judgment of conviction is admissible. When a witness is impeached for bias, memory, or defects in opportunity to observe, and the witness denies the impeachment, extrinsic evidence is admissible, in the judge's discretion.

When a witness is impeached with a prior inconsistent statement, and the witness denies making the inconsistent statement, courts traditionally applied a judge-made rule called the collateral fact rule (CFR) to determine the admissibility of extrinsic evidence of the inconsistent statement. When a witness is impeached by contradiction, and the witness denies the contradiction, the CFR applies.

The CFR is basically a devise to determine when it is worth taking the time to listen to the extrinsic impeachment evidence, usually another witness. If the subject matter of the prior inconsistent statement is relevant to any issue in the case *in addition to* impeachment, the issue is not collateral, it is worth taking the time to listen to the extrinsic evidence, and the extrinsic evidence is admissible. On the other hand, if the *only* relevance of the inconsistent statement is to impeach, then it is not worth taking the time, and the extrinsic evidence is inadmissible.

If the mode of impeachment is contradiction, ask, is the fact contradicted relevant to any issue in the case *in addition to* impeachment? If yes, then the extrinsic evidence is not collateral, and will be received. By contrast, if the *only* relevance of the contradiction is impeachment, it is not worth taking time to listen to the extrinsic evidence, and the evidence is inadmissible.

The CFR rule is a pretty clunky tool to figure out the admissibility of extrinsic impeachment evidence of prior

---

[29]   This is usually stated as, "The cross-examiner must take the witness's answer." The cross-examiner is stuck with the answer, and can't offer extrinsic evidence to prove that the denial is another lie!

[30]   The collateral fact rule does not apply to FRE 608(b) impeachment because extrinsic evidence is *never* admissible when the theory of impeachment is specific acts of untruthfulness.

inconsistent statements and contradiction. The CFR does not apply in California. In California, a party who objects to extrinsic impeachment evidence of a prior inconsistent statement or contradiction, objects under CEC § 352, that it is a waste of court time to admit the extrinsic evidence. Leading authorities on the FRE agree with the California approach, and the CFR is gradually fading away.

§ 10.13   No Impeachment for Religious Belief

FRE 610 and CEC § 789 prohibit evidence of a witness's religious belief, or lack thereof, to attack or support the witness's credibility.[31] In the right situation, religious affiliation may be relevant for another purpose, such a proof of bias.

§ 10.14   Rehabilitation

After a witness is impeached, it is permissible to rehabilitate the witness's credibility. The most immediate way to rehabilitate— and often the most effective—is on redirect examination. If the witness has been impeached on cross, simply ask the witness, on redirect, "Would you care to explain?"

§ 10.14(a).   Rule Against Bolstering Prior to Impeachment

By long tradition, it is improper to bolster a witness's credibility prior to impeachment. This is often called the rule against bolstering prior to impeachment. The rule is mentioned in the FRE and the CEC. FRE 608(a) provides, "[E]vidence of truthful character is admissible only after the witness's character for truthfulness has been attacked." CEC § 790 states that evidence of good character is admissible only after evidence of bad character is admitted.

Prop. 8 applies in California criminal cases, and provides that all relevant evidence is admissible. The effect of Prop. 8 is to overrule CEC § 790, and the rule against bolstering prior to impeachment, in criminal cases.[32] The rule remains viable in civil litigation in California.

---

[31]   Although no cases determine whether Prop. 8 supersedes the ban on impeachment with religious belief, the likely answer is, it doesn't. Even if it does, the judge could use Section 352 to exclude such evidence. In *Brosnahan v. Brown*, 32 Cal. 3d 236, 651 P.2d 274, 186 Cal. Rptr. 30 (1982), the Supreme Court suggested that the voters who enacted Prop. 8 could not have thought they were overturning the ban on religious belief to impeach.

[32]   People v. Harris, 47 Cal. 3d 1047, 1081–1082, 767 P.2d 619, 255 Cal. Rptr. 352 (1989).

§ 10.14(b).   Prior Consistent Statements

In certain situations, a witness who has been impeached can be rehabilitated with evidence that, at an earlier time, the witness made a statement that is consistent with the witness's testimony at trial. Suppose, for example, that Apple testifies on direct examination that the light was red. On cross, Apple is impeached. In some circumstances, Apple's credibility can be repaired with evidence that, at an earlier time, he told a friend the light was red— a prior consistent statement (PCS). The rules provide:

FRE 801(d)(1)(B). Statements That Are Not Hearsay. A statement that meets the following conditions is not hearsay: **(1) A Declarant-witness's Prior Statement**. The declarant testifies and is subject to cross-examination about a prior statement, and the statement: **(B)** is consistent with the declarant's testimony and is offered: (i) to rebut an express or implied charge that the declarant recently fabricated it or acted from a recent improper influence or motive in so testifying; or (ii) to rehabilitate the declarant's credibility as a witness when attacked on another ground.

CEC § 791. Prior Consistent Statement of Witness. Evidence of a statement previously made that is consistent with his testimony at the hearing is inadmissible to support his credibility unless it is offered after: (a) Evidence of a statement made by him that is inconsistent with any part of his testimony at the hearing has been admitted for the purpose of attacking his credibility, and the statement was made before the alleged inconsistent statement; or (b) An express or implied charge has been made that his testimony at the hearing is recently fabricated or is influenced by bias or other improper motive, and the statement was made before the bias, motive for fabrication, or other improper motive is alleged to have arisen.

CEC § 1236. Prior Consistent Statements. Evidence of a statement previously made by a witness is not made inadmissible by the hearsay rule if the statement is consistent with his testimony at the hearing and is offered in compliance with Section 791.

§ 10.14(c).   Not All Impeachment Triggers Rehabilitation with PCS

Not all types of impeachment trigger rehabilitation with a witness's PCS. Most authorities agree that impeachment that takes the form of an attack on a witness's character for truthfulness (FRE 608, 609; CEC § 788) does not trigger rehabilitation with the witness's PCS.

If the cross-examiner states or implies that the witness's direct examination is fabricated, rehabilitation with a PCS is allowed, provided the PCS was made before the motive to fabricate arose.

Does impeachment with a prior inconsistent statement trigger rehabilitation with a PCS? Generally, yes. How about impeachment for bias? If the thrust of the impeachment is that, because of the bias, the witness's testimony is fabricated, slanted, or incomplete, rehabilitation with a PCS is generally allowed. Finally, when a cross-examiner impeaches a witness with lapses in the witness's memory, judges often allow a PCS statement that was uttered when the witness's memory was fresh.

§ 10.14(d).   PCS Offered for Two Purposes

Recall from § 10.4(d), that impeachment with a prior inconsistent statement can be offered for two purposes: (1) For the truth of the matter asserted, in which case the prior inconsistent statement is hearsay; and/or (2) For the limited purpose of impeachment, in which case the prior inconsistent statement is not hearsay because it is not offered for the truth. The same two purposes apply to rehabilitation with a PCS: (1) A PCS may be offered for the truth, in which case it is hearsay; and/or (2) A PCS may be offered for the limited purpose of rehabilitation, in which case the PCS is not hearsay because it is not offered for the truth.

Under the CEC, when impeachment triggers rehabilitation with a PCS, the PCS is admissible to rehabilitate *and* for the truth of the matter asserted (CEC § 1236). The result is the same under the FRE; a PCS is admissible to rehabilitate *and* for TOMA (FRE 801(d)(1)(B)).

§ 10.14(e).   "Recently" Doesn't Mean Recently

FRE 801(d)(1)(B) and CEC § 791(b) mention "recent" fabrication. This is confusing. Under the rules, fabrication does not have to be of recent origin. The witness may have decided weeks or months ago to fabricate.

§ 10.14(f).   The Timing Rule for PCSs

When a cross-examiner asserts that a witness's testimony is fabricated, rehabilitation with a PCS is allowed, provided the PCS was made before the motive to fabricate arose. This is the so-called "timing rule" for PCS, or the "prior to motive" rule. The timing rule applies to the FRE and the CEC.

Consider an example: A little girl was kidnapped on the way home from school. The kidnapper sexually abused the child, and then released her miles from her home. The child was rescued and returned to her parents. When the child told her parents what happened, the police were called. A sheriff's deputy talked to the child, and the child described the abuse and the abuser. Dell was arrested and charged with kidnapping and sexual abuse. A week before Dell's trial, the prosecutor met with the child to prepare her to testify. At trial, the child testified and described what happened in words very similar to what she told the sheriff. On cross-examination, defense counsel asked the child, "Did the prosecutor tell you what to say?" The child answered, "Yes, she told me what to say." Clearly, defense counsel is alleging that the prosecutor influenced the child's testimony. The defense tactic amounts to a charge of fabrication. The timing rule is satisfied because the little girl gave her PCS to the deputy long before speaking with the prosecutor. Thus, it is proper to rehabilitate the child with her prior consistent statement to the deputy. As well, the child's PCS is admissible for the truth.

With PCSs, it is often helpful to create a timeline. On the timeline, arrange by date the prior consistent statement, the motive to fabricate, and the trial testimony.

§ 10.15   Rape Shield Statute

In many rape prosecutions, the defendant admits sex, but claims the alleged victim consented. Prior to the 1970s, judges generally allowed defense counsel to attempt to prove consent by offering evidence that the alleged victim had consented to sex with *other* men. The theory was that an "unchaste" woman was more likely to have consented to sex with the defendant than a "virtuous," "chaste," or "pure" woman. Evidence of unchaste character took three forms. First, if the alleged victim testified, defense counsel could cross-examine the victim, and ask her about the details of any previous sexual relationships with men other than the defendant. Second, defense counsel was permitted to offer witnesses to testify that the alleged victim had a bad reputation in the community for chastity. Third, defense counsel could call the alleged victim's past sexual partners to the witness stand, and have them describe their sexual relations with the victim. Thus, in rape trials, the defendant effectively put the victim "on trial."

In the 1970s, advocates sought reform of rape law. Among other reforms, advocates sought to eliminate the use at trial of evidence of a woman's sexual relations with other men. Advocates argued that the fact that a woman had consensual sex with other men was not relevant to whether she consented to sex with the defendant. This argument carried the day, and states enacted laws called "rape shield statutes" to limit evidence of the alleged victim's prior sexual conduct with others. Rape shield laws apply in all sex offense cases, not just prosecutions for rape.

The FRE rape shield statute is Rule 412, which provides, in part:

FRE 412. Sex-Offense Cases: The Victim

(a) Prohibited Uses. The following evidence is not admissible in a civil or criminal proceeding involving alleged sexual misconduct:

> (1) evidence offered to prove that a victim engaged in other sexual behavior; or
>
> (2) evidence offered to prove a victim's sexual predisposition.

(b) Exceptions.

> **(1) Criminal Cases.** The court may admit the following evidence in a criminal case:
>
> (A) evidence of specific instances of a victim's sexual behavior, if offered to prove that someone other than the defendant was the source of semen, injury, or other physical evidence;
>
> (B) evidence of specific instances of a victim's sexual behavior with respect to the person accused of the sexual misconduct, if offered by the defendant to prove consent or if offered by the prosecutor; and
>
> (C) evidence whose exclusion would violate the defendant's constitutional rights.
>
> **(2) Civil Cases.** In a civil case, the court may admit evidence offered to prove a victim's sexual behavior or sexual predisposition if its probative value substantially outweighs the danger of harm to any victim and of unfair prejudice to any party. The court

may admit evidence of a victim's reputation only if the victim has placed it in controversy.

Pursuant to Rule 412(a), evidence of specific instances of an alleged victim's other sexual behavior is inadmissible as substantive evidence of consent, or to impeach the victim's credibility. As well, character witnesses may not testify to an alleged victim's sexual predisposition.

Subsection (b) contains exceptions to Rule 412's prohibition of evidence of an alleged victim's other sexual behavior. First, a defendant is allowed to prove that he did not cause injuries found on the victim. Sometimes such proof consists of evidence that the victim engaged in sexual behavior with another person. Second, the defendant can offer evidence that he is not the source of semen on the victim, or other physical evidence. Third, Rule 412 makes the judgment that evidence of a prior consensual sexual relationship between the defendant and the victim should be admissible to prove consent. Of course, the fact that a victim previously consented to sex with a defendant does not rule out rape. However, the probative value of a prior consensual relationship between a defendant and an alleged victim can be sufficiently strong to merit receipt of the evidence. Fourth, in rare cases, a defendant's ability to secure a fair trial necessitates receipt of evidence of a victim's sexual behavior with others. This sometimes happens when a defendant's ability to effectively cross-examine the victim or another witness hinges on the ability to ask about the victim's other sexual behavior.

Rule 412(c) establishes procedures governing admission of evidence of a victim's other sexual behavior. A defendant wishing to offer such evidence files a motion at least two weeks before trial, setting forth good cause to admit the evidence. The judge holds a pretrial hearing to consider defendant's motion. The victim has a right to attend the hearing and to address the court.

California's rape shield law typically reaches the same result as FRE 412, exclusion of an alleged victim's other sexual behavior. CEC § 1103(c)(1) excludes evidence of an alleged victim's sexual conduct offered as substantive evidence of consent. Like FRE 412, CEC § 1103(c)(3) allows evidence "of the complaining witness' sexual conduct with the defendant."

CEC § 782 governs evidence of an alleged victim's other sexual behavior offered to impeach the victim's credibility. Under § 782, the court balances the probative value of the evidence against the danger of unfair prejudice.

Courts generally admit evidence that an alleged victim made previous false allegations of rape or sexual assault. False accusations are not "sexual behavior."

§ 10.16   Analysis of Chapter Questions and Exams

This section analyzes questions from earlier sections.

Exam Question: Which Is Which? From § 10.5. This question illustrates the difference between prior inconsistent statements and contradiction. To refresh your memory, here is the question: Ann, Beth, and Charlene devised a plan to rob a bank. Ann's job was to be the getaway driver. Beth and Charlene entered the bank with guns and announced, "This is a robbery." Ann, Beth, and Charlene were caught and are on trial, charged with bank robbery. **Call of the Question**: Discuss the evidence issues in the following paragraphs: (1) During the prosecution's case-in-chief, the prosecutor offers testimony from Bob, a teller at the bank. Bob testifies, "I was working at the bank when Beth and Charlene burst in with guns and said, "This is a robbery." Beth came to my teller window, stuck a gun in my face, and said, 'Put all the money in this bag, and no funny stuff.' " (2) On cross-examination of Bob, defense counsel asks, "Not long after the robbery, didn't you tell a police officer that you could not remember which robber came to your teller window?" (3) On further cross-examination of Bob, defense counsel asks, "Isn't it possible that the robber who came to your window was not Beth, but was someone who looked like Beth?"

(1)   Bob's testimony is relevant eyewitness testimony of the robbery. You should define relevance, and describe why the evidence is relevant. The bar examiners want you to discuss the danger of unfair prejudice, although there is nothing unfairly prejudicial about Bob's testimony. The words spoken by the robbers are relevant, and are admissible against all three defendants under the party admission rule and the co-conspirator exception (*See* §§ 11.24(a), 11.24(e)).

(2)   In number two, the cross-examiner impeaches Bob with Bob's prior inconsistent statement. The cross-examiner's questions are probably sufficient to satisfy the foundation to impeach with a prior inconsistent statement. In California, prior inconsistent statements are admissible to impeach and for the truth of the matter asserted (CEC § 1235). Under the FRE, Bob's prior inconsistent statement is admissible to impeach Bob, but is not admissible for the truth of the matter asserted because it was not made subject to the penalty of perjury (FRE 801(d)(1)(A)).

(3)   The cross-examiner's effort to get Bob to admit the robber who came to Bob's window might not have been Beth is an effort to impeach by contradiction.

Chapter 11

HEARSAY

Hearsay is a large subject. Entire books are written on hearsay. This chapter introduces hearsay, the rule against it, exceptions to the rule, the impact of the Sixth Amendment Confrontation Clause on hearsay in criminal cases, and hearsay on exams.

§ 11.1 Hearsay Defined

FRE 801(c) defines hearsay as "a statement that: (1) the declarant does not make while testifying at the current trial or hearing; and (2) a party offers in evidence to prove the truth of the matter asserted in the statement." The CEC employs different words, but the meaning is the same (CEC § 1200(a)).

A "statement" is a person's oral or written assertion (FRE 801(a); CEC § 225). An assertion is words expressing some fact or opinion. Nonverbal conduct is a "statement" when it is assertive, that is, when a person intends to communicate without words. Thus, when Vic is asked, "Who took your purse?", and Vic points to Dell, Vic's nonverbal conduct is assertive, and a statement.

It is useful to break the definition of hearsay into three parts: (1) The declarant made a statement; (2) The declarant spoke (or wrote or acted) prior to the hearing where the statement is repeated (the statement is out-of-court); and (3) The statement is offered in evidence to prove that the statement is true (the truth of the matter asserted). For words or conduct to be hearsay, all three elements must be present. If one of the elements is missing, the utterance is not hearsay.

Sometimes, the grammatical structure of an utterance influences whether it is a statement for hearsay purposes. Declarative utterances are nearly always statements. For example, "The robber wore a purple ski mask" is a statement, as is, "That guy must have been going a hundred miles an hour." But suppose an utterance takes the form of a question. Is a question a statement of fact? Is, "Why is Jerome here?" a statement? The answer depends on what the utterance is offered to prove. If it is offered to prove that the declarant is asserting Jerome is here, then the question should be considered a statement. Similarly, an utterance in the form of an order—"Get Jerome out of here this instant!"—can be a statement, if it is offered to prove a fact. In the final analysis, grammatical structure should not control whether words are a statement. What is important is whether the speaker intended to assert a fact.

§ 11.2   Rule Against Hearsay

FRE 802 and CEC § 1200(b) state the hearsay rule, or, the rule against hearsay, to be more precise. The rules provide that hearsay is inadmissible unless it meets the requirements of a hearsay exception. Hearsay is excluded because it is sometimes less reliable than testimony in court. Witnesses in court are under oath and subject to cross-examination. The cross-examiner can test the witness's sincerity, memory, accuracy of narration, and whether the witness misperceived events. When a hearsay declarant does not testify, the declarant's words are repeated in court by someone else. Because the declarant is not present, it is not possible to cross-examine the declarant. The inability to cross-examine the declarant is the raison d'etre for the hearsay rule.

What if the declarant comes to court and repeats her own out-of-court statement? For example, Bridgette is on the witness stand, and testifies, "Right after the accident, I turned to my friend, Jamie, and said, 'OMG! Like, the Camaro, like, went through the red light and, like, smashed into the Mustang!' "[1] Is Bridgette's testimony hearsay? Check her statement against the three part definition of hearsay in § 11.1. Regarding the part of Bridgette's testimony where she repeats what she told Jamie: (1) Bridgette, like, made a statement; (2) The statement was, like, out of court; and (3) Bridgette repeats the statement in court for, like, the truth of the matter asserted. (Do you agree that listening to someone repeatedly interject "like" into their speech is irritating? Don't do it in court. The judge will be closer to my age than yours, and she won't *like* it). Bridgett's statement meets the definition of hearsay. But why would we exclude Bridgette's statement under the hearsay rule? Bridgette *can* be cross-examined to test her memory, sincerity, perception, and narration. That's true, but, with some exceptions, Bridgette's statement is considered hearsay.[2]

---

[1]   You can tell from the double and single quote marks that Bridgette is quoting herself. Do not get the idea, however, that quote marks are necessary for hearsay to be present on an exam. Here's an example from a transcript of testimony: Q: What did she say to you? A: She said the Camaro went through the red light and smashed into the Mustang. No quote marks, but clearly hearsay.

[2]   The traditional reason to treat the declarant's words as hearsay when the declarant testifies at trial is that the cross-examiner could not question the declarant *at the time* the out of court statement was made. Why that should make a difference is difficult to understand. Evidence scholars argued that if the declarant testifies, and can be cross-examined about the earlier statement, the statement should be defined as not hearsay. The FRE goes part way in that direction. Out-of-court

§ 11.3   Hearsay Attack Sheet for Exams

Here's an approach to hearsay on exams. You or your professor may favor a different approach. First, examine the facts to see if an out-of-court statement is repeated in court.[3] If so, you have a possible hearsay issue. Let the reader know you know. Second, see if there is a non-hearsay use for the out-of-court statement (*e.g.,* effect on the listener, § 11.4(a)). Third, look for layered hearsay, or, as it is sometimes called, hearsay within hearsay (§ 11.27). Fourth, if you are dealing with hearsay, run through the exceptions that could apply, and discuss them. More than one exception may apply. Fifth, if it is a criminal case, and hearsay is offered against the defendant, discuss the Confrontation Clause (§ 11.29).

§ 11.4   Non-Hearsay Uses of Out-of-Court Statements

An out of court statement is hearsay only if it is offered to prove the truth of the matter asserted. When a statement is offered for some *other* purpose—that is, for a purpose other than the truth of the statement—*and* when the other purpose is *relevant,* the out of court statement may be admissible non-hearsay.[4] This section describes three non-hearsay uses of out-of-court statements.

§ 11.4(a).   Effect on the Listener

Sometimes, the fact that an out-of-court statement was made, and that someone heard it, is relevant.[5] In such cases, the out-of-court statement may be admitted for the non-hearsay purpose of showing the effect on the listener or hearer. In § 2.6, you encountered Sue, who slipped and fell on a banana peel in the produce isle of a grocery store. Twenty minutes *before* Sue slipped, a different customer, Esmerelda, told the produce manager, "Hi, there is a banana peel, on the floor in the produce isle, someone might slip on it." If Esmerelda's statement is offered to prove there really was a banana peel on the floor, the statement is hearsay. Unless a hearsay exception applies, Esmerelda's statement is inadmissible to

---

statements that fall within 801(d)(1) are defined as not hearsay, provided the declarant testifies and is subject to cross-examination. The CEC treats such statements as hearsay within exceptions.

[3]   Most of the time, a witness on the stand repeats an out-of-court statement. Sometimes, an audio recording is played, repeating out-of-court statements. Both situations implicate hearsay.

[4]   The text says "may be admissible" because other rules of evidence could exclude the statement.

[5]   Be clear. Most of the time, the fact that someone heard an out-of-court statement is *not* relevant.

prove a banana peel was on the floor. However, under the law of torts that applies to slip and fall cases, the plaintiff may have to prove that the defendant was on notice of the dangerous condition that caused the accident.[6] Esmerelda's statement to the produce manager, twenty minutes *before* the accident, provides the required notice.[7] Offered for the limited purpose of proving notice, Esmerelda's words are not hearsay because her words are not offered to prove there was a banana peel on the floor.

Dell is charged with the willful, deliberate, and premeditated murder of Roge. Two weeks before Dell shot Roge, Roge told Dell, "I'm having an affair with your partner, and there is nothing you can do about it." Roge's out-of-court statement is admissible for the non-hearsay purpose of proving its effect on Dell. The statement provides Dell a motive to kill. On the other hand, Dell may want to offer the statement to show that he was provoked.

§ 11.4(b).   Verbal Acts, aka, Words of Independent Legal Significance

Sometimes, words have legal consequences whether the words are true or false. In contract law, for example, words of offer and acceptance have consequences, and are admissible as non-hearsay. Such words are called verbal acts. Suppose the Acme Company delivers medical supplies to the XYZ Clinic on credit. The clinic does not pay its bill, and Acme refuses further deliveries on credit. A banker gets involved and asks Acme to resume deliveries on credit. The banker informs Acme that the bank will guarantee payment if XYZ fails to pay. Sure enough, XYZ fails to pay. Acme sues the bank, and offers evidence of the banker's words guaranteeing payment. The bank's attorney raises a hearsay objection. The judge will overrule the objection because the banker's words were verbal acts, creating a contractual obligation.

§ 11.4(c).   Verbal Parts of an Act

Sometimes, conduct is ambiguous, and words that accompany the conduct give it meaning. Suppose Chenguang hands Biyu $1,000 in cash. What just happened? Was it a loan to Biyu? A gift to Biyu? Was Chenguang repaying money she owed Biyu? Was Biyu simply holding the cash while Chenguang tied her shoe? The act was ambiguous. However, what if, as she handed the cash to Biyu, Chenguang said, "Here is your birthday present. Happy Birthday."

---

[6]   *See* Laird v. T.W. Mather, Inc., 51 Cal. 2d 210, 220, 331 P.2d 617 (1958).

[7]   Esmeralda's statement provides notice even if her statement was false! Thus, what is important is not the truth of the statement (hearsay) but the fact that the statement put the grocery store on notice.

The ambiguity is erased. When words accompany ambiguous conduct, and give the conduct meaning, the words are admissible as verbal parts of an act.

§ 11.4(d).   Effect on the Listener, Verbal Acts, and Verbal Parts of an Act Are Not Hearsay

You only need a hearsay exception for hearsay. The effect on the listener doctrine, the verbal acts doctrine, and verbal parts of an act are not hearsay. Nor are they hearsay exceptions. They are non-hearsay uses of out-of-court utterances.

§ 11.5   Hearsay Exceptions

Judges and legislators create exceptions to the rule against hearsay for categories of hearsay that are sufficiently reliable for use in court despite the inability to cross-examine the declarant. The circumstances in which these categories of hearsay are made lower one or more of the risks of hearsay sufficiently to justify receipt of the hearsay. For each hearsay exception, you should know which of the risks is lowered. Is it memory, sincerity, narration, perception, or some combination?

Hearsay exceptions require the declarant to have personal knowledge of the events described (FRE 602; CEC § 702).[8] There is one exception to the rule that a hearsay declarant must have personal knowledge. Personal knowledge is not required for party admissions (*See* § 11.24).

§ 11.6   Unavailability

Sometimes, a hearsay declarant is available to testify at trial. In other cases, the declarant is unavailable. Some hearsay exceptions require a showing of unavailability before the exception applies. In the FRE, exceptions grouped under Rule 803 do not require the declarant to be unavailable. Exceptions collected under Rule 804(b) do require a showing of unavailability. In the CEC, it is necessary to consult each exception to determine whether unavailability is a requirement for the exception.

Common types of unavailability are described in FRE 804(a) and CEC § 240. A declarant may be unavailable due to a privilege not to testify, refusal to testify, failure of memory, death, serious illness, or because the witness is beyond the subpoena power of the court.

---

[8]   *See* People v. Cortez, 63 Cal. 4th 101, 123–124, 369 P.3d 521, 201 Cal. Rptr. 3d 846 (2016).

§ 11.7   Present Sense Impressions

The present sense impression exception is FRE 803(1) and CEC § 1241. The rules state:

> **FRE 803(1). Present Sense Impression**. The following [is] not excluded by the rule against hearsay, regardless of whether the declarant is available as a witness: A statement describing or explaining an event or condition, made while or immediately after the declarant perceived it.

> **CEC § 1241. Contemporaneous Statement**. Evidence of a statement is not made inadmissible by the hearsay rule if the statement: (a) Is offered to explain, qualify, or make understandable conduct of the declarant; and (b) Was made while the declarant was engaged in such conduct.

Present sense impressions are reliable because the risk of memory loss is virtually eliminated. There is no time to forget.

The FRE present sense impression exception admits hearsay statements describing events as the events occur, and statements immediately afterward. The time limit is strict. If a minute or two has gone by since the event, a statement describing the event is not a present sense impression. The event does not have to be exciting. Thus, a statement by a person who is calmly attempting to turn a faucet, "I can't make it turn" is a present sense impression.

The February, 2012 California Bar Examination tested present sense impressions. The following question is reproduced with permission from the California State Bar:

> Paul sued David in federal court for damages for injuries arising from an automobile accident. At trial, in his case-in-chief, Paul testified that he was driving westbound, under the speed limit, in the right-hand lane of a highway having two westbound lanes. He further testified that his passenger, Vera, calmly told him she saw a black SUV behind them weaving recklessly through the traffic. He also testified that about 30 seconds later, he saw David driving a black SUV, which appeared in the left lane and swerved in front of him. He testified David's black SUV hit the front of his car, seriously injuring him and killing Vera. He rested his case. . . . Assuming that all appropriate objections and motions were timely made, should the court have admitted Vera's statement? Discuss.

Because this case is tried in federal court, the Federal Rules of Evidence apply. Vera's statement is relevant to prove that David drove recklessly and caused the accident. Vera's statement is hearsay because it is offered to prove the truth of the matters she asserted in her statement. Vera's statement is a present sense impression. Vera described an event as she perceived it. The fact that Vera is unavailable to testify is immaterial because the availability of the declarant does not matter with present sense impressions. On an exam, you will elaborate on each of these points.

California's contemporaneous statement exception is narrower than the FRE's exception for present sense impressions. First, FRE 803(1) admits statements about the declarant's conduct *and* the conduct of others. CEC § 1241 is limited to explaining the declarant's conduct. Second, the California exception applies only to a statement made "while the declarant was engaged in such conduct," whereas FRE 803(1) applies to statement while an event is occurring *and* to a statement made immediately thereafter.

§ 11.8   Excited Utterances

An excited utterance is a hearsay statement relating to a startling event, made while the declarant was under the psychological excitement caused by the event. Excited utterances are reliable because they are made soon after the event, reducing the danger of memory loss. As well, excited utterances are reliable because the stress of the startling event is thought to reduce lying. The rules state:

> **FRE 803(2). Excited Utterance**. The following [is] not excluded by the rule against hearsay, regardless of whether the declarant is available as a witness: A statement relating to a startling event or condition, made while the declarant was under the stress of excitement that it caused.

> **CEC § 1240. Spontaneous Statement**. Evidence of a statement is not made inadmissible by the hearsay rule if the statement: (a) Purports to narrate, describe, or explain an act, condition, or event perceived by the declarant; and (b) Was made spontaneously while the declarant was under the stress of excitement caused by such perception.

The excited utterance exception has three requirements: (1) A startling event that is perceived by the declarant;[9] (2) The

---

[9]   The declarant must have personal knowledge of the startling event. However, the declarant does not have to be a participant in the event. Thus, statements by bystanders can be excited utterances. Even if the declarant is unknown (*e.g.*, some unknown person at an accident scene blurts out, "The red car ran the light!"), an anonymous statement may be an excited utterance, so long as

statement relates to the startling event;[10] and (3) The statement is made while the person is still under the psychological stress induced by the startling event. In most cases, the litigated issue is whether the declarant was sufficiently upset. On the question of excitement, judges consider the totality of the circumstances. The nature of the event is important. Some events are more startling than others. How much time elapsed from the event to the statement? The more time that goes by, the less likely the declarant remained excited. However, there is no deadline in minutes or hours. Time is simply one factor among others shedding light on excitement. There are cases where 15 minutes is too long, and cases where 15 hours is not too long. If the declarant was injured or in pain, the statement is more likely to be an excited utterance. The declarant's emotional condition is important. Was the declarant crying, hysterical, or emotional? Or, was the declarant calm and relaxed? Words themselves can indicate excitement, and the judge examines the statement for evidence of excitement. On an exam, you should discuss these factors and anything else that indicates presence or absence of excitement.

§ 11.9   State of Mind Exception

The state of mind exception allows admission of hearsay statements describing how a person feels *at the moment* the person speaks. For example, the statement, "My leg hurts!" describes the declarant's physical feeling *at the moment* the declarant spoke. Another example, "I love evidence. It is my favorite course." This statement describes the declarant's mental feeling *at the moment* the declarant spoke.

Statements of then-existing state of mind are considered reliable because the hearsay danger of memory loss is eliminated. To be admissible, a statement must describe how the declarant feels *at the moment*. Thus, there is no time to forget. The rules provide:

> **FRE 803(3). Then-Existing Mental, Emotional, or Physical Condition**. The following [is] not excluded by the rule against hearsay, regardless of whether the declarant is available as a witness: A statement of the

---

circumstantial evidence proves the declarant had personal knowledge, and was sufficiently excited.

[10]   FRE 803(2) requires the statement to relate to the startling event. CEC § 1240 requires the statement to narrate, describe, or explain the startling event. Usually, there is no difference between the CEC and the FRE. It is conceivable that a statement that relates to a startling event might not narrate, describe, or explain the event, thus making the CEC exception narrower than the FRE exception. In practice, the two exceptions are virtually identical.

declarant's then-existing state of mind (such as motive, intent, or plan) or emotional, sensory, or physical condition (such as mental feeling, pain, or bodily health), but not including a statement of memory or belief to prove the fact remembered or believed unless it relates to the validity or terms of the declarant's will.

CEC § 1250. Statement of Declarant's Then Existing Mental or Physical State. (a) Subject to Section 1252 [§ 1252 allows a judge exclude admissible hearsay if the hearsay was made under circumstances that indicate lack of trustworthiness], evidence of a statement of the declarant's then existing state of mind, emotion, or physical sensation (including a statement of intent, plan, motive, design, mental feeling, pain, or bodily health) is not made inadmissible by the hearsay rule when: (1) The evidence is offered to prove the declarant's state of mind, emotion, or physical sensation at that time or at any other time when it is itself an issue in the action; or (2) The evidence is offered to prove or explain acts or conduct of the declarant. (b) This section does not make admissible evidence of a statement of memory or belief to prove the fact remembered or believed.

CEC § 1251. Statement of Declarant's Previously Existing Mental or Physical State. Subject to Section 1252, evidence of a statement of the declarant's state of mind, emotion, or physical sensation (including a statement of intent, plan, motive, design, mental feeling, pain, or bodily health) at a time prior to the statement is not made inadmissible by the hearsay rule if: (a) The declarant is unavailable as a witness; and (b) The evidence is offered to prove such prior state of mind, emotion, or physical sensation when it is itself an issue in the action and the evidence is not offered to prove any fact other than such state of mind, emotion, or physical sensation.

FRE 803(3) and CEC § 1250 operate similarly in practice. CEC § 1251 does not have a counterpart in the FRE. Section 1251 is discussed later.

The state of mind exception admits three categories of hearsay statements: (1) Statements of then-existing physical condition ("My head hurts"); (2) Statements of then-existing mental or emotional condition ("I hate that guy"); and (3) Statements of then-existing intent or plan.

The state of mind exception does *not* admit statements of memory about the past. Thus, the exception does not embrace, "My head hurt yesterday" or "I hated that guy yesterday" or "Yesterday, I went to the Star Wars movie" or "I went to the Star Wars movie" or "The car went through the red light." These are statements of memory.

There is an exception to the rule that the state of mind exception does not include statements of memory. A declarant's statement about the validity or terms of the declarant's will is admissible. Thus, the statement, "I amended my will yesterday to leave everything to my evidence professor" is admissible under the state of mind exception.

Statements of intent or plan are sometimes called "forward looking" statements, in contrast to statements of memory that are "backward looking." The following statements are admissible under the forward looking aspect of the state of mind exception:

"I intend to go to Chicago tomorrow."

"I intend to skip evidence today."

"I'm leaving for class in a few minutes."

"I'm going to the parking lot. I'll be right back."

The state of mind exception gets each of these statements into evidence. Once the statement is in evidence, the jury may draw any reasonable inference from the statement that the jury believes is warranted. Thus, once the state of mind exception admits "I intend to go to Chicago tomorrow," the jury may infer from the statement that the declarant followed up on the intent, and went to Chicago. A two-step process is involved, step one involves hearsay, and step two involves inferential reasoning. First, the state of mind exception gets the statement of intent into evidence. Second, the jury infers conduct by the person, based on the person's intent.

The statement, "I intend to go to Chicago tomorrow" fits squarely into the forward looking aspect of the state of mind exception, and is admissible. But, suppose the statement is a little different: "I intend to go to Chicago tomorrow with Akira." This statement is admissible to prove the declarant's intent to travel to Chicago, and, from intent, the fact of travel to Chicago. But is the statement admissible to prove that Akira went to Chicago?

There has been controversy over whether a declarant's statement of intent to do something in the company of a third person should be admissible to prove the third person's conduct. The most famous case is *Mutual Life Insurance Co. v. Hillmon*, 145 U.S. 285, 12 S. Ct. 909 (1892). In *Hillmon*, the insurance company sought to prove that a man named Walters travelled west from Wichita, Kansas, with a man named Hillmon. The insurance company offered letters written by Walters to his sister and his fiancé, in which Walters wrote, "I intend to go west with a man named Hillmon." Clearly, the letters are admissible to prove Walter's intent to travel west. But are the letters admissible to prove that Walters travelled west with Hillmon? The Supreme Court said yes. Courts, including California courts, generally admit so-called *Hillmon* statements that embrace the declarant's intent to do something with someone else.

Try your hand at the following hearsay statements. Which statements are admissible under the state of mind exception? Answers are in § 11.32.

"I intend to go to Chicago tomorrow."

"I intend to go to Chicago tomorrow, with Anne."

"Anne plans to go to Chicago tomorrow."

"I'm leaving for class in a few minutes."

"Sara and I are leaving for class in a few minutes."

"I'm going to the parking lot. I'll be right back."

"I'm going to meet Angelo in the parking lot. I'll be right back."[11]

"Angelo is going to give me a pound of marijuana for free."

CEC § 1251 admits a declarant's statement describing a state of mind at an earlier time, provided the declarant is now unavailable, and the earlier state of mind is an issue in the case. The FRE does not have a counterpart to CEC § 1251.

There are very few cases under Section 1251. *Estate of Truckenmiller*, 97 Cal. App. 3d 326, 158 Cal. Rptr. 699 (1979) is helpful. Truckenmiller was a 68-year-old widower. Truckenmiller's housekeeper lived in Truckenmiller's home. Norma Wells and her husband were friends of Truckenmiller. Truckenmiller transferred $30,000 of stock to Mrs. Wells. The Wells sold the stock and bought a building. When Truckenmiller died, his administrator claimed that the Wells exerted undue influence on Truckenmiller, in order to force him to transfer the stock. During his lifetime, Truckenmiller told his housekeeper that the Wells had tricked him into giving them the stock. The hearsay question was whether Truckenmiller's statement about being tricked was admissible. The Court of Appeal ruled it admissible under Section 1251.

---

[11]   *See* United States v. Pheaster, 544 F.2d 353 (9th Cir. 1976).

Truckenmiller's statement to his housekeeper about being tricked referred to Truckenmiller's state of mind at a time prior to the statement, Truckenmiller was deceased, and thus unavailable, and Truckenmiller's prior state of mind was an issue in the case.

§ 11.10   Medical Diagnosis or Treatment

The medical diagnosis or treatment exception admits statements that are made to receive medical care. All four hearsay risks are lowered. The patient has an incentive to be truthful with the heath care professional, lowering the risk of insincerity. The risks of misperception and inaccurate narration are reduced because of the patient's motive to be accurate. The risk of memory loss is lowered because, in many cases, the patient is describing recent events. The FRE rule provides:

> **FRE 803(4). Statement Made for Medical Diagnosis or Treatment**. The following [is] not excluded by the rule against hearsay, regardless of whether the declarant is available as a witness: A statement that: (A) is made for— and is reasonably pertinent to—medical diagnosis or treatment; and (B) describes medical history;[12] past or present symptoms or sensations; their inception; or their general cause.

California has the medical diagnosis or treatment exception (CEC § 1253). However, in California, the exception applies only to children's statements in child abuse cases.

Not everything a patient tells a doctor or nurse is covered by the exception. The information must be pertinent to the professional's ability to diagnose or treat. Statements attributing fault are not included because attributions of fault are not pertinent to diagnosis or treatment. Thus, a patient's statement to an emergency room doctor, "It was a head on collision" is pertinent because the doctor needs to know what happened. The patient's further statement, "The idiot in the other car caused it" is not pertinent. The doctor doesn't need to know who caused the crash.

Courts created an exception to the rule that attributions of fault are not pertinent. In child abuse cases, courts rule that a child's statement identifying the abuser is pertinent, and admissible under the medical diagnosis or treatment exception.[13]

---

[12]   "Medical history" is a term of art in medicine. The medical history includes the short- and long-term history of the present illness or injury. Thus, when a professional takes a "history," the professional asks about previous medical matters. The exception covers the medical history.

[13]   *See, e.g.,* People v. Brodit, 61 Cal. App. 4th 1312, 72 Cal. Rptr. 2d 154 (1998).

Statements to doctors and nurses can be admissible under this exception. So can statements to medical technicians, paramedics, and other para-professionals. As well, courts admit statements to mental health professionals.

§ 11.11   Past Recorded Recollection

Sometimes, witnesses forget important details. Section 9.7 discusses techniques to refresh witness memory. Suppose, despite an attorney's effort to trigger a witness's memory, it doesn't work: the witness can't remember! If the witness wrote down a record of the forgotten details, it may be possible to admit the record under the hearsay exception for past recollection recorded. The rules provide:

> **FRE 803(5). Recorded Recollection**. The following [is] not excluded by the rule against hearsay, regardless of whether the declarant is available as a witness: A record that: (A) is on a matter the witness once knew about but now cannot recall well enough to testify fully and accurately; (B) was made or adopted by the witness when the matter was fresh in the witness's memory; and (C) accurately reflects the witness's knowledge. If admitted, the record may be read into evidence but may be received as an exhibit only if offered by an adverse party.[14]

> **CEC § 1237. Past Recollection Recorded**. (a) Evidence of a statement previously made by a witness is not made inadmissible by the hearsay rule if the statement would have been admissible if made by him while testifying, the statement concerns a matter as to which the witness has insufficient present recollection to enable him to testify fully and accurately, and the statement is contained in a writing which: (1) Was made at a time when the fact recorded in the writing actually occurred or was fresh in the witness' memory; (2) Was made (i) by the witness himself or under his direction or (ii) by some other person

---

[14]   The last sentence requires some explanation. With past recollection recorded, the substance of a document is admitted in evidence. Normally, documents are marked as exhibits, formally admitted into evidence, and may be read by the jury during the trial. When the jury retires to deliberate, admitted documents go with the jury to the jury room, and jurors can read the documents. Yet, according to the last sentence of 803(5), a document that is past recollection recorded is not received as an exhibit. The jury never sees the document, and the document is not available to the jury in the jury room during deliberations. Under 803(5), the substance of the document is read aloud to the jury. Why this unusual treatment of a document? The idea is that the document is really just a substitute for the forgetful witness's verbal testimony. Reading it is similar to the witness testifying. Sending the document to the jury room might place too much emphasis on the document.

for the purpose of recording the witness' statement at the time it was made; (3) Is offered after the witness testifies that the statement he made was a true statement of such fact; and (4) Is offered after the writing is authenticated as an accurate record of the statement. (b) The writing may be read into evidence, but the writing itself may not be received in evidence unless offered by an adverse party.

The FRE and CEC exceptions are very similar. With both exceptions, the witness's memory does not have to fail completely. The exceptions apply if the witness's memory is impaired to the point that the witness can't testify fully and accurately. The difference between the FRE and the CEC is that under CEC § 1237, the forgetful witness must testify that the written statement was accurate. FRE 803(5) does not require such testimony.

Understand the progression that leads to past recollection recorded. First, the attorney begins with open-ended questions, intended to elicit testimony from the witness's unassisted memory. Second, if the witness's memory fails on some particular, the attorney attempts to refresh recollection. Third, if efforts to refresh recollection fail, the attorney invokes past recollection recorded. Thus, past recollection is a last resort!

Consider an example: Sam is a teller at a Golden One Credit Union in Stockton. Robbers burst in with guns and rob the place. As the robbers run out and jump in the getaway car, Sam rushes to the front door and shouts, "Hey, somebody write down this license plate number. FRE 803–5" Another teller, Kelly, writes the number on a yellow sticky note. At the robbery trial, Sam testifies for the prosecution, and describes the robbery. Questioning continues:

Q: [Prosecutor] Did you get the license number of the getaway car?

A: Yes.

Q: Do you remember the license plate number?

A: As soon as the robbers ran out, I ran to the door and looked at the license plate on the getaway car. I shouted for someone to write it down, and I recited the plate number as I was looking at the getaway car pull away from the curb. But, to be honest, I can't remember the actual plate number right now.

[Prosecutor]: Your honor, it appears that the witness's memory for the license plate has failed him. May I attempt to refresh his recollection by handing him a piece of paper?

[Court]: Any objection defense counsel?

[Defense counsel]: No, your honor.

[Court] Go ahead.

[Prosecutor]. Thank you your honor. May I approach the witness?

[Court]. Yes.

Q: Sir, I hand you now a piece of paper, and ask that you take a moment to read it.[15] May the record reflect that I am handing a copy of the document to defense counsel?

[Court]: The record will so reflect.

A: Ok. I have read it.

Q: Does the document refresh your recollection about the license plate?

A: Well, I know what the piece of paper says, but to be completely honest, I still don't remember the license plate number.

[Prosecutor]: Your honor, it appears my effort to refresh the witness's recollection has not worked. I would like to lay the foundation to admit the document into evidence as past recollection recorded.

[Court]: You may proceed.

[Prosecutor]: Thank you, your honor. Let me ask you a few questions. First, do you remember calling out the license plate number?

A: Oh yes, I remember that clearly. I knew it was important.

Q: Who actually wrote down the plate number?

A: Kelly wrote it down on a little yellow sticky note, as I shouted it to her.

Q: Who is Kelly?

A: Another teller at the credit union.

Q: How long after the robbery did this happen?

A: Just moments after. The robbers were still piling into their getaway car as the driver pulled away from the curb. I shouted out the numbers and letters to Kelly as the car was leaving.

Q: So, when you stated the plate numbers, your memory of the plate was fresh?

A: Oh sure, I was speaking as I was looking at the plate.

---

[15]   It would be improper for the prosecutor to state the contents of the document. A document that is used to refresh recollection is not evidence, and the jury should not know what the document says.

Q: At the time, did you inspect what Kelly had written on the sticky note?

A: Yes, as soon as the robbers were gone, Kelly showed me the note, and she wrote it down exactly right. I remember that she got it right.

Q: You still have the piece of paper that I handed to you a few minutes ago. Please look at it again. What is it?

A: This is the sticky note that Kelly wrote containing the license plate of the getaway car.

Q: How are you sure?

A: I clearly remember this document. This is the document that Kelly wrote.

Q: Has the document changed in any way since Kelly wrote it?

A: No. It is exactly the same.

[Prosecutor]: Your honor, at this time, the People offer the yellow sticky note into evidence as past recollection recorded.

[Defense counsel]: I object, your honor. Inadequate foundation.

[Court]: Overruled. The foundation is sufficient for the exception, and the witness authenticated the document. As well, it appears from the witness's testimony that this is the original, satisfying the best evidence rule. Counsel, please have your witness read the document to the jury.

[Prosecutor]: Yes, your honor. Please read aloud what is on the document.

A: Sure, the document says "FRE 803–5."

Q: What is the significance of those letters and numbers?

A: That is the license plate of the getaway car. That is what Kelly wrote down as I called it out at the time of the robbery.

Q: Thank you. No further questions, your honor.

The judge was right to overrule defense counsel's objection. The foundation was proper under the FRE and the CEC. The yellow sticky note will not become an exhibit that goes to the jury, but the jury heard the license plate of the getaway car, and that's what the prosecutor wanted.

§ 11.11(a).   Past Recollection Recorded on the California Bar

In 2012, the California bar tested recollection recorded, among other issues. Here is part of the question, reprinted with permission from the California State Bar:

> Paul sued David in federal court for damages for injuries arising from an automobile accident. . . . In his case-in-chief, David testified that Paul was speeding, lost control of his car, and ran into him. David called Molly, who testified that, on the day of the accident, she had been driving on the highway, saw the aftermath of the accident, stopped to help, and spoke with Paul about the accident. She testified further that, as soon a Paul was taken away in an ambulance, she carefully wrote down notes of what Paul had said to her. She testified that she had no recollection of the conversation. David showed her a photocopy of her notes and she identified them as the ones she wrote down immediately after the accident. The photocopy of the notes was admitted into evidence. The photocopy of the notes stated that Paul told Molly that he was at fault because he was driving too fast and that he offered to pay medical expenses for anyone injured. David rested his case. Assuming that all appropriate objections and motions were timely made, should the court have admitted: . . . 2. The photocopy of Molly's notes? Discuss. Answer according to the Federal Rules of Evidence.

This question raises the following issues: (1) Relevance. Relevance is easy because Paul's statement couldn't be more relevant: It is an admission of responsibility! (2) Authentication. Because a document is being offered, it must be authenticated. Molly can do this because she wrote it, and remembers writing it. (3) Best Evidence Rule. David is trying to prove the contents of a writing, so the best evidence rule applies. A photocopy is a duplicate, and duplicates are admissible to the same extent as an original, unless there is reason to be concerned about the correctness of the duplicate, which there does not appear to be here. (4) Layered hearsay. The original (first) layer is Paul's statements to Molly, which is admissible against Paul as a personal admission. The final (second) layer is Molly's note, which is admissible as past recollection recorded. (5) Paul's offer to pay medical expenses is excluded by FRE 409 (See § 2.23). It is an offer to pay medical expenses resulting from an injury, and is not admissible to prove liability for the injury. (6) Do you need to mention competence to testify (FRE 601) and the danger of unfair prejudice (FRE 403)? The witness is an adult. There does not seem to be any reason to discuss testimonial competence. Nor is there a need to discuss the danger of unfair prejudice because there is nothing unfairly prejudicial about this evidence. Your professor may want you to discuss competence and the danger of unfair prejudice. The bar prep courses encourage you to discuss unfair prejudice every time you discuss relevance.

§ 11.12   Business Records Exception

Businesses large and small keep records. So do government agencies. Such records play a daily role in litigation. When records are offered for the truth, they are hearsay. If the requirements of the business records exception are satisfied, the records are admissible. Business records are considered reliable because employees have a duty to produce accurate records. The rules provide:

> **FRE 803(6). Records of a Regularly Conducted Activity**. A record of an act, event, condition, opinion, or diagnosis [is admissible] if: (A) the record was made at or near the time by—or from information transmitted by— someone with [personal] knowledge; (B) the record was kept in the course of a regularly conducted activity or a business, organization, occupation, or calling, whether or not for profit; (C) making the record was a regular practice of that activity; (D) all these conditions are shown by the testimony of the custodian or another qualified witness, or by a certification that complies with Rule 902(11) or (12) or with a statute permitting certification; and (E) neither the source of information nor the method or circumstances of preparation indicate a lack of trustworthiness.[16]

> **CEC § 1271. Admissible Writings**. Evidence of a writing made as a record of an act, condition, or event is not made inadmissible by the hearsay rule when offered to prove the act, condition, or event if: (a) The writing was made in the regular course of a business; (b) The writing was made at or near the time of the act, condition, or event; (c) the custodian or other qualified witness testifies to its identity and the mode of its preparation; and (d) The sources of

---

[16]   With most FRE hearsay exceptions, when a hearsay statement meets the requirements of the exception, the judge does not go on to determine whether the statement is reliable. The fact that the statement meets the requirements of the exception establishes reliability. With business records and public records, however, the FRE provide that even when a document meets the requirements of one of the exceptions, the judge may be persuaded to exclude the particular business or public record because the circumstances under which the document was created raise questions about reliability.

information and method and time of preparation were such as to indicate its trustworthiness.

The FRE and the CEC define "business" broadly. CEC § 1270 provides that business "includes every kind of business, governmental activity, profession, occupation, calling, or operation of institutions, whether carried on for profit or not." The same breadth applies in the FRE. The source of information contained in a business record must have personal knowledge of the facts reported (FRE 602; CEC § 702). The source of the information does not have to write the record. Just about any type of record can qualify, so long as it is prepared in the ordinary course of regularly conducted business or agency activity.

The foundation for a business record is laid by calling the custodian of records to testify at trial. The custodian does not have to have personal knowledge of the facts. Nor does the custodian have to be the preparer of the document. The custodian is familiar with how records are created and maintained at the business or agency. In addition to laying the foundation for the business records exception, the custodian authenticates the document and satisfies the best evidence rule.

Because it takes time to put a custodian of records on the witness stand, the FRE and the CEC contain mechanisms to lay the foundation without the custodian. The FRE allows certification of business records under FRE 902(11) and (12). CEC §§ 1560–1562 create a procedure involving a special subpoena *duces tecum* for business records.[17]

§ 11.13   If the Record Is Silent, It Didn't Happen

FRE 803(7) and CEC § 1272 allow a kind a negative proof. If an event had happened, it would have been recorded in a business record because it was the regular practice of the business to record such events. The fact that the record is silent is evidence the event did not occur.

§ 11.14   Public Records

Government workers generate mountains of paperwork. If a public record is offered for the truth of the matter asserted, it is hearsay. The public records exception paves the way into evidence.

---

[17]   If you become a litigator in California's Superior Courts, you will use the subpoena for records described in Sections 1560 to 1562. You use a form subpoena created by the Judicial Council. If you'd like to see the form, Google California Forms. Click on Browse All Forms. In the dropdown menu, scroll down to subpoena. Click on SUBP–002. The form tells you exactly what you need to do to comply with Sections 1560 to 1562.

In many cases, government documents are admissible under the public records exception *and* the business records exception. Like the business records exception, public records are considered reliable because government employees have a duty to be accurate. The rules provide:

> **FRE 803(8). Public Records**. A record or statement of a public office [is admissible] if: (A) it sets out; (i) the office's activities; (ii) a matter observed while under a legal duty to report, but not including, in a criminal case, a matter observed by law-enforcement personnel; or (iii) in a civil case or against the government in a criminal case, factual findings from a legally authorized investigation; and (B) neither the source of the information nor other circumstances indicate a lack of trustworthiness.

> **CEC § 1280. Record by Public Employee**. Evidence of a writing made as a record of an act, condition, or event is not made inadmissible by the hearsay rule when offered in any civil or criminal proceeding to prove the act, condition, or event if all of the following applies: (a) The writing was made by and within the scope of duty of a public employee. (b) The writing was made at or near the time of the act, condition, or event. (c) The sources of information and method and time of preparation were such as to indicate its trustworthiness.

There is much overlap between CEC § 1280 and FRE 803(8). In criminal cases, however, the FRE limits the use of law enforcement documents against defendants. These limits are not part of CEC § 1280. The idea behind the FRE's limits on law enforcement documents offered against defendants in criminal cases is that the prosecution should prove its case with live witnesses who can be cross-examined, not with police reports. The roots of the FRE's limits lie in the Confrontation Clause of the Sixth Amendment (*See* § 11.29). Under the CEC, a defense attorney would invoke the Confrontation Clause of the Sixth Amendment to object to police reports.

§ 11.14(a). End Run Around FRE 803(8)'s Restrictions?

Suppose a prosecutor operating under the FRE has a law enforcement document that she would like to offer against the defendant under the public records exception. Unfortunately, the document is barred by FRE 803(8)'s limits on police reports offered against criminal defendants. The prosecutor says, "Your honor, I am not offering the document under the public records exception. I know I can't do that. I offer the document under the business records exception which, as the court knows, does not contain those limits on police reports." Pretty clever, huh? Will it work? Probably not. The defense attorney will cite *United States v. Oates*, 560 F.2d 45 (2d Cir. 1977), in which the Second Circuit ruled that when a law enforcement document is barred by the restrictions of Rule 803(8), a prosecutor can't circumvent those restrictions by offering the document as a business record.

§ 11.14(b). Findings of Fact and Conclusions

The public records exception admits public documents containing factual findings and conclusions. In the leading case of *Beech Aircraft Corp. v. Rainey*, 488 U.S. 153, 109 S. Ct. 439 (1988), the Supreme Court ruled that FRE 803(8) authorizes admission of government reports that state conclusions and opinions.

§ 11.15 No Record Exists

FRE 803(10) and CEC § 1284 allow proof that a public record does not exist. The party seeking to prove nonexistence offers evidence that a search was conducted for the record, but the search was unsuccessful. The FRE, but not the CEC, allow a fruitless search to prove that an event did not occur because, if it did occur, a public employee would have documented it.

§ 11.16 Ancient Documents

Hearsay is excluded because it can be unreliable. People don't always tell the truth. Documents are sometimes altered to gain an advantage in court. When a document is decades old, however, there is virtually no chance it was created or altered with the current lawsuit in mind, lowering concerns about tampering. The FRE and the CEC have a hearsay exception for "ancient documents." (FRE 803(16); CEC § 1331). The FRE exception requires the document to be at least 20 years old. The CEC exception requires at least 30 years.

When you see an ancient document on an exam, in addition to discussing the hearsay exception, talk about the special rules regarding authentication of ancient documents. The authentication rules are found at FRE 901(8) and CEC § 643 (*See* § 3.11(i)). Of course, you should also discuss the best evidence rule, or, in California, the secondary evidence rule.

§ 11.17 Learned Treatises

Section 9.15, discussed use of professional books and journal articles to impeach expert witnesses. When a learned treatise is used for the limited purpose of impeachment, the treatise is not offered for the truth, and is not hearsay. However, when the contents of a book or journal article are offered for the truth, the material is hearsay. The FRE and the CEC contain hearsay exceptions for so-called learned treatises. The FRE exception is much broader than the CEC exception. The rules provide:

> **FRE 803(18). Statements in Learned Treatises, Periodicals, or Pamphlets**. A statement contained in a treatise, periodical, or pamphlet [is admissible] if: (A) the statement is called to the attention of an expert witness on cross-examination or relied on by the expert on direct examination; and (B) the publication is established as a reliable authority by the expert's admission or testimony, by another expert's testimony, or by judicial notice. If admitted, the statement may be read into evidence but not received as an exhibit.

> **CEC § 1341. Publications Concerning Facts of General Notoriety and Interest**. Historical works, books of science or art, and published maps or charts, made by persons indifferent between the parties, are not made inadmissible by the hearsay rule when offered to prove facts of general notoriety and interest.

FRE 803(18) is structured so that attorneys can't simply offer books and articles into evidence. A learned treatise must be used in conjunction with an expert witness, who is in a position to explain the contents of the treatise.[18]

§ 11.18   Former Testimony

When a person testifies at an earlier trial, and a transcript of the earlier testimony is offered at a subsequent trial, the earlier testimony is hearsay.[19] The FRE and the CEC have hearsay exceptions for former testimony. Former testimony is reliable because it was under oath and subject to cross-examination. The rules state:

> **FRE 804(b)(1). Former Testimony**. The following [is] not excluded by the rule against hearsay if the declarant is unavailable as a witness: Testimony that: (A) was given as a witness at a trial, hearing, or lawful deposition, whether given during the current proceeding or a different one; and

---

[18]   If attorneys could offer books and articles without an expert on the witness stand to interpret the material, attorneys would bring in boxes of books and articles, and ask the jury to consider them, a task for which the jury is not well equipped.

[19]   The earlier testimony was in court, but, for hearsay purposes, the earlier testimony is out of court; that is, out of *this* court.

(B) is now offered against a party who had—or, in a civil case, whose predecessor in interest had—an opportunity and similar motive to develop it by direct, cross-, or redirect examination.

CEC § 1290. Former Testimony. As used in this article, "former testimony" means testimony given under oath in: (a) Another action or in a former hearing or trial of the same action; (b) A proceeding to determine a controversy conducted by or under the supervision of an agency that has the power to determine such a controversy and is an agency of the United States or a public entity in the United States; (c) A deposition taken in compliance with law in another action; or (d) An arbitration proceeding if the evidence of such former testimony is a verbatim transcript thereof.

CEC § 1291. Former Testimony Offered Against Party to Former Proceeding. (a) Evidence of former testimony is not made inadmissible by the hearsay rule if the declarant is unavailable as a witness and: (1) The former testimony is offered against a person who offered it in evidence in his own behalf on the former occasion or against the successor in interest of such person; or (2) The party against whom the former testimony is offered was a party to the action or proceeding in which the testimony was given and had the right and opportunity to cross-examine the declarant with an interest and motive similar to that which he has at the hearing.

CEC § 1292. Former Testimony Offered Against Person Not a Party to Former Proceeding. (a) Evidence of former testimony is not made inadmissible by the hearsay rule if: (1) The declarant is unavailable as a witness; (2) The former testimony is offered in a civil action; and (3) The issue is such that the party to the action or proceeding in which the former testimony was given had the right and opportunity to cross-examine the declarant with an interest and motive similar to that which the party against whom the testimony is offered has at the hearing.

§ 11.18(a). Basic Requirements

Understand some basic requirements of former testimony. First, the witness at the earlier trial—the declarant—must be unavailable at the subsequent trial. Second, the exception requires that a party at the earlier trial had an opportunity to develop the witness's testimony by direct examination, cross-examination, or redirect examination. In the vast majority of cases, the opportunity was for cross-examination. Actual cross-examination is not necessary. What is required is the opportunity for cross-examination at the earlier trial. Third, keep your eye on whether the party against whom former testimony is offered at the subsequent trial (trial number 2) was a party to the earlier trial (trial number 1).

§ 11.18(b).   Schematic Approach to Former Testimony

Former testimony can be tricky. It is useful to outline the facts in the following manner:

Trial number 1.   Who were the parties to trial number 1? What testimony at trial number 1 is being offered at trial number 2? Who had the opportunity to cross-examine the now-unavailable witness at trial number 1?

Trial number 2.   Who are the parties to trial number 2? Is trial number 2 civil or criminal? It doesn't matter whether trial number 1 was criminal or civil.

With the facts divided into trial number 1 and trial number 2, you are in a position to apply the FRE and the CEC.

If the party against whom former testimony is offered at trial number 2 *was* a party to trial number 1, then it doesn't matter whether trial number 2 is civil or criminal. When the party against former testimony is offered at trial number 2 was *not* a party to trial number 1, then the former testimony exception does not apply if trial number 2 is criminal. Is this giving you a headache?

§ 11.18(c).   When the Party Against Whom Former Testimony Is Offered at Trial Number 2 W*as* a Party to Trial Number 1

When the party against whom former testimony is offered at trial number 2 was a party to trial number 1, and had an opportunity to cross-examine the declarant at trial number 1, with a motive that is similar to the motive at trial number 2, the former testimony is admissible. This is true whether trial number 2 is civil or criminal.

§ 11.18(d). When the Party Against Whom Former Testimony Is Offered at Trial Number 2 Was *Not* a Party to Trial Number 1

This is where things get tricky. When the party to trial number 2 was not a party to trial number 1, the party had no opportunity to cross-examine the now-unavailable declarant at trial number 1. In this scenario, former testimony is only admissible if trial number 2 is civil. If trial number 2 is criminal, former testimony is not admissible against a defendant who was not a party to trial number 1.[20]

§ 11.18(e). FRE 804(b)(1)'s Predecessor in Interest Language

When trial number 2 is civil, and the party against whom former testimony is offered was *not* a party to trial number 1, FRE 804(b)(1) states that former testimony is admissible only if the party to trial number 1 was a predecessor in interest to the party at trial number 2, against whom the former testimony is offered. "Predecessor in interest" is a property concept. When A sells Blackacre to B, A is a predecessor in interest to B. When A dies, and leaves Blackacre to B in her (A's) will, A is a predecessor in interest to B. Courts that apply FRE 804(b)(1) usually ignore the property meaning of predecessor in interest, and interpret the rule to ask whether the party to trial number 1 had a motive to cross-examine that is similar to the motive the party to trial number 2 would have.[21] When the words predecessor in interest are interpreted this way, there is no difference between FRE 804(b)(1) and CEC § 1292.

§ 11.18(f). Examples of Former Testimony

A couple of examples of former testimony will help.

1. Able and Baker are business partners.[22] They owned a building that burned down. Able and Baker filed a claim with their insurance company, but the insurance company refused to pay, claiming that Able deliberately set the fire. Able and Baker sue the insurance company. A year earlier, Able was prosecuted for arson for allegedly burning the building. At the arson trial, Zanny testified for the prosecutor as follows: "Able asked me to help him burn the building. We burned it together. Baker knew about it." At

---

[20] The reason former testimony is inadmissible lies in the constitutional right of the defendant in a criminal case to confront and cross-examine the prosecution's witnesses.

[21] *See* Rich v. Kaiser Gypsum Co., 103 So. 3d 903 (Fla. Ct. App. 2012).

[22] This example is based on *Travelers Fire Insurance Co. v. J.C. Wright and J.B. Wright*, 322 P.2d 417 (Okla. 1958).

the trial against the insurance company, Zanny is unavailable to testify. The insurance company offers Zanny's testimony from the arson trial against Able and Baker. Analyze under the FRE and the CEC. First, use the schematic approach to outline the facts:

Trial number 1:   People v. Able. Baker is not a party to trial number 1. Able had an opportunity and a motive to cross-examine Zanny at trial number 1. Baker had no opportunity to cross-examine Zanny at trial number 1.

Trial number 2:   Able and Baker v. Insurance Company. Trial number 2 is civil.

Under the FRE, Zanny's testimony at trial number 1 is admissible against Able and Baker at trial number 2. As for Able, he was a party to trial number 1, and had an opportunity and motive to cross-examine Zanny that is the same as the motive he would have if Zanny testified at trial number 2. As for Baker, although he was not a party to trial number 1, Able was a party, and Able had an opportunity to cross-examine Zanny with the same motive Baker would have. A court applying FRE 804(b)(1) will ignore the words "predecessor in interest." Under the CEC, Zanny's testimony is admissible against Able under Section 1291, and is admissible against Baker under Section 1292.

2.   Change the facts. Trial number 1 was the civil trial: Able v. Insurance Company. Zanny testified, "Able asked me to help him burn the building. We burned it together. Baker knew about it." Six months following the civil trial, Able and Baker are prosecuted for burning the building. Zanny is unavailable. The prosecutor offers Zanny's testimony from the civil trial against Able and Baker. First, the schematic:

Trial number 1:   Able v. Insurance Company. Able was a party; Baker was not.

Trial number 2:   People v. Able and Baker. Trial number 2 is criminal.

Under the FRE, Zanny's former testimony is admissible against Able, but not Baker because trial number 2 is criminal. The same is true under the CEC. Zanny's testimony is admissible against Able under CEC § 1291. Zanny's testimony is not admissible against Baker, because CEC § 1292 only applies when trial number 2 is civil.

3.   Ahtoh is on trial for murder. At the preliminary hearing, Shelia testified for the prosecution as follows: "I dropped Ahtoh off near the scene about half an hour before it happened." At trial, Shelia is unavailable. The prosecutor offers Shelia's testimony at

the preliminary hearing. Is her testimony admissible under the FRE and/or the CEC? Yes. A preliminary hearing is an adversary proceeding, where a defendant has an opportunity to cross-examine prosecution witnesses. Ahtoh was a party to the preliminary hearing. Shelia's testimony at the prelim is admissible at trial.

4. Melba sued Carla for negligently causing a traffic accident. At trial, Melba offered the following testimony from Zeek, "Carla was speeding toward the intersection. She blasted right through the red light and into Melba's car." Six months later, Carla is prosecuted for speeding, running a red light, and recklessly causing an accident. At the criminal trial, Zeek is unavailable. The prosecutor offers Zeek's former testimony against Carla. The testimony is admissible under the FRE and the CEC.

§ 11.19   Dying Declarations

The dying declaration exception may be the oldest exception. Dying declarations are considered reliable because a person who believes she is dying will not want to meet her maker with a lie upon her lips. The rules provide:

> **FRE 804(b)(2). Statement Under the Belief of Imminent Death**. The following [is] not excluded by the rule against hearsay if the declarant is unavailable as a witness: In a prosecution for homicide or in a civil case, a statement that the declarant, while believing the declarant's death to be imminent, made about its cause or circumstances.

> **CEC § 1242. Dying Declaration**. Evidence of a statement by a dying person respecting the cause and circumstances of his death is not made inadmissible by the hearsay rule if the statement was made upon his personal knowledge and under a sense of immediately impending death.

Both exceptions require the declarant to be unavailable. The CEC requires the declarant to be dead.[23] The FRE requires unavailability, but not death. The FRE and CEC apply in all types of civil cases. In criminal cases, the FRE is narrower than the CEC because the FRE applies only in homicide cases.

Under both exceptions, the proponent must persuade the judge that the declarant thought she was dying. Proof of a sense of impending death may come from the nature of injuries or illness,

---

[23]   Under the CEC, the declarant does not have to die right away. All that is required is that the declarant be dead at the time the hearsay is offered. Some scholars believe Section 1242 does not require the declarant to be deceased.

administration of last rights, statements by the declarant—"I'm dying"—and statements to the declarant—"You ain't gonna make it."

§ 11.20   Statement Against Interest

People don't generally make statements that could get them in trouble unless the statements are true. That's the theory behind the exception for statements against interest: The danger of insincerity is reduced. The rules provide:

> **FRE 804(b)(3). Statement Against Interest**. The following [is] not excluded by the rule against hearsay if the declarant is unavailable as a witness: A statement that: (A) a reasonable person in the declarant's position would have made only if the person believed it to be true because, when made, it was so contrary to the declarant's proprietary or pecuniary interest or had so great a tendency to invalidate the declarant's claim against someone else or to expose the declarant to civil or criminal liability; and (B) if supported by corroborating circumstances that clearly indicate its trustworthiness, it is offered in a criminal case as one that tends to expose the declarant to criminal liability.

> **CEC § 1230. Declarations Against Interest**. Evidence of a statement by a declarant having sufficient knowledge of the subject is not made inadmissible by the hearsay rule if the declarant is unavailable as a witness and the statement, when made, was so far contrary to the declarant's pecuniary or proprietary interest, or so far subjected him to the risk of civil or criminal liability, or so far tended to invalidate a claim by him against another, or created such a risk of making him an object of hatred, ridicule, or social disgrace in the community, that a reasonable person in his position would not have made the statement unless believing it to be true.

The FRE and the CEC exceptions are similar. There are two differences. First, California's exception extends to statements that could subject the declarant to social stigma. The FRE does not include such statements. Second, the FRE provides that when a defendant in a criminal case offers a declaration against interest by an unavailable declarant that implicates the declarant in the crime, and, usually, exculpates the defendant, the statement is admissible only if it is clearly corroborated by other evidence. The CEC does not have this corroboration requirement. The reason for the FRE corroboration requirement is the belief that defendants have an incentive to manufacture false declarations against interest by declarants who are unavailable because they don't exist! To lower this likelihood, the FRE allows such declarations only when corroborative evidence supports the belief the declarant really existed and made the statement.

§ 11.20(a). The *Williamson* Issue

A declaration against interest must be against the declarant's interest—that's what makes it reliable. What if a declarant makes a statement that is against her interest, but the statement also mentions someone else, and gets that person in trouble too! Is the part of the statement that gets the *other person in trouble* admissible as a declaration against interest? This question was addressed by the U.S. Supreme Court in *Williamson v. United States,* 512 U.S. 594, 114 S. Ct. 2431 (1994). The Court ruled that such a statement is admissible only if the part of the statement that mentions the other person is against the *declarant's interest.* With a few changed facts, here is what happened in *Williamson*: Harris was pulled over by the CHP for weaving across lanes on U.S. 101 between San Francisco and San Jose. Harris consented to a search of his car, which revealed 19 kilograms of cocaine. Harris was arrested. During questioning, Harris said, "I was driving the drugs to San Jose for Williamson. When you pulled me over, Williamson was in the car ahead of me. He saw your lights and kept going." Williamson is charged with possession of cocaine for distribution. At Williamson's trial, Harris is dead. The prosecutor offers Harris's statement about transporting the drugs to San Jose for Williamson. The prosecutor argues that Harris' statement is a declaration against *Harris's* interest.[24] There is no doubt that admitting he was transporting drugs was against Harris' penal interest. However, Harris is not on trial. He's dead. It is Williamson who is on trial, and Williamson's attorney argues that the part of Harris's statement that mentioned Williamson is inadmissible because that part of the statement is not against *Harris's* interest. A statement is only admissible under the exception if it is against the *declarant's* interest. As the Court put it, "The question under Rule 804(b)(3) is always whether the statement was sufficiently against the declarant's penal interest that a reasonable person in the declarant's position would not have made the statement unless believing it to be true, and this question can only be answered in light of all the surrounding circumstances."

---

[24]   Harris's statement is not admissible under the co-conspirator exception because Harris was arrested when he spoke, which means the conspiracy was over.

On exams, be on the lookout for the *Williamson* issue. *Williamson* may be lurking when (1) A declarant makes a statement that is against the declarant's interest *and the defendant's* interest, (2) The declarant is unavailable at trial, and (3) The prosecutor offers the statement against the *defendant*. Ask, was the part of the statement that mentions the defendant against the *declarant's interest?*

§ 11.21   Prior Inconsistent Statement

Section 10.4, addresses prior inconsistent statements to impeach. Refer to that section for discussion of prior inconsistent statements. The present section summarizes the hearsay aspect of prior inconsistent statements. When a prior inconsistent statement is offered for the limited purpose of impeachment, it is not hearsay because it is not offered for the truth of the matter asserted. When a prior inconsistent statement is offered both to impeach *and* to prove the truth of the inconsistent statement, it meets the definition of hearsay.

Under the CEC, Section 1235 is a hearsay exception for all prior inconsistent statements. Thus, in California, prior inconsistent statements are admissible to impeach and for the truth.

The FRE is more complicated. Under the FRE, all prior inconsistent statements are admissible for the limited purpose of impeachment, but only some are admissible for the truth. FRE 801(d)(1)(A) provides that only prior inconsistent statements that were made "under penalty of perjury at a trial, hearing, or other proceedings or in a deposition" are admissible for the truth of the matter asserted.

One more FRE detail needs mentioning, although it is a matter more of form than substance. FRE 801(d)(1) allows admission of prior inconsistent statements, prior consistent statements, and out-of-court statements of identification. Rule 801(d)(1) defines these as "not hearsay" despite the fact that each is an out of court statement offered for the truth of the matter asserted. The CEC, by contrast, treats the three as hearsay within exceptions. Thus, FRE 801(d)(1) creates *exemptions* from hearsay rather than *exceptions*. Some professors think the distinction between exemption and exception is worth mentioning. Other professors, influenced by the fact that the distinction makes no difference in practice, tell students, "I don't care whether you call FRE 801(d)(1) exemptions or exceptions; just know how they work."

§ 11.22   Prior Consistent Statement

Section 10.14(b), addresses prior consistent statements to rehabilitate. This section summarizes the hearsay aspect of prior consistent statements. When a prior consistent statement is offered for the limited purpose of rehabilitation, it is not hearsay because it is not offered for the truth. When a prior consistent statement is offered both to rehabilitate and for the truth, it meets the definition of hearsay.

CEC § 1236 creates a hearsay exception for all admissible prior consistent statements. FRE 801(d)(1)(B) is the same, except the FRE calls them not hearsay, rather than hearsay within an exception. Thus, regarding the admissibility of prior consistent statements for the truth, the CEC and the FRE are the same. One calls them an exception, the other calls them an exemption, but it makes no practical difference.

§ 11.23   Out-of-Court Statement of Identification

At trial, it is common for a witness to identify the person who committed a crime. The prosecutor says, "Do you see—here in court—the person who broke into your house?" The witness says, "Yes." The Prosecutor asks, "Please point to the person who broke in, and identify that person by where the person is sitting, and what the person is wearing." The witness answers, "The person who broke into my house is the defendant, seated next to his lawyer, and he is wearing a white shirt and a tie." This in-court identification is not hearsay.

In addition to in-court identifications, FRE 801(d)(1)(C) and CEC § 1238 allow admission of out-of-court identifications. The rules provide:

FRE   801(d)(1)(C). A   Declarant-Witness's   Prior Statement. A statement that meets the following conditions is not hearsay. The declarant testifies and is subject to cross-examination about a prior statement, and the statement: (C) identifies a person as someone the declarant perceived earlier.

CEC   § 1238. Prior   Identification. Evidence of a statement previously made by a witness is not made inadmissible by the hearsay rule if the statement would have been admissible if made by him while testifying and: (a) The statement is an identification of a party or another as a person who participated in a crime or other occurrence; (b) The statement was made at a time when the crime or other occurrence was fresh in the witness' memory; and (c) The evidence of the statement is offered after the witness testifies that he made the identification and that it was a true reflection of his opinion at that time.

Although the CEC rule has more requirements that the FRE, the rules operate similarly in practice, authorizing receipt of out-of-court identifications for the truth.

§ 11.24   Party Admissions

You have heard the saying, "Anything you say can be used against you." In court, the saying is pretty much true. Anything a party said out-of-court, that is relevant, is admissible against the party. Of course, some party statements are excluded by specific rules. For example, if Dell ran over a pedestrian, and Dell visited the pedestrian at the hospital and said, "I'm so sorry, I'd like to pay your medical bills," this statement is excluded by FRE 409 and CEC § 1160. Apart from specific rules, anything a party said out-of-court, that is relevant, is admissible against the party. This use of out-of-court statements for the truth is called party admissions.

With party admissions, personal knowledge is not required. Nor are party admissions admitted because they are reliable. Hearsay is excluded because the declarant cannot be cross-examined. With party admissions, *the declarant is a party*, and a party will not be heard to say, "I can't cross-examine myself." Thus, anything you say can be used against you.

The FRE define party admissions as not hearsay. The CEC defines party admissions as hearsay within exceptions. There is no practical difference.

§ 11.24(a).   Personal Admissions

Anything a party says in her individual or representative capacity is admissible against the party.[25] These are personal admissions. The rules provide:

> **FRE 801(d)(2)(A). Statements That Are Not Hearsay**. A statement that meets the following conditions is not hearsay: **(2) An Opposing Party's Statement**. The statement is offered against an opposing party and: **(A)** Was made by a party in an individual or representative capacity.

---

[25]   Representative capacity refers to a trustee, an executor of an estate, or some similar position.

CEC § 1220. Admission of Party. Evidence of a statement is not made inadmissible by the hearsay rule when offered against the declarant in an action to which he is a party in either his individual or representative capacity, regardless of whether the statement was made in his individual or representative capacity.

The FRE and CEC rules on personal admissions are virtually identical. Of course, the FRE defines them as not hearsay, while the CEC defines them as hearsay within an exception, but this is a distinction without a difference.

Party admissions are offered *against* a party. A party can't use the party admission rule to offer the party's own statements in the party's favor.

§ 11.24(b). Adoptive Admissions

A party can adopt someone else's statement, making the statement the party's own, and thus admissible against the adopting party. For example, Xavier, who is not a party, said, "It is extremely foggy tonight." Dell, who is a party, and who was standing near Xavier, said, "What Xavier says is true." Xavier's statement is admissible against Dell. The rules state:

FRE 801(d)(2)(B). Statements That Are Not Hearsay. A statement that meets the following conditions is not hearsay: (2) An Opposing Party's Statement. The statement is offered against an opposing party and: (B) is one the party manifested that it adopted or believed to be true.

CEC § 1221. Adoptive Admission. Evidence of a statement offered against a party is not made inadmissible by the hearsay rule if the statement is one of which the party, with knowledge of the content thereof, has by words or other conduct manifested his adoption or his belief in its truth.

On exams, the thing that's tricky about adoptive admissions is that the declarant is *not* a party, making it easy to miss the party admission issue. Look for facts indicating that a party adopted a non-party declarant's words.

Another tricky bit is adoption by silence. A non-party makes a statement within earshot and understanding of a party, but the party says nothing. How can saying nothing be an adoption of a statement? Often, it isn't. Sometimes, however, saying nothing is construed as an adoption by silence. This happens when a judge is persuaded that the party heard and understood the statement, there were no impediments to responding to the statement, and a reasonable person in the circumstances would have denied the statement if it were untrue.

In practice, the FRE and CEC rules on adoptive admissions are the same.

§ 11.24(c). Authorized Admissions

When a person is expressly authorized to speak on behalf of another person, the authorized speaker's statements that are within the ambit of the speaker's authority are admissible against the principal.[26] These are called authorized admissions, or statements by speaking agents. The rules provide:

> **FRE 801(d)(2)(C). Statements That Are Not Hearsay**. A statement that meets the following conditions is not hearsay: **(2) An Opposing Party's Statement**. The statement is offered against an opposing party and: **(C)** was made by a person whom the party authorized to make a statement on the subject.

> **CEC § 1222. Authorized Admission**. Evidence of a statement offered against a party is not made inadmissible by the hearsay rule if: (a) The statement was made by a person authorized by the party to make a statement or statements for him concerning the subject matter of the statement; and (b) The evidence is offered either after admission of evidence sufficient to sustain a finding of such authority or, in the court's discretion as to the order of proof, subject to the admission of such evidence.

Authority to speak on behalf of a party is determined by the law of agency. The FRE and the CEC rules on speaking agents are the same.

§ 11.24(d). Employee Admissions

By long tradition, statements by employees were not binding on employers. For example, Felma was employed to drive a truck for Trucking Company. Felma was involved in a traffic accident, and told a police officer, "The brakes failed. They had not been serviced for too long." If Felma is sued, her statement is admissible against her as a personal admission. However, if the company is sued, Felma's statement was not admissible against her employer, Trucking Company. Felma was not a speaking agent for the company. She was hired to drive truck, not make statements binding the company. FRE 801(d)(2)(D) changed the traditional law,

---

[26]   *See* People v. Selivanov, 5 Cal. App. 5th 726, 210 Cal. Rptr. 3d 117 (2017).

admitting statements of employees against the employer, so long as the statement was within the scope of the employee's job, and was made while the person was employed by the employer. Under FRE 801(d)(2)(D), Felma's statement about the brakes is admissible against Trucking Company. The CEC counterpart to FRE 801(d)(2)(D) is CEC § 1224. The rules provide:

> **FRE 801(d)(2)(D). Statements That Are Not Hearsay**. A statement that meets the following conditions is not hearsay: **(2) An Opposing Party's Statement**. The statement is offered against an opposing party and: **(D)** was made by the party's agent or employee on a matter within the scope of that relationship while it existed.

> **CEC § 1224. Statement of Declarant Whose Liability or Breach of Duty Is in Issue**. When the liability, obligation, or duty of a party to a civil action is based in whole or in part upon the liability, obligation, or duty of the declarant, or when the claim or right asserted by a party to a civil action is barred or diminished by a breach of duty by the declarant, evidence of a statement made by the declarant is as admissible against the party as it would be if offered against the declarant in an action involving that liability, obligation, duty, or breach of duty.

At first reading, CEC § 1224 seems to allow statements of employees to be admitted against employers, similar to FRE 801(d)(2)(D). Not so. In *Markely v. Beagle*, 66 Cal. 2d 951, 429 P.2d 129, 59 Cal. Rptr. 809 (1967), the Supreme Court ruled that CEC § 1224 "did not change the settled and apparently universally followed rule that hearsay statements of an agent or employee not otherwise admissible against the principal or employer are not made admissible merely because they may tend to prove negligence of the agent or employee that may be imputed to the principal or employer under the doctrine of *respondeat superior*."[27]

§ 11.24(e). Co-Conspirator Exception

Statements by a conspirator, during the course of, and in furtherance of the conspiracy, are admissible against the other

---

[27]   *See also,* White v. FAV, Inc. 2006 WL 2497890 (Cal. Ct. App. 2006)(not officially published).

In *Beagle*, the great Justice Traynor wrote that the approach he adopted was "settled and apparently universally followed." When Justice Traynor wrote *Beagle* in 1967, the FRE had not been adopted. That happened in 1975. Of course, the FRE departed dramatically from the position Justice Traynor knew to be "universally followed." When FRE 801(d)(2)(D) was adopted, it caused quite a stir, and was considered a major change in the law.

conspirators under the co-conspirator exception.[28] The declarant-conspirator's own words are admissible against the declarant as personal admissions (FRE 801(d)(2)(A); CEC § 1220). It is the co-conspirator exception that gets the words into evidence against the other conspirators. When the conspiracy ends, so does the co-conspirator exception. On exams, watch for the end of the conspiracy, which often happens when some or all of the bad guys are arrested. Statements post-arrest don't fall within the co-conspirator exception because the conspiracy is over for the speaker.

To be admissible under the co-conspirator exception, statements must somehow further or add to the conspiracy. Mere idle chatter among conspirators, or to people outside the conspiracy, does not further the conspiracy, and is not within the exception. Thus, when one conspirator says to another, "We need to steal some guns for the job," this statement furthers the conspiracy, and is admissible under the exception. On the other hand, if a conspirator is bragging to her boyfriend and says, "Me and my mates is gonna do something big, real big," this statement does not further the conspiracy. The statement is admissible against the declarant as a personal admission, but is not admissible against the other conspirators. The rules provide:

> **FRE 801(d)(2)(E). Statements That Are Not Hearsay**. A statement that meets the following conditions is not hearsay: **(2) An Opposing Party's Statement**. The statement is offered against an opposing party and: **(E)** was made by the party's co-conspirator during and in furtherance of the conspiracy.

> **CEC § 1223. Admission of Co-Conspirator**. Evidence of a statement offered against a party is not made inadmissible by the hearsay rule if: (a) The statement was made by the declarant while participating in a conspiracy to commit a crime or civil wrong and in furtherance of the objective of that conspiracy; (b) The statement was made prior to or during the time that the party was participating in that conspiracy; and (c) The evidence is offered either after admission of evidence sufficient to sustain a finding of the facts specified in subdivisions (a)

---

[28] *See* People v. Clark, 63 Cal. 4th 522, 562, 372 P.3d 811, 203 Cal. Rptr. 3d 407 (2016)("Under Evidence Code section 1223, three preliminary facts must be established for evidence of a coconspirator's declaration to be admissible: (1) that the declarant was participating in the conspiracy in question at the time of the declaration, (2) that the declaration furthered or was meant to further the conspiracy's objective, and (3) that the party against whom the evidence is offered was—at the time of the declaration—participating in the conspiracy, or would later participate in it.").

and (b) or, in the court's discretion as to the order of proof, subject to the admission of such evidence.

The party offering an out-of-court statement under the co-conspirator exception must establish the conspiracy. The statement is admissible to prove the conspiracy, but the statement is not sufficient.[29]

A person can join an ongoing conspiracy. A late-joiner is bound by co-conspirator statements uttered before the late-joiner joined.[30]

§ 11.25   Residual Exception

Hearsay statements sometimes come along that seem to be reliable, but don't fit an exception. The FRE has a residual or catchall exception for such statements. The residual exception provides:

> **FRE 807. Residual Exception.** (a) Under the following circumstances, a hearsay statement is not excluded by the rule against hearsay even if the statement is not specifically covered by a hearsay exception in Rule 803 or 804: (1) the statement has equivalent circumstantial guarantees of trustworthiness;[31] (2) it is offered as evidence of a material fact; (3) it is more probative on the point for which it is offered than any other evidence that the proponent can obtain through reasonable efforts; and (4) admitting it will best serve the purposes of these rules and the interests of justice. (b) The statement is admissible only if, before the trial or hearing, the proponent gives an adverse party reasonable notice of the intent to offer the statement and its particulars, including

---

[29]   FRE 801(d)(2) states, "The statement must be considered but does by itself establish the declarant's authority under (C); the existence or scope of the relationship under (D); or the existence of the conspiracy or participation in it under (E)." *See,* People v. Thompson, 1 Cal. 5th 1043, 384 P.3d 693, 210 Cal. Rptr. 3d 693 (2016)(it is necessary to have proof of the conspiracy that is independent of the statement).

[30]   *See* People v. Clark, 63 Cal. 4th 522, 562, 372 P.3d 811, 203 Cal. Rptr. 3d 407 (2016) ("Under Evidence Code section 1223, three preliminary facts must be established for evidence of a coconspirator's declaration to be admissible: (1) that the declarant was participating in the conspiracy in question at the time of the declaration, (2) that the declaration furthered or was meant to further the conspiracy's objective, and (3) that the party against whom the evidence is offered was—at the time of the declaration—participating in the conspiracy, or would later participate in it.").

[31]   By "equivalent circumstantial guarantees of trustworthiness," the residual exception means there is something about the hearsay offered under the residual exception that makes it reliable, similar to hearsay admissible under other exceptions. One or more of the four risks of hearsay is lowered.

the declarant's name and address, so that the party has a fair opportunity to meet it.

The CEC does not have a generally applicable residual exception. The CEC does have a residual exception for reliable statements by children in child sexual abuse cases (CEC § 1228). As well, the California Supreme Court created an exception to the hearsay rule for children's reliable hearsay in juvenile court proceedings to protect abused and neglected children (*In re Cindy L.*, 17 Cal. 4th 15, 947 P.2d 1340, 69 Cal. Rptr. 2d 803 (1997).[32]

When hearsay is offered under a residual exception, the judge considers the totality of circumstances that shed light on reliability, including: Was the statement spontaneous, or was it elicited in response to leading and suggestive questions? Was the declarant consistent over time? What was the declarant's emotional and physical condition when the declarant spoke? Did the declarant have a motive to lie or tell the truth? Is there evidence that corroborates the statement? These and other relevant factors are considered to determine whether hearsay is sufficiently reliable to be admitted.

§ 11.26   Minor Exceptions

The FRE and the CEC contain a number of relatively minor exceptions. FRE 803(9) and CEC § 1281 admit public records of births, deaths, and marriages. FRE 803(11) and (12), and CEC §§ 1315 and 1316, allow records of religious organizations describing births, deaths, family relationships, marriages, and family history, as well as documents certifying that a person performed a marriage or sacrament. FRE 803(13) and CEC § 1312 admit personal family records, such as a family genealogy in a family bible, engraving on a ring, or writing on a burial marker. FRE 803(14) admits certain documents affecting an interest in property, recorded in a government office. The CEC does not have an exact counterpart to FRE 803(14), but CEC § 1330, admits deeds and wills affecting interests in property. FRE 803(15) and CEC § 1330 deal with documents creating interests in property. FRE 803(17) and CEC § 1340 create exceptions for certain commercial documents. FRE 803(19) and CEC § 1313 allow hearsay statements regarding a person's reputation about family history. FRE 803(20) and CEC § 1322 allow admission of statements about property boundaries. FRE 803(21) and CEC § 1324 create a hearsay exception for character evidence in the form of reputation. FRE

---

[32]   In juvenile court dependency proceedings, the California Welfare and Institutions Code creates an additional hearsay exception, this one for reports written by social workers (W&I § 355(b)).

803(22) and (23) and CEC §§ 1300–1302 allow evidence of court judgments.

§ 11.27   Hearsay Within Hearsay—Layered Hearsay

Frequently, a hearsay statement contains within it another hearsay statement—layered hearsay. For example, in a personal injury case, the plaintiff offers a police report against the defendant. In the police report, the officer who wrote the report quoted an eyewitness to the accident, who said, "I saw the whole thing. The brown Fiat turned left, right in front of the other car." There are two hearsay statements. First, the statement by the eyewitness to the accident. Second, the police report that quotes the eyewitness. Consider another example: After the accident, the driver of the Fiat was in the hospital, speaking to a doctor. The Fiat driver told the doctor, "I wasn't watching. I was texting. I turned left, and didn't see the other car. It was my fault." The doctor repeated the driver's words in the patient's medical record. Again, two layers of hearsay. First, the driver's statement to the doctor. Second, the doctor's medical record, in which the doctor repeated what the driver said. Under the FRE and the CEC, with layered hearsay, each layer must meet the requirements of a hearsay exception. The rules state:

> **Rule 805. Hearsay Within Hearsay.** Hearsay within hearsay is not excluded by the rule against hearsay if each part of the combined statements conforms with an exception to the rule.

> **CEC § 1201. Multiple Hearsay.** A statement within the scope of an exception to the hearsay rule is not inadmissible on the ground that the evidence of such statement is hearsay evidence if such hearsay evidence consists of one or more statements each of which meets the requirements of an exception to the hearsay rule.

The CEC and the FRE rules on layered hearsay are the same. When you detect layered hearsay, it is useful to diagram the layers. The original statement is the first statement. If there are only two layers, then the second statement is the final statement. In rare cases, there are three layers, but most of the time, just two. With each layer, determine whether the layer meets the requirement of an exception. Try your hand with the following exercises:

1.   In a personal injury trial, *defendant* offers a police report containing a statement by plaintiff describing the cause of the accident. The witness on the stand is the custodian of records for the police department.

2.   In a personal injury trial, defendant offers plaintiff's medical record from the hospital where plaintiff was treated after the accident. The medical record contains a statement made by plaintiff to a doctor at the hospital, and repeated by the doctor in the record. The witness on the stand is the custodian of records at the hospital.

3.   In a murder prosecution, defendant admits she shot the victim, but claims she acted in self-defense. Defense counsel offers the testimony of Xeno, who will testify that defendant told her (Xeno) that the victim told her (defendant), "I'm (this is the victim speaking) going to get you. You'd better watch your back. Snitches get stitches."

4.   Problem 4 concerns an accident that happened at an intersection in Truckee. Abe was driving a Ford F150 pickup. Ben was driving a Chevy Silverado pickup. Abe is suing Ben for personal injuries sustained in the wreck. A police report was prepared. The following questions offer different versions of what the police report stated. In each case, Abe wants to introduce the police report into evidence against Ben.

a.   The police officer who wrote the police report wrote, "I was sitting in my patrol car, and I saw the Silverado go through the traffic light and strike the F150."

b.   The police officer wrote, "I arrived ten minutes after the accident. I measured skid marks to the back wheels of the Silverado measuring 57 feet."

c.   The police officer wrote, "I arrived less than a minute after the accident, and I heard a bystander say, 'Did you see that crazy Chevy pickup go through the red light?'"

d.   The police officer wrote, "I arrived a few minutes after the accident, and I asked the driver of the Silverado what happened. He told me, 'I must have fallen asleep. I don't know what happened.'"

e.   The police officer wrote, "I arrived a few minutes after the accident. Officer Jenkins approached me and said that he witnessed the accident, and that the Chevy had gone through the red light and hit the Ford."

f.   The police officer wrote, "I arrived a few minutes after the accident, and officer Jenkins told me that she had gotten there just before me, and that she asked the driver of the Chevy what happened, and the Chevy driver said he had been drinking and didn't know what happened."

g.   The police officer wrote, "I arrived 30 minutes after the accident. The scene had been taken care of by other officers who arrived before me. I asked a bystander what happened, and the bystander said he saw the Chevy go through the red light and cause the accident."

In § 11.32, you will find analysis of the Questions.

§ 11.28   Impeach Hearsay Declarant

The FRE and the CEC allow the opponent of hearsay to impeach the declarant, a subject described in § 10.11. (FRE 806; CEC § 1202).

§ 11.29   The Confrontation Clause and Hearsay

The Sixth Amendment to the U.S. Constitution provides that the defendant in a criminal case has the right to confront the prosecution's witnesses. In relevant part, the Confrontation Clause provides: "In all criminal prosecutions, the accused shall enjoy the right . . . to be confronted with the witnesses against him."

The Confrontation Clause gives defendants in criminal cases three rights: (1) The right to face-to-face confrontation with prosecution witnesses. With few exceptions, prosecution witnesses must testify in open court, in the physical presence of the defendant.[33] Witnesses do not have to look at the defendant, except to make an identification. However, the defendant must be able to see and hear government witnesses. (2) The right of confrontation includes the right to cross-examine prosecution witnesses. (3) Although the Confrontation Clause does not mention hearsay, the U.S. Supreme Court interprets the Clause to limit admissibility of certain hearsay offered against defendants in criminal cases.

The leading authority on the impact of the Confrontation Clause on hearsay is *Crawford v. Washington*, 541 U.S. 36, 124 S. Ct. 1354 (2004). Under *Crawford*, if the declarant testifies at trial, and is subject to cross-examination about the out-of-court statement, then the Confrontation Clause is satisfied, and poses no barrier to admission of the hearsay.[34] If the declarant does not testify, the question is whether the hearsay is "testimonial." If the hearsay is not testimonial, then the Confrontation Clause does not

---

[33]   If a child witness would be seriously traumatized by face-to-face confrontation with the defendant in court, the prosecutor may ask the judge to allow the child to testify from a remote location. *See* Maryland v. Craig, 497 U.S. 836, 110 S. Ct. 3157 (1990); Cal. Penal Code § 1347. Most children testify in the traditional way, in the physical presence of the defendant.

[34]   The prosecutor still has to worry about the hearsay rule, of course. But if the declarant testifies at trial, the Confrontation Clause goes away.

bar the hearsay. If the hearsay is testimonial, then the hearsay is inadmissible unless the defendant had a prior opportunity to cross-examine the declarant.[35]

Since *Crawford* was decided in 2004, there have been thousands of appellate decisions grappling with when hearsay is testimonial. The U.S. Supreme Court's 2015 decision in *Ohio v. Clark*, 135 S. Ct. 2173 (2015) is instructive. *Clark* was a child abuse case. Someone hurt three-year-old L.P. The question was, who? The mystery began at L.P.'s Cleveland, Ohio preschool. Darius Clark dropped L.P. off at preschool. A teacher noticed that L.P.'s left eye was bloodshot. The teacher asked, "What happened?" L.P. said, "Nothing." A little later, L.P. said, "I fell." When they moved into a room with brighter light, the teacher saw bruises on L.P.'s face, as though someone whipped him. Alarmed, the teacher notified the head teacher, who asked L.P., "Who did this? What happened to you?" L.P. replied, "Dee Dee." The head teacher asked, "Is Dee big or little?" L.P. said, "Dee is big." The teachers took L.P. to the preschool supervisor, who lifted L.P.'s shirt to reveal more injuries. A report of suspected child abuse was filed, and a child protection social worker (CPS) went to the preschool. Before long, Darius Clark arrived to take L.P. home. Clark, whose nickname is Dee, denied causing the injuries, and quickly left with the child over the objections of the social worker.

CPS searched for L.P., and, the next day, a social worker located L.P. and his little sister at Clark's mother's house. The children were taken to a hospital. A doctor examined L.P. and found a black eye, injuries from a belt on L.P.'s back and stomach, and bruises covering his body. L.P.'s little sister had similar injuries. The children were taken into emergency protective custody.

Why were the children with Clark, who was not related to them? Where were the parents? The father was nowhere to be found. The mother was in Washington, D.C., working as a prostitute. Clark was her pimp. He sent her there while he took "care" of the kids.

A grand jury indicted Clark for physically abusing both children, but Clark said, "I didn't do it. You charged the wrong person. It was the mother who hurt the children." Thus, the question was not whether L.P. was abused, but whodunit?

At Clark's trial, the prosecutor put the preschool teachers on the witness stand to describe what they saw, and to repeat L.P.'s

---

[35]　When hearsay is testimonial, and the declarant does not testify at trial, it is rare that the defendant had a prior opportunity to cross-examine. The opportunity for prior cross-examination does exist with former testimony.

words: "Dee Dee" and "Dee is big." Clark's defense attorney made a two part objection. First, defense counsel argued that repeating L.P.'s words would violate the rule against hearsay. Second, defense counsel argued that repeating L.P.'s words would violate the Confrontation Clause.

The judge overruled defense counsel's objections. The judge ruled that L.P.'s words were admissible under Ohio's residual hearsay exception. As for the Confrontation Clause, the judge ruled that L.P.'s statements were nontestimonial. The teachers repeated L.P.'s words, and Clark was convicted.

Clark appealed his conviction to the Ohio Court of Appeal, where he prevailed. The Court of Appeal ruled that L.P.'s statements to his teachers were testimonial, and should not have been repeated in court. The prosecution appealed to the Ohio Supreme Court, but Ohio's highest court endorsed the position taken by the Court of Appeal: L.P.'s statements were testimonial, and their repetition in court violated Clark's rights under the Confrontation Clause.

The admissibility of hearsay against the defendant in a criminal trial is governed by two sources of law: (1) The rules of evidence, and (2) The Confrontation Clause of the Sixth Amendment. In many cases, the two sources of law reach the same conclusion: hearsay is or is not admissible. Sometimes, however, a hearsay statement that is *admissible* under hearsay law can*not* be used in court because it runs afoul of the Confrontation Clause. Consider, for example, a case in which a prosecutor has a hearsay statement that meets the requirements of a hearsay exception. The statement is admissible under hearsay law. Be that as it may, if the statement is testimonial, and the declarant cannot testify, the statement is inadmissible because it offends the Confrontation Clause. This is precisely what happened in *Ohio v. Clark*. L.P.'s hearsay statements to his teachers were admissible under Ohio's residual hearsay exception. According to the Ohio Supreme Court, however, L.P.'s statements were inadmissible because they were testimonial, and L.P. did not testify.

When you analyze the admissibility of hearsay against a defendant in a criminal case, keep the two sources of law separate. First, conduct a hearsay analysis to determine whether the out-of-court statement is hearsay, and whether it meets the requirements of an exception. If no exception applies, the statement is inadmissible, and it is not necessary to consider the Confrontation Clause. However, if the statement *is* admissible under hearsay law because it meets an exception, then analyze the Confrontation Clause. On that score, ask two questions: First, is the declarant available to testify and be cross-examined? If so, the Confrontation Clause poses no barrier to admission of the hearsay, and this is true whether the hearsay is testimonial or nontestimonial. Second, if the declarant is not available to testify and be cross-examined, is the hearsay testimonial? If yes, the hearsay is inadmissible. If no, the hearsay is admissible.

Do not fall prey to the following error. Some students mistakenly believe "testimonial" is a hearsay exception. It isn't. Testimonial hearsay is a concept under the Confrontation Clause, not a hearsay exception.

So, the issue under the Confrontation Clause is whether hearsay is testimonial. "Testimonial" is a term of art. A hearsay statement can be "testimonial" even though it bears no resemblance to testimony in court. Hearsay is typically testimonial when the primary purpose of the declarant in speaking, or the primary purpose of the person questioning the declarant, is to generate evidence for possible use in future criminal proceedings. For example, a person's answers to questions during formal interrogation at a police station are testimonial because the purpose of the questioning is to gather evidence for use in court.

Under the "primary purpose" test, statements to parents, relatives, friends, and co-workers are almost never testimonial. Hearsay statements to medical and mental health professionals are nontestimonial so long as the professional's motivation for questioning is primarily clinical. On the other hand, if a medical or mental health professional questions a person primarily for legal, evidence-gathering reasons, the person's statements are likely to be testimonial.

Many statements to police officers are testimonial, but not all.[36] The answer depends on the circumstances in which the officer spoke to the declarant. Statements to police are likely to be nontestimonial when police ask questions in the context of an ongoing emergency. Thus, a crime victim's answer to a police officer's question, "What happened?" shortly after the officer arrives in response to a 911 call is often nontestimonial because the question is intended to assess the situation, see whether medical help is necessary, and determine whether the victim and the officer are safe. As the emergency fades, and the officer's attention shifts from dealing with an emergency to gathering evidence, statements become testimonial.

In deciding whether statements to police officers are testimonial, judges consider: (1) Was there an ongoing emergency?

---

[36]   911 calls are nontestimonial when there is an emergency.

(2) Was the declarant safe or in danger? (3) Was medical assistance necessary? (4) Was the declarant alone or protected by others? (5) Was the declarant seeking help? (6) Was the declarant describing events that were happening? Or was the declarant describing past events? (7) How much time elapsed since the crime occurred? (8) What was the level of formality of the questioning?

Returning to the *Clark* case, the Ohio Supreme Court ruled that L.P.'s statements to his teachers—"Dee Dee" and "Dee is big"—were testimonial. The prosecution appealed this ruling to the U.S. Supreme Court. In the U.S. Supreme Court, the fight was not over the hearsay rule. L.P.'s hearsay statements were admissible under Ohio's residual hearsay exception. Rather, the fight focused on whether L.P.'s statements to his preschool teachers were testimonial under the Confrontation Clause. On that score, the Ohio Supreme Court ruled that L.P.'s statements were testimonial because the preschool teachers were required by Ohio's child abuse reporting law to report their suspicions to CPS or police. As such, the Ohio Supreme Court reasoned that the teacher's primary purpose in questioning L.P. was to gather evidence for possible use in future criminal proceedings. The U.S. Supreme Court had to decide whether the Ohio Supreme Court misapplied the meaning of testimonial.

The Supreme Court was unanimous: The Ohio Supreme Court got it wrong. L.P.'s statements to his preschool teachers were not testimonial. Teachers are not transformed into police investigators simply because they are required to report child abuse. The Supreme Court wrote:

> There is no indication that the primary purpose of the conversation was to gather evidence for Clark's prosecution. On the contrary, it is clear that the first objective was to protect L.P. . . . [T]he conversation between L.P. and his teachers was informal and spontaneous. The teachers asked L.P. about his injuries immediately upon discovering them, in the informal setting of a preschool lunchroom and classroom, and they did so precisely as any concerned citizen would talk to a child who might be a victim of abuse. . . .
>
> L.P.'s age fortifies our conclusion that the statements in question were not testimonial. Statements by very young children will rarely, if ever, implicate the Confrontation Clause. . . . [I]t is extremely unlikely that a 3-year-old child in L.P.'s position would intend his statements to be [used as evidence in court]. On the contrary, a young child in these circumstances would

simply want the abuse to end, would want to protect other victims, or would have no discernible purpose at all. . . .

Statements made to someone who is not principally charged with uncovering and prosecuting criminal behavior are significantly less likely to be testimonial than statements given to law enforcement officers. (135 S. Ct. at 2182).

Two Hearsay Exceptions Where the Confrontation Clause Does Not Apply. The Confrontation Clause does not apply to hearsay within the dying declaration exception. Nor does the Confrontation Clause apply to party admissions, including statements that fall within the co-conspirator exception.

Summing Up. When it comes to the Confrontation Clause, remember: (1) The Confrontation Clause applies only in criminal cases, and only when testimonial hearsay is offered against the defendant. (2) In a criminal case, do the hearsay analysis first. If hearsay is inadmissible under hearsay law, you don't need to get to the Confrontation Clause, although, for exam taking purposes, it is probably wise to discuss the Clause. (3) If the declarant testifies at trial, and can be cross-examined about the hearsay statement, the Confrontation Clause poses no barrier to hearsay, and this is true even if the hearsay is testimonial. (4) Discuss whether the hearsay is testimonial.

§ 11.30   *Bruton*

Bruton is an aspect of the Confrontation Clause. Watch for *Bruton* when: (1) Two or more defendants are tried together. If there is only one defendant, *Bruton* does not arise. (2) One of the defendants made an out-of-court, testimonial[37] hearsay statement that implicates the declarant *and* other defendants by name or obvious reference. (3) The out-of-court statement is admissible against the declarant, but not against the other defendants. Why would a statement be admissible against the declarant, but not the other defendants? Won't the statement be admissible against all of the defendants under the co-conspirator exception? If the conspiracy was still ongoing when the declarant spoke, then the statement *will* likely be admissible against all of the defendants under the coconspirator exception. The *Bruton* issue arises when the declarant spoke *after* the conspiracy ended. Often, the conspiracy ended because the declarant had been arrested when the declarant made the statement. *Bruton* often arises after a conspiracy ends due to

---

[37]   If the hearsay statement is not testimonial, there is no Confrontation Clause problem, and no *Bruton* problem. *See* State v. Wilcoxon, 373 P.3d 224, 185 Wash. 2d 324 (2016).

arrest, and one of the defendant's confesses to police and names the other defendants. (4) The declarant does not testify at trial. If the declarant testifies and can be cross-examined, there is no *Bruton* problem.

In *Bruton v. United States*, 391 U.S. 123, 88 S. Ct. 1620 (1968), the Supreme Court ruled that, under the circumstances outlined above, admission of an out-of-court statement violates the Confrontation Clause rights of the non-declarant defendants. A limiting instruction to the jury to consider the statement only against the declarant will not cure the problem. In California, the issue often goes by the name *Aranda* or *Aranda/Bruton*, after *People v. Aranda*, 63 Cal. 2d 518, 407 P.2d 265, 47 Cal. Rptr. 353 (1965).

If a statement that would violate *Bruton* can be redacted sufficiently to remove obvious reference to the non-declarant defendant(s), the statement may be admitted, along with a jury instruction not to consider the statement against the non-declarant defendant.[38] There is controversy over when a redaction is adequate. If there are two defendants, removing the non-declarant defendant's name and replacing it with blanks, or "him," or "the other guy," won't do. In some cases, especially with multiple non-declarant defendants, neutral pronouns may suffice. The Washington Supreme Court observed in *State v. Fisher*, 374 P.3d 1185, 1190, 185 Wash. 2d 836 (2016), "[T]he exact form of the redaction is not dispositive. Rather, . . . the question is whether the redaction obviously refers to the defendant."

In *People v. Song*, 124 Cal. App. 4th 973, 980–981, 22 Cal. Rptr. 3d 118 (2004), the Court of Appeal wrote: "[W]hen the prosecution seeks to introduce an extrajudicial statement of one defendant that implicates a codefendant, the trial court must adopt one of three procedures: (1) in a joint trial, effectively delete direct and indirect identifications of codefendants; (2) grant a severance of trials; or (3) if severance has been denied and effective deletion is not possible, exclude the statement."

§ 11.31   Forfeiture by Wrongdoing

A defendant can forfeit the Sixth Amendment right of confrontation through misconduct that is intended by the defendant to make a witness unavailable to testify at trial. The leading case is *Reynolds v. Unites States*, 98 U.S. 145 (1879). The *Reynolds* Court wrote, "The Constitution gives the accused the right to a trial at which he should be confronted with the witnesses against him; but

---

[38]   *See* People v. Cedeno, 27 N.Y.3d 110, 50 N.E.3d 901, 31 N.Y.S.3d 434 (2016).

if a witness is absent by [defendant's] wrongful procurement, he cannot complain if competent evidence is admitted to supply the place of that which he has kept away. The Constitution does not guarantee an accused person against the legitimate consequences of his own wrongful acts" (p. 158). Thus, a defendant forfeits confrontation when the defendant murders a potential witness to prevent testimony at a forthcoming trial, or threatens a potential witness into silence.

In *Giles v. California*, 554 U.S. 353, 128 S. Ct. 2678 (2008), the Court suggested that forfeiture by wrongdoing applies beyond the situation where a defendant's intent is to prevent testimony in court. Forfeiture by wrongdoing extends to circumstances in which the defendant intends to keep the declarant from making testimonial out-of-court statements in an effort to get help from police or other officials. Referring to domestic violence cases, the Supreme Court wrote:

> Acts of domestic violence often are intended to dissuade a victim from resorting to outside help, and include conduct designed to prevent testimony to police officers or cooperation in criminal prosecutions. Where such an abusive relationship culminates in murder, the evidence may support a finding that the crime expressed the intent to isolate the victim and to stop her from reporting abuse to the authorities or cooperating with a criminal prosecution—rendering her prior statements admissible under the forfeiture doctrine. Earlier abuse, or threats of abuse, intended to dissuade the victim from resorting to outside help would be highly relevant to this inquiry, as would evidence of ongoing criminal proceedings at which the victim would have been expected to testify (128 S. Ct. at 377).

Extending forfeiture by wrongdoing to situations where a perpetrator of child abuse, domestic violence, or elder abuse, threatens, coerces, or harms the victim in order to prevent the victim from obtaining assistance, opens the door to a great deal of otherwise inadmissible testimonial hearsay.

Under the FRE and the CEC, the wrongdoing that forfeits the Sixth Amendment right to confront prosecution witnesses can *also* forfeit the hearsay objection. The rules provide:

FRE 804(b)(6). The following are not excluded by the rule against hearsay if the declarant is unavailable as a witness: A statement offered against a party that wrongfully caused—or acquiesced in wrongfully causing—

the declarant's unavailability as a witness, and did so intending that result.

CEC § 1390. Statements against parties involved in causing unavailability of declarant as a witness. (a) Evidence of a statement is not made inadmissible by the hearsay rule if the statement if offered against a party that has engaged, or aided and abetted, in the wrongdoing that was intended to, and did, procure the unavailability of the declarant as a witness.

Under CEC § 1390, the party seeking to admit hearsay pursuant to subsection (a) must establish the requirements of the subsection by a preponderance of the evidence, at a hearing, held outside the presence of the jury. In making a ruling under Section 1390, the judge may evaluate the reliability of the hearsay.

CEC § 1350 became part of the CEC in 1985. Section 1350 is similar, in some respects, to CEC § 1390, which became part of the Code in 2011. Section 1350 is much narrower than Section 1390, and, in practice, Section 1350 is ignored in favor of Section 1390.

§ 11.32   Analysis of Chapter Questions

Section 11.9 discussed the state of mind exception, and asks whether the following statement are admissible under the exception:

"I intend to go to Chicago tomorrow." Yes. This is a straight forward example of the forward-looking aspect of the state of mind exception.

"I intend to go to Chicago tomorrow with Anne." Yes. Although this statement mentions a third person, courts admit such statements, often referred to as *Hillmon* statements. Under California's state of mind exception (CEC § 1250(a)), the opponent could try to convince the judge to exclude all of the statement, or at least the part of the statement that mentions Anne, based on the argument that "the statement was made under circumstances such as to indicate its lack of trustworthiness." Under the FRE, the opponent could make a FRE 403 objection that the statement mentioning Anne is so unreliable that it should be excluded.

"Anne plans to go to Chicago tomorrow." No. The state of mind exception does not include a statement of someone else's plan or intent.

"I'm leaving for class in a few minutes." Yes.

"Sara and I are leaving for class in a few minutes." Yes— *Hillmon* statement.

"I'm going to the parking lot. I'll be right back." Yes. Easy.

"I'm going to meet Angelo in the parking lot. I'll be right back."[39] Yes—*Hillmon* statement.

"Angelo is going to give me a pound of marijuana for free." No. Again, the state of mind exception does not include one person's belief about what someone else is thinking, intending, or planning.

Layered Hearsay Problems (§ 11.27)

1.   In a personal injury trial, defendant offers a police report containing a statement by plaintiff describing the cause of the accident. The witness on the stand is the custodian of records for the police department.

This is two layers of hearsay. The original statement is the statement by plaintiff. The final statement is the police report. Because the defendant is offering the document against the plaintiff, the original statement by plaintiff is admissible as a party admission. The final statement—the police report—should qualify for admission under the business records exception or the public records exception, or both. The report, including plaintiff's statement, is admissible.

2.   In a personal injury trial, defendant offers plaintiff's medical record from the hospital where plaintiff was treated after the accident. The medical record contains a statement made by plaintiff to a doctor at the hospital, and repeated by the doctor in the record. The witness on the stand is the custodian of records at the hospital.

This is two layers of hearsay. The original statement is plaintiff's statement to the doctor. The final statement is the doctor's medical report, in which the doctor repeated what plaintiff said. The custodian of records is *not* a third layer of hearsay. The plaintiff's statement is being offered against the plaintiff, thus it is admissible as a party admission. When a statement is admissible as a party admission, some professors teach that you don't need to mention whether the hearsay meets other exceptions. All you need is party admission, so why discuss other exceptions? Other professors teach that you should mention all hearsay exceptions that could apply. In this case, plaintiff's statement to the doctor might qualify for the medical diagnosis or treatment exception, provided, of course, that what the plaintiff told the doctor was pertinent to the doctor's ability to treat the plaintiff. Ask your professor her position on whether you should discuss all possible exceptions when a statement is admissible as a party admission.

---

[39]   *See* United States v. Pheaster, 544 F.2d 353 (9th Cir. 1976).

3.   In a murder prosecution, defendant admits she shot the victim, but claims she acted in self-defense. Defense counsel offers the testimony of Xeno, who will testify that defendant told her (Xeno) that the victim told her (defendant), "I'm (this is the victim speaking) going to get you. You'd better watch your back. Snitches get stitches."

Again, we have two layers of hearsay. The original statement is the victim speaking to the defendant. The victim said, "I'm going to get you. You'd better watch your back. Snitches get stitches." The final statement is the defendant speaking to Xeno, and telling Xeno what the victim said. Xeno's testimony is *not* a third layer of hearsay. The original statement by the victim could be admitted under the state of mind exception. As well, the victim's statement could be admitted under the non-hearsay theory of the effect on the listener. The fact that the victim threatened the defendant is relevant to the defendant's claim of self-defense. But we have a problem with the final statement—the defendant's statement to Xeno. There is no hearsay exception for this statement. Nor is there a non-hearsay use of the statement. Thus, it appears that the victim's statement to the defendant is not admissible because there is no hearsay exception for the defendant's statement to Xeno.

4.   Problem 4 concerns an accident that happened at an intersection in Truckee. Abe was driving a Ford F150 pickup. Ben was driving a Chevy Silverado pickup. Abe is suing Ben for personal injuries sustained in the wreck. A police report was prepared. The following questions offer different versions of what the police report stated. In each case, Abe wants to introduce the police report into evidence against Ben.

a.   The police officer who wrote the police report wrote, "I was sitting in my patrol car, and I saw the Silverado go through the traffic light and strike the F150."

This is hearsay, but not layered hearsay. The police report should be admissible as a business record or under the public records exception.

b.   The police officer wrote, "I arrived ten minutes after the accident. I measured skid marks to the back wheels of the Silverado measuring 57 feet."

This, too, is hearsay, but not layered hearsay. The business record exception and/or public records.

c.   The police officer wrote, "I arrived less than a minute after the accident, and I heard a bystander say, 'Did you see that crazy Chevy pickup go through the red light?' "

Now we have layered hearsay. The original statement is by the bystander. The final statement is the police report. The bystander statement is probably an excited utterance. Anonymous bystander statements can be excited utterances (§ 11.8). The police report comes in under business records and/or public records.

d.   The police officer wrote, "I arrived a few minutes after the accident, and I asked the driver of the Silverado what happened. He told me, 'I must have fallen asleep. I don't know what happened.'"

This is layered hearsay. The original statement is by the driver of the Silverado, defendant Ben. The final statement is the police report. If the plaintiff offers the report, Ben's statement is admissible as a party admission. The police report is a business record and/or a public record.

e.   The police officer wrote, "I arrived a few minutes after the accident. Officer Jenkins approached me and said that he witnessed the accident, and that the Chevy had gone through the red light and hit the Ford."

There are two hearsay statements. The original statement is by Officer Jenkins. The final statement is the police report, written by a different police officer. Under the business records exception, it often happens that more than one person working for a company or agency contributes to a document. So long as all the people who contribute to the document are employed by the same business or agency, you can ignore the separate statements they make—the separate layers. If Officer Jenkins and the officer who wrote the report work for the same police agency, ignore the two layers, and treat the document as one layer. If Officer Jenkins works for a different police agency, it is unclear whether you can ignore the layers, or if you have to conclude there are two layers of hearsay.

f.   The police officer wrote, "I arrived a few minutes after the accident, and Officer Jenkins told me that she had gotten there just before me, and that she asked the driver of the Chevy what happened, and the Chevy driver said he had been drinking and didn't know what happened."

Three layers, right? There are three out-of-court statements. The original statement is the Chevy driver to Officer Jenkins. The middle layer is Officer Jenkins speaking to the author of the report, and repeating what the Chevy driver said. The final statement is the police report. The police report is a business record or a public record. If the statement by the Chevy driver is offered against the Chevy driver, it is a party admission. But what about the middle layer? There is no hearsay exception for the middle layer. That means everything "below" the middle layer is inadmissible! However, if Officer Jenkins and the author of the report work for the same police agency, it should be possible to ignore the layers that involved Jenkins and the author. If we do that, then there are only two layers: The party admission by the Chevy driver, and the police report that is a business record or a public record.

g.   The police officer wrote, "I arrived 30 minutes after the accident. The scene had been taken care of by other officers who arrived before me. I asked a bystander what happened, and the bystander said he saw the Chevy go through the red light and cause the accident."

Two layers. The original statement by the bystander, and the final statement is the police report. In this case, 30 minutes is probably too long for the bystander statement to qualify as an excited utterance. No other hearsay exception applies. Thus, the original statement is inadmissible. The police report is admissible as a business record and/or a public record. However, before the police report is admitted, it is necessary to excise the bystander statement because it is not admissible.

Chapter 12

PRIVILEGE

A basic principle of the legal system is that anyone with personal knowledge of relevant facts must testify. Society has a right to every person's evidence.[1] At the same time, society values the ability of people in certain relationships to communicate in private, without fear that what is said in confidence will be disclosed in court. The law creates privileges to shield confidential communications between spouses, attorneys and clients, physicians and patients, psychotherapists and clients, and in certain other contexts. This chapter introduces privileges.

When the Federal Rules of Evidence (FRE) were proposed, the Rules contained detailed privilege rules. Congress rejected the proposed rules, and left the development of federal privilege law to the courts (FRE 501). The California Evidence Code (CEC), like the law in other states, has detailed privilege rules. The CEC privilege rules are extensive, and are not reproduced here in their entirety. Instead, the chapter summarizes the main points of various privileges.

§ 12.1 Attorney-Client Privilege—CEC §§ 950–962

The attorney-client privilege applies in federal court and in all states. Every privilege has a holder, the person to whom the privilege belongs. With the attorney-client privilege, the holder is the client. It is the client's privilege, not the attorney's. However, the attorney is obligated to assert the privilege on the client's behalf. As the holder of the privilege, the client may waive the privilege. The attorney may not waive the privilege without the client's consent. Generally, failure to assert a privilege when the opportunity to do so is available constitutes a waiver.

An attorney is a person licensed to practice law in any state. A client may be an individual, a corporation, or a government agency. The privilege requires a client-attorney relationship. However, the client need not formally retain the attorney. The privilege applies to confidential communications in contemplation of retention. The privilege applies to confidential oral or written communications from the client to the attorney and from the attorney to the client. Communications to the attorney's staff are covered by the privilege.

---

[1]   CEC § 911.

In the past, if an eavesdropper listened in on a confidential conversation between client and attorney, the privilege was lost. California and other states reject the so-called eavesdropper rule. If the attorney and client take reasonable precautions to communicate in private, the privilege applies even if an eavesdropper is listening.

When an attorney retains a physician or psychologist to help the attorney prepare for trial, communications between the client and the doctor are covered by the attorney-client privilege.

The crime-fraud exception to privilege provides that there is no privilege when a client consults an attorney to help the client commit a crime or a civil fraud.

§ 12.2 Physician-Patient Privilege—CEC §§ 990–1007

California, and most, if not all, other states has the physician-patient privilege. The privilege has not been adopted by the federal courts.[2] The patient is the holder of the privilege, although the doctor is required to assert the privilege for the patient. The privilege covers private communications between doctor and patient, as well as information the doctor observes by examining the patient.[3] The physician-patient privilege applies in civil cases, but not criminal prosecutions.

When a patient sues someone for personal injuries, and seeks damages for physical or psychological damage, the patient places her physical or mental condition in issue, waiving, to that extent, the privilege. This waiver is called the patient-litigant exception to privilege.

When a proceeding is commenced to involuntarily commit a person for psychiatric care, the physician-patient privilege does not apply.

§ 12.3 Psychotherapist-Client Privilege—CEC §§ 1010–1027

The psychotherapist-client privilege covers confidential communications between clients and psychotherapists. The client is the holder of the privilege. As with other privileges, the professional is required to assert the privilege on the client's behalf. The privilege applies to individual therapy and group therapy. The

---

[2]   *See* Auer v. Minot, 178 F. Supp. 3d 835 (D. N. D. 2016).

[3]   *See* Snibbe v. Superior Court, 224 Cal. App. 4th 184, 168 Cal. Rptr. 3d 548 (2014) ("Its dual purpose is to protect the patient from the humiliation that might follow the disclosure of his or her ailment and to encourage full disclosure to the physician of information necessary for diagnosis and treatment.").

privilege extends to civil and criminal cases. California appellate courts rule that, in addition to its statutory basis, the psychotherapist-client privilege is grounded in the client's right of privacy guaranteed by the California Constitution.[4]

There is no privilege when a client's mental illness poses a danger to the client or others, such that disclosure of information is needed to help the client. When a person is ordered by a judge to be evaluated by a psychologist or physician, and the court directs the professional to write a report for the court and/or to testify, there is no expectation of privacy in communications, and no privilege. The patient-litigant exception to privilege applies to the psychotherapist-client privilege.[5]

§ 12.4   Clergy-Penitent Privilege—CEC §§ 1030–1034

The CEC has a privilege for confidential "penitential communications" between clergy and members of the congregation. The communication must have some relation to the discipline or practice of the particular religion. Both the penitent and the clergy member hold the privilege.

§ 12.5   Spousal Privileges

There are two spousal privileges: (1) The spousal confidential communications privilege, and (2) The spousal testimonial privilege. The privileges apply in civil and criminal litigation. The privileges do not apply when one spouse is accused of abusing the other spouse or the children.

§ 12.5(a).   Spousal Testimonial Privilege

The spousal testimonial privilege gives a married person the authority to refuse to testify against their spouse. With this privilege, the spouse does not take the witness stand to answer *any* questions. If a visualization helps, visualize an empty witness chair. The privilege requires a valid marriage. The privilege ends when the marriage ends.

Only the witness spouse is a holder of the testimonial privilege. Thus, if the witness spouse is willing to testify against the spouse, the witness spouse may do so, and the non-witness spouse can't prevent the testimony. The point of this privilege is that if the

---

4   *See* Kirchmeyer v. Phillips, 245 Cal. App. 4th 1394, 200 Cal. Rptr. 3d 515 (2016).
5   *See* Manela v. Superior Court, 177 Cal. App. 4th 1139, 99 Cal. Rptr. 3d 736 (2009).

witness spouse does not want to testify against their spouse, the witness spouse can't be forced to testify.

§ 12.5(b).   Spousal Confidential Communications Privilege

The spousal confidential communications privilege has much in common with the other privileges discussed in this chapter. The privilege protects confidential communications between married persons. Both spouses are holders of the privilege. The privilege requires a valid marriage. However, unlike the spousal testimonial privilege, which ends if the marriage ends, the spousal confidential communications privilege protects confidential communications uttered during the marriage, even after the marriage ends.

Suppose Sam and Antha are married. Both are charged with a drug offense. Before trial, the prosecutor offers Antha a very nice plea deal if she will testify against Sam. If Antha will testify, the prosecutor will dismiss all charges against Antha. Antha can turn down the offer, and refuse to testify against Sam. She is the holder of the spousal *testimonial* privilege. If she asserts the spousal testimonial privilege, however, and refuses to testify against Sam, the prosecutor will proceed with the charges against her. If Antha takes the offer, Sam can't keep Antha from testifying because Sam is *not* a holder of the testimonial privilege. Assuming Antha testifies against Sam, Sam *can* raise the confidential communications privilege because he is holder of that privilege. The spousal confidential communications privilege will block Antha from revealing confidential communications between Antha and Sam.

§ 12.6 Official Information Privilege—CEC §§ 1040–1047

The CEC creates privileges for government documents. The evidentiary privilege established by the CEC for government documents is in addition to other laws limiting public access to government documents. Under the CEC, some government documents are absolutely privileged. Other documents are conditionally privileged. With documents in the latter category, the judge balances the need of the government for confidentiality against the benefit to justice of ordering disclosure for use in court.

§ 12.7 Privilege Against Self-Incrimination

The Fifth Amendment to the U.S. Constitution guarantees the privilege against self-incrimination. Two sections of the CEC (930 and 940) reinforce the constitutional right.

Chapter 13

PRESUMPTIONS

Presumptions play almost no role in criminal cases. In civil litigation, presumptions can be important. The CEC has detailed rules on presumptions. FRE has but one rule, Rule 301:

FRE 301. Presumptions in Civil Cases Generally. In a civil case, unless a federal statute or these rules provide otherwise, the party against whom a presumption is directed has the burden of producing evidence to rebut the presumption. But this rule does not shift the burden of persuasion, which remains on the party who had it originally.

§ 13.1 Presumption and Inference Defined and Explained

FRE 301 does not define "presumption." The rule assumes you already know how presumptions work. FRE 301 simply tells you the effect of one type of presumption. Fortunately, the CEC contains useful information on presumptions. Section 600 of the CEC defines "presumption" and "inference." Section 600 provides:

CEC § 600. "Presumption" and "Inference" Defined. (a) A presumption is an assumption of fact that the law *requires* to be made from another fact or group of facts found or otherwise established in the action. A presumption is not evidence. (b) An inference is a deduction of fact that *may* logically and reasonably be drawn from another fact or group of facts found or otherwise established in the action. (emphasis added).

An inference is simply a thought process by which a person reasons from one thing to another—from an item of evidence to a conclusion. As mentioned in § 2.3, you draw inferences all the time. Suppose, for example, that on your driveway this morning you found the local newspaper. It is reasonable to infer that the paper was thrown there by the paper delivery person. You infer how the paper got on the driveway from your experience. You don't actually know how the paper got there because you were asleep when it arrived. Nevertheless, you feel reasonable in concluding that the delivery person threw it there. If the question of who delivered your paper should somehow find its way into litigation, the jury would be permitted to draw the same inference you drew about where the paper came from. The jury would not be required to draw the inference, but could draw it if it so chooses.

An inference, then, is a thought process. A person reasons from one fact to another: You look outside and see someone raise an umbrella: you infer it is raining. You see your friend emerge from the student recreation center all sweaty: you infer she was exercising.

Now, contrast an inference with a presumption. Like an inference, a presumption is not evidence. An inference, like a presumption, is a thought process; a process of reasoning from an item of evidence to a conclusion. The conclusion is the "presumed fact." The evidence leading to the presumed fact is the "basic facts." With a presumption, if the jury finds the basic facts true, then it is *required* to find the presumed fact true.[1]

There is a presumption that a letter correctly addressed and properly mailed with the correct postage was received in the ordinary course of the mail. (CEC § 641). The basic facts are that the letter was correctly addressed and properly mailed with the right postage. If these basic facts are established, then the jury *must* find the existence of the presumed fact, the letter was received in the ordinary course of the mail.

What is the difference between an inference and a presumption? A presumption *requires* the jury to conclude that one fact (presumed fact) exists if another fact (basic facts) exists. Thus, in the case of the properly mailed letter, the jury must conclude that the letter was received in the ordinary course of the mail because a presumption applies. With the newspaper on your driveway, by contrast, the jury would not be compelled to conclude that the delivery person delivered the newspaper to your house. Why? Because there is no presumption that a paper on a driveway was delivered by a delivery person.

Courts and legislatures create presumptions for reasons of convenience, fairness, and policy. Regarding the letter, there are many trials where it is important to determine whether a letter was received. Rather than require burdensome and time consuming proof, it is more convenient to take the short cut of presuming a letter properly sent was received. The presumption is safe because the postal service is usually trustworthy. If the party against whom the presumption operates says the letter never arrived, they are free at trial to offer evidence they didn't get the letter.

---

[1]   The jury is required to find the presumed fact true unless the party against whom the presumption operates offers enough evidence to rebut the presumption.

§ 13.2 Burden of Producing Evidence and Burden of Proof

There are two kinds of rebuttable presumptions: presumptions affecting the burden of proof, and presumptions affecting the burden of producing evidence. Before you can understand the difference between the two, you need to understand two related topics: First, the burden of producing evidence, or, as it is commonly called, the burden of going forward with evidence. Second, the burden of persuasion, also known as the burden of proof.

The burden of producing evidence is the obligation of a party, at the proper point in a trial, to present evidence on an issue (CEC § 550). The evidence produced must be sufficient to permit the jury to act on the evidence. In a negligence action, for example, plaintiff has the burden of producing evidence of defendant's negligence. The penalty for failing to produce evidence is that the judge rules against the party with the burden of production. If the plaintiff in the negligence suit fails to produce evidence of defendant's negligence, the plaintiff is tossed out of court.

The burden of going forward with the evidence (CEC § 550) must be distinguished from the burden of persuasion (burden of proof). The burden of proof is the burden of convincing the jury that a fact is true. CEC § 500 states, "Except as otherwise provided by law, a party has the burden of proof as to each fact the existence or nonexistence of which is essential to the claim for relief or defense that he is asserting."

Evidence law does not determine the facts needed to recover on a cause of action or a claim. Nor does evidence law set forth the elements of defenses. The relevant substantive law, not evidence law, determines what facts must be proven to establish a cause of action or a defense. Thus, in a negligence case, the law of torts determines the elements of negligence. Plaintiff has the burden of proof on each element (CEC § 521). If, at the end of the trial, the plaintiff has not sustained the burden of proof by a preponderance of the evidence, plaintiff's case fails. In the usual case, like the negligence case, the burden of producing evidence and the burden of proof rest, in the first instance, on the same person (CEC § 550(b)).

In criminal cases, the prosecutor has the burden of going forward with evidence of the defendant's guilt, as well as the burden of proof beyond a reasonable doubt (CEC § 520).

Now that you understand the burden of producing evidence and the burden of proof, you arrive at the following important point: The presence in a civil case of a presumption can cause either or both of the burdens to shift from the party who started with the burden(s) to the other party! That is worth repeating. *A presumption can shift the burden of production and/or proof from one party to the other.* If your client has a burden of production or a burden of proof, and you can invoke a presumption, you may be able to shift one or both of those burdens to your opponent.

§ 13.3   Types of Presumptions

There are three types of presumptions: (1) Conclusive presumptions,[2] (2) Rebuttable presumptions affecting the burden of producing evidence, and (3) Rebuttable presumptions affecting the burden of proof (CEC § 601).

A conclusive presumption is not really a presumption at all. A conclusive presumption is a rule of law. When trial lawyers think of presumptions, they have rebuttable presumptions in mind: a presumption that can be rebutted with evidence. A true conclusive presumption cannot be rebutted with any amount of proof—it is irrebuttable. At common law, there was a conclusive presumption that a baby born to a woman cohabiting with her husband, who was not impotent or sterile, was conclusively presumed to be a child of the marriage. This is not really a presumption: It is a rule of law. If the basic facts were established, then the presumed fact was conclusively established, and the party against whom the presumed fact operates was not permitted to introduce evidence to contradict or rebut the existence of the presumed fact. Today, with DNA paternity testing available, this presumption has been softened—it is no longer conclusive.

Throughout the many California Codes—not just the Evidence Code—you will find statutes that state that a particular fact or group of facts is *prima facie* evidence of another fact.[3] CEC § 602 provides that such statutory language creates a rebuttable presumption. However, Section 602 does not tell you whether a statute using the *prima facie* evidence verbiage creates a rebuttable presumption affecting the burden of producing evidence or a rebuttable presumption affecting the burden of proof.

---

[2]   CEC § 620.

[3]   *See e.g.,* Welfare and Institutions Code § 355.1. This statute deals with child abuse and neglect. Subsection (a) provides, "Where the court finds, based upon competent professional evidence, that an injury, injuries, or detrimental condition sustained by a minor is of a nature as would ordinarily not be sustained except as the result of the unreasonable or neglectful acts or omissions of either parent, the guardian, or other person who has the care or custody of the minor, that finding shall be *prima facie* evidence that the minor is a [child who needs the protection of the juvenile court.]" The words *"prima facie evidence"* create a rebuttable presumption affecting the burden of proof.

Sections 603 and 604 tell you which type of rebuttable presumption you are dealing with. If the only thing a presumption does it facilitate the outcome of litigation, then it is a presumption affecting the burden of producing evidence (CEC § 604). On the other hand, if a presumption is intended to serve some important public policy, then it is a presumption affecting the burden of proof (CEC § 605).

The CEC lists the most common presumptions (*See* CEC § 630. et seq.), and tells you whether each is a presumption affecting the burden of producing evidence or a presumption affecting the burden of proof.

§ 13.4 Presumption Affecting Burden of Producing Evidence

Let's examine how a presumption affecting the burden of producing evidence works at trial. We'll use the letter presumption, found in CEC § 641. A letter correctly addressed, with the right postage, and placed in the mail, is presumed to have been delivered in the ordinary course of the mail.[4] It is a presumption affecting the burden of producing evidence. The presumption becomes operative when the basic facts are established which give rise to the presumption. The party seeking to invoke the presumption has the burden of proving the basic facts—correct address, right postage, placed in the mail—usually by a preponderance of the evidence.

There are two possibilities when evidence regarding the basic facts is offered. The party seeking to establish the presumption might fail to prove one or more of the basic facts. In that case, no presumption arises. On the other hand, if the party introduces sufficient evidence to prove the basic facts, then the presumption arises—the presumption is in the case. With the letter, if the proponent establishes the basic facts, then the presumed fact of receipt is established.

What does the party against whom the presumption of receipt operate do? The opponent has four options. (1) Offer no evidence to rebut the basic facts or the presumed fact. (2) Offer evidence rebutting the existence of the basic facts only, and offer no evidence to rebut the presumed fact. (3) Offer evidence rebutting the presumed fact, and don't offer evidence to rebut the basic facts. (4) Offer evidence against the presumed and the basic facts.

---

[4]   How do you prove the ordinary course of the mail? An official government document should work, and the document should be self-authenticating under the FRE. There should be a presumption of authenticity under the CEC.

In the first scenario, the party against whom the presumption operates introduces no evidence to rebut the basic facts or the presumed fact. In this situation, assuming the jury finds the basic facts true, the jury must find that the presumed fact exists, and the judge so instructs the jury. (CEC § 600(a)).

In the second scenario, the party against whom the presumption operates offers evidence rebutting the existence of the basic facts only, and offers no evidence to rebut the presumed fact. For example, the party against whom the presumption operates offers evidence that the letter was not properly addressed. In this scenario, the only dispute is over the basic facts. If the jury resolves the dispute in favor of the existence of the basic facts, the presumption is established, and the jury must find that the presumed fact of delivery exists. If the jury concludes that one of the basic facts is not proven, then the presumption does not arise. The judge instructs the jury that if the jury finds that the basic facts exist, it must find that the presumed fact exists. The judge might instruct the jury, "If you find that the letter was correctly addressed and properly mailed, with the right postage, then you must find that the letter was received in the ordinarily course of the mail."

In the third scenario, the party against whom the presumption operates offers evidence rebutting the existence of the presumed fact only. Thus, the party might offer evidence that letter was not received. When evidence is offered to rebut the presumed fact— delivery of the letter—the judge has to decide whether the evidence is sufficient to sustain a finding by the jury that the presumed fact—delivery—does not exist. If the judge determines that the evidence of non-delivery is sufficient to sustain a finding of non-delivery, then the presumption terminates, it disappears from the case. It is as though the presumption was a bubble, and proof of non-delivery burst the bubble. Indeed, presumptions affecting the burden of producing evidence are often called bursting bubble presumptions.[5] If the judge decides the bubble has burst, then the jury is instructed to determine the question of delivery based on all the evidence. No mention is made of a presumption. Even though the presumption of delivery disappeared when evidence of non-delivery was introduced, the jury may still decide that the letter was delivered. The jury will examine the evidence of the basic facts, that is, addressing, postage, and mailing, and may find, through reasonable, *non-mandatory*, inferences, that the letter was received.

---

[5]   Presumptions that affect the burden of producing evidence are sometimes called Thayer-Wigmore presumptions, named after Professors Thayer and Wigmore. Presumptions that affect the burden of proof are sometimes called Morgan-McCormick presumptions, after Professors Morgan and McCormick.

Thus, the jury may reach the same conclusion it would reach with a presumption of delivery.

When a presumption disappears from a case because it is a presumption affecting the burden of producing evidence, and evidence sufficient to prove the non-existence of the presumed fact was introduced—bursting the bubble—the jury receives no instruction relating to a presumption.

In the fourth scenario, the party against whom the presumption operates offers evidence to rebut the basic facts *and* the presumed facts. The fourth scenario combines scenarios two and three, above.

To summarize the effect of a presumption affecting the burden of producing evidence, once the party seeking the aid of the presumption produces enough evidence to prove the basic facts, the presumption arises. If the party against whom the presumption operates does nothing, the jury will be instructed that if it finds the basic facts exist, it must find the presumed fact exists. If the party against whom the presumption operates offers evidence to rebut the basic facts, but offers no evidence to rebut the presumed fact, then the jury has to resolve the dispute regarding existence of the basic facts. If the jury concludes that the basic facts are not established, then no presumption arises. If, on the other hand, the jury concludes that the basic facts are established, then the presumed fact must be found to exist since the party against whom the presumption operates offered no evidence to rebut the presumed fact. When this type of presumption arises, the party against whom it operates has the burden of going forward with evidence to rebut the presumed fact. If the party against whom the presumption operates offers evidence sufficient to support a finding of the nonexistence of the presumed fact, then the party has met the burden imposed by this type of presumption, and the presumption disappears from the case—the bubble bursts.

§ 13.5 Presumption Affecting Burden of Proof

Now that you have examined presumptions affecting the burden of producing evidence, consider presumptions affecting the burden of proof. (CEC § 606). A presumption affecting the burden of proof shifts the burden of proof of some issue from the party who started with the burden to the other party. By contrast, a presumption affecting the burden of producing evidence *never* shifts the burden of proof. A presumption that shifts the burden of proof does just that—it shifts the burden of proof.

What are the options for a party faced with a presumption that shifts the burden of proof? The options are the same as for a presumption affecting the burden of production. What then is the difference between a presumption that affects the burden of production and a presumption that affects the burden of proof? The difference arises when the party against whom the presumption operates introduces evidence to establish the nonexistence of the presumed fact. If the presumption is one that affects the burden of producing evidence, the presumption disappears, the bubble bursts. But in the case of a presumption that affects the burden of proof, the presumption does not disappear in the face of evidence of the nonexistence of the presumed fact. This is a strong presumption. When a presumption affecting the burden of proof arises, the party against whom it operates has the burden of proving that the presumed fact does not exist.

§ 13.6 Presumptions Under the FRE

As mentioned at the beginning of the chapter, the FRE has only one rule on presumptions, Rule 301. Rule 301 concerns presumptions that affect the burden of producing evidence—bursting bubble presumptions. In practice, there is little difference between the CEC and the FRE. Federal statutes contain numerous presumptions, some of which are presumptions affecting the burden of proof, while others are presumptions affecting the burden of producing evidence. In federal court, presumptions operate the same way as presumptions under the CEC.

Chapter 14

PRACTICE EXAMS, ANSWERS, AND ANALYSIS

Time to apply what you have learned. Chapter 14 contains five practice exams. Questions 1, 2, and 3 are followed by analysis of the evidence issues presented. Questions 4 and 5 are followed by student answers that received high grades. The chapter has two California Bar Examination evidence questions, which are reproduced with the permission of the State Bar. The chapter ends with a set of multiple choice questions.

Question 1

Andrew and Susan worked as bankers at a Wells Fargo Bank branch in Sacramento. In 2018, Andrew and Susan came up with a plan to steal small amounts of money from the bank. Over the course of 2018, Andrew and Susan embezzled more than $300,000 from Wells Fargo. When it became clear to Susan and Andrew that their superiors at the bank suspected them, Susan quit her job and moved to Canada. While in Canada, Susan called Andrew, who was still working at the bank. In a conversation that was secretly recorded by the FBI, Susan advised Andrew on steps he should take to cover up the embezzlement and avoid detection. The FBI had placed a recording device on Andrew's phone. The device recorded calls to and from Andrew's phone, including the call just described. In 2019, Wells Fargo fired Andrew and brought a civil action against Andrew for stealing the $300,000 from the bank. At the civil trial, Wells Fargo offered the testimony of forensic accountant, Rachel. Rachel testified, and described how she was able to use accounting methods to reconstruct Andrew and Susan's scheme to steal from the bank. In the civil case, the jury returned a judgment against Andrew for $300,000. In 2020, prosecutors filed criminal embezzlement charges against Andrew and Susan. Andrew and Susan entered pleas of not guilty. Andrew and Susan are now on trial together in Sacramento, charged with the crime of embezzlement. Andrew and Susan do not testify at the criminal trial.

Call of the question: Assume all proper objections and offers of proof are made. Discuss all evidence issues raised in the following paragraphs. Answer according to the Federal Rules of Evidence and the California Evidence Code. You

should only mention the California Evidence Code if the answer under the California Evidence Code differs from the answer under the Federal Rules of Evidence. The paragraphs are not equally weighted for purposes of grading.

1.   During the prosecution's case-in-chief, the prosecutor offers the testimony of an FBI agent. The agent repeats what Susan and Andrew said to each other during the conversation that was secretly recorded.

2.   At the criminal trial, Rachel is unavailable to testify. During the prosecution's case-in-chief, the prosecutor offers a transcript of Rachel's testimony at the civil trial.

3.   After she was arrested, Susan confessed to the FBI. In her confession, she said, "Andrew and I worked very hard to keep our plan secret. We worked on it together, and we split the money equally." During the prosecution's case-in-chief, the prosecutor offers testimony from the FBI agent to whom Susan confessed. The agent repeats the confession.

4.   During the defense case-in-chief, Andrew offers testimony from Nell, who, for three years, was Andrew's immediate supervisor at Wells Fargo. Nell testifies, "I worked every day with Andrew at our bank branch. I supervised his work. I saw him interact with countless customers over the years. He is an excellent banker, honest and ethical. I never saw him engage in any kind of unethical or illegal behavior. I would have detected anything improper, and I never did."

5.   During the defense case-in-chief, defense counsel offers testimony from John, who knew Rachel for 4 years. John states, "In my opinion, Rachel is a liar."

Question 1—Analysis

1.   Your answer should define relevance, and state how the conversation is relevant. There is really no danger of unfair prejudice, however, your professor may want you to discuss unfair prejudice with most types of evidence. What Susan and Andrew told each other is certainly relevant: it amounts to an admission of guilt. What Susan and Andrew told each other is offered for the truth of the matter asserted, but is admissible under the co-conspirator exception. The conspiracy was still ongoing, and the statements furthered the conspiracy. In the CEC, the co-conspirator rule is an exception to hearsay. In the FRE, the co-conspirator rule is defined as not hearsay. Each speaker's own words are admissible against the speaker as a personal admission, and are admissible against the

other under the co-conspirator rule. Your answer needs to address whether the FBI agent heard the statements as they were made, because the agent was listing in, or whether the agent is simply repeating what is on the recording. If the FBI agent is repeating what is on the recording, there is a violation of the best evidence rule and the secondary evidence rule. The actual recording would need to be admitted. As well, the recording would need to be authenticated. Someone needs to identify the speakers. This is an issue of foundation.

2.   This is primarily a former testimony question. Discuss relevance. The transcript is a layer of hearsay, thus you have layered hearsay. The original statement was the testimony at trial number 1. The final statement is the court reporter's official transcript. The official transcript will need to be authenticated. It should be admissible under the public records exception.

The admissibility of the testimony from trial number one depends on the application of the former testimony exception.

Trial number 1:   Wells Fargo v. Andrew. Andrew had an opportunity to cross-examine Rachel.

Trial number 2:   People v. Andrew and Susan. Trial number 2 is criminal.

Because Andrew was a party to trial number 1, and had an opportunity to cross-examine the now unavailable Rachel, the question is whether Andrew's motive to cross-examine would be the same at trial number 2 as it was a trial number 1. The answer is probably yes. So, Rachel's former testimony may be admissible against Andrew. Clearly, however, the former testimony is not admissible against Susan, who was not a party to trial number 1. Susan should argue that admission at the joint trial of Rachel's testimony would violate Rachel's rights under the Confrontation Clause. Susan should further argue that a limiting instruction— instructing the jury to consider the former testimony only against Andrew—will not cure the problem of Susan's lack of ability to cross examine Rachel.

3.   Number 3 is primarily a *Bruton* issue. Recall that § 11.30 advises you to be on the lookout for *Bruton* when: (1) Two or more defendants are on trial together, (2) The conspiracy was over when one of them made a statement—often to police—that implicated not only the declarant but the other defendants, and (3) The declarant does not testify at trial.

In the exam, the facts raise the *Bruton* issue. It seems unlikely that Susan's statement could be sanitized to remove the

Confrontation Clause problem. What will the jury think if "Andrew" is replaced with a blank space? Won't the jury think, "It has to be Andrew? He's the only other defendant." It may be that the judge should exclude the entire statement.

4.   This is an effort by Andrew to offer evidence of good character as substantive evidence of innocence: Andrew is not the kind of guy who would do such a dishonest thing. Nell has known Andrew long enough and well enough to satisfy the foundation to serve as a character witness. Nell is an opinion character witness. In this case, the part of Nell's testimony where she says Andrew is "honest and ethical" is fine. However, Nell gets too far into specific instances of Andrew's conduct.

5.   This is an effort to impeach Rachel with a character witness. This is allowed by FRE 608(a) and CEC § 790. The testimony is from a character witness who testifies in the form of an opinion, which is allowed. Is four years long enough for the foundation? Probably.

Question 2

Ann, Cindy, and Dawn agreed to rob a bank. During a conversation at a Denny's Restaurant between Ann and Cindy, Cindy said, "We need a getaway car for the bank job. You steal a car, ok?" Ann replied, "Ok, I'll get us a car." Dawn was not present when this conversation occurred. Ann and Cindy did not realize it, but a customer at the next table, Ruth, overheard their conversation. Two days before the robbery, Ann stole a car for use in the robbery. On Saturday, Ann and Cindy entered the bank with guns drawn. Dawn waited outside in the getaway car. Ann and Cindy shouted, "This is a robbery. Put the money in these bags." After bank employees filled the bags with cash, Ann and Cindy ran out of the bank, jumped in the getaway car with Dawn, and sped away. As soon as the getaway car left, a bank employee called 911 and told the operator, "This is Emma Gonzales at First Bank on Main Street. The bank was just robbed by two women. They have guns and they wore masks. They jumped in a green Mazda and left, but I don't know where they are now." The 911 operator notified all police in the area, and the getaway car was soon spotted by a police officer. Following a short chase, Ann, Cindy, and Dawn were arrested. The three were handcuffed and placed in the back of a police car. The three did not realize their conversation in the police car was recorded. While in the police car Cindy said, "How did the cops find us so fast? I think that when we went into the bank we forgot to warn the bank people not to trigger a silent alarm. Damn." In July, six months after the bank robbery, Ann, Cindy, and Dawn were put on trial for bank robbery. At trial, one of the bank tellers testified as follows, "I was working when the bank was robbed. The two robbers entered the bank and shouted that it was a robbery. The two that robbed the bank are sitting there at the defense table. The robbers were the defendants, Ann and Cindy." The trial ended when the judge declared a mistrial. Since the mistrial, the teller who testified died. In November, the prosecutor filed a new complaint charging the three with bank robbery. The trial judge severed the trials, giving each defendant a separate trial.

Call of the question: This question involves the trial in November, in which Dawn is charged with robbing the bank. Dawn is the only defendant on trial. Assume all proper objections and offers of proof are made. Answer according to the Federal Rules of Evidence. Do not mention the California Evidence Code. Discuss all evidence issues in the following paragraphs. The paragraphs are not weighted equally for purposes of grading.

1.   During the prosecution's case-in-chief, the prosecutor offers the testimony of Ruth, who testifies, "I was at Denny's and I overheard a conversation between two women. One of them said, "We need a getaway car for the bank job. You steal a car, ok?" The other woman replied, "Ok, I'll get us a car." On cross-examination of Ruth, defense counsel asks, "Isn't it true that a year ago you were fired from your job for filing false claims for travel expenses?" Ruth answers, "No, I quit that job because I got a better job at another company."

2.   During the prosecution's case-in-chief, the prosecutor offers a bank surveillance videotape that shows the robbery. The video tape contains the words, "This is a robbery. Put the money in these bags."

3.   During the prosecution's case-in-chief, the prosecutor offers the 911 audiotape containing the words, "This is Emma Gonzales at First Bank on Main Street. The bank was just robbed by two women. They have guns and they wore masks. They jumped in a green Mazda and left, but I don't know where they are now."

4.   During the prosecution's case-in-chief, the prosecutor offers the audiotape from the police car in which Cindy said, "How did the cops find us so fast? I think that when we went into the bank we forgot to warn the bank people not to trigger a silent alarm. Damn."

5.   During the prosecution's case-in-chief, the prosecutor offers a transcript of the now-deceased bank teller's testimony from the July trial, in which the teller said, "I was working when the

bank was robbed. The two robbers entered the bank and shouted that it was a robbery. The two that robbed the bank are sitting there at the defense table. The robbers were the defendants, Ann and Cindy."

6.   During the defense case-in-chief, defense counsel offers the testimony of Megan, who testifies, "I have known Dawn for many years. We worked together and socialized together. I know her very well. In my opinion, Dawn is a law abiding, nonviolent person."

7.   On cross-examination of Megan, the prosecutor asks, "Did you know that two years ago, Dawn was arrested for assault with a deadly weapon?"

8.   During the defense case-in-chief, defense counsel offers the testimony of Emily. Emily used to be Ruth's boss. Emily testifies, "I had to fire Ruth from her job because she filed false claims for reimbursement of travel expenses."

9.   During the prosecution's case-in-rebuttal, the prosecutor offers the testimony of Zelda, who testifies, "For five years, I've lived in the same neighborhood as Megan. Over the years, I've heard about Megan's reputation in the community for telling the truth. Megan has a reputation as a liar."

Question 2—Analysis

1.   Ruth's direct testimony is relevant because it repeats evidence of planning for the crime. Ruth will need to identify who was speaking, or the evidence won't be relevant. Assuming Ruth does so, the out-of-court statements by Ann and Cindy meet the requirements of the co-conspirator exception. The statements were during and in furtherance of the conspiracy. Because the co-conspirator exception applies, the evidence is admissible against Dawn. It does not matter that she was not at the restaurant. There is no Confrontation Clause issue here. The Supreme Court has held that the Confrontation Clause does not apply to statements admissible under the co-conspirator exception.

The cross-examination of Ruth is proper. It is proper impeachment to ask a witness about a specific instance of the witness's untruthfulness.

2.   The bank surveillance videotape is relevant. If the videotape is reliable, it is direct evidence of the bank robbery. Your answer should discuss the best evidence rule. It appears the prosecutor is offering the tape itself, although the facts are not entirely clear on this. A foundation will have to be laid to authenticate the tape, and to ensure that it has not been edited.

The words spoken on the video are relevant as evidence of the robbery. The speaker's voice should be identified. Someone who knows the speaker's voice can identify the voice. I suppose that the statement is admissible even if it is not possible to identify the voice. Whoever is speaking is robbing the bank, and other evidence connects Dawn and the others to the robbery. The statement is admissible against Dawn under the co-conspirator exception. The video is not a second layer of hearsay. Machines don't make statements; people do.

3.   The 911 recording is clearly relevant as it is a statement by a person with personal knowledge describing the bank robbery. The recording will need to be authenticated, and evidence will be needed to prove that the recording has not been altered. Emma can testify to identify her voice as the caller. Emma's 911 is hearsay, but it should meet the requirements of the excited utterance exception. A bank robbery is a startling event. Emma's statement descries the event. Finally, Emma made the 911 call right after the robbery, and she was undoubtedly still upset. Her words indicate that she is upset. The fact that guns were involved, and that Emma does not know where the robbers are adds to her emotional state. 911 calls that are made in an emergency are not testimonial for purposes of the Confrontation Clause. It is very likely the 911 call is non-testimonial. The defense will argue that Emma's primary purpose for calling 911 was to provide evidence of a crime, not to help in an emergency. Given the nature of the event, the use of guns, and the fact that Emma does not know where the robbers are, it is likely a court would reject the argument that the 911 call was testimonial. If Emma testifies, and is subject to cross-examination about her 911 call, there would be no Confrontation Clause issue, even if her statement was testimonial.

4.   Cindy's statement is relevant because she implicates all of them in the robbery. You should discuss authentication of the audio recording. Discuss the best evidence rule. Is the conspiracy over so that the co-conspirator exception no longer applies? Probably, because they were under arrest, sitting in a cop car. Cindy's words would be admissible against Cindy as a personal admission, but Cindy is not on trial. Cindy's words might be an excited utterance, which would make her words admissible against Dawn. Cindy's words might be a statement against interest, if Cindy is unavailable at Dawn's trial. However, the facts raise a *Williamson* issue (§ 11.20(a)). Is the part of Cindy's statement that mentions "us" and "we" against *Cindy's* interest?

5.   This is a former testimony problem. Using our schematic approach:

Trial number 1: People v. Ann, Cindy, and Dawn. Dawn had the opportunity cross-examine the now-unavailable bank teller.

Trial number 2: After the mistrial in trial number 1, Dawn is on trial, so trial number 2 is People v. Dawn. Dawn was a party to trial number 1.

The former testimony exception should apply. The declarant is unavailable at trial number 2. Dawn was a party to trial number 1, and had an opportunity to cross-examine the bank teller at trial number 1. Dawn's motive to cross at trial number 1 is very likely the same motive Dawn would have at trial number 2, if the teller testified. There is no Confrontation Clause problem. Even though the former testimony is testimonial, and the declarant is now unavailable, Dawn had an opportunity cross-examine the declarant at the earlier trial. Even though the teller's testimony at trial number 1 did not mention Dawn, the evidence is relevant. The testimony helps to prove the crime.

The transcript of testimony from trial number 1 is itself hearsay. Thus, this is layered hearsay. However, the public records exception will admit the court reporter's transcript of the testimony from trial number 1.

The prosecutor will need to authenticate the transcript and satisfy the best evidence rule.

6. Megan's testimony is admissible, and is a straight forward example of the Mercy Rule. The defendant in a criminal case may offer a character witness to testify that, in the witness's opinion, the defendant is not the type of person who would commit the charged offense. Bank robbery is a crime of violence, and Megan's opinion that Dawn is a law abiding, nonviolent person is pertinent to the crime charged. Megan has known Dawn long enough for Megan to qualify as a character witness.

7. The cross-examination of Megan is proper. (See the last sentence of FRE 405(a)). The prosecutor has the right to test how well Megan knows Dawn. The prosecutor's question is in the correct form. Megan testified as an opinion witness, and the proper impeachment question to an opinion character witness is "Did you know."

8. Under the FRE, Emily's testimony is inadmissible. In question 1, Ruth was impeached by asking Ruth about a specific instance of Ruth's untruthfulness. Ruth denied the untruthful act. The defense attorney has to take Ruth's denial, and may not offer extrinsic evidence to prove that Ruth lied when she denied the impeaching fact. (See FRE 608(b)).

9.   Zelda is offered to impeach Megan's credibility. Zelda's testimony is admissible. (*See* FRE 608(a)). Zelda has enough experience with Megan's reputation to testify as a reputation character witness to impeach Megan's truthfulness.

Question 3

Sue was driving her car in the imaginary state of Calivada. Sue was stopped at a red light. Suddenly, Sue's car was hit from behind by a car driven by Tom. Both cars were damaged beyond repair, and Sue was hospitalized with a severe neck strain—whiplash. Sue is suing Tom for negligence, and seeks damages for property damage to her car and personal injuries, including pain and suffering.

Call of the question: Assume all proper objections and offers of proof are made. Answer according to the Federal Rules of Evidence only. Do not discuss the California Evidence Code. Discuss all evidence issues raised in the following numbered paragraphs. The paragraphs are not weighted equally for purposes of grading.

1.   During Sue's case-in-chief, Sue testifies, "The day after the accident, Tom visited me in my hospital room. He apologized for hitting me, and offered to pay all my expenses, including the hospital bill. I said, 'Thank you for visiting, but don't worry about the bills. I have insurance.'"

2.   On cross-examination of Sue, Tom's attorney asks, "About four years ago, you filed a claim for coverage under a fire insurance policy with Farmers Insurance, and that claim was rejected by Farmers because the claim was not true, didn't you?" Sue replies, "No."

3.   During Sue's case-in-chief, Sue offers the testimony of Ralph to testify as follows: "I have been friends with Tom for 5 years. On three separate occasions when I've been in the car with Tom, he has almost rear ended people because he was not watching where he was going."

4.   During Sue's case-in-chief, Sue offers the testimony of Mary, who is Tom's cousin. Mary will testify as follows: "In my opinion, Tom is a careless driver."

5.   During Sue's case-in-chief, Sue offers the testimony of California Highway Patrol officer Maxwell, who testifies as follows: "I was on duty at the time of the accident. I happened to be parked along the highway where the accident occurred. I was not in my car when the accident happened, and I didn't see the accident. However, the camera on the dashboard of my patrol car recorded the entire accident. From looking at what the camera recorded, I

could clearly see that Tom rear-ended Sue at the intersection, and Tom appeared to be going about 30 mph when he hit Sue."

6.   During Sue's case-in-chief, Sue offers the police report prepared by California Highway Patrol officer Myers, who investigated the accident. Myers' report contains the following statement: "The accident was caused by Tom when he failed to stop, and ran into the back of Sue's car at a speed of approximately 30 mph."

7.   During Tom's case-in-chief, Tom offers testimony from Rachel, an insurance adjuster for Farmers Insurance. Rachael will testify as follows: "I did the investigation of the fire insurance claim Sue filed with our company four years ago. I determined that the claim was false."

Question 3—Analysis

1.   Sue's testimony is relevant. Tom's apology can be interpreted as an admission of responsibility. Tom's offer to pay Sue's medical expenses is barred by FRE 409 (*See* § 2.23). It may be that the judge will admit Tom's apology, and exclude his offer to pay medical expenses. The judge might exclude the entire statement by Tom, if the judge believes the apology and the offer to pay medical expenses are too intertwined to separate. Sue's mention of the fact that she has insurance is interesting. FRE 411 excludes evidence of insurance to prove fault (*See* § 2.24). In this case, though, it was Sue who mentioned insurance, not Tom. Very likely, nothing will be done about the insurance statement. Tom won't object. He does not care if the jury knows Sue has insurance.

2.   This is impeachment with a specific instance of untruthfulness, which is allowed by FRE 608(b) (*See* § 10.7(a)). Tom's attorney has to take Sue's denial, and cannot offer extrinsic evidence that she filed a false claim.

3.   Ralph's testimony is inadmissible. It violates the rule against character to prove that a person acted in conformity with character on a specific occasion. Character is not "in issue" in a negligence case like this. The rule against character evidence applies as much in civil litigation as it does in criminal cases.

4.   Mary's testimony is inadmissible for the same reason Ralph's testimony is inadmissible. Mary's testimony violates the rule against character evidence.

5.   Officer Maxwell's testimony is clearly relevant. The video proves what happened. However, the best evidence rule is violated. Sue is seeking to prove the contents of a writing—the video recording. Thus, the best evidence rule applies, and Sue has not

offered an excuse for the non-production of the original. Officer Maxwell has no personal knowledge of the accident. His testimony is secondary evidence of the content of the video recording, and violates the best evidence rule. The video recording itself needs to be offered. If the recording is offered, it will need to be authenticated. Officer Maxwell could authenticate the tape with testimony that the camera was working properly, the recording offered is the correct recording, and the recording has not been altered. The video recording is not hearsay because machines do not make statements. Don't discuss the business records exception because you are not dealing with hearsay.

6.   Officer Myers' report is likely admissible under the public records exception or the business records exception, or both. The public records exception allows factual findings and conclusions of accident investigations. Is this a proper opinion from a lay witness? I doubt it. This seems like expert testimony, but Officer Myers probably qualifies as an expert.

7.   Rachel's testimony is inadmissible. In question 2, Sue was cross-examined and impeached with a specific instance of untruthfulness. Sue denied it, and Tom's attorney has to take Sue's denial, even if the denial is itself a lie. Extrinsic evidence is not admissible when the theory of impeachment is a prior act of untruthfulness.

Question 4

Nancy is charged with murder, and has pleaded not guilty. The victim was shot and killed in Sacramento, CA, on July 4, 2019. Nancy is on trial in California Superior Court, so use the California Evidence Code only. Do not refer to the Federal Rules of Evidence. At Nancy's trial, the following evidence is offered. Assume that all necessary objections and offers of proof are made. Discuss all evidence issues raised in the following paragraphs. Paragraphs are not weighted equally for grading.

1.   During the prosecution's case-in-chief, the prosecutor offers testimony from Bill, who testifies as follows: "I own a gun shop. On April 1, 2019, Nancy came to my store and purchased a handgun. After the 10-day waiting period, Nancy took the gun with her." Following this testimony, the prosecutor asks Bill, "What kind of gun did Nancy buy?" Bill testifies, "My records indicate that she purchased a Glock 9 millimeter semi-automatic handgun."

2.   During the prosecution's case-in-chief, the prosecutor offers the testimony of Rachel, who is a technician at the police crime lab. Rachel testifies as follows: "I was given the 9 millimeter

bullet taken from the victim's body. I was given a Glock 9 millimeter semi-automatic handgun. I test-fired five rounds from the Glock. I compared the markings on the test-fired bullets against the markings on the bullet retrieved from the victim's body. Based on that comparison, I formed the opinion that the bullet taken from the victim's body was fired from the Glock that I was given."

3.   During the prosecution's case-in-chief, the prosecutor offers testimony from Sylvia, who was the first police officer to arrive at the scene of the shooting. Sylvia testifies as follows: "I arrived on scene just a couple of minutes after the 911 operator got a call that there had been a shooting. The victim was lying in the middle of the street, badly wounded. I asked the victim what happened, and she said, 'Nancy shot me after we had a fight over some money she owes me.' I then asked the victim where I could find Nancy. The victim said, 'She lives a couple of blocks from here, at 321 Maple Street. That's where she shot me, at her house. When she shot me she said, 'That will teach you to mess with me.' "

4.   During the defense case-in-chief, the defense offers the testimony of Ursula, who testifies, "I have known Nancy all her life. We grew up together. Nancy is not a violent person. She would not deliberately hurt someone."

5.   On cross-examination of Ursula, the prosecutor asks, "Did you know that a few months prior to the shooting, Nancy bought a gun?"

Student Answer

The following is a student's answer to this question. The student earned a perfect 100 for her answer. A few minor typos have been corrected. The answer is reproduced with the student's permission.

Question 4—Analysis

1.   Bill's Testimony

Relevance

Evidence must be relevant to be admissible. It is relevant if it has any tendency to make a fact of consequence more or less likely. A fact of consequence is anything that will make a difference in the case. Here, evidence of the purchase of a gun makes it more likely that Nancy is the killer. Because a person with a gun is more likely to shoot someone than someone who did not purchase a gun. This is a material fact, because it goes straight to the fact that Nancy is being charged with. This evidence is relevant.

Uncharged Misconduct Evidence

Plan. Uncharged misconduct evidence is admissible when it is part of a plan. The UME theory of plan can be used to prove motive, intent (mens rea), and actus reus. UME under this theory is allowed when the UME is all part of a continuous undertaking; that the charged act would be in mind when committing the uncharged act. UME does not have to be criminal or even misconduct at all. Buying a gun is perfectly legal, but it can be part of a plan if Nancy was intending to use this gun in the shooting. The prosecution can prove that it was Nancy who committed the UME (bought the gun), and thus it is admissible for the jury to make an inference from the purchase of the gun, and the type of gun that was used that Nancy had the intent, motive, and did the act from this evidence.

Prejudice. Evidence is inadmissible when its probative value is substantially outweighed by its prejudicial effect. This is highly probative as part of a plan because it can show a real intent when there was planning going into an event. Also, it can show act and ID to connect Nancy to the killing. Prejudice is when the jury might use the evidence incorrectly. Just tending to show guilt or innocence is not an incorrect use of evidence, so just because it is highly probative, does not mean it is prejudicial. There is nothing really the jury could misuse this evidence for, and thus the evidence is not unfairly prejudicial.

As plain eyewitness testimony that falls within a UME theory, and has no other bars to admissibility, the evidence is admissible.

2.   Rachel's Testimony

Relevant

As defined above, this evidence is also relevant. Evidence that shows that the bullet in the victim was fired from the gun the expert was given tends to make it more likely that the bullet was fired from the gun the expert was given. However, this is not a material fact if the gun that Rachel was given has nothing to do with the law suit. If the gun is the gun that Nancy bought from Bill then it does go to a material fact because it is central in determining if it was Nancy who shot and killed the victim, and knowing that it was her gun that shot the bullet would help make that determination, because it would be more likely to be her that shot someone with her gun, than someone who did not own the gun. As long as the prosecution can somehow tie the gun they gave Rachel to Nancy, then the testimony is relevant. Otherwise the evidence would be inadmissible as irrelevant because the gun has nothing to do with the lawsuit. Here, we will assume it is the same Glock 9 mm that Nancy bought from Bill.

Expert Testimony

Qualification

The judge determines if an expert is qualified to testify. To qualify as an expert witness, the prosecution must lay the necessary foundation that the expert has knowledge, skill, or training not within lay knowledge, that their testimony will help the jury in some way, and that the testimony is based on facts or data using methods that are reliable that have been reliably applied. Here, it would not be within lay knowledge to know what kinds of guns can make what kinds of markings on bullets. That is not within lay knowledge. For the same reason that it is not within lay knowledge, it would also be helpful for the jury, because figuring out if it was Nancy's gun that shot the bullet, will help them in figuring out if it was Nancy who shot and killed the victim.

Reliable Facts/Data: The expert is allowed to base their testimony on facts/data that a reasonable person in the field would base their opinion on. Here, Rachel says she based her opinion on test-firing the gun, and comparing the markings on the bullet. This would probably be a reasonable way to find out if it was the gun that shot the bullet, but it would have to be established that a reasonable crime lab technician would use these kinds of facts—bullet marking and test firing. This is very likely. Reliable methods, reliably applied: Here, Rachel test-fired 5 rounds, and then compared. This is probably a reliable method, and as long as the prosecution can prove Rachel's system of doing this is also reliable, and that the bullets were kept track of, it should meet this test.

Opinion

Since the foundation is likely established for Rachel to testify as a witness, she is allowed to give her expert opinion on the matter. She makes a conclusory opinion that the bullet was fired from the gun she was given. This is a proper opinion, and an expert is allowed to embrace ultimate factual issues in their opinions. Her opinion is proper as an expert.

There seems to be no other reasons for excluding Rachel's testimony, it is likely admissible expert testimony as long as the relevancy is established by linking Nancy to the gun Rachel was given.

3.   Sylvia's Testimony

There are several pieces of evidence in Sylvia's testimony that need to be discussed separately—her eye witness testimony of the accident, and the victim's statements.

Eye Witness Testimony

Plain eye witness testimony is admissible when relevant. Here it is relevant as defined above because it is about the incident itself, and the scene immediately after the shooting. This will tend to show what happened, which is central to determining if Nancy is guilty or not. There is nothing else about the initial testimony about the scene when the police officer arrived to suggest it would be inadmissible. This first part of the testimony would be admissible.

Victim's Statements About What Happened

Relevant

As defined above, this is relevant—this describes what happened. It is more likely that Nancy shot the victim if the victim says she was the one to shoot her, than if no one had said Nancy shot the victim, and more likely that the incident happened as described. This is a core issue because the jury is determining if Nancy is the killer.

Hearsay

An out of court statement offered for the truth of the matter asserted is generally inadmissible. Here, the statement about what happened that Nancy shot her after they had a fight over money is offered to prove that Nancy shot the victim, and possibly to prove that they fought or that Nancy owed her money to show a motive to kill. They are offering it to prove what happened, and how shot. What is trying to be proved matches the statement and is thus offered for the truth of the matters asserted. It is out of court because it was uttered not at trial in the current proceeding. This is hearsay, and must fit within an exception.

Dying Declaration

An exception to the hearsay rule is the dying declaration. It must be made by a dying person, while they believed death was imminent; it is about the cause/circumstances of their death. Here, it is made by a dying person because the victim was shot and killed—she is now dead—when she made the statement she was a dying person because she was dying from the gun shot. To prove that the victim believed death imminent, it must be proved that the victim subjectively believed it, by looking at all the circumstances surrounding the statement. Here, the victim was lying in the middle of the street, badly wounded. A gunshot wound is likely very severe, and since she was not able to get out of the middle of the street, it makes it seem even more severe. However, she was able to say what happened and where Nancy lived, showing that maybe it wasn't so bad. But ultimately the prosecution would have to prove that the victim herself believed she was about to die to fit the statement within this exception. The prosecution can likely prove this, and the evidence would be admissible. If they cannot prove she believed death was imminent, then they could try to fit the statement into other hearsay exceptions.

Excited Utterance

The excited utterance exception also makes hearsay admissible. The prosecution must prove that there was a startling event, that the statement describes or narrates the event, and that the statement was made while the declarant was still under the stress of the event. Here, there was a startling event—being shot is probably very startling. The statement describes the event and how it took place—Nancy shot her, after a fight. The prosecution would have to prove that the victim was still under the stress of the event by looking at all the circumstances surrounding the statement. Here, the injury was very bad since it was a gun shot, it was said to the first police officer who arrived—so probably not long after, Nancy had not been apprehended yet, and the scene had not been secured in any way, and the injury had not been treated at all. Likely this statement would fit into the excited utterance exception, if it cannot fit into the dying declaration.

Victim's Statements About What Nancy Said to Her When She Shot Her

This statement, which includes Nancy's statement, is layered hearsay, and thus even if the victim's statement fits within a hearsay exception, Nancy's statement must also fit within a hearsay exception for the statement to be admissible in court. It is hearsay because it is out of court—earlier when Nancy was doing the shooting, and offered for the truth of the matter asserted, because while they are not trying to prove that this will teach the victim a lesson, when you apply the "what is the declarant really saying test," it can be inferred that she is saying she is shooting the victim on purpose—something the prosecution will want to prove. Thus, it is hearsay, and needs its own exception. This would easily fall under a party admission, however. A party admission includes personal admissions, and anything you say can be used against you. Nancy is a party, and she is the one who made the statement, so the prosecution is now allowed to use it against her. This statement meets the exception.

Confrontation Clause

The confrontation clause can be a constitutional bar to admissible hearsay when it is offered against a D in a criminal case, where the declarant does not testify, and the D did not have a prior opportunity to cross examine the declarant about the statement, and the statement is testimonial. The confrontation clause does not apply to hearsay when it fits within the dying declaration exception. Thus, if the statement fits within the dying declaration, the confrontation clause is not violated. Additionally, a party admission cannot violate the confrontation clause either. However, if the statements come in under an excited utterance rather than the dying declaration, a confrontation clause issue might exist. Here, they are hearsay that fall within an exception. They are offered against a D in a criminal trial, and the declarant is not testifying— she is dead. And the D never had a prior opportunity to cross examine. Next, the statement must be testimonial too. Testimonial means the primary purpose of the statement was to generate a statement for court to be used at trial. Or that a reasonable person would know that the statement's primary purpose would be for trial. An ongoing emergency is usually found not be testimonial, even though it is given to the police. Here, the statement was given before the victim had gotten any help for her injury, the injury was very severe, and the shooter was still at large. Questions about who shot the victim, and where they live could be testimonial in a different situation because they are information gathering, but because the shooter was still on the loose, the primary purpose was probably to catch the shooter, and prevent anyone else from getting hurt, rather than to collect information for trial. This is emphasized by the fact that the statement was to the first police officer to get to the scene, and the scene had not been secured, because the emergency was still continuing. Thus, likely none of the victim's statements are testimonial, and even if the statements come in under the excited utterance exception, they would not violate the confrontation clause.

All the evidence is relevant hearsay within an exception, the entire testimony is admissible.

4. Ursula's Testimony

Relevant

As defined above, this evidence is relevant. That Nancy is not violent would tend to prove she is not a murderer, and being a murderer is central to determining if she murdered someone. Thus this evidence is relevant.

Character Evidence

Evidence of a person's character is generally inadmissible to prove that a person acted in conformity with their character on a particular occasion. Here, the defense is offering evidence that Nancy is not violent (a character trait) to show that on the day the victim died, Nancy acted peacefully and did not shoot the victim (acting in conformity). Thus, this is character evidence. An exception, however, is when a defendant in a criminal case offers evidence of their pertinent good character trait to help prove innocent. Then character evidence in the form of reputation or opinion character witness is allowed. This is an opinion character witness. And thus, as long as the necessary foundation is met, it would be admissible. The foundation is required to be that the witness knew the D for a long time—long enough and in context to form an opinion. Here, they grew up together, and that is probably long enough to form an opinion. Further, she does have an opinion as she is giving it to the court. This would be a qualified and proper witness for character evidence. The evidence is admissible.

5.   Cross Exam of Ursula

Impeachment—Specific Instances

An opposing party may impeach a character witness by questioning about specific instances of the person the character witness is testifying about. They can ask specific instances pertinent to the character trait the witness is testifying about in order to test how good of a character witness they are—how much they really know the person they are testifying about. This evidence is likely admissible.

Question 5

Travis is an excellent skier. Travis decided to go skiing at a ski resort near Lake Tahoe, California. Travis took the ski lift to the top of the mountain, and decided to ski down the most difficult ski run. A sign at the entrance to the ski run said, "Difficult run. Recommended for experienced skiers only." Half way down the run, Travis hit a tree and was seriously injured. Travis is suing the ski resort based on the theory that the resort was negligent in allowing people to use the ski run on which Travis was injured. The ski resort denies any negligence.

Apply the Federal Rules of Evidence (FRE) and the California Evidence Code (CEC). However, you should only mention the CEC if there is a difference between the FRE and the CEC on a particular issue. Assume all proper objections and offers of proof are made. Discuss all evidence issues in the numbered paragraphs. Paragraphs are not weighted equally for grading.

1.   Travis's lawyer offers the testimony of Mark Jones as an expert on ski safety. You may assume Mr. Jones is qualified to testify. Jones testifies as follows: "In my opinion, this particular ski run should not have been open to the public. It was far too

dangerous. Allowing people to ski on that run fell below the standard of care in the ski industry, and was negligent."

2.   Travis's lawyer offers the testimony of Thor Billings, who states: "After this accident, the ski resort replaced the sign at the top of the run. The new sign states: 'EXTREMELY DANGEROUS RUN, WITH EXPOSED TREES AND ROCKS; ENTER AT YOUR OWN RISK.'"

3.   Travis testifies and describes his view of how the accident happened. During his testimony, Travis says, "I knew it was a difficult run, but I am an experienced skier. The ski run was so steep I could not control my skis, and I slammed into a tree." On cross-examination, defense counsel asks, "Isn't it a fact that a couple of weeks after the accident you told your friend Helmut that you ran into the tree because you were distracted?" Travis, replies, "I never said that." On further cross-examination, defense counsel asks, "Isn't it true that you were injured in two other ski accidents because you were not looking where you were going?" Travis replies, "No."

4.   Travis's lawyer offers the testimony of Roger Williams, who used to work for the ski resort as the head ski instructor, who states: "On two occasions, people told me that the run was extremely dangerous, and they almost got hurt." On cross-examination of Roger, the ski resort's lawyer asks, "Isn't it a fact that you were fired from the ski resort because you stole money from the resort?" Roger answers, "I quit. I wasn't fired, and I didn't steal any money."

5.   During the defense, case-in-chief, the ski resort offer testimony from Nancy Nichols, who is the general manager of the ski resort. Nancy states: "I fired Roger for stealing from the company."

Student Answer

The following answer earned a perfect score of 100. Interestingly, this is the same student who wrote the 100 on question 4. Indeed, during evidence that year, students took four exams. This particular student got perfect scores on every question: four 100s! Grading was anonymous. Pretty impressive, yes?

Question 5—Analysis

1.   Mark's Testimony

Relevant

Evidence is relevant if it has any tendency to make a fact of consequence more or less likely. A fact of consequence is something that will make a difference in the outcome of the case. Here, the evidence is relevant because it is about how safe the run was. Testimony about how safe the run was tends to make it more likely that it is what the expert says it is. And how safe the run is is central to determining if the resort was negligent because that is what the entire suit is about. This evidence is relevant.

Expert Testimony

As a qualified expert, Mark may state his opinion that can help the jury in their determination. His opinion may embrace the ultimate factual issues, but not the ultimate legal issues. Here, the opinions that the ski run should not have been open to the public, and that the run was much too dangerous are just opinions that will help the jury in determining negligence. The statement that the ski run fell below the standard of care in the ski industry parrots the language of the cause of action on an element that the jury will need to find to find liability. Even though the language is the same, it is an ultimate factual issue, because it does not draw the ultimate conclusion of liability or not. Parroting the language of the necessary elements is proper expert testimony. The statement that they were negligent, however, embraces the ultimate legal issue that is for the jury to determine. This statement is the entire cause of action of what the jury needs to determine, and is an improper expert opinion. If the statement that the ski resort was negligent is redacted, this is admissible evidence.

2.   Thor's Testimony

Relevant

This evidence is relevant—as defined above—because a person who puts up a warning sign is more likely to have done something wrong than someone who does not put up a warning sign after an accident. A person who puts up a warning sign of danger is more likely to actually believe that the run is dangerous than a person who does not. This tends to show the slope is dangerous and thus the resort was negligent for not having the warning signs earlier. This is central to the case—it is what the case is all about, so it is a fact of consequence. The evidence is relevant.

Subsequent Remedial Measures

Subsequent remedial measures are measures taken after an accident that would have made the accident or injury less likely had they been there prior to the accident. They are not admissible, for policy reasons, to prove negligence or liability. The sign would have made the accident less likely because rather than just saying the run was "difficult," which an excellent skier would think would be fine to go down, the run is now much more warning as "dangerous" and thus would have made it less likely for even an excellent skier to attempt. Thus, this is a measure that would have made it less likely. So, Travis cannot use it to prove negligence or strict liability under the FRE, and he cannot use it to prove negligence under the CEC. He is trying to prove negligence, so it would be inadmissible under both. Unless Travis can find another use for the evidence, such as feasibility, if it is in issue (but that does not seem to be in issue yet, as no one from the ski resort has denied that they could have made a better warning sign or made the run any safer). It can also show ownership or control, but those are not disputed here. The only logical relevance of this evidence is to show negligence, thus it is inadmissible.

3.   Travis's Testimony

Travis's testimony is just eye witness testimony as to what happened. It is relevant because it tends to be more likely that it happened the way he says, rather than a way that he did not say. What happened is key to determining if the ski resort is liable or not. The evidence is relevant, as defined above, and his testimony is admissible.

Cross Exam—Impeachment with Prior Inconsistent Statement

Travis is a witness, and his truthfulness is relevant because the jury needs to know if they can believe his testimony or not. Here, the evidence of saying something different is relevant to show that Travis is changing his story, and thus should not be believed on the witness stand. The evidence also is relevant to show that what Travis previously said is how the accident happened—that Travis was distracted. This is relevant to show that the ski resort is not liable because they did not cause the accident if Travis's distraction caused the accident. This is also material as it is what the whole case is about.

On cross examination, a party can impeach the witness with evidence of prior inconsistent statements. Here, they are using a statement that Travis said prior to the trial, and it is that he ran into the tree because he was distracted. This is inconsistent with his current testimony because he said he ran into the tree because the run was too steep and he could not control his skis. This is a different cause and thus inconsistent. This evidence would be admissible for impeachment.

An out of court statement offered for the truth of the matter asserted is generally inadmissible. Here the statement was to his friend, not at the trial, so it is out of court. If the cross examiner wants to prove that it was being distracted that caused the accident rather than how steep the slope was, they would be trying to prove the truth of what Travis said out of court. Thus, they need to find an exception to the rule against hearsay. Prior inconsistent statement is an exception, but applies differently under the FRE than the CEC.

Under the FRE the statement would not be admissible for the truth of the matter asserted. A prior inconsistent statement is only admissible for the truth under the FRE if it was given under penalty of perjury. Statements to friends are not given under penalty of perjury, and thus it could only be used for the sole purpose of impeachment, and not to prove that Travis was actually distracted and that is what cause the accident—only that the jury cannot believe anything that Travis says because he keeps changing his story. Under the CEC, the statement can be used for the truth of the matter asserted, and for impeachment purposes. While out of court statements are generally inadmissible to prove the truth under the general hearsay rule, the CEC allows them in when it is offered as a prior inconsistent statement. Thus it could be used both to prove that Travis is a liar, and that the cause of the accident was because Travis was distracted.

Cross Exam—Impeachment with Specific Instances of Negligence

Evidence of a person's character trait is generally inadmissible to prove that the person acted in conformity with that trait on a particular occasion. In civil cases, there are no exceptions to this, except if character is in issue (it is never in issue in negligence cases) or if to impeach for the character of untruthfulness. This evidence is offered as character evidence because it is offered to show that he was acting negligently on two separate occasions proves that he is negligent and was probably acting negligently on this occasion. Here, character is not in issue because this is negligence, and the evidence is offered to prove that Travis is negligent, rather than untruthful. Thus, the evidence is inadmissible character evidence.

4.   Roger's Testimony

Relevant Testimony

Relevance

There are two theories of relevance of these statements. First, they are relevant to prove that the slope is dangerous, because someone saying it is tends to show that it is, and that is a material fact, because if the slope is dangerous, the ski resort is more likely to be liable. Next, it is admissible to prove notice, because that is an element of a claim for negligence that the person be on notice of a dangerous condition to be held liable for it.

Hearsay

Evidence of an out of court statement offered to prove the truth of the matter asserted is inadmissible, generally. The statements are out of court, being repeated in court because they were said prior to trial. Thus, the evidence would be inadmissible to show that the run was extremely dangerous, and that two people almost got hurt. Thus, they would need a hearsay exception to get this evidence in for the truth. There are no applicable hearsay exceptions for the statements, and thus they could not be offered for the truth of the matter asserted.

Not Hearsay

Evidence that is inadmissible for one reason, but admissible for another is admissible with a limiting instruction to not use the evidence in the way that is inadmissible. Here, there is another theory of relevance to get this statement in—the Effect on the Listener Doctrine. Effect on the listener is applicable when trying to prove what effect the statement had on the listener, rather than the truth of what was said. Here, it is relevant that two people told the head ski instructor that the run was very dangerous because it shows that the ski resort employees were on notice of how dangerous the run was, and did not do anything about it. This would tend to show that the ski resort was negligent by not fixing a dangerous condition that they knew about. Thus, the evidence would be admissible to show notice.

Cross Examination

Relevance

This evidence is relevant to show that Travis is not truthful. A person who steals is untruthful and more likely to be lying on the witness stand than someone who is truthful. This is a relevant fact because it is necessary for the jury to determine . . . if Travis is a truthful person . . . . The evidence is relevant.

Character evidence, as defined above, is generally inadmissible. That is the relevance of this evidence—it is a specific instance of being untruthful: stealing, to show that Travis is untruthful, and acting in conformity with his untruthful character on a particular occasion (today, on the witness stand). Thus, the evidence is inadmissible character evidence unless there is a valid exception to get it in. Under the FRE, specific instances of untruthfulness are admissible to impeach a witness by showing their untruthful character, and is an exception to the general rule against character evidence. Here, there is a specific instance of being untruthful—stealing money from the resort. The only requirement is that the cross-examiner have a good faith basis for a belief that the specific instance they are asking about did in fact happen. As long as this is met, this is a proper mode of impeachment to show that Travis is not a truthful person, and the jury cannot trust what he has to say on the witness stand.

Under the CEC, in civil cases, because Prop, 8 does not apply, specific instances are inadmissible for impeachment. The evidence is inadmissible under the CEC.

5.   Nancy's Testimony

Relevance

For the same reason impeachment by specific instances of untruthfulness is relevant, this is too, because it is the same thing: evidence of Travis being untruthful. CEC: it was already established the CEC does not allow impeachment by specific instances of untruthfulness. The evidence is still inadmissible. FRE: Impeachment by specific instances of untruthfulness is only admissible when the witness is asked about the specific instance on the witness stand. Once the witness answers the question, no extrinsic evidence is allowed to prove the impeaching fact. The cross-examiner must take the witness's answer for what it is, and not offer any extrinsic evidence later. It cannot be re-characterized as contradiction evidence once the witness is off the stand. Extrinsic evidence is inadmissible to impeach by specific instances of untruthfulness. This evidence is inadmissible.

Author's Note. The same student wrote the answers to questions 4 and 5. Her answers are remarkable. I know for sure that when I was a student, I could not have written anything approaching her work. Most students in my evidence course who earn A grades do not write as much and as well as she did. So, don't think that you have to perform at her level to earn a good grade, or to pass the bar exam. I provided her answers, with her permission, to give you a sense of what is possible.

California Bar Examination Questions

The California bar exam tests on the FRE and the CEC. Two essays follow. To see what the bar examiners thought to be excellent answers, go to the State Bar website. You will find the questions and model answers.

CAL BAR, JULY, 2014: QUESTION 2

Pete was a passenger on ABC Airlines (ABC), and was severely injured when the plane in which he was flying crashed because of a fuel line blockage.

Pete sued ABC in federal court, claiming that its negligent maintenance of the plane was the cause of the crash.

At trial, Pete's counsel called Wayne, a delivery person, who testified that he was in the hanger when the plane was being prepared for flight, and heard Mac, an ABC mechanic say to Sal, an ABC supervisor: "Hey, the fuel feed reads low, Boss, and I just cleared some gunk from the line. Shouldn't we do a complete systems check of the fuel line and fuel valves?" Wayne further testified that Sal replied: "Don't worry, a little stuff is normal for this fuel and doesn't cause any problems."

On cross-examination, ABC's counsel asked Wayne: "Isn't it true that when you applied for a job you claimed that you had graduated from college when, in fact, you never went to college?" Wayne answered, "Yes."

ABC then called Chuck, its custodian of records, who identified a portion of the plane's maintenance record detailing the relevant preflight inspection. Chuck testified that all of ABC's maintenance records are stored in his office. After asking Chuck about the function of the maintenance records and their method of preparation, ABC offered into evidence the following excerpt: "Preflight completed; all okay. Fuel line strained and all valves cleared and verified by Mac." Chuck properly authenticated Sal's signature next to the entry.

Assuming all appropriate objections and motions were timely made, did the court properly:

1.   Admit Wayne's testimony about Mac's question to Sal? Discuss.

2.   Admit Wayne's testimony about Sal's answer? Discuss.

3.   Permit ABC to ask Wayne about college? Discuss.

4.   Admit the excerpt from the maintenance record? Discuss.

Answer according to the Federal Rules of Evidence.

CAL BAR, JULY, 2012: QUESTION 3

Vicky was killed on a rainy night. The prosecution charged Dean, a business rival, with her murder. It alleged that, on the night in question, he hid in the bushes outside her home and shot her when she returned from work.

At Dean's trial in a California court, the prosecution called Whitney, Dean's wife, to testify. One week after the murder, Whitney had found out that Dean had been dating another woman and had moved out, stating the marriage was over. Still angry, Whitney was willing to testify against Dean. After Whitney was called to the stand, the court took a recess. During the recess, Dean and Whitney reconciled. Whitney decided not to testify against Dean. The trial recommenced and the prosecutor asked Whitney if she saw anything on Dean's shoes the night of the murder. When Whitney refused to answer, the court threatened to hold her in contempt. Reluctantly, Whitney testified that she saw mud on Dean's shoes.

The prosecution then called Ella, Dean's next-door neighbor. Ella testified that, on the night Vicky was killed, she was standing by an open window in her kitchen, which was about 20 feet from an open window in Dean's kitchen. She also testified that she saw Dean and Whitney and she heard Dean tell Whitney, "I just killed the gal who stole my biggest account." Dean and Whitney did not know that Ella overheard their conversation.

Dean called Fred, a friend, to testify. Fred testified that, on the day after Vicky was killed, he was having lunch in a coffee shop when he saw Hit, a well-known gangster, conversing at the next table with another gangster, Gus. Fred testified that he heard Gus ask Hit if he had "taken care of the assignment concerning Vicky," and that Hit then drew his index finger across his own throat.

Assuming appropriate objections and motions were timely made, did the court properly: (1) Allow the prosecution to call Whitney? Discuss. (2) Admit the testimony of (a) Whitney? Discuss. (b) Ella? Discuss. (c) Fred? Discuss.

Answer according to California law.

Multiple Choice Questions

To give you some practice with multiple choice questions, try your hand at the following 15 questions. Answers and analysis follow the questions.

Questions 1, 2, and 3 are based on the following facts. An auto accident occurred at an intersection in the city. The car driven by Abe broadsided the car driven by Beth. Both drivers were injured, and were transported by ambulance to the hospital. Beth is suing Abe for causing the accident. Abe denies liability.

1.   At the hospital, Abe told the physician treating him, "I guess I didn't see the stop sign. My phone was ringing, and I was

looking down for my phone." The physician wrote Abe's statement verbatim in Abe's medical record. At trial, Beth offers the medical record into evidence. Abe's attorney makes a hearsay objection. How should the judge rule? For this question, use the Federal Rules of Evidence.

A.   Sustain the objection because this is layered hearsay, and the medical record is inadmissible hearsay.

B.   Overrule the objection because the medical record is a verbal act, and not hearsay, while Abe's words are a party admission.

C.   Sustain the objection because Abe was apparently not represented by an attorney when he made the statement.

— D.   Overrule the objection because the medical record is a business record and Abe's statement is a personal party admission.

2.   At the hospital, two days after the accident, Beth was speaking with the physician treating her, Dr. Zahn. Dr. Zahn asked Beth, "I understand your back hurts. Have you ever injured your back in the past, before this accident?" Beth replied, "A year ago, I fell off a ladder and twisted my back, but I went to my doctor at that time, and there was no lasting injury. My back has been fine until the car accident." At trial, Beth calls Dr. Zahn as a witness, and asks the doctor to repeat what Beth told the doctor at the hospital. Abe makes a hearsay objection. How should the judge rule? For this question, use the Federal Rules of Evidence.

A.   Sustain the objection because Beth cannot use her own, self-serving statements as evidence.

B.   Sustain the objection because what Beth told the doctor is not relevant to the car accident.

— C.   Overrule the objection because Beth's statement to the doctor is a statement of medical history.

D.   Overrule the objection because Beth's statement to the doctor is a statement then-existing state of mind.

3.   For question 3, use the facts of question 2, above, but answer the question by applying the California Evidence Code.

A.   Overrule the objection because Beth's statement to the doctor is a statement of medical history.

— B.   Sustain the objection because Beth's statement to the doctor is inadmissible hearsay.

C. Overrule the objection because Beth's statement to the doctor is admissible under the state of mind exception.

D. Sustain the objection because the probative value of Beth's statement to the doctor is substantially outweighed by the danger of unfair prejudice to Abe.

4.   Dell is on trial for arson, which he denies. At trial, Dell testifies that he was at home when the fire was started in another city. During the prosecution's case in rebuttal, the prosecutor offers evidence that a year ago, Dell broke into a jewelry store and made off with a large amount of valuable jewelry. Dell's attorney objects to evidence of the jewelry store burglary and theft. How should the judge rule?

A. The judge should overrule the objection because character is in issue, and the evidence is relevant to prove Dell's bad character.

B. The judge should overrule the objection because the evidence is irrelevant.

C. The judge should sustain the objection even if the evidence has some modest relevance.

D. The judge should overrule the objection because the evidence proves a plan.

5.   Sam is on trial for murder. During the defense case-in-chief, Sam offers the testimony of Zeek, who testifies that he and Sam were fishing when the murder happened. On cross-examination of Zeek, the prosecutor asks, "Isn't it true that you lied on your federal taxes last year? Zeek replies, "That is not true." During the prosecutor's case-in-rebuttal, the prosecutor calls Rachel, an employee of the tax authority, who will testify that she audited Zeek's tax return for last year, and that Zeek's tax return was false. Sam's attorney objects to any testimony from Rachel. How should the judge rule? Apply the Federal Rules of Evidence.

A. The judge should sustain the objection because of the theory of impeachment. *extrinsic evidence never admissible*

B. The judge should sustain the objection because Rachel's testimony would be irrelevant to a fact of consequence in the action.

C. The judge should overrule the objection because Rachel's testimony tends to contradict Zeek's answer that he did not lie on his taxes, and contradiction is a proper theory of impeachment.

D. The judge should overrule the objection because Zeek's answer on cross-examination was a lie, and a witness cannot get away with a lie on the witness stand.

Questions 6 and 7 are based on the following facts. Cristiano is charged with murder. Cristiano admits he shot the victim, but Cristiano claims he acted in self-defense, after the victim attacked him. During the defense case-in-chief, Cristiano offers testimony from Renoldo, who will testify that on three occasions in the past, Renoldo saw the victim start fights with strangers. The prosecutor objects to Renoldo's testimony.

6.   How should the judge rule under the Federal Rules of Evidence?

A. Sustain the objection because the testimony is in the form of specific instances, and is inadmissible for that reason.

B. Sustain the objection because the testimony has no tendency to prove whether the victim started the fight with Cristiano.

C. Overrule the objection because a defendant who claims self-defense is permitted to offer character evidence that the victim was the first aggressor.

D. Overrule the objection because the victim's character as a violent person is in issue.

7.   How should the judge rule under the California Evidence Code?

A. Overrule the objection because a defendant claiming self-defense may attack the victim's character with specific instances of the victim's prior violence.

B. Sustain the objection because, although a defendant claiming self-defense may attack the victim's character, the evidence must be in the form of opinion or reputation, not specific instances.

C. Overrule the objection so long as Renoldo has known the victim long enough for Renoldo to qualify as a character witness.

D. Sustain the objection because evidence of the victim's prior violence violates the rule against character evidence to prove that a person acted in conformity with their character on a specific occasion.

8.   Dell is on trial, charged with sexually abusing 7-year-old Claire. Dell denies the charge. At trial, the prosecutor calls Claire as a witness. Defense counsel objects to any testimony from Claire because she is incompetent. The judge will probably take which of the following actions? Apply the Federal Rules of Evidence.

A.   The judge will rule that Claire is not a competent witness because she is a child.

B.   Because the rules of evidence state that every person is competent to be a witness, judges no longer hold competency examinations of children, and the judge will allow Claire to testify.

C.   The judge will order that Claire be examined by a psychologist to see if she understands the difference between the truth and a lie, and the duty to tell the truth in court.

— D.   Given's Claire's age, the judge probably will conduct a competency examination by asking her questions to determine if she understands the difference between truth and lies, and the duty to testify truthfully.

Questions 9 and 10 are based on the following facts. Dell is on trial for the murder of Vic. Dell pleads not guilty, based on the claim that he killed Vic in self-defense. During the defense case-in-chief, the only evidence offered by Dell is his own testimony. Dell testifies as follow: "I was walking down the street, minding my own business, when Vic jumped out from behind a bush and attacked me with a knife. I was able to get the knife away from him, and, when he charged me, I stabbed him in self-defense." During the prosecutor's case-in-rebuttal, the prosecutor offers the following testimony from Danielle, "I knew Vic for ten years. In my opinion, Vic was a nonviolent person."

9.   Apply the Federal Rules of Evidence to answer this question. Dell objects to any testimony from Danielle. How should the judge rule?

A.   Overrule the objection because character is in issue in this case.

B.   Sustain the objection because the prosecutor cannot be the first to offer a character witness to testify that the victim was a peaceful person. If the defendant first attacks the victim's character for violence with a character witness, then the prosecutor can offer a rebuttal character witness, who testifies that the victim was peaceful. In this case, Dell did not offer a character witness to testify that

Vic was a violent person. Therefore, the prosecutor cannot be the first to offer a character witness to describe Vic as a peaceful person.

C.   Overrule the objection despite the fact that Dell did not offer a character witness to attack the victim's character for violence. Dell's testimony triggers the prosecutor's ability to offer a character witness to testify about Vic's peacefulness.

404 2c

D.   Sustain the objection because, although the prosecutor is allowed to offer a character witness to testify to Vic's peacefulness, the character witness must describe Vic's reputation for peacefulness, and cannot offer the character witness's personal opinion of Vic's character.

10.   Apply the California Evidence Code to answer this question. Dell objects to any testimony from Danielle. How should the judge rule?

A.   Overrule the objection because character is in issue in this case.

B.   Sustain the objection because the prosecutor cannot be the first to offer a character witness to testify that the victim was a peaceful person. If the defendant first attacks the victim's character for violence, then the prosecutor can offer rebuttal character evidence. In this case, Dell did not offer character evidence that Vic was a violent person. Therefore, the prosecutor cannot be the first to offer a character witness to describe Vic as a peaceful person.

C.   Overrule the objection despite the fact that Dell did not offer a character witness to attack the victim's character for violence. Dell's testimony triggers the prosecutor's ability to offer a character witness to testify about Vic's peacefulness.

D.   Sustain the objection because, although the prosecutor is allowed to offer a character witness to testify to Vic's peacefulness, the character witness must describe Vic's reputation for peacefulness, and cannot offer the character witness's personal opinion of Vic's character.

11.   Pam sues Dorothy for personal injuries caused in an auto accident in which Dorothy's car rear ended Pam's car at a stop sign. At trial, Rachel testifies for Pam as follows: "I was standing on the corner, waiting for the bus. I was looking at my phone, when I heard tires squealing. I looked up just in time to see Dorothy's car

slam into the back of Pam's car." On cross-examination of Rachel, the following cross-examination occurs by Dorothy's attorney:

Q: Rachel, a week after the accident, did you have a conversation, with your mother, about the accident?

A: Yes.

Q: And during that conversation, didn't you tell your mother that you didn't look up until after the cars collided?

At that moment, Pam's attorney says, "Your honor I object. This question calls for improper impeachment and hearsay." How should the judge rule on the objection?

    A.   Under the CEC and the FRE, the judge should overrule the objection and admit the answer for impeachment and to prove the truth of the matter asserted.

— B.   Under the CEC, the judge should overrule the objection and admit the statement for impeachment and for the truth of the matter asserted. Under the FRE, the judge should overrule the objection regarding impeachment, but sustain the hearsay objection.

    C.   Under the CEC, the judge should overrule the objection regarding impeachment, but sustain the hearsay objection. Under the FRE, the judge should overrule the objection and allow the statement to impeach and to prove the truth of the matter asserted.

    D.   Under the CEC and the FRE, the judge should overrule the objection, and allow the answer both to impeach and to prove the truth of the matter asserted.

12.   The Golden One Credit Union, in Davis, CA, was robbed on May 2nd. Megan is charged with the crime. Megan does not deny the crime occurred, but she raises an alibi. Megan claims she was hundreds of miles away, in San Diego, when the credit union was robbed. Megan seeks to prove that the robbery was committed by Athina. Megan offers testimony from Glenn, who testifies" "On May 1st, I was in Middletown, which is a two hour drive from Davis. I was in the Cow Poke Café, and I heard Athina say, 'Tomorrow I'm headed to Davis.'" The prosecutor objects to Glenn's testimony. How should the judge rule?

    A.   Sustain the objection because Glenn's testimony about what Athina said is inadmissible hearsay.

B. Overrule the objection because Glenn heard what Athina said, and the evidence is admissible under the effect on the listener doctrine, which is not hearsay.

C. Sustain the objection because Glenn's testimony about what Athina said violates the Confrontation Clause.

D. Overrule the objection because, although Glenn's testimony about what Athina said is hearsay, the hearsay meets the requirements of a hearsay exception.

— forward looking statement exception

Questions 13 and 14 are based on the following facts. Dorothy is on trial for murder in California Superior Court in San Jose. Dorothy enters a plea of not guilty. Dorothy claims she was in Reno, Nevada, when the crime occurred. The victim was shot in the head with a high powered shotgun that basically blew off the top of the victim's head. The crime occurred on May 23.

13. During the prosecution's case-in-chief, the pathologist who performed the autopsy on the victim testifies and describes how the victim died. The prosecutor hands the doctor a photo taken of the victim lying on the autopsy table. The photo shows the top half of the victim's skull missing, just above the nose. The photo is very gruesome. The defense attorney objects to allowing the jury to see the photograph. The judge is most likely to:

A. Sustain the objection because the doctor can explain the injuries that caused death without the gruesome picture, which will undoubtedly impact the jury emotionally. The probative value of the photo is substantially outweighed by the danger of unfair prejudice to the defendant.

B. Sustain the objection because the cause of death is not disputed.

C. Overrule the objection because the defendant has forfeited any objection due to her own wrongdoing.

D. Overrule the objection if the photo will help the jury understand the doctor's testimony. —

14. Mimi is Dorothy's best friend. The prosecutor offers a recording of a telephone call between Mimi and her dad on May 21, in which Mimi said, "Hi dad, Dorothy and I will be headed to San Jose tomorrow from Reno. Want to meet for dinner?" Defense counsel makes a hearsay objection to the recording of the phone call. How should the judge rule?

A. The judge should sustain the objection because Mimi's intent cannot be used to prove Dorothy's conduct.

B.   The judge should overrule the objection and allow Mimi's entire statement into evidence.

C.   The judge should sustain the objection because Mimi's statement is hearsay within hearsay, and not admissible.

D.   The judge should sustain the objection because the prosecutor did not properly authenticate the recording.

15.   Abe is on trial, charged with burglary. Apply the Federal Rules of Evidence. The prosecutor offers the police report written by the detective who investigated the burglary. Abe's attorney objects to the police report on hearsay grounds. The judge should:

A.   Admit the police report under the public records exception.

B.   Admit the police report under the business records exception.

— C.   Exclude the police report because it is inadmissible hearsay.

D.   Exclude the police report because it violates the best evidence rule.

Answers and Analysis of Multiple Choice Questions

1.   The correct answer is D. The answer itself specifies the hearsay exceptions that apply.

A.   is wrong because, while the record is layered hearsay, both layers are admissible. The original statement by Abe is a party admission (FRE 801(d)(2)(A)). The medical record that repeats Abe's statement is a business record (FRE 803(6)).

B.   is wrong because the medical record is not a verbal act. The record is hearsay within an exception.

C.   is wrong because there is no right to counsel that applies in this context.

2.   The correct answer is C. Beth's words are words of medical history, admissible under the medical diagnosis or treatment exception, FRE 803(4). Beth's words are pertinent to Dr. Zahn's ability to diagnose and treat Beth.

A.   is wrong. Self-serving statements are admissible if they meet the requirements of a hearsay exception.

B.   is wrong. Beth's statement is relevant because it has a tendency to prove that it was the car accident that caused her injuries, not the fall from the ladder.

D.   is wrong because Beth's statement is a statement of memory, not admissible under the state of mind exception (803(3)).

3.   The correct answer is B. Beth's statement is hearsay. It does not meet the requirements of a hearsay exception. California has the medical diagnosis or treatment exception, but it only applies in child abuse cases (CEC § 1253). Beth spoke two days after the car accident, so her statement is not an excited utterance, called a spontaneous statement in the CEC (CEC § 1240).

A.   is wrong. It is true that Beth's words are words of medical history. In California, however, there is no hearsay exception for words of medical history.

C.   is wrong because Beth's words are backward looking. Her words are a statement of memory, inadmissible under the state of mind exception (CEC § 1250(b)).

D.   is wrong. The probative value vs. unfair prejudice answer is usually wrong. The professor throws it in because she can't think of a better "wrong" answer.

4.   The correct answer is C. This is character evidence. The only relevance of the evidence is to prove that Dell is a criminal, and, because he is a criminal, he probably acted in conformity with his criminal character and committed the charged crime.

A.   is wrong. Character is not in issue in an arson case.

B.   is wrong. Evidence of the jewelry store crime is evidence of criminality—it is character evidence. Evidence of bad character is relevant. The evidence in this cases does not have much probative value, but, to be relevant, evidence only has to have "any" tendency to prove a fact of consequence. The evidence is relevant.

D.   is wrong because the jewelry store heist is not part of a plan. Even under the broad theory of plan used in California, this is not a plan.

5.   The correct answer is A. The theory of impeachment is a specific instance of untruthfulness, which is permitted by FRE 608(b). Rule 608(b) provides that, while the question is proper, the cross-examiner must take the witness's answer. Extrinsic evidence is never admissible with this theory of impeachment. It is clear that Rachel's testimony is extrinsic evidence that is inadmissible.

B. is wrong. Rachel's testimony might have some minimal probative value regarding Zeek's credibility. However, Rule 608(b) is categorical—no extrinsic evidence, period.

C. is wrong. It is a common mistake, when the theory of impeachment is a specific act of untruthfulness, and extrinsic evidence is offered, for students to view the extrinsic evidence as contradiction (it is) and to admit the testimony under the contradiction theory. The reason this is wrong goes back to the language of Rule 608(b). The rule says extrinsic evidence is not admissible. The rule does not say, "Go ahead and re-characterize this as contradiction." The rule says extrinsic evidence is not admissible, and the rule means what it says.

D. is wrong. To repeat, Rule 608(b) says extrinsic evidence is not admissible. Even if the witness is lying when the witness denies the lie, it doesn't matter. Extrinsic evidence is not admissible with this theory of impeachment. Got it?!

6.   The correct answer is A. FRE 404(a)(2)(B) allows a defendant who claims self-defense to attack the victim's character for violence. However, the defendant is limited to a character witness who testifies in the form of reputation or opinion (FRE 405(a)). Specific instances of the victim's prior violence are not admissible to prove the victim was the first aggressor.

B. is wrong because specific instances would be relevant to prove the victim started the fight. The specific instances are relevant, but are not admissible because the FRE does not allow them.

C. is wrong. It is true that a defendant who claims self-defense may attack the victim's character for violence, but the rules limit the defendant's evidence to a character witness.

D. is wrong because character is not in issue. (See § 6.7).

7.   The correct answer is A. In California, CEC § 1103(a) allows a defendant who claims self-defense to attack the victim's character for violence, in an effort to prove the victim was the first aggressor. Unlike under the FRE, the CEC allows the defendant to offer specific instances of the victim's violence for this purpose.

B. is wrong because, in California, the attack on the victim's character can take the form of specific instances or a character witness.

C. is wrong because there is no requirement that Renoldo have known the victim for any period of time. This answer is mixing up the foundation to testify as a character witness with what is required to testify to specific instances. All that is required to testify to specific instances is personal knowledge of the instances.

D. is wrong because, although evidence of the victim's violence is offered as character evidence, this use of the evidence is allowed.

8.   The correct answer is D. Despite the fact that the FRE and the CEC state that all persons are competent witnesses, judges routinely question young children to determine competence. The attorney opposing a child's testimony must object. The judge may ask the questions, or may permit the attorneys to question the child. When children are asked simple questions they understand, the vast majority of children as young as five are competent to testify.

A. is wrong because children are competent witnesses.

B. is wrong. Although it is true that the rules provide every person is competent, judges still conduct competency examinations for child witnesses when there are legitimate questions about competence.

C. is wrong. Although a judge would have authority to appoint a psychologist to evaluate a child's competence, this is very rarely done. In the vast majority of cases, the judge's questions are sufficient to determine that a child is or is not competent.

9.   Question 9 requires you to use the FRE. The correct answer is C. This is an application of FRE 404(a)(2)(C), which, in homicide cases, allows the prosecutor to offer a character witness to testify to the victim's peacefulness after the defendant offers evidence—but not character evidence—that the victim was the first aggressor.

A. is wrong because character is not in issue.

B. is wrong, although tempting for the student who does not understand 404(a)(2)(C). Rule 404(a)(2)(C) is the one situation where the FRE allow the prosecutor to be the first to offer a character witness to provide substantive evidence.

D. is wrong because under the FRE (and the CEC) a character witness can always testify in the form of reputation or opinion.

10. Question 10 requires you to use the CEC. The CEC does not have a counterpart to FRE 404(a)(2)(C). So, in California, the correct answer is B.

A.   is wrong because character is not in issue.

C.   is wrong because the CEC does not have a counterpart to FRE 404(a)(2)(C).

D.   is wrong because, like the FRE, the CEC allows a character witness to testify in the form of reputation or opinion. Of course, D is also wrong for the same reason C is wrong: the prosecutor can't be the first under the CEC of offer evidence of the victim's character for peacefulness.

11. Question 11 deals with impeachment by prior inconsistent statement. Some professors want you to discuss the traditional four part foundation to impeach with a prior inconsistent statement. The questions are: Was a prior statement made? When? Who was present? What was the subject matter of the statement? The foundation is probably adequate in this question. One of the important differences between the CEC and the FRE is the use of prior inconsistent statements to prove the truth of the matter asserted. *See* §§ 10.4(d), 11.21.

The correct answer is B. Under the CEC and the FRE, the statement is admissible to impeach. However, under the FRE, the statement is not admissible for the truth of the matter asserted because the out-of-court statement was not made under oath (FRE 801(d)(1)(A)). In the CEC, § 1235 creates a hearsay exception for all prior inconsistent statements.

A.   is wrong because, under the FRE, the prior inconsistent statement is not admissible for the truth of the matter asserted.

C.   is wrong in two respects. First, under the CEC, the statement is admissible to impeach and for the truth of the matter asserted. Second, under the FRE, the statement is admissible to impeach, but not for the truth of the matter asserted.

D.   is wrong, for the reasons explained above.

12. The correct answer is D. Glenn's repetition of Athina's statement is hearsay, but it is admissible under the forward looking aspect of the state of mind exception.

A.   is wrong because D is right.

B.   The effect on the listener doctrine does not work here. In order for the effect on the listener doctrine to apply, the effect on the listener has to be relevant. In this case, what Glenn heard Athina say is not relevant. What Athina said is relevant, but it does not matter that Glenn heard it.

C.   is wrong because the Confrontation Clause applies when the prosecution offers hearsay against the defendant in a criminal case. Here, the defendant is the one offering the hearsay against the prosecution. The prosecution does not enjoy the protections of the Sixth Amendment.

13.   The correct answer is D. In homicide cases, gruesome photos are admissible so long as the photo helps the jury understand the expert's testimony. In this case, the crime was ugly, and the picture is, of necessity, ugly too.

A.   is wrong because, although the photo does have some potential to tempt the jury to decide the case on an improper basis, the photo is probative and will help the jury understand the pathologist's testimony. Again, murder is not pretty.

B.   is wrong. Even though there is no dispute that the victim died from a shotgun blast, the prosecutor is typically allowed to prove its case the way it wishes. The photo will help the jury understand what happened, and understand the pathologist's testimony. Because the burden of proof on the prosecutor is heavy, the prosecution is entitled to prove its case in the way that the prosecutor thinks best.

C.   is wrong because the forfeiture by wrongdoing doctrine applies to hearsay and confrontation, not the admissibility of an autopsy photo. Dorothy has the right to object to the photo as too gruesome.

14.   The correct answer is B. Mimi's hearsay statement is admissible under the forward looking aspect of the state of mind exception. Mimi's statement is a classic *Hillmon* statement. You remember from the famous *Hillmon* case that the insurance company needed to prove that Walters went west from Wichita. The company offered letters Walters wrote to his sister and his fiancé, in which Walters stated he planned to go west from Wichita with a man named Hillmon. The Supreme Court ruled the letters were admissible to prove that Walters intended to travel west with Hillmon. This aspect of the state of mind exception is controversial, but so-called *Hillmon* statements are admissible.

A.   is wrong. The argument against allowing Hillmon statements is that the state of mind exception should not include one person's statement that mentions what another person may do. But the courts have rejected this position. Thus, A is wrong.

C. is wrong because Mimi's statement is admissible under the state of mind exception.

D. is wrong because defense counsel objected on the basis of hearsay, not authentication. Failure to make an authentication objection waives any error regarding authentication.

15. The correct answer is C. The police report is not admissible under the public records exception because it is a police report. Because the report is inadmissible under the public records exception, the prosecutor can't use the business records exception to do an end run around the limitation on police reports contained in the public records exception. The police report is hearsay not within any exception.

A. and B.are wrong for the reason stated above.

D. is wrong. There was no objection based on the best evidence rule. Moreover, there is no reason to think the prosecutor is offering anything other than the original or a duplicate.

Appendix A

FEDERAL RULES OF EVIDENCE

The Federal Rules of Evidence are reproduced below.

ARTICLE I
GENERAL PROVISIONS

Rule 101. Scope; Definitions

(a) Scope. These rules apply to proceedings in United States courts. The specific courts and proceedings to which the rules apply, along with exceptions, are set out in Rule 1101.

(b) Definitions. In these rules:

(1) "civil case" means a civil action or proceeding;

(2) "criminal case" includes a criminal proceeding;

(3) "public office" includes a public agency;

(4) "record" includes a memorandum, report, or data compilation;

(5) a "rule prescribed by the Supreme Court" means a rule adopted by the Supreme Court under statutory authority; and

(6) a reference to any kind of written material or any other medium includes electronically stored information.

Rule 102. Purpose

These rules should be construed so as to administer every proceeding fairly, eliminate unjustifiable expense and delay, and promote the development of evidence law, to the end of ascertaining the truth and securing a just determination.

Rule 103. Rulings on Evidence

(a) Preserving a Claim of Error. A party may claim error in a ruling to admit or exclude evidence only if the error affects a substantial right of the party and:

(1) If the ruling admits evidence, a party, on the record:

(A) Timely objects or moves to strike; and

(B) States the specific ground, unless it was apparent from the context; or

(2) If the ruling excludes evidence, a party informs the court of its substance by an offer of proof, unless the substance was apparent from the context.

(b) Not Needing to Renew an Objection or Offer of Proof. Once the court rules definitively on the record—either before or at trial—a party need not renew an objection or offer of proof to preserve a claim of error for appeal.

(c) Court's Statement About the Ruling; Directing an Offer of Proof. The court may make any statement about the character or form of the evidence, the objection made, and the ruing. The court may direct that an offer of proof be made in question-and-answer form.

(d) Preventing the Jury from Hearing Inadmissible Evidence. To the extent practicable, the court must conduct a jury trial so that inadmissible evidence is not suggested to the jury by any means.

(e) Taking Notice of Plain Error. A court may take notice of a plain error affecting a substantial right, even if the claim of error was not properly preserved.

Rule 104.   Preliminary Questions

(a) In General. The court must decide any preliminary question about whether a witness is qualified, a privilege exists, or evidence is admissible. In so deciding, the court is not bound by evidence rules, except those on privilege.

(b) Relevance That Depends on a Fact. When the relevance of evidence depends on whether a fact exists, proof must be introduced sufficient to support a finding that the fact does exist. The court may admit the proposed evidence on the condition that the proof be introduced later.

(c) Conducting a Hearing So That the Jury Cannot Hear It. The court must conduct any hearing on a preliminary question so that the jury cannot hear it if:

(1) the hearing involves the admissibility of a confession;

(2) a defendant in a criminal case is a witness and so requests; or

(3) justice so requires.

(d) Cross-Examining a Defendant in a Criminal Case. By testifying on a preliminary question, a defendant in a criminal case does not become subject to cross-examination on other issues in the case.

(e) Evidence Relevant to Weight and Credibility. This rule does not limit a party's right to introduce before the jury evidence that is relevant to the weight or credibility of other evidence.

Rule 105.   Limiting Evidence That Is Not Admissible Against Other Parties or for Other Purposes

If the court admits evidence that is admissible against a party or for a purpose—but not against another party or for another purpose—the court, on timely request, must restrict the evidence to its proper scope and instruct the jury accordingly.

Rule 106.   Remainder of or Related Writings or Recorded Statements

If a party introduces all or part of a writing or recorded statement, an adverse party may require the introduction, at that time, of any other part—or any other writing or recorded statement—that in fairness ought to be considered at the same time.

ARTICLE II

JUDICIAL NOTICE

Rule 201.   Judicial Notice of Adjudicative Facts

(a) Scope. This rule governs judicial notice of an adjudicative fact only, not a legislative fact.

(b) Kinds of Facts That May Be Judicially Noticed. The court may judicially notice a fact that is not subject to reasonable dispute because it:

(1) Is generally known within the trial court's territorial jurisdiction; or

(2) Can be accurately and readily determined from sources whose accuracy cannot reasonably be questioned.

(c) Taking Notice. The Court:

(1) May take judicial notice on its own; or

(2) Must take judicial notice if a party requests it and the court is supplied with the necessary information.

(d) Timing. The court may take judicial notice at any stage of the proceeding.

(e) Opportunity to Be Heard. On timely request, a party is entitled to be heard on the propriety of taking judicial notice and the nature of the fact to be noticed. If the court takes judicial notice before notifying a party, the party, on request, is still entitled to be heard.

(f) Instructing the Jury. In a civil case, the court must instruct the jury to accept the noticed fact as conclusive. In a criminal case, the court must instruct the jury that it may or may not accept the noticed fact as conclusive.

ARTICLE III
PRESUMPTIONS IN CIVIL CASES

Rule 301.   Presumptions in Civil Cases Generally

In a civil case, unless a federal statute or these rules provide otherwise, the party against whom a presumption is directed has the burden of proceeding evidence to rebut the presumption. But this rule does not shift the burden of persuasion, which remains on the party who had it originally.

Rule 302.   Applying State Law to Presumptions in Civil Cases

In a civil case, state law governs the effect of a presumption regarding a claim or defense for which state law supplies the rule of decision.

ARTICLE IV
RELEVANCE AND ITS LIMITS

Rule 401.   Test for Relevant Evidence

Evidence is relevant if:

(a) It has any tendency to make a fact more or less probable than it would be without the evidence; and

(b) The fact is of consequence in determining the action.

Rule 402.   General Admissibility of Relevant Evidence

Relevant evidence is admissible unless any of the following provides otherwise:

- The United States Constitution;
- A federal statute;
- These rules; or
- Other rules prescribed by the Supreme Court.

Irrelevant evidence is not admissible.

Rule 403.   Excluding Relevant Evidence for Prejudice, Confusion, Waste of Time, or Other Reasons

The court may exclude relevant evidence if its probative value is substantially outweighed by a danger of one or more of the following: unfair prejudice, confusing the issues, misleading the jury, undue delay, wasting time, or needlessly presenting cumulative evidence.

Rule 404.   Character Evidence; Crimes or Other Acts

(a) Character Evidence.

    (1) Prohibited Uses. Evidence of a person's character or character trait is not admissible to prove that on a particular occasion the person acted in accordance with the character or trait.

    (2) Exceptions for a Defendant or Victim in a Criminal Case. The following exceptions apply in a criminal case:

        (A) A defendant may offer evidence of the defendant's pertinent trait, and if the evidence is admitted, the prosecutor may offer evidence to rebut it;

        (B) subject to the limitations in Rule 412, a defendant may offer evidence of an alleged victim's pertinent trait, and if the evidence is admitted, the prosecutor may:

            (i)   Offer evidence to rebut it; and

            (ii) offer evidence of the defendant's same trait; and

        (C) in a homicide case, the prosecutor may offer evidence of the alleged victim's trait of peacefulness to rebut evidence that the victim was the first aggressor.

    (3) Exceptions for a Witness. Evidence of a witness's character may be admitted under Rules 607, 608, and 609.

(b) Crimes, Wrongs, or Other Acts.

    (1) Prohibited Uses. Evidence of a crime, wrong, or other act is not admissible to prove a person's character in order to show that on a particular occasion the person acted in accordance with the character.

(2) Permitted Uses; Notice in a Criminal Case. This evidence may be admissible for another purpose, such as providing motive, opportunity, intent, preparation, plan, knowledge, identity, absence of mistake, or lack of accident. On request by a defendant in a criminal case, the prosecutor must:

> **(A)** provide reasonable notice of the general nature of any such evidence that the prosecutor intends to offer at trial; and

> **(B)** do so before trial—or during trial if the court, for good cause, excuses lack of pretrial notice.

Rule 405.   Methods of Proving Character

(a) By Reputation or Opinion. When evidence of a person's character or character trait is admissible, it may be proved by testimony about the person's reputation or by testimony in the form of an opinion. On cross-examination of the character witness, the court may allow an inquiry into relevant specific instances of the person's conduct.

(b) By Specific Instances of Conduct. When a person's character or character trait is an essential element of a charge, claim, or defense, the character or trait may also be proved by relevant specific instances of the person's conduct.

Rule 406.   Habit; Routine Practice

Evidence of a person's habit or an organization's routine practice may be admitted to prove that on a particular occasion the person or organization acted in accordance with the habit or routine practice. The court may admit this evidence regardless of whether it is corroborated or whether there was an eyewitness.

Rule 407.   Subsequent Remedial Measures

When measures are taken that would have made an earlier injury or harm less likely to occur, evidence of the subsequent measures is not admissible to prove:

- Negligence;

- Culpable conduct;

- A defect in a product or its design; or

- A need for a warning or instruction.

But the court may admit this evidence for another purpose, such as impeachment or—if disputed—proving ownership, control, or the feasibility of precautionary measures.

Rule 408.   Compromise Offers and Negotiations

(a) Prohibited Uses. Evidence of the following is not admissible—on behalf of any party—either to prove or disprove the validity or amount of a disputed claim or to impeach by a prior inconsistent statement or a contradiction:

(1) Furnishing, promising, or offering—or accepting, promising to accept, or offering to accept—a valuable consideration in compromising or attempting to compromise the claim; and

(2) Conduct or a statement made during compromise negotiations about the claim—except when offered in a criminal case and when the negotiations related to a claim by a public office in the exercise of its regulatory, investigative, or enforcement authority.

(b) Exceptions. The court may admit this evidence for another purpose, such as proving a witness's bias or prejudice, negating a contention of undue delay, or proving an effort to obstruct a criminal investigation or prosecution.

Rule 409.   Payment of Medical and Similar Expenses

Evidence of furnishing, promising to pay, or offering to pay medical, hospital, or similar expenses resulting from an injury is not admissible to prove liability for the injury.

Rule 410.   Pleas, Plea Discussions, and Related Statements

(a) Prohibited Uses. In a civil or criminal case, evidence of the following is not admissible against the defendant who made the plea or participated in the plea discussions;

(1) A guilty plea that was later withdrawn;

(2) A nolo contendere plea;

(3) A statement made during a proceeding on either of those pleas under Federal Rule of Criminal Procedure 11 or a comparable state procedure; or

(4) A statement made during plea discussions with an attorney for the prosecuting authority if the discussions did not result in a guilty plea or they resulted in a later-withdrawn guilty plea.

(b) Exceptions. The court may admit a statement described in Rule 410(a) (3) or (4):

(1) in any proceeding in which another statement made during the same plea or plea discussions has been introduced, if in fairness the statements ought to be considered together; or

(2) in a criminal proceeding for perjury or false statement, if the defendant made the statement under oath, on the record, and with counsel present.

Rule 411.   Liability Insurance

Evidence that a person was or was not insured against liability is not admissible to prove whether the person acted negligently or otherwise wrongfully, But the court may admit this evidence for another purpose, such as proving a witness's bias or prejudice or proving agency, ownership, or control.

Rule 412.   Sex-Offense Cases: The Victim's Sexual Behavior or Predisposition

(a) Prohibited Uses. The following evidence is not admissible in a civil or criminal proceeding involving alleged sexual misconduct:

(1) Evidence offered to prove that a victim engaged in other sexual behavior; or

(2) Evidence offered to prove a victim's sexual predisposition.

(b) Exceptions.

(1) Criminal Cases. The court may admit the following evidence in a criminal case:

(A) evidence of specific instances of a victim's sexual behavior, if offered to prove that someone other than the defendant was the source of semen, injury, or other physical evidence;

(B) evidence of specific instances of a victim's sexual behavior with respect to the person accused of the sexual misconduct, if offered by the defendant to prove consent or if offered by the prosecutor; and

(C) evidence whose exclusion would violate the defendant's constitutional rights.

(2) Civil Cases. In a civil case, the court may admit evidence offered to prove a victim's sexual behavior or sexual predisposition if its probative value substantially outweighs the danger of harm to any victim and of unfair prejudice to any party. The court may admit evidence of a victim's reputation only if the victim has placed it in controversy.

(c) Procedure to Determine Admissibility.

(1) Motion. If a party intends to offer evidence under Rule 412(b), the party must:

(A) file a motion that specifically describes the evidence and states the purpose for which it is to be offered;

(B) do so at least 14 days before trial unless the court, for good cause, sets a different time;

(C) serve the motion on all parties; and

(D) notify the victim or, when appropriate, the victim's guardian or representative.

(2) Hearing. Before admitting evidence under this rule, the court must conduct an in camera hearing and give the victim and parties a right to attend and be heard. Unless the court orders otherwise, the motion, related materials, and the record of the haring must be and remain sealed.

(d) Definition of "Victim." In this rule, "victim" includes an alleged victim.

Rule 413.   Similar Crimes in Sexual-Assault Cases

(a) Permitted Uses. In a criminal case in which a defendant is accused of a sexual assault, the court may admit evidence that the defendant committed any other sexual assault. The evidence may be considered on any matter to which it is relevant.

(b) Disclosure to the Defendant. If the prosecutor intends to offer this evidence, the prosecutor must disclose it to the defendant, including witnesses' statements or a summary of the expected testimony. The prosecutor must do so at least 15 days before trial or at a later time that the court allows for good cause.

(c) Effect on the Other Rules. This rule does not limit the admission or consideration of evidence under any other rule.

(d) Definition of "Sexual Assault." In this rule and Rule 415, "sexual assault" means a crime under federal law or under state law. (as "state" is defined in 18 U.S.C. § 513) involving:

(1) any conduct prohibited by 18 U.S.C. chapter 109A;

(2) contact, without consent, between any part of the defendant's body—or an object—and another person's genitals or anus;

(3) contact, without consent, between the defendant's genitals or anus and any part of another person's body;

(4) deriving sexual pleasure or gratification from inflicting death, bodily injury, or physical pain on another person; or

(5) an attempt or conspiracy to engage in conduct described in subparagraphs (1)–(4).

Rule 414.   Similar Crimes in Child-Molestation Cases

(a) Permitted Uses. In a criminal case in which a defendant is accused of child molestation, the court may admit evidence that the defendant committed any other child molestation. The evidence may be considered on any matter to which it is relevant.

(b) Disclosure to the Defendant. If the prosecutor intends to offer this evidence, the prosecutor must disclose it to the defendant, including witnesses' statements or a summary of the expected testimony. The prosecutor must do so at least 15 days before trial or at a later time that the court allows for good cause.

(c) Effect on Other Rules. This rule does not limit the admission or consideration of evidence under any other rule.

(d) Definition of "Child" and "Child Molestation." In this rule and Rule 415:

(1) "child" means a person below the age of 14; and

(2) "child molestation" means a crime under federal law or under state law (as "state" is defined in 18 U.S.C. § 513) involving:

(A) any conduct prohibited by 18 U.S.C. chapter 109A and committed with a child:

(B) any conduct prohibited by 18 U.S.C. chapter 110;

(C) contact between any part of the defendant's body—or an object—and a child's genitals or anus;

(D) contact between the defendant's genitals or anus and any part of a child's body;

(E) deriving sexual pleasure or gratification from inflicting death, bodily injury, or physical pain on a child; or

(F) an attempt or conspiracy to engage in conduct described in subparagraphs (A)–(E).

Rule 415.   Similar Acts in Civil Cases Involving Sexual Assault or Child Molestation

(a) Permitted Uses. In a civil case involving a claim for relief based on a party's alleged sexual assault or child molestation, the court may admit evidence that the party committed any other sexual assault or child molestation. The evidence may be considered as provided in Rules 413 and 414.

(b) Disclosure to the Opponent. If a party intends to offer this evidence, the party must disclose it to the party against whom it will be offered, including witnesses' statements or a summary of the expected testimony. The party must do so at least 15 days before trial or at a later time that the court allows for good cause.

(c) Effect on Other Rules. This rule does not limit the admission or consideration of evidence under any other rule.

ARTICLE V
PRIVILEGES

Rule 501.   Privilege in General

The common law—as interpreted by United States courts in the light of reason and experience—governs a claim of privilege unless any of the following provides otherwise:

- the United States Constitution;
- a federal statute; or
- rules prescribed by the Supreme Court.

But in a civil case, state law governs privilege regarding a claim or defense for which state law supplies the rule of decision.

ARTICLE VI

WITNESSES

Rule 601.   Competency to Testify in General

Every person is competent to be a witness unless these rules provide otherwise. But in a civil case, state law governs the witness's competency regarding a claim or defense for which state law supplies the rule of decision.

Rule 602.   Need for Personal Knowledge

A witness may testify to a matter only if evidence is introduced sufficient to support a finding that the witness has personal knowledge of the matter. Evidence to prove personal knowledge may consist of the witness's own testimony. This rule does not apply to a witness's expert testimony under Rule 703.

Rule 603.   Oath or Affirmation to Testify Truthfully

Before testifying, a witness must give an oath or affirmation to testify truthfully. It must be in a form designed to impress that duty on the witness's conscience.

Rule 604.   Interpreter

An interpreter must be qualified and must give an oath or affirmation to make a true translation.

Rule 605.   Judge's Competency as a Witness

The presiding judge may not testify as a witness at the trial. A party need not object to preserve the issue.

Rule 606.   Juror's Competency as a Witness

(a) At the Trial. A juror may not testify as a witness before the other jurors at the trial. If a juror is called to testify, the court must give a party an opportunity to object outside the jury's presence.

(b) During an Inquiry into the Validity of a Verdict or Indictment.

(1) Prohibited Testimony or Other Evidence. During an inquiry into the validity of a verdict or indictment, a juror may not testify about any statement made or incident that occurred during the jury's deliberations; the effect of anything on that juror's or another juror's vote; or any juror's mental processes concerning the verdict or indictment. The court may not receive a juror's affidavit or evidence of a juror's statement on these matters.

(2) **Exceptions**. A juror may testify about whether:

(A) extraneous prejudicial information was improperly brought to the jury's attention;

(B) an outside influence was improperly brought to bear on any juror; or

(C) a mistake was made in entering the verdict on the verdict form.

Rule 607.   Who May Impeach a Witness

Any party, including the party that called the witness, may attack the witness's credibility.

Rule 608.   A Witness's Character for Truthfulness or Untruthfulness

(a) Reputation or Opinion Evidence. A witness's credibility may be attacked or supported by testimony about the witness's reputation for having a character for truthfulness or untruthfulness, or by testimony in the form of an opinion about the character. But evidence of truthful character is admissible only after the witness's character for truthfulness has been attacked.

(b) Specific Instances of Conduct. Except for a criminal conviction under Rule 609, extrinsic evidence is not admissible to prove specific instances of a witness's conduct in order to attack or support the witness's character for truthfulness. But the court may, on cross-examination, allow them to be inquired into if they are probative of the character for truthfulness or untruthfulness of:

(1) The witness; or

(2) Another witness whose character the witness being cross-examined has testified about

By testifying on another matter, a witness does not waive any privilege against self-incrimination for testimony that relates only to the witness's character for truthfulness.

Rule 609.   Impeachment by Evidence of a Criminal Conviction

(a) In General. The following rules apply to attacking a witness's character for truthfulness by evidence of a criminal conviction.

(1) for a crime that, in the convicting jurisdiction, was punishable by death or by imprisonment for more than one year, the evidence:

(A) must be admitted, subject to Rule 403, in a civil case or in a criminal case in which the witness is not a defendant; and

(B) must be admitted in a criminal case in which the witness is a defendant, if the probative value of the evidence outweighs its prejudicial effect to that defendant; and

(2) for any crime regardless of the punishment, the evidence must be admitted if the court can readily determine that establishing the elements of the crime required proving—or the witness's admitting—a dishonest act or false statement.

(b) Limit on Using the Evidence After 10 Years. This subdivision (b) applies if more than 10 years have passed since the witness's conviction or release from confinement for it, whichever is later. Evidence of the conviction is admissible only if:

(1) its probative value, supported by specific facts and circumstances, substantially outweighs its prejudicial effects; and

(2) the proponent gives an adverse party reasonable written notice of the intent to use it so that the party has a fair opportunity to contest its use.

(c) Effect of a Pardon, Annulment, or Certificate of Rehabilitation. Evidence of a conviction is not admissible if:

(1) the conviction has been the subject of a pardon, annulment, certificate of rehabilitation, or other equivalent procedure based on a finding that the person has been rehabilitated, and the person has not been convicted of a later crime punishable by death or by imprisonment for more than one year; or

(2) the conviction has been the subject of a pardon, annulment, or other equivalent procedure based on a finding of innocence.

(d) Juvenile Adjudications. Evidence of a juvenile adjudication is admissible under this rule only if:

(1) it is offered in a criminal case;

(2) the adjudication was of a witness other than the defendant;

(3) an adult's conviction for that offense would be admissible to attack the adult's credibility; and

(4) admitting the evidence is necessary to fairly determine guilt or innocence.

(e) Pendency of an Appeal. A conviction that satisfies this rule is admissible even if an appeal is pending. Evidence of the pendency is also admissible.

Rule 610.   Religious Beliefs or Opinions

Evidence of a witness's religious beliefs or opinions is not admissible to attack or support the witness's credibility.

Rule 611.   Mode and Order of Examining Witnesses and Presenting Evidence

(a) Control by the Court; Purposes. The court should exercise reasonable control over the mode and order of examining witnesses and presenting evidence so as to:

(1) Make those procedures effective for determining the truth;

(2) Avoid wasting time; and

(3) Protect witnesses from harassment or undue embarrassment.

(b) Scope of Cross-Examination. Cross-examination should not go beyond the subject matter of the direct examination and matters affecting the witness's credibility. The court may allow inquiry into additional matters as if on direct examination.

(c) Leading Questions. Leading questions should not be used on direct examination except as necessary to develop the witness's testimony. Ordinarily, the court should allow leading questions:

(1) On cross-examination; and

(2) When a party calls a hostile witness, an adverse party, or a witness identified with an adverse party.

Rule 612.   Writing Used to Refresh a Witness's Memory

(a) Scope. This rule gives an adverse party certain options when a witness uses a writing to refresh memory:

(1) While testifying; or

(2) Before testifying, if the court decides that justice requires the party to have those options.

(b) Adverse Party's Options; Deleting Unrelated Matter. Unless 18 U.S.C. § 3500 provides otherwise in a criminal case, an adverse party is entitled to have the writing produced at the hearing, to inspect it, to cross-examine the witness about it, and to introduce in evidence any portion that relates to the witness's testimony. If the producing party claims that the writing includes unrelated matter, the court must examine the writing in camera, delete any unrelated portion, and order that the rest be delivered to the adverse party. Any portion deleted over objection must be preserved for the record. [18 U.S.C. § 3500 deals with disclosure of witness statements]

(c) Failure to Produce or Deliver the Writing. If a writing is not produced or is not delivered as ordered, the court may issue any appropriate order. But if the prosecution does not comply in a criminal case, the court must strike the witness's testimony or—if justice so requires—declare a mistrial.

Rule 613.   Witness's Prior Statement

(a) Showing or Disclosing the Statement During Examination. When examining a witness about the witness's prior statement, a party need not show it or disclose its contents to the witness. But the party must, on request, show it or disclose its contents to an adverse party's attorney.

(b) Extrinsic Evidence of a Prior Inconsistent Statement. Extrinsic evidence of a witness's prior inconsistent statement is admissible only if the witness is given an opportunity to explain or deny the statement and an adverse party is given an opportunity to examine the witness about it, or if justice so requires. This subdivision (b) does not apply to an opposing party's statement under Rule 801(d)(2) [party admissions].

Rule 614.   Court's Calling or Examining a Witness

(a) Calling. The court may call a witness on its own or at a party's request. Each party is entitled to cross-examine the witness.

(b) Examining. The court may examine a witness regardless of who calls the witness.

(c) Objections. A party may object to the court's calling or examining a witness either at that time or at the next opportunity when the jury is not present.

Rule 615. Excluding Witnesses

At a party's request, the court must order witnesses excluded so that they cannot hear other witnesses' testimony. Or the court may do so on its own. But this rule does not authorize excluding:

(a) a party who is a natural person;

(b) an officer or employee of a party that is not a natural person, after being designated as the party's representative by its attorney;

(c) a person whose presence a party shows to be essential to presenting the party's claim or defense; or

(d) a person authorized by statute to be present.

ARTICLE VII
OPINIONS AND EXPERT TESTIMONY

Rule 701. Opinion Testimony by Lay Witnesses

If a witness is not testifying as an expert, testimony in the form of an opinion is limited to one that is:

(a) rationally based on the witness's perception;

(b) helpful to clearly understanding the witness's testimony or to determining a fact in issue; and

(c) not based on scientific, technical, or other specialized knowledge within the scope of Rule 702.

Rule 702. Testimony by Expert Witnesses

A witness who is qualified as an expert by knowledge, skill, experience, training, or education may testify in the form of an opinion or otherwise if:

(a) the expert's scientific, technical, or other specialized knowledge will help the trier of fact to understand the evidence or to determine a fact in issue;

(b) the testimony is based on sufficient facts or data;

(c) the testimony is the product of reliable principles and methods; and

(d) the expert has reliably applied the principles and methods to the facts of the case.

Rule 703. Bases of an Expert's Opinion Testimony

An expert may base an opinion on facts or data in the case that the expert has been made aware of or personally observed. If experts in the particular field would reasonably rely on those kinds of facts or data in forming an opinion on the subject, they need not be admissible for the opinion to be admitted. But if the facts or data would otherwise be inadmissible, the proponent of the opinion may disclose them to the jury only if their probative value in helping the jury evaluate the opinion substantially outweighs their prejudicial effect.

Rule 704. Opinion on an Ultimate Issue

(a) In General—Not Automatically Objectionable. An opinion is not objectionable just because it embraces an ultimate issue.

(b) Exception. In a criminal case, an expert witness must not state an opinion about whether the defendant did or did not have a mental state or condition that constitutes an element of the crime charged or of a defense. Those matters are for the trier of fact alone.

Rule 705. Disclosing the Facts or Date Underlying an Expert's Opinion

Unless the court orders otherwise, an expert may state an opinion—and give the reasons for it—without first testifying to the underlying facts or data. But the expert may be required to disclose those facts or data on cross-examination.

Rule 706. Court-Appointed Expert Witnesses

(a) Appointment Process. On a party's motion or on its own, the court may order the parties to show cause why expert witnesses should not be appointed and may ask the parties to submit nominations. The court may appoint any expert that the parties agree on and any of its own choosing. But the court may only appoint someone who consents to act.

(b) Expert's Role. The court must inform the expert of the expert's duties. The court may do so in writing and have a copy filed with the clerk or may do so orally at a conference in which the parties have an opportunity to participate. The expert:

> **(1)** must advise the parties of any findings the expert makes;
>
> **(2)** may be deposed by any party;
>
> **(3)** may be called to testify by the court or any party; and
>
> **(4)** may be cross-examined by any party, including the party that called the expert.

(c) Compensation. The expert is entitled to a reasonable compensation, as set by the court. The compensation is payable as follows:

(1) in a criminal case or in a civil case involving just compensation under the Fifth Amendment, from any funds that are provided by law; and

(2) in any other civil case, by the parties in the proportion and at the time that the court directs—and the compensation is then charged like other costs.

(d) Disclosing the Appointment to the Jury. The court may authorize disclosure to the jury that the court appointed the expert.

(e) Parties' Choice of Their Own Experts. This rule does not limit a party in calling its own experts.

ARTICLE VIII

HEARSAY

Rule 801. Definitions That Apply to This Article; Exclusions from Hearsay

(a) Statement. "Statement" means a person's oral assertion, written assertion, or nonverbal conduct, if the person intended it as an assertion.

(b) Declarant. "Declarant" means the person who made the statement.

(c) Hearsay. "Hearsay" means a statement that:

(1) the declarant does not make while testifying at the current trial or hearing; and

(2) a party offers in evidence to prove the truth of the matter asserted in the statement.

(d) Statements That Are Not Hearsay. A statement that meets the following conditions is not hearsay:

(1) A Declarant-Witness's Prior Statement. The declarant testifies and is subject to cross-examination about a prior statement, and the statement:

(A) is inconsistent with the declarant's testimony and was given under penalty of perjury at a trial, hearing, or other proceeding or in a deposition;

(B) is consistent with the declarant's testimony and is offered: (i) to rebut an express or implied charge that the declarant recently fabricated it or acted from a recent improper influence or motive in so testifying; or; or (ii) to rehabilitate the declarants credibility as a witness when attacked on another ground; or

(C) identifies a person as someone the declarant perceived earlier.

(2) An Opposing Party's Statement. The statement is offered against an opposing party and:

(A) was made by the party in an individual or representative capacity;

(B) is one the party manifested that it adopted or believed to be true;

(C) was made by a person whom the party authorized to make a statement on the subject;

(D) was made by the party's agent or employee on a matter within the scope of that relationship and while it existed; or

(E) was made by the party's coconspirator during and in furtherance of the conspiracy

The statement must be considered but does not by itself establish the declarant's authority under (C); the existence or scope of the relationship under (D); or the existence of the conspiracy or participation in it under (E).

Rule 802.   The Rule Against Hearsay

Hearsay is not admissible unless any of the following provides otherwise:

- a federal statute;
- these rules; or
- other rules prescribed by the Supreme Court.

Rule 803.   Exceptions to the Rule Against Hearsay— Regardless of Whether the Declarant is Available as a Witness

The following are not excluded by the rule against hearsay, regardless of whether the declarant is available as a witness:

(1) Present Sense Impression. A statement describing or explaining an event or condition, made while or immediately after the declarant perceived it.

(2) Excited Utterance. A statement relating to a startling event or condition, made while the declarant was under the stress of excitement that it caused.

(3) Then-Existing Mental, Emotional, or Physical Condition. A statement of the declarant's then-existing state of mind (such as motive, intent, or plan) or emotional, sensory, or physical condition (such as mental feeling, pain, or bodily health), but not including a statement of memory or belief to prove that fact remembered or believed unless it relates to the validity or terms of the declarant's will.

(4) Statement Made for Medical Diagnosis or Treatment. A Statement that:

(A) is made for—and is reasonably pertinent to—medical diagnosis or treatment; and

(B) describes medical history; past or present symptoms or sensations; their inception; or their general cause.

(5) Recorded Recollection. A record that:

(A) is on a matter the witness once knew about but now cannot recall well enough to testify fully and accurately;

(B) was made or adopted by the witness when the matter was fresh in the witness's memory; and

(C) accurately reflects the witness's knowledge.

If admitted, the record may be read into evidence but may be received as an exhibit only if offered by an adverse party.

(6) Records of a Regularly Conducted Activity. A record of an act, event, condition, opinion, or diagnosis if:

(A) the record was made at or near the time by—or from information transmitted by—someone with knowledge;

(B) the record was kept in the course of a regularly conducted activity of a business, organization, occupation, or calling, whether or not for profit;

(C) making the record was a regular practice of that activity;

(D) all these conditions are shown by the testimony of the custodian or another qualified witness, or by a certification that complies with Rule 902(11) or (12) or with a statute permitting certification; and

(E) neither the source of information nor the method or circumstances of preparation indicate a lack of trustworthiness.

(7) Absence of a Record of a Regularly Conducted Activity. Evidence that a matter is not included in a record described in paragraph (6) if:

(A) the evidence is admitted to prove that the matter did not occur or exist;

(B) a record was regularly kept for a matter of that kind; and

(C) neither the possible source of the information nor other circumstances indicate a lack of trustworthiness.

(8) Public Records. A record or statement of a public office if:

(A) it sets out:

(i) the office's activities;

(ii) a matter observed while under a legal duty to report, but not including, in a criminal case, a matter observed by law-enforcement personnel; or

(iii) in a civil case or against the government in a criminal case, factual findings from a legally authorized investigation; and

(B) neither the source of information nor other circumstances indicate a lack of trustworthiness.

(9) Public Records of Vital Statistics. A record of a birth, death, or marriage, if reported to a public office in accordance with a legal duty.

(10) Absence of a Public Record. Testimony—or a certification under Rule 902—that a diligent search failed to disclose a public record or statement if the testimony or certification is admitted to prove that:

(A) the record or statement does not exist; or

(B) a matter did not occur or exist, if a public office regularly kept a record or statement of a matter of that kind.

(11) Records of Religious Organizations Concerning Personal or Family History. A statement of birth, legitimacy, ancestry, marriage, divorce, death, relationship by blood or marriage, or similar facts of personal or family history, contained in a regularly kept record of a religious organization.

(12) Certificates of Marriage, Baptism, and Similar Ceremonies. A statement of fact contained in a certificate:

> **(A)** made by a person who is authorized by a religious organization or by law to perform the act certified;
>
> **(B)** attesting that the person performed a marriage or similar ceremony or administered a sacrament; and
>
> **(C)** purporting to have been issued at the time of the act or within a reasonable time after it.

(13) Family Records. A statement of fact about personal or family history contained in a family record, such as a Bible, genealogy, chart, engraving on a ring, inscription on a portrait, or engraving on an urn or burial marker.

(14) Records of Documents That Affect an Interest in Property. The record of a document that purports to establish or affect an interest it property if:

> **(A)** The record is admitted to prove the content of the original recorded document, along with its signing and its delivery by each person who purports to have signed it;
>
> **(B)** The record is kept in a public office; and
>
> **(C)** A statute authorizes recording documents of that kind in that office.

(15) Statements in Documents That Affect an Interest in Property. A statement contained in a document that purports to establish or affect an interest in property if the matter stated was relevant to the document's purpose—unless later dealings with the property are inconsistent with the truth of the statement or the purport of the document.

(16) Statements in Ancient Documents. A statement in a document that is at least 20 years old and whose authenticity is established.

(17) Market Reports and Similar Commercial Publications. Market quotations, lists, directories, or other complications that are generally relied on by the public or by persons in particular occupations.

(18) Statements in Learned Treatises, Periodicals, or Pamphlets. A statement contained in a treatise, periodical, or pamphlet if:

> **(A)** The statement is called to the attention of an expert witness on cross-examination or relied on by the expert on direct examination; and

> **(B)** The publication is established as a reliable authority by the expert's admission or testimony, by another expert's testimony, or by judicial notice.

If admitted, the statement may be read into evidence but not received as an exhibit.

(19) Reputation Concerning Personal or Family History. A reputation among a person's family by blood, adoption, or marriage—or among a person's associates or in the community—concerning the person's birth, adoption, legitimacy, ancestry, marriage, divorce, death, relationship by blood, adoption, or marriage, or similar facts of personal or family history.

(20) Reputation Concerning Boundaries or General History. A reputation in a community—arising before the controversy—concerning boundaries of land in the community or customs that affect the land, or concerning general historical events important to that community, state, or nation.

(21) Reputation Concerning Character. A reputation among a person's associates or in the community concerning the person's character.

(22) Judgment of a Previous Conviction. Evidence of a final judgment of conviction if:

> **(A)** The judgment was entered after a trial or guilty plea, but not a nolo contendere plea;

> **(B)** The conviction was for a crime punishable by death or by imprisonment for more than a year;

> **(C)** The evidence is admitted to prove any fact essential to the judgment; and

(D) When offered by the prosecutor in a criminal case for a purpose other than impeachment, the judgment was against the defendant.

The pendency of an appeal may be shown but does not affect admissibility.

(24) [Other Exceptions.] [Transferred to Rule 807.]

Rule 804.   Exceptions to the Rule Against Hearsay—When the Declarant Is Unavailable as a Witness

(a) Criteria for Being Unavailable. A declarant is considered to be unavailable as a witness if the declarant:

(1) is exempted from testifying about the subject matter of the declarant's statement because the court rules that a privilege applies;

(2) refuses to testify about the subject matter despite a court order to do so;

(3) testifies to not remembering the subject matter;

(4) cannot be present or testify at the trial or hearing because of death or a then-existing infirmity, physical illness, or mental illness; or

(5) is absent from the trial or hearing and the statement's proponent has not been able, by process or other reasonable means, to procure:

(A) the declarant's attendance, in the case of hearsay exception under Rule 804(b)(1) or (6); or

(B) the declarant's attendance or testimony, in the case of a hearsay exception under Rule 804(b)(2), (3), or (4).

But this subdivision (a) does not apply if the statement's proponent procured or wrongfully caused the declarant's unavailability as a witness in order to prevent the declarant from attending or testifying.

(b) The Exceptions. The following are not excluded by the rule against hearsay if the declarant is unavailable as a witness:

(1) Former Testimony. Testimony that:

(A) was given as a witness at a trial, hearing, or lawful deposition, whether given during the current proceeding or a different one; and

(B) is now offered against a party who had—or, in a civil case, whose predecessor in interest had—an opportunity and similar motive to develop it by direct, cross-, or redirect examination.

(2) Statement Under the Belief of Imminent Death. In a prosecution for homicide or in a civil case, a statement that the declarant, while believing the declarant's death to be imminent, made about its cause or circumstances.

(3) Statement Against Interest. A statement that:

(A) a reasonable person in the declarant's position would have made only if the person believed it to be true because, when made, it was so contrary to the declarant's proprietary or pecuniary interest or had so great a tendency to invalidate the declarant's claim against someone else or to expose the declarant to civil or criminal liability; and

(B) is supported by corroborating circumstances that clearly indicate its trustworthiness, if it is offered in a criminal case as one that tends to expose the declarant to criminal liability.

(4) Statement of Personal or Family History. A statement about:

(A) the declarant's own birth, adoption, legitimacy, ancestry, marriage, divorce, relationship by blood, adoption, or marriage, or similar facts of personal or family history, even though the declarant had no way of acquiring personal knowledge about that fact; or

(B) another person concerning any of these facts, as well as death, if the declarant was related to the person by blood, adoption, or marriage or was so intimately associated with the person's family that the declarant's information is likely to be accurate.

(5) [Other exceptions.] [Transferred to Rule 807.]

(6) Statement Offered Against a Party That Wrongfully Caused the Declarant's Unavailability. A statement offered against a party that wrongfully caused—or acquiesced in wrongfully causing—the declarant's unavailability as a witness, and did so intending that result.

Rule 805.   Hearsay Within Hearsay

Hearsay within hearsay is not excluded by the rule against hearsay if each part of the combined statements conforms with an exception to the rule.

Rule 806.   Attacking and Supporting the Declarant's Credibility

When a hearsay statement—or a statement described in Rule 801(d)(2)(C), (D), or (E)—has been admitted in evidence, the declarant's credibility may be attacked, and then supported, by any evidence that would be admissible for those purposes if the declarant had testified as a witness. The court may admit evidence of the declarant's inconsistent statement or conduct, regardless of when it occurred or whether the declarant had an opportunity to explain or deny it. If the party against whom the statement was admitted calls the declarant as a witness, the party may examine the declarant on the statement as if on cross-examination.

Rule 807.   Residual Exception

(a) In General. Under the following circumstances, a hearsay statement is not excluded by the rule against hearsay even if the statement is not specifically covered by a hearsay exception in Rule 803 or 804:

(1) the statement has equivalent circumstantial guarantees of trustworthiness;

(2) it is offered as evidence of a material fact;

(3) it is more probative on the point for which it is offered than any other evidence that the proponent can obtain through reasonable efforts; and

(4) admitting it will best serve the purposes of these rules and the interests of justice.

(b) Notice. The statement is admissible only if, before the trial or hearing, the proponent gives an adverse party reasonable notice of the intent to offer the statement and its particulars, including the declarant's name and address, so that the party has a fair opportunity to meet it.

ARTICLE IX

AUTHENTICATION AND IDENTIFICATION

Rule 901.   Authenticating or Identifying Evidence

(a) In General. To satisfy the requirement of authenticating or identifying an item of evidence, the proponent must produce evidence sufficient to support a finding that the item is what the proponent claims it is.

(b) Examples. The following are examples only—not a complete list—of evidence that satisfies the requirement:

> **(1) Testimony of a Witness with Knowledge**. Testimony that an item is what it is claimed to be.
>
> **(2) Nonexpert Opinion About Handwriting**. A nonexpert's opinion that handwriting is genuine, based on a familiarity with it that was not acquired for the current litigation.
>
> **(3) Comparison by an Expert Witness or the Trier of Fact**. A comparison with an authenticated specimen by an expert witness or the trier of fact.
>
> **(4) Distinctive Characteristics and the Like**. The appearance, contents, substance, internal patterns, or other distinctive characteristics of the item, taken together with all the circumstances.
>
> **(5) Opinion About a Voice**. An opinion identifying a person's voice—whether heard firsthand or through mechanical or electronic transmission or recording—based on hearing the voice at any time under circumstances that connect it with the alleged speaker.
>
> **(6) Evidence About a Telephone Conversation**. For a telephone conversation, evidence that a call was made to the number assigned at the time to:
>
>> **(A)** a particular person, if circumstances, including self-identification, show that the person answering was the one called; or
>>
>> **(B)** a particular business, if the call was made to a business and the call related to business reasonably transacted over the telephone.
>
> **(7) Evidence About Public Records**. Evidence that:
>
>> **(A)** a document was recorded or filed in a public office as authorized by law; or
>>
>> **(B)** a purported public record or statement is from the office where items of this kind are kept.
>
> **(8) Evidence About Ancient Documents or Data Compilations**. For a document or date compilation, evidence that it:

(A) is in a condition that creates no suspicion about its authenticity;

(B) was in a place where, if authentic, it would likely be; and

(C) is at least 20 years old when offered.

(9) Evidence About a Process or System. Evidence describing a process or system and showing that it produces an accurate result.

(10) Methods Provided by a Statute or Rule. Any method of authentication or identification allowed by a federal statute or a rule prescribed by the Supreme Court.

Rule 902.   Evidence That Is Self-Authenticating

The following items of evidence are self-authenticating; they require no extrinsic evidence of authenticity in order to be admitted:

(1) Domestic Public Documents That are Sealed and Signed. A document that bears:

(A) a seal purporting to be that of the United States; any state, district, commonwealth, territory, or insular possession of the United States; the former Panama Canal Zone; the Trust Territory of the Pacific Islands; a political subdivision of any of these entities; or a department, agency, or officer of any entity named above; and

(B) a signature purporting to be an execution or attestation.

(2) Domestic Public Documents That Are Not Sealed but Are Signed and Certified. A document that bears no seal if:

(A) it bears the signature of any officer or employee of an entity named in Rule 902(1)(A); and

(B) another public officer who has a seal and official duties within that same entity certifies under seal— or its equivalent—that the signer has the official capacity and that the signature is genuine.

(3) Foreign Public Documents. A document that purports to be signed or attested by a person who is authorized by a foreign country's law to do so. The document must be accompanied by a final certification that certifies the genuineness of the signature and official position of the signer or attester—or of any foreign official whose certificate of genuineness relates to the signature or attestation or is in a chain of certificates of genuineness relating to the signature or attestation. The certification may be made by a secretary of a United States embassy or legation; by a consul general, vice consul, or consular agent of the United States; or by a diplomatic or consular official of the foreign country assigned or accredited to the United States. If all parties have been given a reasonable opportunity to investigate the document's authenticity and accuracy, the court may, for good cause, either:

> **(A)** order that it be treated as presumptively authentic without final certification; or

> **(B)** allow it to be evidenced by an attested summary with or without final certification.

(4) Certified Copies of Public Records. A copy of an official record—or a copy of a document that was recorded or filed in a public office as authorized by law—if the copy is certified as correct by:

> **(A)** The custodian or another person authorized to make the certification; or

> **(B)** A certificate that complies with Rule 902(1), (2), or (3), a federal statute, or a rule prescribed by the Supreme Court.

(5) Official Publications. A book, pamphlet, or other publication purporting to be issued by a public authority.

(6) Newspapers and Periodicals. Printed material purporting to be a newspaper or periodical.

(7) Trade Inscriptions and the Like. An inscription, sign, tag, or label purporting to have been affixed in the course of business and indicating origin, ownership, or control.

(8) Acknowledged Documents. A document accompanied by a certificate of acknowledgment that is lawfully executed by a notary public or another officer who is authorized to take acknowledgements.

(9) Commercial Paper and Related Documents.

(10) Presumptions Under a Federal Statute. A signature, document, or anything else that a federal statute declares to be presumptively or prima facie genuine or authentic.

(11) Certified Domestic Records of a Regularly Conducted Activity. The original or a copy of a domestic record that meets the requirement of Rule 803(6)(A)-(C), as shown by a certification of the custodian or another qualified person that complies with a federal statute or a rule prescribed by the Supreme Court. Before the trial or hearing, the proponent must give an adverse party reasonable written notice of the intent to offer the record— and must make the record and certification available for inspection—so that the party has a fair opportunity to challenge them.

(12) Certified Foreign Records of a Regularly Conducted Activity. In a civil case, the original or a copy of a foreign record that meets the requirements of Rule 902(11), modified as follows: the certification, rather than complying with a federal statute or Supreme Court rule, must be signed in a manner that, if falsely made, would subject the maker to a criminal penalty in the country where the certification is signed. The proponent must also meet the notice requirements of Rule 902(11).

Rule 903.   Subscribing Witness's Testimony

A subscribing witness's testimony is necessary to authenticate a writing only if required by the law of the jurisdiction that governs its validity.

ARTICLE X
CONTENTS OF WRITINGS, RECORDINGS, AND PHOTOGRAPHS

Rule 1001.   Definitions That Apply to This Article

In this article:

(a) A "writing" consists of letters, words, numbers, or their equivalent set down in any form.

(b) A "recording" consists of letters, words, numbers, or their equivalent recorded in any manner.

(c) "Photograph" means a photographic image or its equivalent stored in any form.

(d) An "original" of a writing or recording means the writing or recording itself or any counterpart intended to have the same effect by the person who executed or issued it. For electronically stored information, "original" means any printout—or other output readable by sight—if it accurately reflects the information. An "original" of a photograph includes the negative or a print from it.

(e) A "duplicate" means a counterpart produced by a mechanical, photographic, chemical, electronic, or other equivalent process or technique that accurately reproduces the original.

Rule 1002.   Requirement of the Original

An original writing, recording, or photograph is required in order to prove its content unless these rules or a federal statute provides otherwise.

Rule 1003.   Admissibility of Duplicates

A duplicate is admissible to the same extent as the original unless a genuine question is raised about the original's authenticity or the circumstances make it unfair to admit the duplicate.

Rule 1004.   Admissibility of Other Evidence of Content

An original is not required and other evidence of the content of a writing, recording, or photograph is admissible if:

(a) all the originals are lost or destroyed, and not by the proponent acting in bad faith;

(b) an original cannot be obtained by any available judicial process;

(c) the party against whom the original would be offered had control of the original; was at that time put on notice, by pleadings or otherwise, that the original would be a subject of proof at the trial or hearing; and fails to produce it at the trial or hearing; or

(d) the writing, recording, or photograph is not closely related to a controlling issue.

Rule 1005.   Copies of Public Records to Prove Content

The proponent may use a copy to prove the content of an official record—or of a document that was recorded or filed in a public office as authorized by law—if these conditions are met; the record or document is otherwise admissible; and the copy is certified as correct in accordance with Rule 902(4) or is testified to be correct by a witness who has compared it with the original. If no such copy can be obtained by reasonable diligence, then the proponent may use other evidence to prove the content.

Rule 1006.   Summaries to Prove Content

The proponent may use a summary, chart, or calculation to prove the content of voluminous writings, recordings, or photographs that cannot be conveniently examined in court. The proponent must make the originals or duplicates available for examination or copying, or both, by other parties at a reasonable time and place. And the court may order the proponent to produce them in court.

Rule 1007.   Testimony or Admission of a Party to Prove Content

The proponent may prove the content of a writing, recording, or photograph by the testimony, deposition, or written statement of the party against whom the evidence is offered. The proponent need not account for the original.

Rule 1008.   Functions of the Court and Jury

Ordinarily, the court determines whether the proponent has fulfilled the factual conditions for admitting other evidence of the content of a writing, recording, or photograph under Rule 1004 or 1005. But in a jury trial, the jury determines—in accordance with Rule 104(b)—any issue about whether:

(a) an asserted writing, recording, or photograph ever existed;

(b) another one produced at the trial or hearing is the original; or

(c) other evidence of content accurately reflects the content.

ARTICLE XI

MISCELLANEOUS RULES

Rule 1101.   Applicability of Rules

(a) To Courts and Judges. These rules apply to proceedings before:

- United States district courts;
- United States bankruptcy and magistrate judges;
- United States courts of appeals;
- the United States Court of Federal Claims; and
- the district courts of Guam, the Virgin Islands, and the Northern Mariana Islands.

(b) To Cases and Proceedings. These rules apply in:

- civil cases and proceedings, including bankruptcy, admiralty, and maritime cases;

- criminal cases and proceedings; and

- contempt proceedings, except those in which the court may act summarily.

(c) Rules on Privilege. The rules on privilege apply to all stages of a case or proceeding.

(d) Exceptions. These rules—except for those on privilege—do not apply to the following:

    (1) the court's determination, under Rule 104(a), on a preliminary question of fact governing admissibility;

    (2) grand-jury proceedings; and

    (3) miscellaneous proceedings such as:

- extradition or rendition;

- issuing an arrest warrant, criminal summons, or search warrant;

- a preliminary examination in a criminal case;

- sentencing; granting or revoking probation or supervised release; and

- considering whether to release on bail or otherwise.

(e) Other Statutes and Rules. A federal statute or a rule prescribed by the Supreme Court may provide for admitting or excluding evidence independently from these rules.

Appendix B

CALIFORNIA EVIDENCE CODE

Appendix B contains selected sections of the California Evidence Code.

WORDS AND PHRASES DEFINED

§ 110. Burden of producing evidence.

"Burden of producing evidence" means the obligation of a party to introduce evidence sufficient to avoid a ruling against him on the issue.

§ 115. Burden of proof.

"Burden of proof" means the obligation of a party to establish by evidence a requisite degree of belief concerning a fact in the mind of the trier of fact or the court. The burden of proof may require a party to raise a reasonable doubt concerning the existence or nonexistence of a fact or that he establish the existence or nonexistence of a fact by a preponderance of the evidence, by clear and convincing proof, or by proof beyond a reasonable doubt. Except as otherwise provided by law, the burden of proof requires proof by a preponderance of the evidence.

§ 120. Civil action.

"Civil action" includes civil proceedings.

§ 125. Conduct.

"Conduct" includes all active and passive behavior, both verbal and nonverbal.

§ 135. Declarant.

"Declarant" is a person who makes a statement.

§ 140. Evidence.

"Evidence" means testimony, writings, material objects, or other things presented to the senses that are offered to prove the existence or nonexistence of a fact.

§ 190. Proof.

"Proof" is the establishment by evidence of a requisite degree of belief concerning a fact in the mind of the trier of fact or the court.

323

§ 210.   Relevant evidence.

"Relevant evidence" means evidence, including evidence relevant to the credibility of a witness or hearsay declarant, having any tendency in reason to prove or disprove any disputed fact that is of consequence to the determination of the action.

§ 225.   Statement.

"Statement" means (a) oral or written verbal expression or (b) nonverbal conduct of a person intended by him as a substitute for oral or written verbal expression.

§ 240.   Unavailable as a witness.

(a) Except as otherwise provided in subdivision (b), "unavailable as a witness" means that the declarant is any of the following:

(1) Exempted or precluded on the ground of privilege from testifying concerning the matter to which his or her statement is relevant.

(2) Disqualified from testifying to the matter.

(3) Dead or unable to attend or to testify at the hearing because of then existing physical or mental illness or infirmity.

(4) Absent from the hearing and the court is unable to compel his or her attendance by its process.

(5) Absent from the hearing and the proponent of his or her statement has exercised reasonable diligence but has been unable to procure his or her attendance by the court's process.

(b) A declarant is not unavailable as a witness if the exemption, preclusion, disqualification, death, inability, or absence of the declarant was brought about by the procurement or wrongdoing of the proponent of his or her statement for the purpose of preventing the declarant from attending or testifying.

(c) Expert testimony which establishes that physical or mental trauma resulting from an alleged crime has caused harm to a witness of sufficient severity that the witness is physically unable to testify or is unable to testify without suffering substantial trauma may constitute a sufficient showing of unavailability pursuant to paragraph (3) of subdivision (a). As used in this section, the term "expert" means a physician and surgeon, including a psychiatrist, or any person described by subdivision (b), (c), or (e) of Section 1010.

The introduction of evidence to establish the unavailability of a witness under this subdivision shall not be deemed procurement of unavailability, in absence of proof to the contrary.

§ 250.   Writing.

"Writing" means handwriting, typewriting, printing, photostating, photographing, photocopying, transmitting by electronic mail or facsimile, and every other means of recording upon any tangible thing, any form of communication or representation, including letters, words, pictures, sounds, or symbols, or combinations thereof, and any record thereby created, regardless of the manner in which the record has been stored.

§ 255.   Original.

"Original" means the writing itself or any counterpart intended to have the same effect by a person executing or issuing it. An "original" of a photograph includes the negative or any print therefrom. If data are stored in a computer or similar device, any printout or other output readable by sight, shown to reflect the data accurately, is an "original."

§ 260.   Duplicate.

A "duplicate" is a counterpart produced by the same impression as the original, or from the same matrix, or by means of photography, including enlargements and miniatures, or by mechanical or electronic rerecording, or by chemical reproduction, or by other equivalent technique which accurately reproduces the original.

GENERAL PROVISIONS

§ 300.   Applicability of code.

Except as otherwise provided by statute, this code applies in every action before the Supreme Court or a court of appeal or superior court, including proceedings in such actions conducted by a referee, court commissioner, or similar officer, but does not apply in grand jury proceedings.

§ 320.   Power of court to regulate order of proof.

Except as otherwise provided by law, the court in its discretion shall regulate the order of proof.

§ 350.   Only relevant evidence admissible.

No evidence is admissible except relevant evidence.

§ 351.   Admissibility of relevant evidence.

Except as otherwise provided by statute, all relevant evidence is admissible.

§ 352.   Discretion of court to exclude evidence.

The court in its discretion may exclude evidence if its probative value is substantially outweighed by the probability that its admission will (a) necessitate undue consumption of time or (b) create substantial danger of undue prejudice, of confusing the issues, or of misleading the jury.

§ 353.   Erroneous admission of evidence; effect.

A verdict or finding shall not be set aside, nor shall the judgment or decision based thereon be reversed, by reason of the erroneous admission of evidence unless:

(a) There appears of record an objection to or a motion to exclude or to strike the evidence that was timely made and so stated as to make clear the specific ground of the objection or motion; and

(b) The court which passes upon the effect of the error or errors is of the opinion that the admitted evidence should have been excluded on the ground stated and that the error or errors complained of resulted in a miscarriage of justice.

§ 354.   Erroneous exclusion of evidence; effect. A verdict or finding shall not be set aside, nor shall the judgment or decision based thereon be reversed, by reason of the erroneous exclusion of evidence unless the court which passes upon the effect of the error or errors is of the opinion that the error or errors complained of resulted in a miscarriage of justice and it appears of record that:

(a) The substance, purpose, and relevance of the excluded evidence was made known to the court by the questions asked, an offer of proof, or by any other means;

(b) The rulings of the court made compliance with subdivision (a) futile; or

(c) The evidence was sought by questions asked during cross-examination or recross-examination.

§ 355.   Limited admissibility.

When evidence is admissible as to one party or for one purpose and is inadmissible as to another party or for another purpose, the court upon request shall restrict the evidence to its proper scope and instruct the jury accordingly.

§ 356.   Entire act, declaration, conversation, or writing to elucidate part offered.

Where part of an act, declaration, conversation, or writing is given in evidence by one party, the whole on the same subject may be inquired into by an adverse party; when a letter is read, the answer may be given; and when a detached act, declaration, conversation, or writing is given in evidence, any other act, declaration, conversation, or writing which is necessary to make it understood may also be given in evidence.

§ 400.   "Preliminary fact" defined.

As used in this article, "preliminary fact" means a fact upon the existence or nonexistence of which depends the admissibility or inadmissibility of evidence. The phrase "the admissibility or inadmissibility of evidence" includes the qualification or disqualification of a person to be a witness and the existence or nonexistence of a privilege.

§ 401.   "Proffered evidence" defined.

As used in this article, "proffered evidence" means evidence, the admissibility or inadmissibility of which is dependent upon the existence or nonexistence of a preliminary fact.

§ 402.   Procedure for determining foundational and other preliminary facts.

(a)   When the existence of a preliminary fact is disputed, its existence or nonexistence shall be determined as provided in this article.

(b)   The court may hear and determine the question of the admissibility of evidence out of the presence or hearing of the jury; but in a criminal action, the court shall hear and determine the question of the admissibility of a confession or admission of the defendant out of the presence and hearing of the jury if any party so requests.

(c)   A ruling on the admissibility of evidence implies whatever finding of fact is prerequisite thereto; a separate or formal finding is unnecessary unless required by statute.

§ 403.   Determination of foundational and other preliminary facts where relevancy, personal knowledge, or authenticity is disputed.

(a)   The proponent of the proffered evidence has the burden of producing evidence as to the existence of the preliminary fact, and the proffered evidence is inadmissible unless the court finds that there is evidence sufficient to sustain a finding of the existence of the preliminary fact, when:

(1)   The relevance of the proffered evidence depends on the existence of the preliminary fact;

(2)　The preliminary fact is the personal knowledge of a witness concerning the subject matter of his testimony;

(3)　The preliminary fact is the authenticity of a writing; or

(4)　The proffered evidence is of a statement or other conduct of a particular person and the preliminary fact is whether that person made the statement or so conducted himself.

(b)　Subject to Section 702, the court may admit conditionally the proffered evidence under this section, subject to evidence of the preliminary fact being supplied later in the course of the trial.

(c)　If the court admits the proffered evidence under this section, the court:

(1)　May, and on request shall, instruct the jury to determine whether the preliminary fact exists and to disregard the proffered evidence unless the jury finds that the preliminary fact does exist.

(2)　Shall instruct the jury to disregard the proffered evidence if the court subsequently determines that a jury could not reasonably find that the preliminary fact exists.

§ 404.　Determination of whether proffered evidence is incriminatory.

Whenever the proffered evidence is claimed to be privileged under Section 940, the person claiming the privilege has the burden of showing that the proffered evidence might tend to incriminate him; and the proffered evidence is inadmissible unless it clearly appears to the court that the proffered evidence cannot possibly have a tendency to incriminate the person claiming the privilege.

§ 405.　Determination of foundational and other preliminary facts in other cases.

With respect to preliminary fact determinations not governed by Section 403 or 404:

(a)　When the existence of a preliminary fact is disputed, the court shall indicate which party has the burden of producing evidence and the burden of proof on the issue as implied by the rule of law under which the question arises. The court shall determine the existence or nonexistence of the preliminary fact and shall admit or exclude the proffered evidence as required by the rule of law under which the question arises.

(b)　If a preliminary fact is also a fact in issue in the action:

(1)　The jury shall not be informed of the court's determination as to the existence or nonexistence of the preliminary fact.

(2)   If the proffered evidence is admitted, the jury shall not be instructed to disregard the evidence if its determination of the fact differs from the court's determination of the preliminary fact.

§ 406.   Evidence affecting weight or credibility.

This article does not limit the right of a party to introduce before the trier of fact evidence relevant to weight or credibility.

WEIGHT OF EVIDENCE

§ 410.   "Direct evidence" defined.

As used in this chapter, "direct evidence" means evidence that directly proves a fact, without an inference or presumption, and which in itself, if true, conclusively establishes that fact.

§ 411.   Direct evidence of one witness sufficient.

Except where additional evidence is required by statute, the direct evidence of one witness who is entitled to full credit is sufficient for proof of any fact.

§ 412.   Party having power to produce better evidence.

If weaker and less satisfactory evidence is offered when it was within the power of the party to produce stronger and more satisfactory evidence, the evidence offered should be viewed with distrust.

§ 413.   Party's failure to explain or deny evidence.

In determining what inferences to draw from the evidence or facts in the case against a party, the trier of fact may consider, among other things, the party's failure to explain or to deny by his testimony such evidence or facts in the case against him, or his willful suppression of evidence relating thereto, if such be the case.

JUDICIAL NOTICE

§ 450.   Judicial notice may be taken only as authorized by law.

Judicial notice may not be taken of any matter unless authorized or required by law.

§ 451.   Matters which must be judicially noticed.

Judicial notice shall be taken of the following:

(a)   The decisional, constitutional, and public statutory law of this state and of the United States and the provisions of any charter described in Section 3, 4, or 5 of Article XI of the California Constitution.

(b) Any matter made a subject of judicial notice by Section 11343.6, 11344.6, or 18576 of the Government Code or by Section 1507 of Title 44 of the United States Code.

(c) Rules of professional conduct for members of the bar adopted pursuant to Section 6076 of the Business and Professions Code and rules of practice and procedure for the courts of this state adopted by the Judicial Council.

(d) Rules of pleading, practice, and procedure prescribed by the United States Supreme Court, such as the Rules of the United States Supreme Court, the Federal Rules of Civil Procedure, the Federal Rules of Criminal Procedure, the Admiralty Rules, the Rules of the Court of Claims, the Rules of the Customs Court, and the General Orders and Forms in Bankruptcy.

(e) The true signification of all English words and phrases and of all legal expressions.

(f) Facts and propositions of generalized knowledge that are so universally known that they cannot reasonably be the subject of dispute.

§ 452.   Matters which may be judicially noticed.

Judicial notice may be taken of the following matters to the extent that they are not embraced within Section 451:

(a) The decisional, constitutional, and statutory law of any state of the United States and the resolutions and private acts of the Congress of the United States and of the Legislature of this state.

(b) Regulations and legislative enactments issued by or under the authority of the United States or any public entity in the United States.

(c) Official acts of the legislative, executive, and judicial departments of the United States and of any state of the United States.

(d) Records of (1) any court of this state or (2) any court of record of the United States or of any state of the United States.

(e) Rules of court of (1) any court of this state or (2) any court of record of the United States or of any state of the United States.

(f) The law of an organization of nations and of foreign nations and public entities in foreign nations.

(g) Facts and propositions that are of such common knowledge within the territorial jurisdiction of the court that they cannot reasonably be the subject of dispute.

(h) Facts and propositions that are not reasonably subject to dispute and are capable of immediate and accurate determination by resort to sources of reasonably indisputable accuracy.

§ 452.5. Criminal conviction records; computer-generated records and electronically digitized copies; admissibility.

(a) The official acts and records specified in subdivisions (c) and (d) of Section 452 include any computer-generated official court records, as specified by the Judicial Council which relate to criminal convictions, when the record is certified by a clerk of the superior court pursuant to Section 69844.5 of the Government Code at the time of computer entry.

(b) An official record of conviction certified in accordance with subdivision (a) of Section 1530 is admissible pursuant to Section 1280 to prove the commission, attempted commission, or solicitation of a criminal offense, prior conviction, service of a prison term, or other act, condition, or event recorded by the record.

§ 453. Compulsory judicial notice upon request.

The trial court shall take judicial notice of any matter specified in Section 452 if a party requests it and:

(a) Gives each adverse party sufficient notice of the request, through the pleadings or otherwise, to enable such adverse party to prepare to meet the request; and

(b) Furnishes the court with sufficient information to enable it to take judicial notice of the matter.

§ 454. Information that may be used in taking judicial notice.

(a) In determining the propriety of taking judicial notice of a matter, or the tenor thereof:

(1) Any source of pertinent information, including the advice of persons learned in the subject matter, may be consulted or used, whether or not furnished by a party.

(2) Exclusionary rules of evidence do not apply except for Section 352 and the rules of privilege.

(b) Where the subject of judicial notice is the law of an organization of nations, a foreign nation, or a public entity in a foreign nation and the court resorts to the advice of persons learned in the subject matter, such advice, if not received in open court, shall be in writing.

§ 455.   Opportunity to present information to court.

With respect to any matter specified in Section 452 or in subdivision (f) of Section 451 that is of substantial consequence to the determination of the action:

(a)   If the trial court has been requested to take or has taken or proposes to take judicial notice of such matter, the court shall afford each party reasonable opportunity, before the jury is instructed or before the cause is submitted for decision by the court, to present to the court information relevant to (1) the propriety of taking judicial notice of the matter and (2) the tenor of the matter to be noticed.

(b)   If the trial court resorts to any source of information not received in open court, including the advice of persons learned in the subject matter, such information and its source shall be made a part of the record in the action and the court shall afford each party reasonable opportunity to meet such information before judicial notice of the matter may be taken.

§ 456.   Noting denial of request to take judicial notice.

If the trial court denies a request to take judicial notice of any matter, the court shall at the earliest practicable time so advise the parties and indicate for the record that it has denied the request.

§ 457.   Instructing jury on matter judicially noticed.

If a matter judicially noticed is a matter which would otherwise have been for determination by the jury, the trial court may, and upon request shall, instruct the jury to accept as a fact the matter so noticed.

§ 458.   Judicial notice by trial court in subsequent proceedings.

The failure or refusal of the trial court to take judicial notice of a matter, or to instruct the jury with respect to the matter, does not preclude the trial court in subsequent proceedings in the action from taking judicial notice of the matter in accordance with the procedure specified in this division.

BURDEN OF PROOF; BURDEN OF PRODUCING EVIDENCE; PRESUMPTIONS

§ 500.   Party who has the burden of proof.

Except as otherwise provided by law, a party has the burden of proof as to each fact the existence or nonexistence of which is essential to the claim for relief or defense that he is asserting.

§ 520.   Claim that person is guilty of crime or wrongdoing.

The party claiming that a person is guilty of crime or wrongdoing has the burden of proof on that issue.

§ 521.   Claim that person did not exercise care.

The party claiming that a person did not exercise a requisite degree of care has the burden of proof on that issue.

§ 522.   Claim that person is or was insane.

The party claiming that any person, including himself, is or was insane has the burden of proof on that issue.

§ 550.   Party who has the burden of producing evidence.

(a)   The burden of producing evidence as to a particular fact is on the party against whom a finding on that fact would be required in the absence of further evidence.

(b)   The burden of producing evidence as to a particular fact is initially on the party with the burden of proof as to that fact.

PRESUMPTIONS AND INFERENCES

§ 600.   "Presumption" and "inference" defined.

(a)   A presumption is an assumption of fact that the law requires to be made from another fact or group of facts found or otherwise established in the action. A presumption is not evidence.

(b)   An inference is a deduction of fact that may logically and reasonably be drawn from another fact or group of facts found or otherwise established in the action.

§ 601.   Classification of presumptions.

A presumption is either conclusive or rebuttable. Every rebuttable presumption is either (a) a presumption affecting the burden of producing evidence or (b) a presumption affecting the burden of proof.

§ 602.   Statute making one fact prima facie evidence of another fact.

A statute providing that a fact or group of facts is prima facie evidence of another fact establishes a rebuttable presumption.

§ 603.   "Presumption affecting the burden of producing evidence" defined.

A presumption affecting the burden of producing evidence is a presumption established to implement no public policy other than to facilitate the determination of the particular action in which the presumption is applied.

§ 604.   Effect of presumption affecting burden of producing evidence.

The effect of a presumption affecting the burden of producing evidence is to require the trier of fact to assume the existence of the presumed fact unless and until evidence is introduced which would support a finding of its nonexistence, in which case the trier of fact shall determine the existence or nonexistence of the presumed fact from the evidence and without regard to the presumption. Nothing in this section shall be construed to prevent the drawing of any inference that may be appropriate.

§ 605.   "Presumption affecting the burden of proof" defined.

A presumption affecting the burden of proof is a presumption established to implement some public policy other than to facilitate the determination of the particular action in which the presumption is applied, such as the policy in favor of establishment of a parent and child relationship, the validity of marriage, the stability of titles to property, or the security of those who entrust themselves or their property to the administration of others.

§ 606.   Effect of presumption affecting burden of proof.

The effect of a presumption affecting the burden of proof is to impose upon the party against whom it operates the burden of proof as to the nonexistence of the presumed fact.

CONCLUSIVE PRESUMPTIONS

§ 620.   Conclusive presumptions.

The presumptions established by this article, and all other presumptions declared by law to be conclusive, are conclusive presumptions.

§ 622.   Facts recited in written instrument.

The facts recited in a written instrument are conclusively presumed to be true as between the parties thereto, or their successors in interest; but this rule does not apply to the recital of a consideration.

§ 623.   Estoppel by own statement or conduct.

Whenever a party has, by his own statement or conduct, intentionally and deliberately led another to believe a particular thing true and to act upon such belief, he is not, in any litigation arising out of such statement or conduct, permitted to contradict it.

§ 624.   Estoppel of tenant to deny title of landlord.

A tenant is not permitted to deny the title of his landlord at the time of the commencement of the relation.

PRESUMPTIONS AFFECTING THE BURDEN OF PRODUCING EVIDENCE

§ 630.   Presumptions affecting the burden of producing evidence.

The presumptions established by this article, and all other rebuttable presumptions established by law that fall within the criteria of Section 603, are presumptions affecting the burden of producing evidence.

§ 631.   Money delivered by one to another.

Money delivered by one to another is presumed to have been due to the latter.

§ 632.   Thing delivered by one to another.

A thing delivered by one to another is presumed to have belonged to the latter.

§ 633.   Obligation delivered up to the debtor.

An obligation delivered up to the debtor is presumed to have been paid.

§ 634.   Person in possession of order on self.

A person in possession of an order on himself for the payment of money, or delivery of a thing, is presumed to have paid the money or delivered the thing accordingly.

§ 635.   Obligation possessed by creditor.

An obligation possessed by the creditor is presumed not to have been paid.

§ 636.   Payment of earlier rent or installments.

The payment of earlier rent or installments is presumed from a receipt for later rent or installments.

§ 637.   Ownership of things possessed.

The things which a person possesses are presumed to be owned by him.

§ 638.   Property ownership acts.

A person who exercises acts of ownership over property is presumed to be the owner of it.

§ 639.   Judgment correctly determines rights of parties.

A judgment, when not conclusive, is presumed to correctly determine or set forth the rights of the parties, but there is no presumption that the facts essential to the judgment have been correctly determined.

§ 640.   Writing truly dated.

A writing is presumed to have been truly dated.

§ 641.   Letter received in ordinary course of mail.

A letter correctly addressed and properly mailed is presumed to have been received in the ordinary course of mail.

§ 643.   Authenticity of ancient document.

A deed or will or other writing purporting to create, terminate, or affect an interest in real or personal property is presumed to be authentic if it:

(a)   Is at least 30 years old;

(b)   Is in such condition as to create no suspicion concerning its authenticity;

(c)   Was kept, or if found was found, in a place where such writing, if authentic, would be likely to be kept or found; and

(d)   Has been generally acted upon as authentic by persons having an interest in the matter.

§ 644.   Book purporting to be published by public authority.

A book, purporting to be printed or published by public authority, is presumed to have been so printed or published.

§ 645.   Book purporting to contain reports of cases.

A book, purporting to contain reports of cases adjudged in the tribunals of the state or nation where the book is published, is presumed to contain correct reports of such cases.

§ 645.1. Printed materials purporting to be particular newspaper or periodical.

Printed materials, purporting to be a particular newspaper or periodical, are presumed to be that newspaper or periodical if regularly issued at average intervals not exceeding three months.

§ 646.   Res ipsa loquitur; instruction.

(a)   As used in this section, "defendant" includes any party against whom the res ipsa loquitur presumption operates.

(b) The judicial doctrine of res ipsa loquitur is a presumption affecting the burden of producing evidence.

(c) If the evidence, or facts otherwise established, would support a res ipsa loquitur presumption and the defendant has introduced evidence which would support a finding that he was not negligent or that any negligence on his part was not a proximate cause of the occurrence, the court may, and upon request shall, instruct the jury to the effect that:

(1) If the facts which would give rise to res ipsa loquitur presumption are found or otherwise established, the jury may draw the inference from such facts that a proximate cause of the occurrence was some negligent conduct on the part of the defendant; and

(2) The jury shall not find that a proximate cause of the occurrence was some negligent conduct on the part of the defendant unless the jury believes, after weighing all the evidence in the case and drawing such inferences therefrom as the jury believes are warranted, that it is more probable than not that the occurrence was caused by some negligent conduct on the part of the defendant.

PRESUMPTIONS AFFECTING THE BURDEN OF PROOF

§ 660. Presumptions affecting the burden of proof.

The presumptions established by this article, and all other rebuttable presumptions established by law that fall within the criteria of Section 605, are presumptions affecting the burden of proof.

§ 662. Owner of legal title to property is owner of beneficial title.

The owner of the legal title to property is presumed to be the owner of the full beneficial title. This presumption may be rebutted only by clear and convincing proof.

§ 663. Ceremonial marriage.

A ceremonial marriage is presumed to be valid.

§ 664. Official duty regularly performed.

It is presumed that official duty has been regularly performed. This presumption does not apply on an issue as to the lawfulness of an arrest if it is found or otherwise established that the arrest was made without a warrant.

§ 665. Ordinary consequences of voluntary act.

A person is presumed to intend the ordinary consequences of his voluntary act. This presumption is inapplicable in a criminal action to establish the specific intent of the defendant where specific intent is an element of the crime charged.

§ 667. Death of person not heard from in five years.

A person not heard from in five years is presumed to be dead.

§ 668. Unlawful intent.

An unlawful intent is presumed from the doing of an unlawful act. This presumption is inapplicable in a criminal action to establish the specific intent of the defendant where specific intent is an element of the crime charged.

§ 669. Due care; failure to exercise.

(a) The failure of a person to exercise due care is presumed if:

(1) He violated a statute, ordinance, or regulation of a public entity;

(2) The violation proximately caused death or injury to person or property;

(3) The death or injury resulted from an occurrence of the nature which the statute, ordinance, or regulation was designed to prevent; and

(4) The person suffering the death or the injury to his person or property was one of the class of persons for whose protection the statute, ordinance, or regulation was adopted.

(b) This presumption may be rebutted by proof that:

(1) The person violating the statute, ordinance, or regulation did what might reasonably be expected of a person of ordinary prudence, acting under similar circumstances, who desired to comply with the law; or

(2) The person violating the statute, ordinance, or regulation was a child and exercised the degree of care ordinarily exercised by persons of his maturity, intelligence, and capacity under similar circumstances, but the presumption may not be rebutted by such proof if the violation occurred in the course of an activity normally engaged in only by adults and requiring adult qualifications.

§ 670. Payments by check.

(a) In any dispute concerning payment by means of a check, a copy of the check produced in accordance with Section 1550 of the Evidence Code, together with the original bank statement that reflects payment of the check by the bank on which it was drawn or a copy thereof produced in the same manner, creates a presumption that the check has been paid.

(b) As used in this section:

(1) "Bank" means any person engaged in the business of banking and includes, in addition to a commercial bank, a savings and loan association, savings bank, or credit union.

(2) "Check" means a draft, other than a documentary draft, payable on demand and drawn on a bank, even though it is described by another term, such as "share draft" or "negotiable order of withdrawal."

COMPETENCY

§ 700.   General rule as to competency.

Except as otherwise provided by statute, every person, irrespective of age, is qualified to be a witness and no person is disqualified to testify to any matter.

§ 701.   Disqualification of witness.

(a) A person is disqualified to be a witness if he or she is:

(1) Incapable of expressing himself or herself concerning the matter so as to be understood, either directly or through interpretation by one who can understand him; or

(2) Incapable of understanding the duty of a witness to tell the truth.

(b) In any proceeding held outside the presence of a jury, the court may reserve challenges to the competency of a witness until the conclusion of the direct examination of that witness.

§ 702.   Personal knowledge of witness.

(a) Subject to Section 801, the testimony of a witness concerning a particular matter is inadmissible unless he has personal knowledge of the matter. Against the objection of a party, such personal knowledge must be shown before the witness may testify concerning the matter.

(b) A witness' personal knowledge of a matter may be shown by any otherwise admissible evidence, including his own testimony.

§ 703.   Judge as witness.

(a) Before the judge presiding at the trial of an action may be called to testify in that trial as a witness, he shall, in proceedings held out of the presence and hearing of the jury, inform the parties of the information he has concerning any fact or matter about which he will be called to testify.

(b) Against the objection of a party, the judge presiding at the trial of an action may not testify in that trial as a witness. Upon such objection, the judge shall declare a mistrial and order the action assigned for trial before another judge.

(c) The calling of the judge presiding at a trial to testify in that trial as a witness shall be deemed a consent to the granting of a motion for mistrial, and an objection to such calling of a judge shall be deemed a motion for mistrial.

(d) In the absence of objection by a party, the judge presiding at the trial of an action may testify in that trial as a witness.

§ 704. Juror as witness.

(a) Before a juror sworn and impaneled in the trial of an action may be called to testify before the jury in that trial as a witness, he shall, in proceedings conducted by the court out of the presence and hearing of the remaining jurors, inform the parties of the information he has concerning any fact or matter about which he will be called to testify.

(b) Against the objection of a party, a juror sworn and impaneled in the trial of an action may not testify before the jury in that trial as a witness. Upon such objection, the court shall declare a mistrial and order the action assigned for trial before another jury.

(c) The calling of a juror to testify before the jury as a witness shall be deemed a consent to the granting of a motion for mistrial, and an objection to such calling of a juror shall be deemed a motion for mistrial.

(d) In the absence of objection by a party, a juror sworn and impaneled in the trial of an action may be compelled to testify in that trial as a witness.

OATH AND CONFRONTATION

§ 710. Oath required.

Every witness before testifying shall take an oath or make an affirmation or declaration in the form provided by law, except that a child under the age of 10 or a dependent person with a substantial cognitive impairment, in the court's discretion, may be required only to promise to tell the truth.

§ 711.   Confrontation.

At the trial of an action, a witness can be heard only in the presence and subject to the examination of all the parties to the action, if they choose to attend and examine.

EXPERT WITNESSES GENERALLY

§ 720.   Qualification as an expert witness.

(a)   A person is qualified to testify as an expert if he has special knowledge, skill, experience, training, or education sufficient to qualify him as an expert on the subject to which his testimony relates. Against the objection of a party, such special knowledge, skill, experience, training, or education must be shown before the witness may testify as an expert.

(b)   A witness' special knowledge, skill, experience, training, or education may be shown by any otherwise admissible evidence, including his own testimony.

§ 721.   Cross-examination of expert witness.

(a)   Subject to subdivision (b), a witness testifying as an expert may be cross-examined to the same extent as any other witness and, in addition, may be fully cross-examined as to (1) his or her qualifications, (2) the subject to which his or her expert testimony relates, and (3) the matter upon which his or her opinion is based and the reasons for his or her opinion.

(b)   If a witness testifying as an expert testifies in the form of an opinion, he or she may not be cross-examined in regard to the content or tenor of any scientific, technical, or professional text, treatise, journal, or similar publication unless any of the following occurs:

(1)   The witness referred to, considered, or relied upon such publication in arriving at or forming his or her opinion.

(2)   The publication has been admitted in evidence.

(3)   The publication has been established as a reliable authority by the testimony or admission of the witness or by other expert testimony or by judicial notice.

If admitted, relevant portions of the publication may be read into evidence but may not be received as exhibits.

APPOINTMENT OF EXPERT WITNESS BY COURT

§ 730.   Appointment of expert by court.

When it appears to the court, at any time before or during the trial of an action, that expert evidence is or may be required by the court or by any party to the action, the court on its own motion or on motion of any party may appoint one or more experts to investigate, to render a report as may be ordered by the court, and to testify as an expert at the trial of the action relative to the fact or matter as to which the expert evidence is or may be required. The court may fix the compensation for these services, if any, rendered by any person appointed under this section, in addition to any service as a witness, at the amount as seems reasonable to the court.

Nothing in this section shall be construed to permit a person to perform any act for which a license is required unless the person holds the appropriate license to lawfully perform that act.

INTERPRETERS AND TRANSLATORS

§ 750.   Rules relating to witnesses apply to interpreters and translators.

A person who serves as an interpreter or translator in any action is subject to all the rules of law relating to witnesses.

METHOD AND SCOPE OF EXAMINATION

§ 760.   Direct examination.

"Direct examination" is the first examination of a witness upon a matter that is not within the scope of a previous examination of the witness.

§ 761.   Cross-examination.

"Cross-examination" is the examination of a witness by a party other than the direct examiner upon a matter that is within the scope of the direct examination of the witness.

§ 762.   Redirect examination.

"Redirect examination" is an examination of a witness by the direct examiner subsequent to the cross-examination of the witness.

§ 763.   Recross-examination.

"Recross-examination" is an examination of a witness by a cross-examiner subsequent to a redirect examination of the witness.

§ 764.   Leading question.

A "leading question" is a question that suggests to the witness the answer that the examining party desires.

EXAMINATION OF WITNESSES

§ 765.   Court to control mode of interrogation.

(a) The court shall exercise reasonable control over the mode of interrogation of a witness so as to make interrogation as rapid, as distinct, and as effective for the ascertainment of the truth, as may be, and to protect the witness from undue harassment or embarrassment.

(b)   With a witness under the age of 14 or a dependent person with a substantial cognitive impairment, the court shall take special care to protect him or her from undue harassment or embarrassment, and to restrict the unnecessary repetition of questions. The court shall also take special care to ensure that questions are stated in a form which is appropriate to the age or cognitive level of the witness. The court may, in the interests of justice, on objection by a party, forbid the asking of a question which is in a form that is not reasonably likely to be understood by a person of the age or cognitive level of the witness.

§ 766.   Responsive answers.

A witness must give responsive answers to questions, and answers that are not responsive shall be stricken on motion of any party.

§ 767.   Leading questions.

(a)   Except under special circumstances where the interests of justice otherwise require:

(1)   A leading question may not be asked of a witness on direct or redirect examination.

(2)   A leading question may be asked of a witness on cross-examination or recross-examination.

(b)   The court may, in the interests of justice permit a leading question to be asked of a child under 10 years of age or a dependent person with a substantial cognitive impairment in a case involving a prosecution under Section 273a, 273d, 288.5, 368, or any of the acts described in Section 11165.1 or 11165.2 of the Penal Code.

§ 768.   Writings.

(a)   In examining a witness concerning a writing, it is not necessary to show, read, or disclose to him any part of the writing.

(b)   If a writing is shown to a witness, all parties to the action must be given an opportunity to inspect it before any question concerning it may be asked of the witness.

§ 769.   Inconsistent statement or conduct.

In examining a witness concerning a statement or other conduct by him that is inconsistent with any part of his testimony at the hearing, it is not necessary to disclose to him any information concerning the statement or other conduct.

§ 770. Evidence of inconsistent statement of witness; exclusion; exceptions.

Unless the interests of justice otherwise require, extrinsic evidence of a statement made by a witness that is inconsistent with any part of his testimony at the hearing shall be excluded unless:

(a) The witness was so examined while testifying as to give him an opportunity to explain or to deny the statement; or

(b) The witness has not been excused from giving further testimony in the action.

§ 771. Production of writing used to refresh memory.

(a) Subject to subdivision (c), if a witness, either while testifying or prior thereto, uses a writing to refresh his memory with respect to any matter about which he testifies, such writing must be produced at the hearing at the request of an adverse party and, unless the writing is so produced, the testimony of the witness concerning such matter shall be stricken.

(b) If the writing is produced at the hearing, the adverse party may, if he chooses, inspect the writing, cross-examine the witness concerning it, and introduce in evidence such portion of it as may be pertinent to the testimony of the witness.

(c) Production of the writing is excused, and the testimony of the witness shall not be stricken, if the writing:

(1) Is not in the possession or control of the witness or the party who produced his testimony concerning the matter; and

(2) Was not reasonably procurable by such party through the use of the court's process or other available means.

§ 772. Order of examination.

(a) The examination of a witness shall proceed in the following phases: direct examination, cross-examination, redirect examination, recross-examination, and continuing thereafter by redirect and recross-examination.

(b) Unless for good cause the court otherwise directs, each phase of the examination of a witness must be concluded before the succeeding phase begins.

(c) Subject to subdivision (d), a party may, in the discretion of the court, interrupt his cross-examination, redirect examination, or recross-examination of a witness, in order to examine the witness upon a matter not within the scope of a previous examination of the witness.

(d) If the witness is the defendant in a criminal action, the witness may not, without his consent, be examined under direct examination by another party.

§ 773. Cross-examination.

(a) A witness examined by one party may be cross-examined upon any matter within the scope of the direct examination by each other party to the action in such order as the court directs.

(b) The cross-examination of a witness by any party whose interest is not adverse to the party calling him is subject to the same rules that are applicable to the direct examination.

§ 774. Re-examination.

A witness once examined cannot be reexamined as to the same matter without leave of the court, but he may be reexamined as to any new matter upon which he has been examined by another party to the action. Leave may be granted or withheld in the court's discretion.

§ 775. Court may call witnesses.

The court, on its own motion or on the motion of any party, may call witnesses and interrogate them the same as if they had been produced by a party to the action, and the parties may object to the questions asked and the evidence adduced the same as if such witnesses were called and examined by an adverse party. Such witnesses may be cross-examined by all parties to the action in such order as the court directs.

§ 777. Exclusion of witness.

(a) Subject to subdivisions (b) and (c), the court may exclude from the courtroom any witness not at the time under examination so that such witness cannot hear the testimony of other witnesses.

(b) A party to the action cannot be excluded under this section.

(c) If a person other than a natural person is a party to the action, an officer or employee designated by its attorney is entitled to be present.

§ 778. Recall of witness.

After a witness has been excused from giving further testimony in the action, he cannot be recalled without leave of the court. Leave may be granted or withheld in the court's discretion.

CREDIBILITY GENERALLY

§ 780.   Testimony; proof of truthfulness; considerations.

Except as otherwise provided by statute, the court or jury may consider in determining the credibility of a witness any matter that has any tendency in reason to prove or disprove the truthfulness of his testimony at the hearing, including but not limited to any of the following:

(a) His demeanor while testifying and the manner in which he testifies.

(b) The character of his testimony.

(c) The extent of his capacity to perceive, to recollect, or to communicate any matter about which he testifies.

(d) The extent of his opportunity to perceive any matter about which he testifies.

(e) His character for honesty or veracity or their opposites.

(f) The existence or nonexistence of a bias, interest, or other motive.

(g) A statement previously made by him that is consistent with his testimony at the hearing.

(h) A statement made by him that is inconsistent with any part of his testimony at the hearing.

(i) The existence or nonexistence of any fact testified to by him.

(j) His attitude toward the action in which he testifies or toward the giving of testimony.

(k) His admission of untruthfulness.

§ 782.   Sexual offenses; evidence of sexual conduct of complaining witness; procedure for admissibility; treatment of resealed affidavits.

(a) In any of the circumstances described in subdivision (c), if evidence of sexual conduct of the complaining witness is offered to attack the credibility of the complaining witness under Section 780, the following procedure shall be followed.

ATTACKING OR SUPPORTING CREDIBILITY

§ 785.   Parties may attack or support credibility.

The credibility of a witness may be attacked or supported by any party, including the party calling him.

§ 786.   Character evidence generally.

Evidence of traits of his character other than honesty or veracity, or their opposites, is inadmissible to attack or support the credibility of a witness.

§ 787.   Specific instances of conduct.

Subject to Section 788, evidence of specific instances of his conduct relevant only as tending to prove a trait of his character is inadmissible to attack or support the credibility of a witness.

§ 788.   Prior felony conviction.

For the purpose of attacking the credibility of a witness, it may be shown by the examination of the witness or by the record of the judgment that he has been convicted of a felony unless:

(a)   A pardon based on his innocence has been granted to the witness by the jurisdiction in which he was convicted.

(b)   A certificate of rehabilitation and pardon has been granted to the witness under the provisions of Chapter 3.5 (commencing with Section 4852.01) of Title 6 of Part 3 of the Penal Code.

(c)   The accusatory pleading against the witness has been dismissed under the provisions of Penal Code Section 1203.4, but this exception does not apply to any criminal trial where the witness is being prosecuted for a subsequent offense.

(d)   The conviction was under the laws of another jurisdiction and the witness has been relieved of the penalties and disabilities arising from the conviction pursuant to a procedure substantially equivalent to that referred to in subdivision (b) or (c).

§ 789.   Religious belief.

Evidence of his religious belief or lack thereof is inadmissible to attack or support the credibility of a witness.

§ 790.   Good character of witness.

Evidence of the good character of a witness is inadmissible to support his credibility unless evidence of his bad character has been admitted for the purpose of attacking his credibility.

§ 791.   Prior consistent statement of witness.

Evidence of a statement previously made by a witness that is consistent with his testimony at the hearing is inadmissible to support his credibility unless it is offered after:

(a)   Evidence of a statement made by him that is inconsistent with any part of his testimony at the hearing has been admitted for the purpose of attacking his credibility, and the statement was made before the alleged inconsistent statement; or

(b) An express or implied charge has been made that his testimony at the hearing is recently fabricated or is influenced by bias or other improper motive, and the statement was made before the bias, motive for fabrication, or other improper motive is alleged to have arisen.

HYPNOSIS OF WITNESSES

§ 795. Testimony of hypnosis subject; admissibility; conditions.

(a) The testimony of a witness is not inadmissible in a criminal proceeding by reason of the fact that the witness has previously undergone hypnosis for the purpose of recalling events that are the subject of the witness's testimony, if all of the following conditions are met:

(1) The testimony is limited to those matters that the witness recalled and related prior to the hypnosis.

(2) The substance of the prehypnotic memory was preserved in a writing, audio recording, or video recording prior to the hypnosis.

(3) The hypnosis was conducted in accordance with all of the following procedures:

(A) A written record was made prior to hypnosis documenting the subject's description of the event, and information that was provided to the hypnotist concerning the subject matter of the hypnosis.

(B) The subject gave informed consent to the hypnosis.

(C) The hypnosis session, including the pre- and post-hypnosis interviews, was video recorded for subsequent review.

(D) The hypnosis was performed by a licensed medical doctor, psychologist, licensed clinical social worker, or a licensed marriage and family therapist experienced in the use of hypnosis and independent of and not in the presence of law enforcement, the prosecution, or the defense.

(4) Prior to admission of the testimony, the court holds a hearing pursuant to Section 402 at which the proponent of the evidence proves by clear and convincing evidence that the hypnosis did not so affect the witness as to render the witness's prehypnosis recollection unreliable or to substantially impair the ability to cross-examine the witness concerning the witness's prehypnosis

recollection. At the hearing, each side shall have the right to present expert testimony and to cross-examine witnesses.

(b) Nothing in this section shall be construed to limit the ability of a party to attack the credibility of a witness who has undergone hypnosis, or to limit other legal grounds to admit or exclude the testimony of that witness.

EXPERT AND OTHER OPINION TESTIMONY

§ 800.   Lay witness; opinion testimony.

If a witness is not testifying as an expert, his testimony in the form of an opinion is limited to such an opinion as is permitted by law, including but not limited to an opinion that is:

(a)   Rationally based on the perception of the witness; and

(b)   Helpful to a clear understanding of his testimony.

§ 801.   Expert witnesses; opinion testimony.

If a witness is testifying as an expert, his testimony in the form of an opinion is limited to such an opinion as is:

(a)   Related to a subject that is sufficiently beyond common experience that the opinion of an expert would assist the trier of fact; and

(b)   Based on matter (including his special knowledge, skill, experience, training, and education) perceived by or personally known to the witness or made known to him at or before the hearing, whether or not admissible, that is of a type that reasonably may be relied upon by an expert in forming an opinion upon the subject to which his testimony relates, unless an expert is precluded by law from using such matter as a basis for his opinion.

§ 802.   Statement of basis of opinion.

A witness testifying in the form of an opinion may state on direct examination the reasons for his opinion and the matter (including, in the case of an expert, his special knowledge, skill, experience, training, and education) upon which it is based, unless he is precluded by law from using such reasons or matter as a basis for his opinion. The court in its discretion may require that a witness before testifying in the form of an opinion be first examined concerning the matter upon which his opinion is based.

§ 803.   Opinion based on improper matter.

The court may, and upon objection shall, exclude testimony in the form of an opinion that is based in whole or in significant part on matter that is not a proper basis for such an opinion. In such case, the witness may, if there remains a proper basis for his opinion, then state his opinion after excluding from consideration the matter determined to be improper.

§ 805.   Opinion on ultimate issue.

Testimony in the form of an opinion that is otherwise admissible is not objectionable because it embraces the ultimate issue to be decided by the trier of fact.

OPINION TESTIMONY ON PARTICULAR MATTERS

§ 870.   Opinion as to sanity.

A witness may state his opinion as to the sanity of a person when:

(a)   The witness is an intimate acquaintance of the person whose sanity is in question;

(b)   The witness was a subscribing witness to a writing, the validity of which is in dispute, signed by the person whose sanity is in question and the opinion relates to the sanity of such person at the time the writing was signed; or

(c)   The witness is qualified under Section 800 or 801 to testify in the form of an opinion.

GENERAL PROVISIONS RELATING TO PRIVILEGES

§ 911.   Refusal to be or have another as witness, or disclose or produce any matter.

Except as otherwise provided by statute:

(a)   No person has a privilege to refuse to be a witness.

(b)   No person has a privilege to refuse to disclose any matter or to refuse to produce any writing, object, or other thing.

(c)   No person has a privilege that another shall not be a witness or shall not disclose any matter or shall not produce any writing, object, or other thing.

§ 917.   Presumption that certain communications are confidential; privileged character of electronic communications.

(a)   If a privilege is claimed on the ground that the matter sought to be disclosed is a communication made in confidence in the course of the lawyer-client, physician-patient, psychotherapist-patient, clergy-penitent, husband-wife, sexual assault counselor-victim, or domestic violence counselor-victim relationship, the communication is presumed to have been made in confidence and the opponent of the claim of privilege has the burden of proof to establish that the communication was not confidential.

(b)   A communication between persons in a relationship listed in subdivision (a) does not lose its privileged character for the sole reason that it is communicated by electronic means or because persons involved in the delivery, facilitation, or storage of electronic communication may have access to the content of the communication.

§ 919.   Admissibility   where   disclosure   erroneously compelled; claim of privilege; coercion.

(a)   Evidence of a statement or other disclosure of privileged information is inadmissible against a holder of the privilege if:

(1)   A person authorized to claim the privilege claimed it but nevertheless disclosure erroneously was required to be made; or

(2)   The presiding officer did not exclude the privileged information as required by Section 916.

(b)   If a person authorized to claim the privilege claimed it, whether in the same or a prior proceeding, but nevertheless disclosure erroneously was required by the presiding officer to be made, neither the failure to refuse to disclose nor the failure to seek review of the order of the presiding officer requiring disclosure indicates consent to the disclosure or constitutes a waiver and, under these circumstances, the disclosure is one made under coercion.

PRIVILEGE OF DEFENDANT IN CRIMINAL CASE

§ 930.   Privilege not to be called as a witness and not to testify.

To the extent that such privilege exists under the Constitution of the United States or the State of California, a defendant in a criminal case has a privilege not to be called as a witness and not to testify.

PRIVILEGE AGAINST SELF-INCRIMINATION

§ 940.   Privilege against self-incrimination.

To the extent that such privilege exists under the Constitution of the United States or the State of California, a person has a privilege to refuse to disclose any matter that may tend to incriminate him.

LAWYER-CLIENT PRIVILEGE

§ 950.   Lawyer.

As used in this article, "lawyer" means a person authorized, or reasonably believed by the client to be authorized, to practice law in any state or nation.

§ 951.   Client.

As used in this article, "client" means a person who, directly or through an authorized representative, consults a lawyer for the purpose of retaining the lawyer or securing legal service or advice from him in his professional capacity, and includes an incompetent (a) who himself so consults the lawyer or (b) whose guardian or conservator so consults the lawyer in behalf of the incompetent.

§ 952.   Confidential communication between client and lawyer.

As used in this article, "confidential communication between client and lawyer" means information transmitted between a client and his or her lawyer in the course of that relationship and in confidence by a means which, so far as the client is aware, discloses the information to no third persons other than those who are present to further the interest of the client in the consultation or those to whom disclosure is reasonably necessary for the transmission of the information or the accomplishment of the purpose for which the lawyer is consulted, and includes a legal opinion formed and the advice given by the lawyer in the course of that relationship.

§ 953.   Holder of the privilege.

As used in this article, "holder of the privilege" means:

(a)   The client, if the client has no guardian or conservator.

(b)   A guardian or conservator of the client, if the client has a guardian or conservator.

(c)   The personal representative of the client if the client is dead, including a personal representative appointed pursuant to Section 12252 of the Probate Code.

(d)   A successor, assign, trustee in dissolution, or any similar representative of a firm, association, organization, partnership, business trust, corporation, or public entity that is no longer in existence.

§ 954.   Lawyer-client privilege.

Subject to Section 912 and except as otherwise provided in this article, the client, whether or not a party, has a privilege to refuse to disclose, and to prevent another from disclosing, a confidential communication between client and lawyer if the privilege is claimed by:

(a)   The holder of the privilege;

(b)   A person who is authorized to claim the privilege by the holder of the privilege; or

(c) The person who was the lawyer at the time of the confidential communication, but such person may not claim the privilege if there is no holder of the privilege in existence or if he is otherwise instructed by a person authorized to permit disclosure.

The relationship of attorney and client shall exist between a law corporation as defined in Article 10 (commencing with Section 6160) of Chapter 4 of Division 3 of the Business and Professions Code and the persons to whom it renders professional services, as well as between such persons and members of the State Bar employed by such corporation to render services to such persons. The word "persons" as used in this subdivision includes partnerships, corporations, limited liability companies, associations and other groups and entities.

§ 955.   When lawyer required to claim privilege.

The lawyer who received or made a communication subject to the privilege under this article shall claim the privilege whenever he is present when the communication is sought to be disclosed and is authorized to claim the privilege under subdivision (c) of Section 954.

§ 956.   Exception: Crime or fraud.

There is no privilege under this article if the services of the lawyer were sought or obtained to enable or aid anyone to commit or plan to commit a crime or a fraud.

§ 956.5. Exception: Prevention of criminal act likely to result in death or substantial bodily harm.

There is no privilege under this article if the lawyer reasonably believes that disclosure of any confidential communication relating to representation of a client is necessary to prevent a criminal act that the lawyer reasonably believes is likely to result in the death of, or substantial bodily harm to, an individual.

§ 957.   Exception: Parties claiming through deceased client.

There is no privilege under this article as to a communication relevant to an issue between parties all of whom claim through a deceased client, regardless of whether the claims are by testate or intestate succession, nonprobate transfer, or inter vivos transaction.

§ 958.   Exception: Breach of duty arising out of lawyer-client relationship.

There is no privilege under this article as to a communication relevant to an issue of breach, by the lawyer or by the client, of a duty arising out of the lawyer-client relationship.

§ 959.   Exception: Lawyer as attesting witness.

There is no privilege under this article as to a communication relevant to an issue concerning the intention or competence of a client executing an attested document of which the lawyer is an attesting witness, or concerning the execution or attestation of such a document.

PRIVILEGE NOT TO TESTIFY AGAINST SPOUSE

§ 970.   Spouse's privilege not to testify against spouse; exceptions.

Except as otherwise provided by statute, a married person has a privilege not to testify against his spouse in any proceeding.

§ 971.   Privilege not to be called as a witness against spouse.

Except as otherwise provided by statute, a married person whose spouse is a party to a proceeding has a privilege not to be called as a witness by an adverse party to that proceeding without the prior express consent of the spouse having the privilege under this section unless the party calling the spouse does so in good faith without knowledge of the marital relationship.

§ 972.   Exceptions to privilege.

A married person does not have a privilege under this article in:

(a)   A proceeding brought by or on behalf of one spouse against the other spouse.

(b)   A proceeding to commit or otherwise place his or her spouse or his or her spouse's property, or both, under the control of another because of the spouse's alleged mental or physical condition.

(c)   A proceeding brought by or on behalf of a spouse to establish his or her competence.

(d)   A proceeding under the Juvenile Court Law, Chapter 2 (commencing with Section 200) of Part 1 of Division 2 of the Welfare and Institutions Code.

(e)   A criminal proceeding in which one spouse is charged with:

(1)   A crime against the person or property of the other spouse or of a child, parent, relative, or cohabitant of either, whether committed before or during marriage.

PRIVILEGE FOR CONFIDENTIAL
MARITAL COMMUNICATIONS

§ 980.   Confidential marital communication privilege.

Subject to Section 912 and except as otherwise provided in this article, a spouse (or his guardian or conservator when he has a guardian or conservator), whether or not a party, has a privilege during the marital relationship and afterwards to refuse to disclose, and to prevent another from disclosing, a communication if he claims the privilege and the communication was made in confidence between him and the other spouse while they were husband and wife.

§ 981.   Exception: Crime or fraud.

There is no privilege under this article if the communication was made, in whole or in part, to enable or aid anyone to commit or plan to commit a crime or a fraud.

§ 982.   Commitment or similar proceedings.

There is no privilege under this article in a proceeding to commit either spouse or otherwise place him or his property, or both, under the control of another because of his alleged mental or physical condition.

§ 983.   Competency proceedings.

There is no privilege under this article in a proceeding brought by or on behalf of either spouse to establish his competence.

§ 984.   Proceeding between spouses.

There is no privilege under this article in:

(a)   A proceeding brought by or on behalf of one spouse against the other spouse.

(b)   A proceeding between a surviving spouse and a person who claims through the deceased spouse, regardless of whether such claim is by testate or intestate succession or by inter vivos transaction.

§ 985.   Criminal proceedings.

There is no privilege under this article in a criminal proceeding in which one spouse is charged with:

(a)   A crime committed at any time against the person or property of the other spouse or of a child of either.

(b)   A crime committed at any time against the person or property of a third person committed in the course of committing a crime against the person or property of the other spouse.

(c)   Bigamy.

(d)   A crime defined by Section 270 or 270a of the Penal Code.

§ 987.   Communication offered by spouse who is criminal defendant.

There is no privilege under this article in a criminal proceeding in which the communication is offered in evidence by a defendant who is one of the spouses between whom the communication was made.

PHYSICIAN-PATIENT PRIVILEGE

§ 990.   Physician.

As used in this article, "physician" means a person authorized, or reasonably believed by the patient to be authorized, to practice medicine in any state or nation.

§ 991.   Patient.

As used in this article, "patient" means a person who consults a physician or submits to an examination by a physician for the purpose of securing a diagnosis or preventive, palliative, or curative treatment of his physical or mental or emotional condition.

§ 992.   Confidential communication between patient and physician.

As used in this article, "confidential communication between patient and physician" means information, including information obtained by an examination of the patient, transmitted between a patient and his physician in the course of that relationship and in confidence by a means which, so far as the patient is aware, discloses the information to no third persons other than those who are present to further the interest of the patient in the consultation or those to whom disclosure is reasonably necessary for the transmission of the information or the accomplishment of the purpose for which the physician is consulted, and includes a diagnosis made and the advice given by the physician in the course of that relationship.

§ 993.   Holder of the privilege.

As used in this article, "holder of the privilege" means:

(a)   The patient when he has no guardian or conservator.

(b)   A guardian or conservator of the patient when the patient has a guardian or conservator.

(c)   The personal representative of the patient if the patient is dead.

§ 994.   Physician-patient privilege.

Subject to Section 912 and except as otherwise provided in this article, the patient, whether or not a party, has a privilege to refuse to disclose, and to prevent another from disclosing, a confidential communication between patient and physician if the privilege is claimed by:

(a) The holder of the privilege;

(b) A person who is authorized to claim the privilege by the holder of the privilege; or

(c) The person who was the physician at the time of the confidential communication, but such person may not claim the privilege if there is no holder of the privilege in existence or if he or she is otherwise instructed by a person authorized to permit disclosure.

The relationship of a physician and patient shall exist between a medical or podiatry corporation as defined in the Medical Practice Act and the patient to whom it renders professional services, as well as between such patients and licensed physicians and surgeons employed by such corporation to render services to such patients. The word "persons" as used in this subdivision includes partnerships, corporations, limited liability companies, associations, and other groups and entities.

§ 995.   When physician required to claim privilege.

The physician who received or made a communication subject to the privilege under this article shall claim the privilege whenever he is present when the communication is sought to be disclosed and is authorized to claim the privilege under subdivision (c) of Section 994.

§ 996.   Patient-litigant exception.

There is no privilege under this article as to a communication relevant to an issue concerning the condition of the patient if such issue has been tendered by:

(a) The patient;

(b) Any party claiming through or under the patient;

(c) Any party claiming as a beneficiary of the patient through a contract to which the patient is or was a party; or

(d) The plaintiff in an action brought under Section 376 or 377 of the Code of Civil Procedure for damages for the injury or death of the patient.

§ 997.   Exception: crime or tort.

There is no privilege under this article if the services of the physician were sought or obtained to enable or aid anyone to commit or plan to commit a crime or a tort or to escape detection or apprehension after the commission of a crime or a tort.

§ 998.   Criminal proceeding.

There is no privilege under this article in a criminal proceeding.

§ 999.   Communication relating to patient condition in proceeding to recover damages; good cause.

There is no privilege under this article as to a communication relevant to an issue concerning the condition of the patient in a proceeding to recover damages on account of the conduct of the patient if good cause for disclosure of the communication is shown.

§ 1000.   Parties claiming through deceased patient.

There is no privilege under this article as to a communication relevant to an issue between parties all of whom claim through a deceased patient, regardless of whether the claims are by testate or intestate succession or by inter vivos transaction.

§ 1001.   Breach of duty arising out of physician-patient relationship.

There is no privilege under this article as to a communication relevant to an issue of breach, by the physician or by the patient, of a duty arising out of the physician-patient relationship.

§ 1002.   Intention of decreased patient concerning writing affecting property interest.

There is no privilege under this article as to a communication relevant to an issue concerning the intention of a patient, now deceased, with respect to a deed of conveyance, will, or other writing, executed by the patient, purporting to affect an interest in property.

§ 1004.   Commitment or similar proceeding.

There is no privilege under this article in a proceeding to commit the patient or otherwise place him or his property, or both, under the control of another because of his alleged mental or physical condition.

§ 1005.   Proceeding to establish competence.

There is no privilege under this article in a proceeding brought by or on behalf of the patient to establish his competence.

§ 1006. Required report.

There is no privilege under this article as to information that the physician or the patient is required to report to a public employee, or as to information required to be recorded in a public office, if such report or record is open to public inspection.

§ 1007. Proceeding to terminate right, license or privilege.

There is no privilege under this article in a proceeding brought by a public entity to determine whether a right, authority, license, or privilege (including the right or privilege to be employed by the public entity or to hold a public office) should be revoked, suspended, terminated, limited, or conditioned.

PSYCHOTHERAPIST-PATIENT PRIVILEGE

§ 1010. Psychotherapist.

As used in this article, "psychotherapist" means a person who is, or is reasonably believed by the patient to be:

(a) A person authorized to practice medicine in any state or nation who devotes, or is reasonably believed by the patient to devote, a substantial portion of his or her time to the practice of psychiatry.

(b) A person licensed as a psychologist under Chapter 6.6 (commencing with Section 2900) of Division 2 of the Business and Professions Code.

(c) A person licensed as a clinical social worker under Article 4 (commencing with Section 4996) of Chapter 14 of Division 2 of the Business and Professions Code, when he or she is engaged in applied psychotherapy of a nonmedical nature. . . .

§ 1010.5. Privileged communication between patient and educational psychologist.

A communication between a patient and an educational psychologist, licensed under Article 5 (commencing with Section 4986) of Chapter 13 of Division 2 of the Business and Professions Code, shall be privileged to the same extent, and subject to the same limitations, as a communication between a patient and a psychotherapist described in subdivisions (c), (d), and (e) of Section 1010.

§ 1011. Patient.

As used in this article, "patient" means a person who consults a psychotherapist or submits to an examination by a psychotherapist for the purpose of securing a diagnosis or preventive, palliative, or curative treatment of his mental or emotional condition or who submits to an examination of his mental or emotional condition for the purpose of scientific research on mental or emotional problems.

§ 1012. Confidential communication between patient and psychotherapist.

As used in this article, "confidential communication between patient and psychotherapist" means information, including information obtained by an examination of the patient, transmitted between a patient and his psychotherapist in the course of that relationship and in confidence by a means which, so far as the patient is aware, discloses the information to no third persons other than those who are present to further the interest of the patient in the consultation, or those to whom disclosure is reasonably necessary for the transmission of the information or the accomplishment of the purpose for which the psychotherapist is consulted, and includes a diagnosis made and the advice given by the psychotherapist in the course of that relationship.

§ 1013. Holder of the privilege.

As used in this article, "holder of the privilege" means:

(a)   The patient when he has no guardian or conservator.

(b)   A guardian or conservator of the patient when the patient has a guardian or conservator.

(c)   The personal representative of the patient if the patient is dead.

§ 1014. Psychotherapist-patient privilege; application to individuals and entities.

Subject to Section 912 and except as otherwise provided in this article, the patient, whether or not a party, has a privilege to refuse to disclose, and to prevent another from disclosing, a confidential communication between patient and psychotherapist if the privilege is claimed by:

(a)   The holder of the privilege.

(b)   A person who is authorized to claim the privilege by the holder of the privilege.

(c)   The person who was the psychotherapist at the time of the confidential communication, but the person may not claim the privilege if there is no holder of the privilege in existence or if he or she is otherwise instructed by a person authorized to permit disclosure.

§ 1015. When psychotherapist required to claim privilege.

The psychotherapist who received or made a communication subject to the privilege under this article shall claim the privilege whenever he is present when the communication is sought to be disclosed and is authorized to claim the privilege under subdivision (c) of Section 1014.

§ 1016. Exception: Patient-litigant exception.

There is no privilege under this article as to a communication relevant to an issue concerning the mental or emotional condition of the patient if such issue has been tendered by:

    (a)   The patient;

    (b)   Any party claiming through or under the patient;

    (c)   Any party claiming as a beneficiary of the patient through a contract to which the patient is or was a party; or

    (d)   The plaintiff in an action brought under Section 376 or 377 of the Code of Civil Procedure for damages for the injury or death of the patient.

§ 1017. Exception: Psychotherapist appointed by court or board of prison terms.

    (a)   There is no privilege under this article if the psychotherapist is appointed by order of a court to examine the patient, but this exception does not apply where the psychotherapist is appointed by order of the court upon the request of the lawyer for the defendant in a criminal proceeding in order to provide the lawyer with information needed so that he or she may advise the defendant whether to enter or withdraw a plea based on insanity or to present a defense based on his or her mental or emotional condition.

    (b)   There is no privilege under this article if the psychotherapist is appointed by the Board of Prison Terms to examine a patient pursuant to the provisions of Article 4 (commencing with Section 2960) of Chapter 7 of Title 1 of Part 3 of the Penal Code.

§ 1018. Exception: Crime or tort.

There is no privilege under this article if the services of the psychotherapist were sought or obtained to enable or aid anyone to commit or plan to commit a crime or a tort or to escape detection or apprehension after the commission of a crime or a tort.

§ 1019. Exception: Parties claiming through deceased patient.

There is no privilege under this article as to a communication relevant to an issue between parties all of whom claim through a deceased patient, regardless of whether the claims are by testate or intestate succession or by inter vivos transaction.

§ 1020. Exception: Breach of duty arising out of psychotherapist-patient relationship.

There is no privilege under this article as to a communication relevant to an issue of breach, by the psychotherapist or by the patient, of a duty arising out of the psychotherapist-patient relationship.

§ 1023. Exception: Proceeding to determine sanity of criminal defendant.

There is no privilege under this article in a proceeding under Chapter 6 (commencing with Section 1367) of Title 10 of Part 2 of the Penal Code initiated at the request of the defendant in a criminal action to determine his sanity.

§ 1024. Exception: Patient dangerous to himself or others.

There is no privilege under this article if the psychotherapist has reasonable cause to believe that the patient is in such mental or emotional condition as to be dangerous to himself or to the person or property of another and that disclosure of the communication is necessary to prevent the threatened danger.

§ 1025. Exception: Proceeding to establish competence.

There is no privilege under this article in a proceeding brought by or on behalf of the patient to establish his competence.

§ 1026. Exception: Required report.

There is no privilege under this article as to information that the psychotherapist or the patient is required to report to a public employee or as to information required to be recorded in a public office, if such report or record is open to public inspection.

§ 1027. Exception: Child under 16 victim of crime.

There is no privilege under this article if all of the following circumstances exist:

(a) The patient is a child under the age of 16.

(b) The psychotherapist has reasonable cause to believe that the patient has been the victim of a crime and that disclosure of the communication is in the best interest of the child.

CLERGY PENITENT PRIVILEGES

§ 1030.   Member of the clergy.

As used in this article, a "member of the clergy" means a priest, minister, religious practitioner, or similar functionary of a church or of a religious denomination or religious organization.

§ 1031.   Penitent.

As used in this article, "penitent" means a person who has made a penitential communication to a member of the clergy.

§ 1032.   Penitential communication.

As used in this article, "penitential communication" means a communication made in confidence, in the presence of no third person so far as the penitent is aware, to a member of the clergy who, in the course of the discipline or practice of the clergy member's church, denomination, or organization, is authorized or accustomed to hear those communications and, under the discipline or tenets of his or her church, denomination, or organization, has a duty to keep those communications secret.

§ 1033.   Privilege of penitent.

Subject to Section 912, a penitent, whether or not a party, has a privilege to refuse to disclose, and to prevent another from disclosing, a penitential communication if he or she claims the privilege.

§ 1034.   Privilege of clergy.

Subject to Section 912, a member of the clergy, whether or not a party, has a privilege to refuse to disclose a penitential communication if he or she claims the privilege.

OFFICIAL INFORMATION AND
IDENTITY OF INFORMER

§ 1040.   Privilege for official information.

(a)   As used in this section, "official information" means information acquired in confidence by a public employee in the course of his or her duty and not open, or officially disclosed, to the public prior to the time the claim of privilege is made.

(b)   A public entity has a privilege to refuse to disclose official information, and to prevent another from disclosing official information, if the privilege is claimed by a person authorized by the public entity to do so and:

(1)   Disclosure is forbidden by an act of the Congress of the United States or a statute of this state; or

(2) Disclosure of the information is against the public interest because there is a necessity for preserving the confidentiality of the information that outweighs the necessity for disclosure in the interest of justice; but no privilege may be claimed under this paragraph if any person authorized to do so has consented that the information be disclosed in the proceeding. In determining whether disclosure of the information is against the public interest, the interest of the public entity as a party in the outcome of the proceeding may not be considered.

(c) Notwithstanding any other provision of law, the Employment Development Department shall disclose to law enforcement agencies, in accordance with the provisions of subdivision (k) of Section 1095 and subdivision (b) of Section 2714 of the Unemployment Insurance Code, information in its possession relating to any person if an arrest warrant has been issued for the person for commission of a felony.

§ 1041. Privilege for identity of informer.

(a) Except as provided in this section, a public entity has a privilege to refuse to disclose the identity of a person who has furnished information as provided in subdivision (b) purporting to disclose a violation of a law of the United States or of this state or of a public entity in this state, and to prevent another from disclosing such identity, if the privilege is claimed by a person authorized by the public entity to do so and:

(1) Disclosure is forbidden by an act of the Congress of the United States or a statute of this state; or

(2) Disclosure of the identity of the informer is against the public interest because there is a necessity for preserving the confidentiality of his identity that outweighs the necessity for disclosure in the interest of justice; but no privilege may be claimed under this paragraph if any person authorized to do so has consented that the identity of the informer be disclosed in the proceeding. In determining whether disclosure of the identity of the informer is against the public interest, the interest of the public entity as a party in the outcome of the proceeding may not be considered.

(b) This section applies only if the information is furnished in confidence by the informer to:

(1) A law enforcement officer;

(2) A representative of an administrative agency charged with the administration or enforcement of the law alleged to be violated; or

(3) Any person for the purpose of transmittal to a person listed in paragraph (1) or (2).

(c) There is no privilege under this section to prevent the informer from disclosing his identity.

PRIVILEGE TO PROTECT SECRECY OF VOTE

§ 1050. Privilege to protect secrecy of vote.

If he claims the privilege, a person has a privilege to refuse to disclose the tenor of his vote at a public election where the voting is by secret ballot unless he voted illegally or he previously made an unprivileged disclosure of the tenor of his vote.

IMMUNITY OF NEWSMAN FROM CITATION FOR CONTEMPT

§ 1070. Refusal to disclose news source.

(a) A publisher, editor, reporter, or other person connected with or employed upon a newspaper, magazine, or other periodical publication, or by a press association or wire service, or any person who has been so connected or employed, cannot be adjudged in contempt by a judicial, legislative, administrative body, or any other body having the power to issue subpoenas, for refusing to disclose, in any proceeding as defined in Section 901, the source of any information procured while so connected or employed for publication in a newspaper, magazine or other periodical publication, or for refusing to disclose any unpublished information obtained or prepared in gathering, receiving or processing of information for communication to the public.

EVIDENCE OF CHARACTER, HABIT, OR CUSTOM

§ 1100. Manner of proof of character.

Except as otherwise provided by statute, any otherwise admissible evidence (including evidence in the form of an opinion, evidence of reputation, and evidence of specific instances of such person's conduct) is admissible to prove a person's character or a trait of his character.

§ 1101. Evidence of character to prove conduct.

(a) Except as provided in this section and in Sections 1102, 1103, 1108, and 1109, evidence of a person's character or a trait of his or her character (whether in the form of an opinion, evidence of reputation, or evidence of specific instances of his or her conduct) is inadmissible when offered to prove his or her conduct on a specified occasion.

(b)　Nothing in this section prohibits the admission of evidence that a person committed a crime, civil wrong, or other act when relevant to prove some fact (such as motive, opportunity, intent, preparation, plan, knowledge, identity, absence of mistake or accident, or whether a defendant in a prosecution for an unlawful sexual act or attempted unlawful sexual act did not reasonably and in good faith believe that the victim consented) other than his or her disposition to commit such an act.

(c)　Nothing in this section affects the admissibility of evidence offered to support or attack the credibility of a witness.

§ 1102. Opinion and reputation evidence of character of criminal defendant to prove conduct.

In a criminal action, evidence of the defendant's character or a trait of his character in the form of an opinion or evidence of his reputation is not made inadmissible by Section 1101 if such evidence is:

(a)　Offered by the defendant to prove his conduct in conformity with such character or trait of character.

(b)　Offered by the prosecution to rebut evidence adduced by the defendant under subdivision (a).

§ 1103. Character evidence of crime victim to prove conduct; evidence of defendant's character or trait for violence; evidence of manner of dress of victim; evidence of complaining witness' sexual conduct.

(a)　In a criminal action, evidence of the character or a trait of character (in the form of an opinion, evidence of reputation, or evidence of specific instances of conduct) of the victim of the crime for which the defendant is being prosecuted is not made inadmissible by Section 1101 if the evidence is:

(1)　Offered by the defendant to prove conduct of the victim in conformity with the character or trait of character.

(2)　Offered by the prosecution to rebut evidence adduced by the defendant under paragraph (1).

(b)　In a criminal action, evidence of the defendant's character for violence or trait of character for violence (in the form of an opinion, evidence of reputation, or evidence of specific instances of conduct) is not made inadmissible by Section 1101 if the evidence is offered by the prosecution to prove conduct of the defendant in conformity with the character or trait of character and is offered after evidence that the victim had a character for violence or a trait of character tending to show violence has been adduced by the defendant under paragraph (1) of subdivision (a).

(c) (1)   Notwithstanding any other provision of this code to the contrary, and except as provided in this subdivision, in any prosecution under Section 261, 262, or 264.1 of the Penal Code, or under Section 286, 288a, or 289 of the Penal Code, or for assault with intent to commit, attempt to commit, or conspiracy to commit a crime defined in any of those sections, except where the crime is alleged to have occurred in a local detention facility, as defined in Section 6031.4, or in a state prison, as defined in Section 4504, opinion evidence, reputation evidence, and evidence of specific instances of the complaining witness' sexual conduct, or any of that evidence, is not admissible by the defendant in order to prove consent by the complaining witness.

(2)   Notwithstanding paragraph (3), evidence of the manner in which the victim was dressed at the time of the commission of the offense shall not be admissible when offered by either party on the issue of consent in any prosecution for an offense specified in paragraph (1), unless the evidence is determined by the court to be relevant and admissible in the interests of justice. The proponent of the evidence shall make an offer of proof outside the hearing of the jury. The court shall then make its determination and at that time, state the reasons for its ruling on the record. For the purposes of this paragraph, "manner of dress" does not include the condition of the victim's clothing before, during, or after the commission of the offense.

(3)   Paragraph (1) shall not be applicable to evidence of the complaining witness' sexual conduct with the defendant.

(4)   If the prosecutor introduces evidence, including testimony of a witness, or the complaining witness as a witness gives testimony, and that evidence or testimony relates to the complaining witness' sexual conduct, the defendant may cross-examine the witness who gives the testimony and offer relevant evidence limited specifically to the rebuttal of the evidence introduced by the prosecutor or given by the complaining witness.

(5)   Nothing in this subdivision shall be construed to make inadmissible any evidence offered to attack the credibility of the complaining witness as provided in Section 782.

(6)   As used in this section, "complaining witness" means the alleged victim of the crime charged, the prosecution of which is subject to this subdivision.

§ 1104.   Character trait for care or skill.

Except as provided in Sections 1102 and 1103, evidence of a trait of a person's character with respect to care or skill is inadmissible to prove the quality of his conduct on a specified occasion.

§ 1105.   Habit or custom to prove specific behavior.

Any otherwise admissible evidence of habit or custom is admissible to prove conduct on a specified occasion in conformity with the habit or custom.

§ 1106.   Sexual harassment, sexual assault, or sexual battery cases; opinion or reputation evidence of plaintiff's sexual conduct; inadmissibility; exception; cross-examination.

(a)   In any civil action alleging conduct which constitutes sexual harassment, sexual assault, or sexual battery, opinion evidence, reputation evidence, and evidence of specific instances of plaintiff's sexual conduct, or any of such evidence, is not admissible by the defendant in order to prove consent by the plaintiff or the absence of injury to the plaintiff, unless the injury alleged by the plaintiff is in the nature of loss of consortium.

(b)   Subdivision (a) shall not be applicable to evidence of the plaintiff's sexual conduct with the alleged perpetrator.

(c)   If the plaintiff introduces evidence, including testimony of a witness, or the plaintiff as a witness gives testimony, and the evidence or testimony relates to the plaintiff's sexual conduct, the defendant may cross-examine the witness who gives the testimony and offer relevant evidence limited specifically to the rebuttal of the evidence introduced by the plaintiff or given by the plaintiff.

(d)   Nothing in this section shall be construed to make inadmissible any evidence offered to attack the credibility of the plaintiff as provided in Section 783.

§ 1107.   Intimate partner battering and its effects; expert testimony in criminal actions; sufficiency of foundation; abuse and domestic violence; applicability to Penal Code; impact on decisional law.

(a)   In a criminal action, expert testimony is admissible by either the prosecution or the defense regarding intimate partner battering and its effects, including the nature and effect of physical, emotional, or mental abuse on the beliefs, perceptions, or behavior of victims of domestic violence, except when offered against a criminal defendant to prove the occurrence of the act or acts of abuse which form the basis of the criminal charge.

§ 1108. Evidence of another sexual offense by defendant; disclosure; construction of section.

(a)   In a criminal action in which the defendant is accused of a sexual offense, evidence of the defendant's commission of another sexual offense or offenses is not made inadmissible by Section 1101, if the evidence is not inadmissible pursuant to Section 352.

§ 1109. Evidence of defendant's other acts of domestic violence.

(a) (1)   Except as provided in subdivision (e) or (f), in a criminal action in which the defendant is accused of an offense involving domestic violence, evidence of the defendant's commission of other domestic violence is not made inadmissible by Section 1101 if the evidence is not inadmissible pursuant to Section 352.

OTHER EVIDENCE AFFECTED OR EXCLUDED BY EXTRINSIC POLICIES

§ 1151. Subsequent remedial conduct.

When, after the occurrence of an event, remedial or precautionary measures are taken, which, if taken, previously, would have tended to make the event less likely to occur, evidence of such subsequent measures is inadmissible to prove negligence or culpable conduct in connection with the event.

§ 1152. Offers to compromise.

(a)   Evidence that a person has, in compromise or from humanitarian motives, furnished or offered or promised to furnish money or any other thing, act, or service to another who has sustained or will sustain or claims that he or she has sustained or will sustain loss or damage, as well as any conduct or statements made in negotiation thereof, is inadmissible to prove his or her liability for the loss or damage or any part of it. . . .

§ 1153. Offer to plead guilty or withdrawn plea of guilty by criminal defendant.

Evidence of a plea of guilty, later withdrawn, or of an offer to plead guilty to the crime charged or to any other crime, made by the defendant in a criminal action is inadmissible in any action or in any proceeding of any nature, including proceedings before agencies, commissions, boards, and tribunals.

§ 1155. Liability insurance.

Evidence that a person was, at the time a harm was suffered by another, insured wholly or partially against loss arising from liability for that harm is inadmissible to prove negligence or other wrongdoing.

§ 1160. Admissibility of expressions of sympathy or benevolence; definitions.

(a) The portion of statements, writings, or benevolent gestures expressing sympathy or a general sense of benevolence relating to the pain, suffering, or death of a person involved in an accident and made to that person or to the family of that person shall be inadmissible as evidence of an admission of liability in a civil action. A statement of fault, however, which is part of, or in addition to, any of the above shall not be inadmissible pursuant to this section.

HEARSAY EVIDENCE

§ 1200. The hearsay rule.

(a) "Hearsay evidence" is evidence of a statement that was made other than by a witness while testifying at the hearing and that is offered to prove the truth of the matter states.

(b) Except as provided by law, hearsay evidence is inadmissible.

(c) This section shall be known and may be cited as the hearsay rule.

§ 1201. Multiple hearsay.

A statement within the scope of an exception to the hearsay rule is not inadmissible on the ground that the evidence of such statement is hearsay evidence if such hearsay evidence consists of one or more statements each of which meets the requirements of an exception to the hearsay rule.

§ 1202. Credibility of hearsay declarant.

Evidence of a statement or other conduct by a declarant that is inconsistent with a statement by such declarant received in evidence as hearsay evidence is not inadmissible for the purpose of attacking the credibility of the declarant though he is not given and has not had an opportunity to explain or to deny such inconsistent statement or conduct. Any other evidence offered to attack or support the credibility of the declarant is admissible if it would have been admissible had the declarant been a witness at the hearing. For the purposes of this section, the deponent of a deposition taken in the action in which it is offered shall be deemed to be a hearsay declarant.

CONFESSIONS AND ADMISSIONS

§ 1220. Admission of party.

Evidence of a statement is not made inadmissible by the hearsay rule when offered against the declarant in an action to which he is a party in either his individual or representative capacity, regardless of whether the statement was made in his individual or representative capacity.

§ 1221. Adoptive admission.

Evidence of a statement offered against a party is not made inadmissible by the hearsay rule if the statement is one of which the party, with knowledge of the content thereof, has by words or other conduct manifested his adoption or his belief in its truth.

§ 1222. Authorized Admission.

Evidence of a statement offered against a party is not made inadmissible by the hearsay rule if:

(a) The statement was made by a person authorized by the party to make a statement or statements for him concerning the subject matter of the statement; and

(b) The evidence is offered either after admission of evidence sufficient to sustain a finding of such authority or, in the court's discretion as to the order of proof, subject to the admission of such evidence.

§ 1223. Admission of Co-Conspirator.

Evidence of a statement offed against a party is not made inadmissible by the hearsay rule if:

(a) The statement was made by the declarant while participating in a conspiracy to commit a crime or civil wrong and in furtherance of the objective of that conspiracy;

(b) The statement was made prior to or during the time that the party was participating in that conspiracy; and

(c) The evidence is offered either after admission of evidence sufficient to sustain a finding of the facts specified in subdivision (a) and (b) or, in court's discretion as to the order of proof, subject to the admission of such evidence.

§ 1224. Statement of Declarant Whose Liability or Breath of Duty is in Issue.

When the liability, obligation, or duty of a party to a civil action is based in whole or in part upon the liability, obligation, or duty of the declarant, or when the claim or right asserted by a party to a civil action is barred or diminished by a breath of duty by the declarant, evidence of a statement made by the declarant is an admissible against the party as it would be if offered against the declarant in an action involving that liability, obligation, duty, or breach of duty.

DECLARATIONS AGAINST INTEREST

§ 1230.   Declarations against interest.

Evidence of a statement by a declarant having sufficient knowledge of the subject is not made inadmissible by the hearsay rule if the declarant is unavailable as a witness and the statement, when made, was so far contrary to the declarant's pecuniary or proprietary interest, or so far subjected him to the risk of civil or criminal liability, or so far tended to render invalid a claim by him against another, or created such a risk of making him an object of hatred, ridicule, or social disgrace in the community, that a reasonable man in his position would not have made the statement unless he believed it to be true.

PRIOR STATEMENTS OF WITNESSES

§ 1235.   Inconsistent statements.

Evidence of a statement made by a witness is not made inadmissible by the hearsay rule if the statement is inconsistent with his testimony at the hearing and is offered in compliance with Section 770.

§ 1236.   Prior consistent statements.

Evidence of a statement previously made by a witness is not made inadmissible by the hearsay rule if the statement is consistent with his testimony at the hearing and is offered in compliance with Section 791.

§ 1237.   Past recollection recorded.

(a)   Evidence of a statement previously made by a witness is not made inadmissible by the hearsay rule if the statement would have been admissible if made by him while testifying, the statement concerns a matter as to which the witness has insufficient present recollection to enable him to testify fully and accurately, and the statement is contained in a writing which:

(1)   Was made at a time when the fact recorded in the writing actually occurred or was fresh in the witness' memory;

(2)   Was made (i) by the witness himself or under his direction or (ii) by some other person for the purpose of recording the witness' statement at the time it was made;

(3) Is offered after the witness testifies that the statement he made was a true statement of such fact; and

(4) Is offered after the writing is authenticated as an accurate record of the statement.

(b) The writing may be read into evidence, but the writing itself may not be received in evidence unless offered by an adverse party.

§ 1238. Prior identification.

Evidence of a statement previously made by a witness is not made inadmissible by the hearsay rule if the statement would have been admissible if made by him while testifying and:

(a) The statement is an identification of a party or another as a person who participated in a crime or other occurrence;

(b) The statement was made at a time when the crime or other occurrence was fresh in the witness' memory; and

(c) The evidence of the statement is offered after the witness testifies that he made the identification and that it was a true reflection of his opinion at that time.

SPONTANEOUS, CONTEMPORANEOUS, AND DYING DECLARATIONS

§ 1240. Spontaneous statement.

Evidence of a statement is not made inadmissible by the hearsay rule if the statement:

(a) Purports to narrate, describe, or explain an act, condition, or event perceived by the declarant; and

(b) Was made spontaneously while the declarant was under the stress of excitement caused by such perception.

§ 1241. Contemporaneous statement.

Evidence of a statement is not made inadmissible by the hearsay rule if the statement:

(a) Is offered to explain, qualify, or make understandable conduct of the declarant; and

(b) Was made while the declarant was engaged in such conduct.

§ 1242. Dying declaration.

Evidence of a statement made by a dying person respecting the cause and circumstances of his death is not made inadmissible by the hearsay rule if the statement was made upon his personal knowledge and under a sense of immediately impending death.

STATEMENTS OF MENTAL OR PHYSICAL HEALTH

§ 1250. Statement of declarant's then existing mental or physical state.

(a) Subject to Section 1252, evidence of a statement of the declarant's then existing state of mind, emotion, or physical sensation (including a statement of intent, plan, motive, design, mental feeling, pain, or bodily health) is not made inadmissible by the hearsay rule when:

(1) The evidence is offered to prove the declarant's state of mind, emotion, or physical sensation at that time or at any other time when it is itself an issue in the action; or

(2) The evidence is offered to prove or explain acts or conduct of the declarant.

(b) This section does not make admissible evidence of a statement of memory or belief to prove the fact remembered or believed.

§ 1251. Statement of declarant's previously existing mental or physical state.

Subject to Section 1252, evidence of a statement of the declarant's state of mind, emotion, or physical sensation (including a statement of intent, plan, motive, design, mental feeling, pain, or bodily health) at a time prior to the statement is not made inadmissible by the hearsay rule if:

(a) The declarant is unavailable as a witness; and

(b) The evidence is offered to prove such prior state of mind, emotion, or physical sensation when it is itself an issue in the action and the evidence is not offered to prove any fact other than such state of mind, emotion, or physical sensation.

§ 1252. Restriction on admissibility of statement of mental or physical state.

Evidence of a statement is inadmissible under this article if the statement was made under circumstances such as to indicate its lack of trustworthiness.

§ 1253. Statements for purposes of medical diagnosis or treatment; contents of statement; child abuse or neglect; age limitations.

Subject to Section 1252, evidence of a statement is not made inadmissible by the hearsay rule if the statement was made for purposes of medical diagnosis or treatment and describes medical history, or past or present symptoms, pain, or sensations, or the inception or general character of the cause or external source thereof insofar as reasonably pertinent to diagnosis or treatment. This section applies only to a statement made by a victim who is a minor at the time of the proceedings, provided the statement was made when the victim was under the age of 12 describing any act, or attempted act, of child abuse or neglect. "Child abuse" and "child neglect," for purposes of this section, have the meanings provided in subdivision (c) of Section 1360. In addition, "child abuse" means any act proscribed by Chapter 5 (commencing with Section 281) of Title 9 of Part 1 of the Penal Code committed against a minor.

STATEMENTS RELATING TO WILLS AND TO CLAIMS AGAINST ESTATES

§ 1260. Statements concerning declarant's will or revocable trust.

(a) Evidence of a statement made by a declarant who is unavailable as a witness that he has or has not made a will, or has or has not revoked his will, or that identifies his will, is not made inadmissible by the hearsay rule.

(b) Evidence of a statement is inadmissible under this section if the statement was made under circumstances such as to indicate its lack of trustworthiness.

§ 1261. Statement of decedent offered in action against his estate.

(a) Evidence of a statement is not made inadmissible by the hearsay rule when offered in an action upon a claim or demand against the estate of the declarant if the statement was made upon the personal knowledge of the declarant at a time when the matter had been recently perceived by him and while his recollection was clear.

(b) Evidence of a statement is inadmissible under this section if the statement was made under circumstances such as to indicate its lack of trustworthiness.

BUSINESS RECORDS

§ 1270. A business.

As used in this article, "a business" includes every kind of business, governmental activity, profession, occupation, calling, or operation of institutions, whether carried on for profit or not.

§ 1271. Admissible writings.

Evidence of a writing made as a record of an act, condition, or event is not made inadmissible by the hearsay rule when offered to prove the act, condition, or event if:

(a) The writing was made in the regular course of a business;

(b) The writing was made at or near the time of the act, condition, or event;

(c) The custodian or other qualified witness testifies to its identity and the mode of its preparation; and

(d) The sources of information and method and time of preparation were such as to indicate its trustworthiness.

§ 1272. Absence of entry in business records.

Evidence of the absence from the records of a business of a record of an asserted act, condition, or event is not made inadmissible by the hearsay rule when offered to prove the nonoccurrence of the act or event, or the nonexistence of the condition, if:

(a) It was the regular course of that business to make records of all such acts, conditions, or events at or near the time of the act, condition, or event and to preserve them; and

(b) The sources of information and method and time of preparation of the records of that business were such that the absence of a record of an act, condition, or event is a trustworthy indication that the act or event did not occur or the condition did not exist.

OFFICIAL RECORDS AND OTHER OFFICIAL WRITINGS

§ 1280. Record by public employee.

Evidence of a writing made as a record of an act, condition, or event is not made inadmissible by the hearsay rule when offered in any civil or criminal proceeding to prove the act, condition, or event if all of the following applies:

(a) The writing was made by and within the scope of duty of a public employee.

(b) The writing was made at or near the time of the act, condition, or event.

(c) The sources of information and method and time of preparation were such as to indicate its trustworthiness.

§ 1281. Vital statistics records.

Evidence of a writing made as a record of a birth, fetal death, death, or marriage is not made inadmissible by the hearsay rule if the maker was required by law to file the writing in a designated public office and the writing was made and filed as required by law.

§ 1284. Statement of absence of public record.

Evidence of a writing made by the public employee who is the official custodian of the records in a public office, reciting diligent search and failure to find a record, is not made inadmissible by the hearsay rule when offered to prove the absence of a record in that office.

FORMER TESTIMONY

§ 1290. Former testimony.

As used in this article, "former testimony" means testimony given under oath in:

(a) Another action or in a former hearing or trial of the same action;

(b) A proceeding to determine a controversy conducted by or under the supervision of an agency that has the power to determine such a controversy and is an agency of the United States or a public entity in the United States;

(c) A deposition taken in compliance with law in another action; or

(d) An arbitration proceeding if the evidence of such former testimony is a verbatim transcript thereof.

§ 1291. Former testimony offered against party to former proceeding.

(a) Evidence of former testimony is not made inadmissible by the hearsay rule if the declarant is unavailable as a witness and:

(1) The former testimony is offered against a person who offered it in evidence in his own behalf on the former occasion or against the successor in interest of such person; or

(2) The party against whom the former testimony is offered was a party to the action or proceeding in which the testimony was given and had the right and opportunity to cross-examine the declarant with an interest and motive similar to that which he has at the hearing.

(b) The admissibility of former testimony under this section is subject to the same limitations and objections as though the declarant were testifying at the hearing, except that former testimony offered under this section is not subject to:

(1) Objections to the form of the question which were not made at the time the former testimony was given.

(2) Objections based on competency or privilege which did not exist at the time the former testimony was given.

§ 1292. Former testimony offered against person not a party to former proceeding.

(a) Evidence of former testimony is not made inadmissible by the hearsay rule if:

(1) The declarant is unavailable as a witness;

(2) The former testimony is offered in a civil action; and

(3) The issue is such that the party to the action or proceeding in which the former testimony was given had the right and opportunity to cross-examine the declarant with an interest and motive similar to that which the party against whom the testimony is offered has at the hearing.

(b) The admissibility of former testimony under this section is subject to the same limitations and objections as though the declarant were testifying at the hearing, except that former testimony offered under this section is not subject to objections based on competency or privilege which did not exist at the time the former testimony was given.

JUDGMENTS

§ 1300. Judgment of conviction of crime punishable as felony.

Evidence of a final judgment adjudging a person guilty of a crime punishable as a felony is not made inadmissible by the hearsay rule when offered in a civil action to prove any fact essential to the judgment whether or not the judgment was based on a plea of nolo contendere.

REPUTATION AND STATEMENTS CONCERNING COMMUNITY HISTORY, PROPERTY INTERESTS, AND CHARACTER

§ 1320. Reputation concerning community history.

Evidence of reputation in a community is not made inadmissible by the hearsay rule if the reputation concerns an event of general history of the community or of the state or nation of which the community is a part and the event was of importance to the community.

§ 1322. Reputation concerning boundary or custom affecting land.

Evidence of reputation in a community is not made inadmissible by the hearsay rule if the reputation concerns boundaries of, or customs affecting, land in the community and the reputation arose before controversy.

§ 1324. Reputation concerning character.

Evidence of a person's general reputation with reference to his character or a trait of his character at a relevant time in the community in which he then resided or in a group with which he then habitually associated is not made inadmissible by the hearsay rule.

DISPOSITIVE INSTRUMENTS AND ANCIENT WRITINGS

§ 1330. Recitals in writings affecting property.

Evidence of a statement contained in a deed of conveyance or a will or other writing purporting to affect an interest in real or personal property is not made inadmissible by the hearsay rule if:

(a) The matter stated was relevant to the purpose of the writing;

(b) The matter stated would be relevant to an issue as to an interest in the property; and

(c) The dealings with the property since the statement was made have not been inconsistent with the truth of the statement.

§ 1331. Recitals in ancient writings.

Evidence of a statement is not made inadmissible by the hearsay rule if the statement is contained in a writing more than 30 years old and the statement has been since generally acted upon as true by persons having an interest in the matter.

COMMERCIAL, SCIENTIFIC, AND SIMILAR PUBLICATIONS

§ 1340. Publications relied upon as accurate in the course of business.

Evidence of a statement, other than an opinion, contained in a tabulation, list, directory, register, or other published compilation is not made inadmissible by the hearsay rule if the compilation is generally used and relied upon as accurate in the course of a business as defined in Section 1270.

§ 1341. Publications concerning facts of general notoriety and interests.

Historical works, books of science or art, and published maps or charts, made by persons indifferent between the parties, are not made inadmissible by the hearsay rule when offered to prove facts of general notoriety and interest.

DECLARANT UNAVAILABLE AS A WITNESS

§ 1350. Unavailable declarant; hearsay rule.

(a) In a criminal proceeding charging a serious felony, evidence of a statement made by a declarant is not made inadmissible by the hearsay rule if the declarant is unavailable as a witness, and all of the following are true:

(1) There is clear and convincing evidence that the declarant's unavailability was knowingly caused by, aided by, or solicited by the party against whom the statement is offered for the purpose of preventing the arrest or prosecution of the party and is the result of the death by homicide or the kidnapping of the declarant.

(2) There is no evidence that the unavailability of the declarant was caused by, aided by, solicited by, or procured on behalf of, the party who is offering the statement.

(3) The statement has been memorialized in a tape recording made by a law enforcement official, or in a written statement prepared by a law enforcement official and signed by the declarant and notarized in the presence of the law enforcement official, prior to the death or kidnapping of the declarant.

(4) The statement was made under circumstances which indicate its trustworthiness and was not the result of promise, inducement, threat, or coercion.

(5) The statement is relevant to the issues to be tried.

(6) The statement is corroborated by other evidence which tends to connect the party against whom the statement is offered with the commission of the serious felony with which the party is charged. The corroboration is not sufficient if it merely shows the commission of the offense or the circumstances thereof.

(b) If the prosecution intends to offer a statement pursuant to this section, the prosecution shall serve a written notice upon the defendant at least 10 days prior to the hearing or trial at which the prosecution intends to offer the statement, unless the prosecution shows good cause for the failure to provide that notice. In the event that good cause is shown, the defendant shall be entitled to a reasonable continuance of the hearing or trial.

(c) If the statement is offered during trial, the court's determination shall be made out of the presence of the jury. If the defendant elects to testify at the hearing on a motion brought pursuant to this section, the court shall exclude from the examination every person except the clerk, the court reporter, the bailiff, the prosecutor, the investigating officer, the defendant and his or her counsel, an investigator for the defendant, and the officer having custody of the defendant. Notwithstanding any other provision of law, the defendant's testimony at the hearing shall not be admissible in any other proceeding except the hearing brought on the motion pursuant to this section. If a transcript is made of the defendant's testimony, it shall be sealed and transmitted to the clerk of the court in which the action is pending.

(d) As used in this section, "serious felony" means any of the felonies listed in subdivision (c) of Section 1192.7 of the Penal Code or any violation of Section 11351, 11352, 11378, or 11379 of the Health and Safety Code.

(e) If a statement to be admitted pursuant to this section includes hearsay statements made by anyone other than the declarant who is unavailable pursuant to subdivision (a), those hearsay statements are inadmissible unless they meet the requirements of an exception to the hearsay rule.

§ 1360. Statements describing an act or attempted act of child abuse or neglect; criminal prosecutions; requirements.

(a) In a criminal prosecution where the victim is a minor, a statement made by the victim when under the age of 12 describing any act of child abuse or neglect performed with or on the child by another, or describing any attempted act of child abuse or neglect with or on the child by another, is not made inadmissible by the hearsay rule if all of the following apply:

(1) The statement is not otherwise admissible by statute or court rule.

(2) The court finds, in a hearing conducted outside the presence of the jury, that the time, content, and circumstances of the statement provide sufficient indicia of reliability.

(3) The child either:

(A) Testifies at the proceedings.

(B) Is unavailable as a witness, in which case the statement may be admitted only if there is evidence of the child abuse or neglect that corroborates the statement made by the child.

(b) A statement may not be admitted under this section unless the proponent of the statement makes known to the adverse party the intention to offer the statement and the particulars of the statement sufficiently in advance of the proceedings in order to provide the adverse party with a fair opportunity to prepare to meet the statement.

(c) For purposes of this section, "child abuse" means an act proscribed by Section 273a, 273d, or 288.5 of the Penal Code, or any of the acts described in Section 11165.1 of the Penal Code, and "child neglect" means any of the acts described in Section 11165.2 of the Penal Code.

PHYSICAL ABUSE

§ 1370.   Threat of infliction of injury.

(a) Evidence of a statement by a declarant is not made inadmissible by the hearsay rule if all of the following conditions are met:

(1)   The statement purports to narrate, describe, or explain the infliction or threat of physical injury upon the declarant.

(2)   The declarant is unavailable as a witness pursuant to Section 240.

(3)   The statement was made at or near the time of the infliction or threat of physical injury. Evidence of statements made more than five years before the filing of the current action or proceeding shall be inadmissible under this section.

(4)   The statement was made under circumstances that would indicate its trustworthiness.

(5)   The statement was made in writing, was electronically recorded, or made to a physician, nurse, paramedic, or to a law enforcement official.

(b)   For purposes of paragraph (4) of subdivision (a), circumstances relevant to the issue of trustworthiness include, but are not limited to, the following:

(1)   Whether the statement was made in contemplation of pending or anticipated litigation in which the declarant was interested.

(2)   Whether the declarant has a bias or motive for fabricating the statement, and the extent of any bias or motive.

(3)   Whether the statement is corroborated by evidence other than statements that are admissible only pursuant to this section.

(c)   A statement is admissible pursuant to this section only if the proponent of the statement makes known to the adverse party the intention to offer the statement and the particulars of the statement sufficiently in advance of the proceedings in order to provide the adverse party with a fair opportunity to prepare to meet the statement.

REQUIREMENT OF AUTHENTICATION

§ 1400.   Authentication.

Authentication of a writing means (a) the introduction of evidence sufficient to sustain a finding that it is the writing that the proponent of the evidence claims it is or (b) the establishment of such facts by any other means provided by law.

§ 1401.   Authentication required.

(a)   Authentication of a writing is required before it may be received in evidence.

(b)   Authentication of a writing is required before secondary evidence of its content may be received in evidence.

§ 1402.   Authentication of altered writings.

The party producing a writing as genuine which has been altered, or appears to have been altered, after its execution, in a part material to the question in dispute, must account for the alteration or appearance thereof. He may show that the alteration was made by another, without his concurrence, or was made with the consent of the parties affected by it, or otherwise properly or innocently made, or that the alteration did not change the meaning or language of the instrument. If he does that, he may give the writing in evidence, but not otherwise.

MEANS OF AUTHENTICATING AND PROVING WRITINGS

§ 1410.   Article not exclusive.

Nothing in this article shall be construed to limit the means by which a writing may be authenticated or proved.

§ 1411.   Subscribing witness' testimony unnecessary.

Except as provided by statute, the testimony of a subscribing witness is not required to authenticate a writing.

§ 1412.   Use of other evidence when subscribing witness' testimony required.

If the testimony of a subscribing witness is required by statute to authenticate a writing and the subscribing witness denies or does not recollect the execution of the writing, the writing may be authenticated by other evidence.

§ 1413. Witness to the execution of a writing.

A writing may be authenticated by anyone who saw the writing made or executed, including a subscribing witness.

§ 1414. Admission of authenticity; acting upon writing as authentic.

A writing may be authenticated by evidence that:

(a) The party against whom it is offered has at any time admitted its authenticity; or

(b) The writing has been acted upon as authentic by the party against whom it is offered.

§ 1415. Authentication by handwriting evidence.

A writing may be authenticated by evidence of the genuineness of the handwriting of the maker.

§ 1416. Proof of handwriting by person familiar therewith.

A witness who is not otherwise qualified to testify as an expert may state his opinion whether a writing is in the handwriting of a supposed writer if the court finds that he has personal knowledge of the handwriting of the supposed writer. Such personal knowledge may be acquired from:

(a) Having seen the supposed writer write;

(b) Having seen a writing purporting to be in the handwriting of the supposed writer and upon which the supposed writer has acted or been charged;

(c) Having received letters in the due course of mail purporting to be from the supposed writer in response to letters duly addressed and mailed by him to the supposed writer; or

(d) Any other means of obtaining personal knowledge of the handwriting of the supposed writer.

§ 1417. Comparison of handwriting by trier of fact.

The genuineness of handwriting, or the lack thereof, may be proved by a comparison made by the trier of fact with handwriting (a) which the court finds was admitted or treated as genuine by the party against whom the evidence is offered or (b) otherwise proved to be genuine to the satisfaction of the court.

§ 1418.   Comparison of writing by expert witness.

The genuineness of writing, or the lack thereof, may be proved by a comparison made by an expert witness with writing (a) which the court finds was admitted or treated as genuine by the party against whom the evidence is offered or (b) otherwise proved to be genuine to the satisfaction of the court.

§ 1419.   Exemplars when writing is more than 30 years old.

Where a writing whose genuineness is sought to be proved is more than 30 years old, the comparison under Section 1417 or 1418 may be made with writing purporting to be genuine, and generally respected and acted upon as such, by persons having an interest in knowing whether it is genuine.

§ 1420.   Authentication by evidence of reply.

A writing may be authenticated by evidence that the writing was received in response to a communication sent to the person who is claimed by the proponent of the evidence to be the author of the writing.

§ 1421.   Authentication by content.

A writing may be authenticated by evidence that the writing refers to or states matters that are unlikely to be known to anyone other than the person who is claimed by the proponent of the evidence to be the author of the writing.

PRESUMPTIONS AFFECTING ACKNOWLEDGED WRITINGS AND OFFICIAL WRITINGS

§ 1450.   Classification of presumptions in article.

The presumptions established by this article are presumptions affecting the burden of producing evidence.

§ 1451.   Acknowledged writings.

A certificate of the acknowledgment of a writing other than a will, or a certificate of the proof of such a writing, is prima facie evidence of the facts recited in the certificate and the genuineness of the signature of each person by whom the writing purports to have been signed if the certificate meets the requirements of Article 3 (commencing with Section 1180) of Chapter 4, Title 4, Part 4, Division 2 of the Civil Code.

§ 1452.   Official seals.

A seal is presumed to be genuine and its use authorized if it purports to be the seal of:

(a) The United States or a department, agency, or public employee of the United States.

(b) A public entity in the United States or a department, agency, or public employee of such public entity.

(c) A nation recognized by the executive power of the United States or a department, agency, or officer of such nation.

(d) A public entity in a nation recognized by the executive power of the United States or a department, agency, or officer of such public entity.

(e) A court of admiralty or maritime jurisdiction.

(f) A notary public within any state of the United States.

§ 1453. Domestic official signatures.

A signature is presumed to be genuine and authorized if it purports to be the signature, affixed in his official capacity, of:

(a) A public employee of the United States.

(b) A public employee of any public entity in the United States.

(c) A notary public within any state of the United States.

§ 1454. Foreign official signatures.

A signature is presumed to be genuine and authorized if it purports to be the signature, affixed in his official capacity, of an officer, or deputy of an officer, of a nation or public entity in a nation recognized by the executive power of the United States and the writing to which the signature is affixed is accompanied by a final statement certifying the genuineness of the signature and the official position of (a) the person who executed the writing or (b) any foreign official who has certified either the genuineness of the signature and official position of the person executing the writing or the genuineness of the signature and official position of another foreign official who has executed a similar certificate in a chain of such certificates beginning with a certificate of the genuineness of the signature and official position of the person executing the writing. The final statement may be made only by a secretary of an embassy or legation, consul general, consul, vice consul, consular agent, or other officer in the foreign service of the United States stationed in the nation, authenticated by the seal of his office.

PROOF OF THE CONTENT OF A WRITING

§ 1520. Content of writing; proof.

The content of a writing may be proved by an otherwise admissible original.

§ 1521. Secondary evidence rule.

(a) The content of a writing may be proved by otherwise admissible secondary evidence. The court shall exclude secondary evidence of the content of writing if the court determines either of the following:

(1) A genuine dispute exists concerning material terms of the writing and justice requires the exclusion.

(2) Admission of the secondary evidence would be unfair.

(b) Nothing in this section makes admissible oral testimony to prove the content of a writing if the testimony is inadmissible under Section 1523 (oral testimony of the content of a writing).

(c) Nothing in this section excuses compliance with Section 1401 (authentication).

(d) This section shall be known as the "Secondary Evidence Rule."

§ 1522. Additional grounds for exclusion of secondary evidence.

(a) In addition to the grounds for exclusion authorized by Section 1521, in a criminal action the court shall exclude secondary evidence of the content of a writing if the court determines that the original is in the proponent's possession, custody, or control, and the proponent has not made the original reasonably available for inspection at or before trial. This section does not apply to any of the following:

(1) A duplicate as defined in Section 260.

(2) A writing that is not closely related to the controlling issues in the action.

(3) A copy of a writing in the custody of a public entity.

(4) A copy of a writing that is recorded in the public records, if the record or a certified copy of it is made evidence of the writing by statute.

(b) In a criminal action, a request to exclude secondary evidence of the content of a writing, under this section or any other law, shall not be made in the presence of the jury.

§ 1523. Oral testimony of the content of a writing; admissibility.

(a) Except as otherwise provided by statute, oral testimony is not admissible to prove the content of a writing.

(b) Oral testimony of the content of a writing is not made inadmissible by subdivision (a) if the proponent does not have possession or control of a copy of the writing and the original is lost or has been destroyed without fraudulent intent on the part of the proponent of the evidence.

(c) Oral testimony of the content of a writing is not made inadmissible by subdivision (a) if the proponent does not have possession or control of the original or a copy of the writing and either of the following conditions is satisfied:

(1) Neither the writing nor a copy of the writing was reasonably procurable by the proponent by use of the court's process or by other available means.

(2) The writing is not closely related to the controlling issues and it would be inexpedient to require its production.

(d) Oral testimony of the content of a writing is not made inadmissible by subdivision (a) if the writing consists of numerous accounts or other writings that cannot be examined in court without great loss of time, and the evidence sought from them is only the general result of the whole.

§ 1530. Copy of writing in official custody.

(a) A purported copy of a writing in the custody of a public entity, or of an entry in such a writing, is prima facie evidence of the existence and content of such writing or entry if:

(1) The copy purports to be published by the authority of the nation or state, or public entity therein in which the writing is kept;

§ 1531. Certification of copy for evidence.

For the purpose of evidence, whenever a copy of a writing is attested or certified, the attestation or certificate must state in substance that the copy is a correct copy of the original, or of a specified part thereof, as the case may be.

§ 1532. Official record of recorded writing.

(a) The official record of a writing is prima facie evidence of the existence and content of the original recorded writing if:

(1) The record is in fact a record of an office of a public entity; and

(2) A statute authorized such a writing to be recorded in that office.

(b) The presumption established by this section is a presumption affecting the burden of producing evidence.

PHOTOGRAPHIC COPIES AND PRINTED REPRESENTATIONS OF WRITINGS

§ 1550. Photographic copies made as business records.

A nonerasable optical image reproduction provided that additions, deletions, or changes to the original document are not permitted by the technology, a photostatic, microfilm, microcard, miniature photographic, or other photographic copy or reproduction, or an enlargement thereof, of a writing is as admissible as the writing itself if the copy or reproduction was made and preserved as a part of the records of a business (as defined by Section 1270) in the regular course of that business. The introduction of the copy, reproduction, or enlargement does not preclude admission of the original writing if it is still in existence. A court may require the introduction of a hard copy printout of the document.

§ 1550. Types of evidence as writing admissible as the writing itself.

(a) If made and preserved as a part of the records of a business, as defined in Section 1270, in the regular course of that business, the following types of evidence of a writing are as admissible as the writing itself:

(1) A nonerasable optical image reproduction or any other reproduction of a public record by a trusted system, as defined in Section 12168.7 of the Government Code, if additions, deletions, or changes to the original document are not permitted by the technology.

(2) A photostatic copy or reproduction.

(3) A microfilm, microcard, or miniature photographic copy, reprint, or enlargement.

(4) Any other photographic copy or reproduction, or an enlargement thereof.

(b) The introduction of evidence of a writing pursuant to subdivision (a) does not preclude admission of the original writing if it is still in existence. A court may require the introduction of a hard copy printout of the document.

PRODUCTION OF BUSINESS RECORDS

§ 1560. Compliance with subpoena duces tecum for business records.

(a)   As used in this article:

(1)   "Business" includes every kind of business described in Section 1270.

(2)   "Record" includes every kind of record maintained by a business.

(b)   Except as provided in Section 1564, when a subpoena duces tecum is served upon the custodian of records or other qualified witness of a business in an action in which the business is neither a party nor the place where any cause of action is alleged to have arisen, and the subpoena requires the production of all or any part of the records of the business, it is sufficient compliance therewith if the custodian or other qualified witness delivers by mail or otherwise a true, legible, and durable copy of all of the records described in the subpoena to the clerk of the court or to another person described in subdivision (d) of Section 2026.010 of the Code of Civil Procedure, together with the affidavit described in Section 1561, within one of the following time periods:

(1)   In any criminal action, five days after the receipt of the subpoena.

(2)   In any civil action, within 15 days after the receipt of the subpoena.

(3)   Within the time agreed upon by the party who served the subpoena and the custodian or other qualified witness.

(c)   The copy of the records shall be separately enclosed in an inner envelope or wrapper, sealed, with the title and number of the action, name of witness, and date of subpoena clearly inscribed thereon; the sealed envelope or wrapper shall then be enclosed in an outer envelope or wrapper, sealed, and directed as follows:

(1)   If the subpoena directs attendance in court, to the clerk of the court.

(2)   If the subpoena directs attendance at a deposition, to the officer before whom the deposition is to be taken, at the place designated in the subpoena for the taking of the deposition or at the officer's place of business.

(3)   In other cases, to the officer, body, or tribunal conducting the hearing, at a like address.

(d) Unless the parties to the proceeding otherwise agree, or unless the sealed envelope or wrapper is returned to a witness who is to appear personally, the copy of the records shall remain sealed and shall be opened only at the time of trial, deposition, or other hearing, upon the direction of the judge, officer, body, or tribunal conducting the proceeding, in the presence of all parties who have appeared in person or by counsel at the trial, deposition, or hearing. Records that are original documents and that are not introduced in evidence or required as part of the record shall be returned to the person or entity from whom received. Records that are copies may be destroyed.

(e) As an alternative to the procedures described in subdivisions (b), (c), and (d), the subpoenaing party in a civil action may direct the witness to make the records available for inspection or copying by the party's attorney, the attorney's representative, or deposition officer as described in Section 2020.420 of the Code of Civil Procedure, at the witness' business address under reasonable conditions during normal business hours. Normal business hours, as used in this subdivision, means those hours that the business of the witness is normally open for business to the public. When provided with at least five business days' advance notice by the party's attorney, attorney's representative, or deposition officer, the witness shall designate a time period of not less than six continuous hours on a date certain for copying of records subject to the subpoena by the party's attorney, attorney's representative, or deposition officer. It shall be the responsibility of the attorney's representative to deliver any copy of the records as directed in the subpoena. Disobedience to the deposition subpoena issued pursuant to this subdivision is punishable as provided in Section 2020.240 of the Code of Civil Procedure.

§ 1561. Affidavit accompanying records.

(a) The records shall be accompanied by the affidavit of the custodian or other qualified witness, stating in substance each of the following:

(1) The affiant is the duly authorized custodian of the records or other qualified witness and has authority to certify the records.

(2) The copy is a true copy of all the records described in the subpoena duces tecum, or pursuant to subdivision (e) of Section 1560 the records were delivered to the attorney, the attorney's representative, or deposition officer for copying at the custodian's or witness' place of business, as the case may be.

(3) The records were prepared by the personnel of the business in the ordinary course of business at or near the time of the act, condition, or event.

(4) The identity of the records.

(5) A description of the mode of preparation of the records.

(b) If the business has none of the records described, or only part thereof, the custodian or other qualified witness shall so state in the affidavit, and deliver the affidavit and those records that are available in one of the manners provided in Section 1560.

(c) Where the records described in the subpoena were delivered to the attorney or his or her representative or deposition officer for copying at the custodian's or witness' place of business, in addition to the affidavit required by subdivision (a), the records shall be accompanied by an affidavit by the attorney or his or her representative or deposition officer stating that the copy is a true copy of all the records delivered to the attorney or his or her representative or deposition officer for copying.

§ 1562. Admissibility of affidavit and copy of records.

If the original records would be admissible in evidence if the custodian or other qualified witness had been present and testified to the matters stated in the affidavit, and if the requirements of Section 1271 have been met, the copy of the records is admissible in evidence. The affidavit is admissible as evidence of the matters stated therein pursuant to Section 1561 and the matters so stated are presumed true. When more than one person has knowledge of the facts, more than one affidavit may be made. The presumption established by this section is a presumption affecting the burden of producing evidence.

Appendix C

DIFFERENCES BETWEEN FRE & CEC

Rules	Differences
Rule of Completeness FRE 106; CEC § 356. Treatise §§ 2.9–2.11. When one party offers part of a document into evidence, fairness dictates that the other party be allowed to offer the rest of the document, so the court has "the entire story."	FRE 106 applies only to documents, whereas CEC § 356 applies to documents, acts, and conversations. Thus, CEC § 356 is broader than FRE 106. In practice, however, the rules operate similarly because judges apply FRE 106 expansively so as to avoid unfairness.
Subsequent Remedial Measures FRE 407; CEC § 1151. Treatise § 2.21. Evidence of subsequent remedial measures is inadmissible under the FRE and the CEC to prove negligence.	Regarding claims of negligence, the FRE and the CEC are the same. FRE 407 also bars subsequent remedial measures in strict product liability cases. By contrast, the California Supreme Court interpreted CEC § 1151 not to bar subsequent remedial measures in strict liability cases.
Authentication FRE 901–902; CEC 1400 et seq. Treatise, Chapter 3. For the most part, the FRE and the CEC operate similarly when it comes to authentication and identification.	FRE 902 provides that certain documents are self-authenticating. (Treatise § 3.12). CEC § 1450 et seq., reaches a similar result by a different procedure. Under the CEC, certain documents are presumed genuine. (Treatise § 3.13).

Rules	Differences
Ancient Documents FRE 901(b)(8)(C), 803(16); CEC §§ 643, 1331. Treatise §§ 3.11(i), 11.16. The FRE and the CEC have authentication and hearsay rules on so-called ancient documents.	Under FRE, a document must be at least 20 years old to be an ancient document. Under the CEC, a document must be at least 30 years old.
Plain Error FRE 103(e). Treatise § 4.5. Plain error is error that was not preserved for appeal by proper objection or offer of proof, but which the appellate court nevertheless considers because the error in the trial court was very serious, and probably affected the outcome of the trial.	The CEC does not have a rule on plain error. In California, a party who failed to preserve error would have to argue that error in the trial court rendered the proceeding fundamentally unfair, depriving the party of due process of law.
Best and Secondary Evidence Rules FRE 1001 et seq.; CEC § 1521. Treatise Chapter 5. The FRE uses the traditional best evidence rule, which provides that when a party seeks to prove the contents of a writing, the party must produce the original writing. California abandoned the best evidence rule, and replaced it with the secondary evidence rule.	Despite the different names, the FRE best evidence rule, and the CEC secondary evidence rule, operate very similarly in practice.
Character Evidence FRE 404(a); CEC §§ 1101–1104 Treatise Chapter 6. 1. Criminal Defendant Offers Evidence of Defendant's Good Character FRE 404(a)(2)(A); 405(a); CEC	

Rules	Differences
§ 1102. Treatise § 6.9. The FRE and the CEC are the same when the defendant in a criminal case offers evidence of the defendant's good character to prove innocence. The character evidence is offered as substantive evidence to prove that the defendant is not the type of person who would commit such an offense. The evidence must take the form of a character witness who testifies in the form of opinion or reputation.	
2. Criminal Defendant Offers Evidence of Victim's Character. FRE 404(a)(2)(B); CEC § 1103(a). Treatise § 6.12. Both the FRE and the CEC allow the defendant in a criminal case to offer character evidence of the victim's violence, as substantive evidence, to prove that the victim was the first aggressor.	2. Criminal Defendant Offers Evidence of Victim's Character. Under the FRE, when a defendant attacks a victim's character, the defendant is limited to a character witness who testifies in the form of reputation or opinion. Under the CEC, the defendant who attacks a victim's character may use a character witness who testifies in the form of reputation or opinion. In addition, under the CEC, the defendant may offer specific instances of the victim's violence to prove the victim's character for violence. The FRE does not allow the defendant to use specific instances to prove the victim's character for violence. Treatise § 6.12(c).
3. Under the FRE, in a homicide prosecution, after the defendant offers evidence that	3. The CEC has no counterpart to FRE 404(a)(2)(C).

Rules	Differences
the victim was the first aggressor, the prosecutor may offer a character witness to testify that the victim was a peaceful person. FRE 404(a)(2)(C). Treatise § 6.13.	
Abolition of the Rule Against Character Evidence FRE 413–415; CEC §§ 1108–1109. Treatise § 6.15.	The FRE and the CEC abolish the rule against character evidence in sex offense cases. The CEC goes further, abolishing the rule in elder abuse, child abuse, and domestic violence cases.
Testimonial Competence FRE 601; CEC §§ 700–791. Treatise § 9.1. In court, the FRE and the CEC operate identically.	FRE 601 provides that every person is competent to testify as a witness. CEC § 700 is to the same effect. CEC § 701 retains two of the common law elements of testimonial competence. However, the FRE and the CEC operate virtually identically in practice.
Expert Testimony FRE 703; CEC § 801. Treatise § 9.12. The FRE and the CEC provide that experts may base opinion testimony on the kinds of facts and data that experts in their field reasonably rely on. Experts may rely on hearsay and other evidence that would be inadmissible in evidence, provided it is the type of information reasonably relied on by experts in the field.	When an expert relies on inadmissible information, FRE 703 provides that "the proponent of the opinion may disclose [the inadmissible information] to the jury only if [its] probative value in helping the jury evaluate the opinion substantially outweighs [the information's] prejudicial effect." The CEC does not have this balancing test for opinion testimony based on inadmissible evidence. In *People v. Sanchez*, 63 Cal. 4th 665 (2016), the Supreme Court limited the admissibility of hearsay supporting expert testimony. *See* Treatise § 9.12.

Rules	Differences
Learned Treatises FRE 803(18); CEC §§ 721(b), 1341. Treatise §§ 9.15, 11.17. Learned treatises (*e.g.*, books on science and medicine, articles in the professional literature) are often used during cross-examination of expert witnesses. Learned treatises can be used to impeach an expert (*e.g.*, the treatise is inconsistent with the expert's opinion) and/or for the truth of the words written in the treatise (hearsay).	Learned treatises can be used to impeach experts under the FRE and the CEC. When it comes to offering a learned treatise for the truth of the contents of the treatise, the FRE rule (803(18)) is much broader than the CEC rule (CEC § 1341).
Impeachment by Conviction FRE 609; CEC § 788. Treatise § 10.6. The FRE and the CEC allow a witness to be impeached with evidence that the witness was convicted of certain crimes.	FRE 609 allows impeachment with felonies and misdemeanors that involve lying/deceit—so-called *crimen falsi* crimes (FRE 609(a)(2)). When a conviction fits within Rule 609(a)(2), the conviction can be used to impeach, and the judge does not balance the probative value of the conviction for purposes of impeachment against the danger of unfair prejudice. A 609(a)(2) conviction is automatically admissible to impeach. FRE 609(a)(1) allows impeachment with felonies (not misdemeanors) that are not *crimen falsi*. When a felony is offered to impeach under FRE 609(a)(1), the judge balances the probative value of the conviction for purposes of impeachment against the danger of unfair prejudice. If the witness to be

Rules	Differences
	impeached is the defendant in a criminal case, a special balancing test is used that is more protective of the defendant, that is, the balancing test is more likely to exclude use of the conviction to impeach.
	FRE 609(b) creates a rebuttable presumption that a conviction more than ten years old cannot be used to impeach. The CEC contains no such restriction, although a California judge might well exclude such as old conviction as irrelevant to a witness's credibility at the time of trial.
	CEC § 788 allows impeachment with felony convictions, but not misdemeanors. Not all felonies can be used to impeach under Section 788. Only felonies that are *crimen falsi* or that involve moral turpitude (readiness to do evil) are admissible.
	Prop 8. states that all relevant evidence is admissible. California courts rule that Prop. 8 does not make misdemeanor convictions admissible. However, the conduct underlying the misdemeanor conviction may be used to impeach, provided it is relevant to a witness's credibility.

Rules	Differences
Collateral Fact Rule (CFR) Treatise § 10.12. The Collateral Fact Rule is a judge-made rule that governs the admissibility of extrinsic evidence to impeach regarding prior inconsistent statements and contradiction.	The CFR is falling into disuse in federal court. California does not use the CFR. In California, and increasingly in federal courts and other state courts, the admissibility of extrinsic evidence to impeach with prior inconsistent statements and contradiction is governed by FRE 403. The judge determines whether it is worth taking the trial time to allow the extrinsic evidence to impeach.
Impeachment with Specific Instances of Misconduct FRE 608(b); CEC § 787. Treatise § 10.7. FRE 608(b) allows a witness to be impeached by asking the witness about specific instances of the witness's untruthful conduct. If the witness denies the specific instance, the impeaching attorney cannot offer extrinsic evidence to prove the witness really did commit the specific instance. California is among the minority of states that does not allow this mode of impeachment. CEC § 787.	CEC § 787 does not does not allow impeachment with specific instances of misconduct. In criminal cases, however, Prop. 8 effectively abolished Section 787. As a result, in California criminal cases, it is proper to impeach a witness by asking the witness about specific instances of the witness's untruthful conduct. (Treatise § 10.7(b)). In criminal cases, then, CEC § 787 and FRE 608(b) are the same. In criminal cases, CEC § 787 is broader than FRE 608(b). FRE 608(b) is limited to specific acts of untruthfulness. CEC § 787 allows impeachment with specific acts of untruthfulness *and* specific acts of moral turpitude, in criminal cases. In civil cases, CEC § 787 remains good law because Prop. 8 applies only to criminal cases. Thus, in civil litigation in California, impeachment with specific

In civil cases (handwritten annotation)

Rules	Differences
	instances of untruthfulness is not allowed.
Present Sense Impression Hearsay Exception FRE 803(1); CEC § 1241. Treatise § 11.7. The FRE and the CEC contain a hearsay exception for present sense impressions.	The CEC present sense impression exception is narrower than the FRE exception. The FRE exception applies to acts of the declarant, and to acts of others (*e.g.*, "Look at that guy standing on the wall. He might fall.") The CEC exception applies only to conduct of the declarant. The FRE exception extends to statements made during or immediately after an event. The CEC exception is limited to statements made while the declarant was engaged in conduct. Thus, the CEC exception does not extend to statements immediately after an event.
Medical Diagnosis or Treatment Hearsay Exception FRE 803(4); CEC § 1253. Treatise § 11.10. The FRE and the CEC have a hearsay exception for statements made for purposes of obtaining diagnostic or treatment services.	The CEC medical diagnosis or treatment exception applies only to children's hearsay statements in child abuse cases. The FRE exception is much broader, applying to any statement made for purposes of diagnosis or treatment, that is pertinent to the professional's ability to diagnose or treat.
Public Records Hearsay Exception FRE 803(8); CEC § 1280. Treatise § 11.14. The FRE and the CEC contain a hearsay exception for public documents.	The FRE and the CEC public records exceptions are similar. The FRE exception contains limits on the admissibility of police reports against defendants in criminal cases; limits that are not found in the CEC exception.

Rules	Differences
Former Testimony Hearsay Exception FRE 804(b)(1); CEC §§ 1290–1292. Treatise § 11.18. The FRE and the CEC contain a hearsay exception for former testimony.	The language of the FRE and the CEC exceptions differs. In practice, however, the rules operate quite similarly.
Dying Declaration Hearsay Exception FRE 804(b)(2); CEC § 1242. Treatise § 11.19. The FRE and the CEC contain a hearsay exception for dying declarations.	The dying declaration exceptions are similar in the FRE and the CEC. There are two differences. First, the FRE exception requires the declarant to be unavailable at trial, but the declarant does not have to be dead. The CEC exception requires the declarant to be deceased at the time of trial. Second, the CEC exception applies more broadly than the FRE exception. Both exceptions apply in civil litigation. In criminal litigation, the FRE exception applies only in homicide prosecutions. The CEC applies in all criminal cases.
Statement Against Interest Hearsay Exception FRE 804(b)(3); CEC § 1230. Treatise § 11.20. The FRE and the CEC contain a hearsay exception for statements against interest.	The CEC and the FRE exceptions operate similarly in practice. The CEC exception extends to declarations against social interest. The FRE exception does not extend to declarations against social interest.
Employee Admissions Hearsay Exception FRE 801(d)(2)(D); CEC § 1224. Treatise § 11.24(d). The FRE contains a hearsay exemption for statements by a	The California Supreme Court interpreted the CEC exception to exclude most employee statements offered against the employer. Thus, the CEC exception is much narrower

Rules	Differences
party's employee on a matter within the scope of the employment relationship, uttered while the declarant worked for the party. The CEC has an exception that, on the surface, looks like it would cover the same territory.	than the FRE exception.
Residual Hearsay Exception FRE 807; CEC § 1228. Treatise § 11.25. The FRE has a residual hearsay exception that can apply in any kind of litigation. California's residual exception is much narrower.	Unlike the FRE residual exception, which applies in all kinds of litigation, the CEC residual exception applies only to hearsay statements by children in child sexual abuse cases.

Table of Cases

Aguilar, People v., 167
Anderson, People v., 4
Aranda, People v., 229
Arias, People v., 21
Auer v. Minot, 238
Barnes, United States v., 58
Barreiro v. State Bar, 79
Beech Aircraft Corp. v. Rainey, 203
Beechum, United States v., 128
Brodit, People v., 194
Brosnahan v. Brown, 175
Bruton v. United States, 229
Bryant, People v., 10
Carter-Scanlon, Marriage of, 81
Castro, People v., 167
Cedeno, People v., 229
Chambers v. Mississippi, 4
Chapman v. California, 64
Cindy L., In re, 220
Clark, People v., 21, 151, 217, 219
Collins, People v., 167
Cook, In re, 82
Cortez, People v., 187
Crawford v. Washington, 223
Daubert v. Merrell Dow Pharmaceuticals, Inc., 152
Davis, State v., 58
DeHoyos, People v., 140
Diaz, People v., 35
Doolin, People v., 30
Downin, People v., 57
Eleck, State v., 57, 58
Ewoldt, People v., 123, 132
Fisher, State v., 229
Ford, State v., 58
Forklift, Inc. v. Capacity of Texas, Inc., 81
Frye v. United States, 151
Garlinger, People v., 151
Giles v. California, 230
Gould v. Maryland Sound Industries, Inc., 83
Green, People v., 58
Hall, People v., 134
Hamilton, People v., 34
Harpenau, Marriage of, 82
Harris, People v., 21, 175
Hassan, United States v., 58
Hawkins v. Suntrust Bank, 81

Hennessy v. Penril Datacomm Networks, 81
Holmes v. South Carolina, 4
Huddleston v. United States, 121
Hughes, State v., 101
Jackson, People v., 86, 151
Kace v. Liang, 150
Kearley v. State, 58
Kelly, People v., 151
Kirchmeyer v. Phillips, 239
Koch, State v., 58
Kowalski v. Gagne, 81
Laird v. T.W. Mather, Inc., 18, 186
Landry, People v., 26, 61
Lapage, State v., 127
Licudine v. Cedars-Siani Medical Center, 81, 83
Lockley v. Law Office of Cantrell, Green, Pekich, Cruz & McCort, 80, 81
Luce v. United States, 166
Manela v. Superior Court, 239
Manuel, State v., 57, 58
Markely v. Beagle, 217
Maryland v. Craig, 223
McGee v. Cessna Aircraft Co., 35
Medina, People v., 168
Michelson v. United States, 171
Mickel, People v., 3, 4
Mutual Life Insurance Co. v. Hillmon, 192
Oates, United States v., 203
Ohio v. Clark, 224
Old Chief v. United States, 28
Palermo, State v., 58
Pena-Rodriguez v. Colorado, 137
Pheaster, United States v., 193, 232
Ranlet, People v., 10
Reynolds v. Unites States, 229
Rich v. Kaiser Gypsum Co., 207
Rock v. Arkansas, 4
Sanchez, People v., 147, 154
Sanghera, People v., 167
Selivanov, People v., 216
Seumanu, People v., 140
Smallwood, People v., 121
Snibbe v. Superior Court, 238
Song, People v., 229
Stamps, People v., 50
Stitely, People v., 34

Stoll, People v., 101
Streeter, People v., 35
Sublet v. State, 57
Sullivan v. Doe, 80
Tassell, People v., 123
Thompson v. Los Angeles, 29
Thompson, People v., 125, 219
Tienda v. State, 57
Travelers Fire Insurance Co. v.
   J.C. Wright, and J.B. Wright,
   207
Truckenmiller, Estate of, 193
Tuggles, People v., 172
Tully, People v., 117
Valentine, People v., 29
Vicks, In re, 81
Wagner, People v., 100, 155, 172
Wheeler, People v., 167, 168, 169
White v. FAV, Inc., 217
Wilcoxon, State, 228
Williamson v. United States, 211
Woods, United States v., 129

Index

References are to Section

Admissions by Parties, § 11.24
Affirmation, § 9.4
Ancient Documents
Authentication, § 3.11(i)
Hearsay, § 11.16
Aranda, § 11.30
Authentication, §§ 3.6–3.16
Bench Conference, § 2.11
Best Evidence Rule. Chapter 5
Bias, § 10.8, § 10.12, § 10.13
Bolstering Credibility, Rule
   Against Abolished, § 10.14(a)
Bruton, § 11.30
Business Records Exception,
   § 11.12
Capacity to Observe, § 10.8
Chain of Custody, § 3.14
Character Evidence. Chapter 6
Abolition of Rule Against Character
   Evidence, § 6.15
Character Witness, § 6.6, § 10.9,
   § 10.10
Credibility, § 6.2(b), § 6.4, § 6.14
Defined, § 6.1, § 6.2
Exceptions to Rule Against Character
   Evidence, § 6.4
Good Character Evidence Offered by
   Defendant, § 6.4, § 6.9
Impeachment, § 6.2(b), § 6.4, § 6.14,
   § 10.6(b), § 10.9
In Issue, § 6.2(c), § 6.7, § 6.9(g)
Mercy Rule, § 6.4, § 6.9
Methods of Proving Character, § 6.5
Opinion, § 6.6(b)
Reputation, § 6.6(a)
Rule Against Character Evidence,
   § 6.3
Sex Offense Cases, § 6.15
Specific Instances of Conduct,
   § 6.6(c), § 6.7, § 6.9(b), § 6.9(i),
   § 6.12(c)
Substantive Evidence, § 6.2(a), § 6.4,
   § 6.9(f), § 6.12(a)
Victim's Character, § 6.4, § 6.12
Circumstantial Evidence, § 2.3
Co-Conspirator Exception,
   § 11.24(e), § 11.29
Collateral Fact Rule, § 10.4(c),
   § 10.12
Competence to Testify, § 9.1

Confrontation Clause, §§ 11.29–
   11.31
Consistent Statements,
   §§ 10.14(b)–10.14(f)
Contradiction, § 10.5, § 10.12
Conviction, Impeachment With,
   § 2.13, § 10.6
Crawford **and Testimonial**
   Hearsay, § 11.29
Cross-Examination. Chapter 10,
   § 9.14, § 11.29
Daubert Test for Scientific
   Evidence. See Expert
   Testimony
Dead Man's Statute, § 9.2
Demeanor, § 10.2
Demonstrative Evidence, § 1.2
Direct Evidence, § 2.3
Dying Declarations, § 11.19,
   § 11.29
Electronic Communications,
   authentication, § 3.15
Email, § 3.15
Excited Utterances, § 11.8
Expert Testimony, § 2.13, §§ 9.8–
   9.16
Bases for Expert Testimony, § 12
Cross-Examination of Experts, § 9.14
Daubert Test, § 9.16
Frye Test, § 9.16
General Acceptance Test, § 9.16
Hearsay as Basis of Expert
   Testimony, § 9.12
Hypothetical Question, § 9.10
Inadmissible Evidence as Basis for
   Expert Testimony, § 9.12
Kelly Test, § 9.16
Learned Treatises, § 9.15
Opinion, § 9.10
Novel Scientific Evidence, § 9.16
Qualification, § 9.9
Reasonable Certainty, § 9.11
Scientific Evidence, § 9.16
Ultimate Issues, § 9.13
Extrinsic Evidence, § 10.4(c),
   § 10.7(a), § 10.8, § 10.12
Facebook, § 3.15
Facts of Consequence, § 2.2(a)
Forfeiture by Wrongdoing, § 11.31
Former Testimony, § 11.18

Foundation. Chapter 3, § 6.6(a), § 6.6(b), § 6.11, § 10.4(a), § 10.9, § 11.11, § 11.12

Frye Test for Scientific Evidence. See Expert Testimony

General Acceptance Test. See Expert Testimony

Habit. Chapter 7

Handwriting, § 3.11(b)

Harmless Error, § 4.4

Hearsay

Admissions by parties, § 11.24

Ancient Documents Exception, § 11.16

Bruton, § 11.30

Business Records Exception, § 11.12

Co-Conspirator Exception, § 11.24(e)

Confrontation Clause, § 11.29

Crawford and Testimonial Hearsay, § 11.29

Defined, § 11.1

Dying Declarations, § 11.19

Effect on the Listener, § 11.4(a)

Excited Utterances, § 11.8

Forfeiture by Wrongdoing, § 11.31

Former Testimony, § 11.18

Hillmon Statements, § 11.19, § 11.32

Impeach Hearsay Declarant, § 10.11, § 11.28

Identification, Out-of-Court Statements of, § 11.23

Layered Hearsay, § 11.27

Learned Treatises, § 9.15, § 11.17

Masked Hearsay, § 5.10

Medical Diagnosis or Treatment Exception, § 11.10

Non-Hearsay Used of Out-of-Court Statements, § 11.4

Past Recollection Recorded Exception, § 11.11

Personal Knowledge of Declarant, § 11.5

Public Records Exception, § 11.14

Present Sense Impressions, § 11.7

Prior Consistent Statements, § 10.14(b), § 10.14(d), § 11.22

Prior Inconsistent Statements, § 10.4(d), § 10.11, § 11.21

Residual Exception, § 11.25

Rule Against Hearsay, § 11.2

State of Mind Exception, § 11.9

Statements Against Interest, § 11.20

Testimonial Hearsay, § 11.29

Unavailability, § 11.6

Verbal Acts, and Verbal Parts of an Act, § 11.4(b), § 11.4(c)

Williamson Issue, § 11.20(a)

Hillmon Statements, § 11.19, § 11.32

Hypothetical Question, § 9.10

Identification of Persons, § 11.23

Identification of Things, § 3.6

Impeach a Verdict, § 9.1(a)

Impeachment of Witnesses. Chapter 10

Inference, § 2.3, § 13.1

Insurance, § 2.24

Judicial Notice, § 5.11

Kelly Test. See Expert Testimony

Lay Witnesses. Chapter 9

Layered Hearsay, § 11.27

Leading Questions, § 10.1

Learned Treatises, § 9.15, § 11.17

Limited Admissibility, §§ 2.6–2.8

Material Facts, § 2.2(a), § 2.2(b)

Medical Diagnosis or Treatment, § 11.10

Medical Expenses, Offer to Pay, § 2.23

Memory Lapse to Impeach, § 10.8, § 10.12

Moral Turpitude, § 10.6(f), § 10.7(b)

Motion

Motion to Strike. Chapter 4

Motion to Exclude Convictions to Impeach, § 10.6(e)

Novel Scientific Evidence. See Expert Testimony

Oath, § 9.4

Objection. Chapter 4, § 2.15, § 3.6

Offer of Proof. Chapter 4

Party Admissions, § 11.24

Past Recollection Recorded Exception, § 11.11

Personal Knowledge, § 9.3, § 11.5, § 11.8, § 11.24

Photos, § 2.11

Plain Error, § 4.5

Preliminary Facts. Chapter 3

Present Sense Impressions, § 11.7

Presumptions. Chapter 13

Burden of Producing Evidence, § 13.2

Burden of Proof, § 13.2

Conclusive Presumptions, § 13.3

Defined, § 13.1

Inference, § 13.1

Presumptions Affecting the Burden of Producing Evidence, §§ 13.2–13.5

Presumptions Affecting the Burden of Proof, §§ 13.2–13.3, § 13.5

Prior Bad Acts. See Uncharged Misconduct

Prior Consistent Statements, § 10.14(b)– § 10.14(f), § 11.22

Prior Inconsistent Statements, §§ 10.3–10.5, § 10.12, § 11.21

Privilege

Attorney-Client, § 1.1, § 12.1

Clergy-Penitent Privilege, § 12.4

Official Information Privilege, § 12.6

Physician-Patient Privilege, § 12.2

Privilege Renders Declarant Unavailable for Hearsay Purposes, § 11.6

Psychotherapist-Patient, § 3.3, § 12.3

Self-Incrimination, Privilege Against, § 12.7

Spousal Privileges, § 12.5

Proposition 8, § 2.17, § 10.6, § 10.7(b), § 10.13, § 10.14(a)

Public Records

Authentication, § 3.11(h)

Public Records Hearsay Exception, § 11.14

Rape Shield Statute, § 6.12(b), § 6.15

Real Evidence, § 1.2

Reasonable Certainty, § 9.11

Re-Direct Examination, § 10.1

Refreshing Witness Recollection, § 9.7

Rehabilitation of Witnesses, § 10.14

Relevance. Chapter 2

Religious Belief, § 10.13

Reply Letter Doctrine, § 3.11(c), § 3.15

Residual Exception, § 11.25

Reversible Error, § 4.4

Rule in the Queen's Case, § 10.4, § 10.4(b)

Rule of Completeness, §§ 2.9–2.11

Scientific Evidence. See Expert Testimony

Secondary Evidence Rule. Chapter 5

Self-Authentication, § 3.8, § 3.12, § 3.13

State of Mind Exception, § 11.9

Statements Against Interest, § 11.20

Subsequent Remedial Measures, § 2.21

Telephone Calls, § 3.11(g)

Testimonial Hearsay, § 11.29

Text Messages, § 3.15

Third Party Culpability Evidence, § 8.13

Ultimate Issues, § 9.13

Uncharged Misconduct Evidence (UME). Chapter 8

Accident, Disproof, § 8.10

Doctrine of Chances, § 8.10

Intent, §§ 8.9–8.10

Memory, § 10.8

Modus Operandi, § 8.11k

Motive, § 8.8, § 8.9

Not Character Evidence, § 8.2, § 8.3

Plan, § 8.7, § 8.9

Proof of UME, § 8.4

Third Party Culpability Evidence, § 8.13

Unfair Prejudice, § 8.5

Unfair Prejudice, § 2.5, §§ 2.12–2.19, § 8.5, § 10.6

Unique Item, Foundation for, § 3.14

Voices, Identification of, § 1.33(f)

Voucher Rule, § 1.4

Williamson **Issue,** § 11.29(a)

Witnesses

Affirmation, § 9.4

Bias, § 10.8

Bolstering, Rule Against Abolished, § 10.14

Capacity to Observe, § 10.8

Character Witness to Impeach, § 10.9

Child Witnesses, § 9.1

Competence to Testify § 9.1

Contradiction, § 10.5

Conviction, Impeachment with, § 10.6

Credibility, § 1.3

Cross-Examination, § 10.1

Dead Man's Statute, § 9.2

Demeanor, § 10.2

Direct Examination, § 10.1

Excluding Witnesses While Not Testifying, § 9.6

Expert Witnesses, §§ 9.8–9.16

Extrinsic Evidence, § 10.3, § 10.4, § 10.4(c), § 10.6(c), § 10.7(a)

Impeach a Character Witness, § 10.10

Impeachment, § 10.1, § 10.3, § 10.6, § 10.11

Judge as Witness, § 9.1(a)

Juror as Witness, § 9.1(a)

Leading Questions, § 10.1

Memory, § 10.8

Oath, § 9.4

Opinion Testimony, § 9.5

Personal Knowledge, § 9.3

Prior Inconsistent Statements, §§ 10.3–10.4

Re-Direct Examination, § 10.1, § 10.14

Refreshing Recollection, § 9.7

Rehabilitation, § 10.14

Religious Belief, No Impeachment, § 10.13

Testimonial Competence, § 9.1

Untruthfulness, Specific Instance of to Impeach, § 10.7, § 10.12